Prophets Without Honour

PROPHETS WITHOUT HONOUR

A Background to
Freud,
Kafka,
Einstein
and Their World

FREDERIC V. GRUNFELD

McGraw-Hill Book Company
New York St. Louis San Francisco Bogotá Guatemala
Hamburg Lisbon Madrid Mexico Montreal Panama
Paris San Juan São Paulo Tokyo Toronto

Reprinted by arrangement with
Holt, Rinehart and Winston

Library of Congress Cataloging in Publication Data

Grunfeld, Frederic V.
    Prophets without honour.

    Bibliography: p.
    Includes index.
    1. Jews in Germany—Intellectual life.   2. Jews in
Austria—Intellectual life.   3. Germany—Civilization—
Jewish influences.   4. Austria—Civilization—
Jewish influences.   5. Jews—Biography.   I. Title.
[DS135.G33G8 1980] 943'.004924   80-17497
ISBN 0-07-025087-1 (pbk.)

Designer: Helene Berinsky
First McGraw-Hill Paperback edition, 1980
1 2 3 4 5 6 7 8 9 0   DODO   8 7 6 5 4 3 2 1 0

Thanks are due the following copyright holders for permission to quote from the books listed
below:

"In Memory of Sigmund Freud" copyright 1940 renewed © 1968 by W. H. Auden. Reprinted
from *Collected Poems*, by W. H. Auden, by permission of Random House Inc.
Excerpts from *Illuminations* by Walter Benjamin are reprinted by permission of Harcourt Brace
Jovanovich, Inc., copyright © 1955 by Suhrkamp Verlag, Frankfurt a.M.; English translation
copyright © 1968 by Harcourt Brace Jovanovich, Inc. Walter Benjamin's *Gesammelte Schriften*
copyright © 1972 and *Briefe* copyright © 1966, as well as *Über Walter Benjamin* copyright © 1968 and
Zur Aktualität Walter Benjamins copyright © 1972, all by Suhrkamp Verlag, Frankfurt.
From *The Born-Einstein Letters* with commentaries by Max Born. The Born Letters © 1971 by
G.V.R. Born, I. Newton-John, M. Pryce; the Einstein letters © 1971 by the Estate of Albert
Einstein; commentaries © 1971 by G.V.R. Born; translation © 1971 by I. Newton-John. Used by
permission of Walker and Company. Also used by permission of Macmillan, London and
Basingstoke.
Hermann Broch's *The Death of Virgil*, translated by Jean Starr Untermeyer, copyright 1946 by
Pantheon Books, a Division of Random House Inc., New York, used also by permission of
Routledge & Kegan Paul Ltd., London.
Alfred Doeblin's *Werke in Einzelausgeben* copyright by Walter Verlag AG, Olten and used by
permission of Niedieck Linder AG Zurich.
Excerpts from *Ideas and Opinions* by Albert Einstein. Copyright 1954 by Crown Publishers, Inc.
Used by permission of Crown Publishers, Inc.
Lion Feuchtwanger's *The Devil in France* copyright 1940 by Hutchinson & Co. London.
From Paper II, "Analysis of a Phobia in a Five-Year-Old Boy," in the *Collected Papers of Sigmund
Freud*, Volume 3, edited by Ernest Jones, M.D., authorized translation by Alix and James
Strachey, published by Basic Books, Inc., Publishers, New York, by arrangement with The
Hogarth Press Ltd. and The Institute of Psycho-Analysis, London. From Paper XI, "Contribu-
tions to the Psychology of Love," (also, From Paper X, " 'The Antithetical Sense of Primal
Words',") in the *Collected Papers of Sigmund Freud*, Volume 4, edited by Ernest Jones, M.D.,

For Franz, Elli and Lauten

A prophet is not without honour, save
in his own country, and in his own house.

—*St. Matthew 13:57*

CONTENTS

AUTHOR'S NOTE TO THE PAPERBACK EDITION

Much of this book concerns a neglected literature which I cannot expect anyone else to have read, for it is only now being rediscovered in Germany and remains largely untranslated into other languages. Since the work of writers like Wolfskehl, Lasker-Schüler and Doeblin is virtually unknown in the English-speaking world, I have quoted from them as often and profusely as possible in order to give them a belated chance to speak for themselves.

I have made my own translations of both poetry and prose except where standard English versions already exist—as in the case of Harry Zohn's rendering of Walter Benjamin's *Illuminations*, the Joan Riviere edition of Freud's *Collected Papers*, Willa and Edwin Muir's translations of Kafka, Richard and Clara Winston's edition of the *Letters* of Thomas Mann, and Jean Starr Untermeyer's translation of Hermann Broch's *The Death of Virgil*. Occasionally, in spite of an existing English version, I have ventured to make a new translation of my own.

Sources and acknowledgments will be found starting on page 305, where all quotations are identified by page and line number. Though this method of annotation may be slightly more cumbersome, it seemed preferable to constantly interrupting the narrative with footnote numbers. The illustrations are to be found on pages 163 to 174.

One reviewer of the original edition referred to it as a "German-Jewish Hall of Fame." It was intended, however, as a collective biography rather than a catalogue. I might just as easily have chosen a dozen other representative figures for this composite portrait of a lost culture. Yet I had to stop somewhere—hence many equally important writers and poets are given unavoidably short shrift in the following pages.

Another point requires further amplification: my passing reference (on page 31) to kindly old Theodor Mommsen as a "chauvinist historian," to which a critic took particular exception. Conventional wisdom has it that Mommsen was a liberal: certainly he himself thought he was pleading for tolerance when he wrote his 1880 essay, *Auch ein Wort über unser Judenthum* (Another Word about Our Jews). Yet it is a peculiarly grudging and double-edged affair, in which he agrees with the nationalists that an "inequality exists between the German occidental and the Semitic blood," and concedes that "Jews are an element of national decomposition, as they were in the Roman empire." His conclusion was that Jews should mend their peculiar ways, change their religion and become good Germans. Surely "chauvinist" is not too strong a word to characterize this attitude.

April, 1980

Prophets Without Honour

I

A FAMILY RESEMBLANCE

*No people is more difficult to understand
than the Jews.*
                    —ELIAS CANETTI, Crowds and Power

In 1838 the romantic poet Heinrich Heine wrote of "the deep affinity that prevails between these two ethical nations, Jews and Germans," who were jointly destined to create a New Jerusalem in Germany—"a modern Palestine," as he put it, which would emerge as "the home of philosophy, the mother soil of prophecy and the citadel of pure spirituality."

Though it did not turn out quite as he had hoped, neither did Heine's splendid vision go altogether unfulfilled. For well over a half century the confluence of these two intellectual traditions, the German and the Jewish, produced such an outpouring of literature, music and ideas that, had it not been for its infamous finale, the cultural historians would now be writing of it as a golden age second only to the Italian Renaissance. It was a time of great poets and painters, of composers, philosophers, scholars, critics; of Expressionism, Dadaism and a new sense of compassion in the arts; of Mahler's *Lied von der Erde*, Freud's *The Interpretation of Dreams* and Kafka's *The Trial*.

For the Jews of Germany and Austria, only recently emerged from the mental and physical isolation of ghetto life, it was a time of difficulties and rebuffs, but also of what Albert Einstein called "undreamed-of possibilities." He was speaking from personal experience when he described the "burning enthusiasm" with which so many Jews joined the rush into the arts and sciences. They may have been newcomers to the German universities, but it

1

seemed as though they had been preparing for the entrance examinations for a thousand years.

Their bibliophile traditions as "people of the book" took them, almost as a matter of course, into medicine and mathematics as well as literature and music. Their grandfathers had studied the Talmud. They, no less attentively, read Kant, Goethe and Hegel. Karl Marx (son of a lawyer and grandson of not one, but two, orthodox rabbis) unconsciously reverted to an old kabalist technique when he "turned Hegel upside down" in order to formulate his own dialectical materialism. In the sciences, though most professorships still remained closed to them, new doors were constantly opening. Once they had access to the tools of German scholarship, as one observer noted, "what leaps into the past and future they were able to make!" The botanist Ferdinand Julius Cohen, for example, became the founder of bacteriology; Paul Ehrlich, experimenting in his private laboratory, produced the first practical form of chemotherapy; Franz Boas, originally a student of physics, went on to become the "Papa Franz" of cultural anthropology.

There was a price to be paid for joining the modern world, but for the most part they were willing enough to pay it. Emancipation from the ghetto also implied assimilation with the prevailing patterns of German society. At the beginning of the century the "ticket of admission to European culture," as Heine called it, was the baptismal certificate—usually Protestant in northern Germany (for Heine, Marx, Felix Mendelssohn and many others) but Catholic in Bavaria and the Hapsburg empire. Conversion tended to be a matter of good form rather than an act of faith. The poet Hugo von Hofmannsthal once described his grandfather's conversion as "being in accord with a perfectly natural trend, perhaps the only possible one at the beginning of the nineteenth century, to step out of an isolation that no longer made any sense, and to enter what was generally considered the cultivated sphere." Time, too, played its part in transforming the silk manufacturer's grandson into the perfect model of the Austrian nobleman of letters: certainly nothing could be more quintessentially Viennese than the libretto that Hofmannsthal wrote for Der Rosenkavalier in 1909. By then, of the family's antecedents, only a faintly nostalgic memory remained:

> *Ganz vergessener Völker Müdigkeiten*
> *Kann ich nicht abtun von meinen Lidern. . . .*

> The weariness of wholly forgotten peoples
> Cannot be brushed from my eyelids.

Less conspicuous families than the baronets von Hofmannsthal were often able to blend entirely into the social background after converting to Christianity. A generation or two later, no one remembered that Johann Strauss, Sr. ("Strauss the magic fiddler," as Richard Wagner described him, "the demon of Vienna's innate musical spirit"), was the son of a baptized Jewish tavernkeeper from Budapest, or that Franz Marc, one of the major painters of the "Blue Rider" school, was a descendant of Dr. Israel Markus, personal physician of the bishop of Bamberg. A recent biographer of the philosopher Ludwig Wittgenstein felt obliged to explain to his readers that "the Wittgenstein family . . . is of Jewish descent. It is not, contrary to what has often been stated, related to the princes of the same name." The mistake was a perfectly natural one to make under the circumstances—though it seems improbable that Wittgenstein himself would have deliberately encouraged it. Many German Jews bore the names of localities which, with the addition of a *von* or *zu*—like that of the Prince zu Löwenstein, for example—also furnished some of the most eminent entries in the *Almanac de Gotha*.

Even those who stopped short of conversion, however, tended to abandon the more visible aspects of the Jewish faith. German life was becoming increasingly secular: by the 1880s Friedrich Nietzsche no longer doubted that "God is dead." By the same token, baptism as such ceased to be the touchstone of social assimilation. In fashionable circles one's religious affiliation came to count for less than the cut of one's lapels and the crispness of one's consonants. Benjamin Disraeli, who had witnessed the same process at work in England—and participated in it—summed it up rather maliciously in a fictional portrait of a Jewish lady, of nervous and uncertain faith, who "felt persuaded that the Jews would not be so much disliked if they were better known; that all they had to do was to imitate as closely as possible the habits and customs of the nation among whom they chanced to live; and she really did believe that eventually, such was the progressive spirit of the age, a difference in religion would cease to be regarded, and that a respectable Hebrew, particularly if well dressed and well mannered, might be able to pass through society without being discovered, or at least noticed."

Most of the emancipated German Jews likewise did their best to become outwardly indistinguishable from their neighbors. As a measure of the enthusiasm with which they joined in the prevailing fashions of the age, they gave their children Wagnerian names

like Siegmund or Siegfried, and even Wagner's antisemitic diatribes in *Das Judentum in der Musik* (The Jews in Music) failed to
discourage them. For their surnames they might acquire the en-
nobling *von* if possible, or else one of the more accessible titles,
such as *Doktor* or *Geheimrat* (privy counselor). Those who were in
the public eye, especially actors and journalists, tended to change
their names, if necessary, to something neutral-sounding or inconspicuous. Friedrich Gundolf, for example, the literary critic who
wrote definitively on "Shakespeare and the German *Geist*," short-
ened his name from Gundelfinger at the suggestion of his mentor,
the symbolist poet Stefan George. The socialist leader Ferdinand
Lassalle, who founded the German Social Democratic movement,
added two letters to his name while on a visit to Paris as a young
man: the French ending improved his political prospects in Germany (Lassal, the original name, had been derived from his
father's birthplace, the town of Loslau in Upper Silesia). Jakob van
Hoddis, one of the first Expressionist poets, was proud of having
created his nom de plume as a quasi-anagram of the original, Hans
Davidsohn.

This, too, was a way of stepping out of "an isolation that no
longer made any sense." Most German-Jewish names had been
acquired in arbitrary ways not very long before, when the old
Hebrew names of the ghetto were exchanged for duly registered
German ones. Some of them, indeed, had been bestowed by big-
oted officials with the express purpose of humiliating the bearer.
The so-called *galizische Ekelnamen* (Galician loathing-names), for
example, had been passed out en masse among the Jewish inhabitants of Austrian Poland by government officials who thought they
were being funny when they stigmatized some defenseless villager
with a surname like Urin, Kalfuss (bald-foot), Dintenfass (ink-
bottle) or Streisand (blotting-sand).

Since the possessors of such names were under no compulsion
to keep them (at least until the Nazis came to power), it seemed to
involve no particular disrespect for one's forebears to change them
into something that sounded less ridiculous to German ears. Still
the cumulative effect of these and countless other adjustments of
the kind was to cause serious concern about the survival of Jewish
traditions in the German-speaking world. Among their
coreligionists in Eastern Europe, the *Yekkes*—an unflattering
nickname for German Jews—acquired the reputation of being
"four-fifths German and only one-fifth Jewish." So long as the
assimilation process continued unabated, there was every reason
to believe that their ethnic identity would soon reach the vanishing

point. Einstein, though he regarded himself as *"pas très juif,"* was one of many prominent critics disturbed by "the loosening fabric of Jewish society" and the moral dilemma of "the Jew who has lost touch with his own people."

Yet it was precisely this problematic stratum of "marginal Jews"—the so-called *Grenzjuden*—which supplied most of the artists and intellectuals who helped to create the most exciting epoch in German intellectual history. The very precariousness of their position astride the two cultures gave them an extraordinary vantage point from which to survey the European cultural landscape. Hence the "impertinence" of Heinrich Heine in writing the best-loved German poetry of the Romantic age, as well as the most scathing criticism of nineteenth-century Prussian absolutism—for which the German nationalists have not forgiven him to this day. (There is still no adequate monument to Heine in Düsseldorf, his birthplace.)

If the image were more appropriate, Heine might be called the patron saint of emancipated Jews; and quite apart from that he was certainly the most important literary figure of the post-Goethe epoch. "Standing all alone," as Ford Madox Ford describes him, "Heine, perhaps the most exquisite of all the world's lyricists since the great Greeks, perhaps the greatest of all the world's realistic-bitter romantics. . . ." Heine was still in his twenties when, single-handed, he established the tradition of the German-Jewish literary gadfly. His ballads and love lyrics—"The Lorelei," "On Wings of Song," "Im wunderschönen Monat Mai" and a dozen others, known to the rest of the world chiefly in settings by Schubert, Schumann and Mendelssohn—were sung and recited throughout Germany, and made him a celebrity almost overnight. His political sarcasm in prose, however, cost him most of the goodwill he had earned with his poetry. As one of his editors noted, he had the disconcerting habit of "thinking aloud the moment an impression strikes him, without reflecting that the whole world is listening to him"—a habit that nearly landed him in prison, but brought him to Paris instead, at the age of thirty-three, to spend the last twenty-six years of his life as a displaced poet, exiled from his reading public and his mother tongue. Although he accepted a yearly stipend from the privy purse of Louis Philippe, he refused to become a naturalized French citizen. "The stone-cutter who is called upon to adorn my tombstone will find no one to protest when he engraves these words: 'Here lies a German poet.'" His own mixed feelings toward his ambiguous role in German literature are summed up with a typically ironic smile in the poem in which he encounters a brown-eyed lass who asks him who he is and what ails him. He answers (in Ford Madox Ford's translation):

> I am a German poet
> Known throughout Germany,
> And when they mention the best-known names
> They have to talk of me.
>
> And that which ails me, little one,
> Ails a-many in Germany;
> And when they talk of men's bitterest pains
> They must mention my agony.

Heine often spoke to his French friends about his homesickness. As the composer Hector Berlioz wrote in a letter to Heine: "What infinite tenderness breathes through the secret recesses of your heart for the country which you have so often satirized, this land fruitful in poets, this country of dreaming genius—this Germany, in fact, whom you call your old grandmother, and who loves you so well notwithstanding." Still, in spite of his nostalgia the poet really preferred the free air of Paris, where he could write the most shamelessly outspoken essays and verses about himself, his friends, his family in Hamburg, German politics and, of course, music, painting and literature. It was easier for a man of his temperament to live among the French; easier, too, to live with French women. He ended up by marrying a grisette who knew nothing of his poetry; it gave him the delicious sensation of being loved incognito. His lines, "At night I think of Germany/ And then there is no sleep for me"—

> Denk ich an Deutschland in der Nacht
> Dann bin ich um den Schlaf gebracht

—have achieved a kind of immortality even in the country to which they refer. But a more elaborate variation of the theme occurs in one of his *Salon* poems, addressed to a girl identified only as Angélique—it has been described as the world's first political poem disguised as a love lyric. The translation is by Louis Untermeyer:

> While in your arms and in our kisses
>   I find love's sweet and happiest season,
> My Germany you must never mention—
>   I cannot bear it: there is a reason.
>
> Oh, silence your chatter on anything German;
>   You must not plague me or ask me to share it.
> Be still when you think of my home or my kindred—
>   There is a reason: I cannot bear it.

Like other baptized Jews, Heine found that his "ticket of admission" to Europe did little to lighten the burden of what he called the *tausendjährige Familienübel,* the "thousand-year-old family misfortune, brought with us from the valley of the Nile." Nor did he make any attempt to disavow it. In 1840 he wrote an impassioned defense of the persecuted Jews of Damascus, then being butchered by an Egyptian vice regent in league with the French consul. But when he published the magnificent "Hebrew Melodies" that form part of his masterpiece, the *Romancero,* he felt obliged to deny the rumor that his return to belief in a personal God had conducted him "to the threshold of any church, let alone its bosom." By then he was already half paralyzed by the illness that confined him to his "mattress grave" for a decade prior to his death in 1856, but to the very end he remained what he had always been, a free-thinker of what we would now call the Existentialist persuasion. His nostalgia for the faith of his fathers tended to take a culinary rather than religious turn. Both in poetry and in prose he spoke often and longingly about his childhood memories of traditional Jewish food—a curious *idée fixe* in a man surrounded by the pleasures of French cuisine. "In my mind's eye," he writes in *The Rabbi of Bacharach,* "I saw again the carp with brown raisin sauce which my aunt knew how to make so well for the Friday evening meal: I saw again the steamed mutton with garlic and horseradish, with which one can waken the dead, and the soup with its rapturous, floating meatballs—my soul melted like the notes of an amorous nightingale."

This was about as much of the past as most of the marginal Jews took with them into the modern world: the memory of their mother's cooking and, perhaps, a vague sense of kinship with other people belonging to the same "community of suffering." Sigmund Freud, who prided himself on his Jewishness while professing to be an unbeliever, declared in his last years that he had always felt linked to his Jewish friends by "the hidden secret of a common psychic structure"—but of what intangibles that might consist he did not venture to say. As he himself was the first to realize, some of the strongest emotions and darkest instincts were the very ones that could least be expressed in words.

Gustav Landauer, the utopian socialist writer whose ties to Judaism were even more tenuous than Freud's, thought of himself, nonetheless, as belonging to an esoteric mystical community that included Moses, Jesus and Spinoza. He sensed his own Jewishness, he wrote, in his body language: "in my gestures, my facial expression, my bearing, my appearance, and these signs are to me proof that it lives in all that I am and undertake." Like Heine he was also in love with Germany and repeatedly stressed his identity as a German writer: "My language and that of my children is German,"* he wrote in 1913. "My being German and being Jewish do no harm to each other and do much for each other's sake. . . . I experience this strange and intimate dualistic unity as something precious."

In practical terms this twofold legacy was never an easy one to live with. Most of the intellectuals were uncomfortable with it: only a few actually welcomed its influence. "I am German and I am Jewish," wrote the novelist Jakob Wassermann, "one as much as the other, and neither can be separated from the other." The trouble was that, as members of a tiny minority of one or two percent in an ocean of Germans and Austrians, it was easy enough for them to learn the ways of the majority, but as the poet Ludwig Jacobowski pointed out, they could "have no idea of what it means 'to be Jewish.' " Most of them, indeed, had only the vaguest notion of what they or their parents had left behind. Otto Weininger, the literary prodigy of turn-of-the-century Vienna, wrote a brilliant farrago of nonsense attacking his own Jewishness in a book called *Sex and Character*, and then, to underscore the point, committed suicide at twenty-three in a room especially rented for the occasion, in the house where Beethoven had died.

There was no literary school or coterie to which Weininger might have turned for guidance, nor a concerted program that might have given the German-speaking Jews as a whole some specific ethnic or political cohesion. Politically and socially they were a thoroughly fragmented minority. Most of them tended to support liberal causes, but all shades of political opinion were represented. Some marched with the militant nationalists, others provided the backbone of radical and pacifist movements. Ideologically there seemed to be no common denominator except, perhaps, the very lack of one. "The Jew," wrote Weininger from the depths of his neurotic self-abnegation, "is the *Grenzverwischer*, the eraser of boundaries, the formless one."

It was a curious charge to level at a people whose history, from Moses to Einstein, had displayed such an intense preoccupation with "the Law"—though the accusation might, with more justice, have been applied to the Viennese Jewish literati of the 1900s, who could write convincing and utterly delightful feuilletons on both sides of almost any question. For that matter, there was much to be

---

*The language of his grandson Mike Nichols, however, is English.

said for a certain mental flexibility: the trigger-happy Weininger, who berated the Jews for "always having another alternative, many alternatives," was simply too young to appreciate the importance of not making up one's mind too hastily or with too much finality. Peter Altenberg, the genial and magnificent poet who led a charmed but shabby life in the Bohemian cafés of Vienna, could have enlightened him on this point:* much of his poetry is an advertisement for the virtues of ambivalence:

> Our lives contain so many nuances—
> One woman says, "Healer of my ailing soul!"
> The other, "How terrible he looks!" . . .
> One says, "A romantic without a heart!"
> The other, "A hearty one without romance!"
> And each sees a "for" and an "against"—
> And neither senses that "for" and "against" are one
> In a man, in whom "for" and "against" exist at the same time.

Yet if there was a besetting sin—or a family resemblance— among the German-Jewish intellectuals, it revealed itself not in their occasional vacillations but, on the contrary, in the fierce concentration they were apt to bestow on the work they chose to do, the problems they wanted to solve. The poet-critic Walter Benjamin, whose adventures are related in Chapter VII, provides a typical case in point: according to his friends he was a "perfect fanatic in everything pertaining to his work." As a young man he became fascinated with Kant's concept of the *unendliche Aufgabe,* the never-ending problem, and though he dropped the idea of writing his Ph.D. thesis on "knowledge as the never-ending problem," in a sense he spent the rest of his life in pursuit of the never-ending solution. It was the equivalent of Einstein's lifelong quest for a unified field theorem that would encompass all physical phenomena, Marx's search for an all-embracing historical method, or what Ernest Jones called Freud's "divine passion" for understanding the origin and nature of human behavior.

A century earlier, Goethe had already been struck by the intensity of the work ethic among the Jews he knew: it seemed to be the touchstone of Jewish character *(jüdisches Wesen)* as he saw it. "Energy is the basis of everything," *(Energie der Grund von allem)* he decided. "Every Jew, no matter how insignificant, is engaged in some decisive and immediate pursuit of a goal. . . ." It seems not

*See also F. Scott Fitzgerald in *The Crack-Up:* "The test of a first-rate intelligence is the ability to hold two opposed ideas in the mind at the same time, and still retain the ability to function."

entirely a coincidence that it was Einstein who later applied this principle to the whole universe, demonstrating that the very essence of all matter—Kant's "thing-in-itself"—is nothing other than "the sum total of its energy."

The work ethic happened to be a Calvinist invention, and one of the cornerstones of the Protestant Reformation. Yet too much energy, too visibly expended on intellectual pursuits, was generally regarded as undignified and alien to German ways. Freud, as a young hospital resident, was only half facetious when he promised his fiancée that, for the sake of good form, he would henceforth "try to live more like the Gentiles—modestly, learning and practicing the usual things and not striving after discoveries and delving too deep." He was unable to keep his promise: instead, he got into the habit of working sixteen or eighteen hours a day. A self-diagnosed obsessive, he was perfectly conscious of being under a kind of ancestral obligation to display "the industry, the tenacious enthusiasm . . . the talent normally expected from Jews."

Of all the time-honored ethnic traditions, this was perhaps the hardest to leave behind at the baptismal font. Even the elegant Felix Mendelssohn, raised as a proper Protestant by a banker father who wanted to spare him the aggravations of being Jewish, never really learned the gentlemanly art of relaxation. The actor Eduard Devrient, who helped Mendelssohn produce his famous revival of Bach's *St. Matthew Passion* in 1829, writes in his memoirs that even as a young man Mendelssohn had an unfortunate way of making everybody nervous. "The habit of constant occupation, instilled by his mother, made rest intolerable to him. To spend any time in mere talk caused him to look frequently at his watch, by which he often gave offense; his impatience was only satisfied when something was being done, such as music, reading, chess, etc." Devrient thought that far too much had been expected of this boy prodigy who had composed the *Midsummer Night's Dream* Overture at the age of seventeen:

> Of middle height, slender frame, and of uncommon muscular power, a capital gymnast, swimmer, walker, rider, and dancer, the leading feature of his outward and inner nature was an extraordinary sensitiveness. Excitement stimulated him to the verge of frenzy, from which he was restored only by his sound, death-like sleep. . . . His brain had from childhood been taxed excessively, by the university course, study of modern languages, drawing and much else, and to these were added the study of music in its profoundest sense. . . . His bearing retained from his boyhood the slight rocking of the head and upper part of the body, and shifting from foot to foot; it was

always easy to see whether he was pleased or otherwise when any new music was going on, by his nods and shakes of the head.

Mendelssohn was the early Victorian composer par excellence (Victoria and Albert both sang rapturously to his accompaniment when he visited Buckingham Palace in the 1840s)—especially in such solid and reassuring works as "Hark, the Herald Angels Sing" and "Oh Rest in the Lord." Yet certain features of his portrait call to mind the composer of a far more problematic, heaven-storming kind of music:

> Mahler, who is below middle height, has a delicate, slender and spare body, though of extraordinary strength and suppleness, hardly equalled even by the tallest. In Budapest he used to carry his sister Justi, who is heavier than he is, fully dressed in her winter clothes and fur coat, up three flights of stairs every day to save her having to walk up, since she was very ill.

> It fascinated me to find the same intensity and high intellectual pitch in his talk as in his rehearsing. . . . His sudden plunge into reflective silence, then the friendly glance with which he picked up a sensible observation; then the unexpected twitches of furtive pain across his face; even the curious irregularity of his walk—now he would stamp, stand stock-still; now rush ahead—all this confirmed and strengthened the impression of someone demoniac.

The first of these reminiscences comes from the pen of Natalie Bauer-Lechner, the violinist who was Gustav Mahler's closest friend for several years before he married the formidable Alma Schindler. The second is by Bruno Walter, afterward the foremost Mahler conductor of his generation. But everyone who knew Mahler noted the bow-string tension of this difficult man, who created a new kind of stream-of-consciousness music that shattered all existing limitations of length and breadth in order to be, as he said, "cosmic and inexhaustible like the world and life itself." That, too, was a kind of never-ending problem which he was still in the midst of solving when he died of rheumatic heart disease in 1911, leaving behind the unfinished manuscript of the tenth and most cosmic symphony of all.

Mahler's daily work schedule in the 1890s, as described by Natalie Bauer-Lechner, sounds like a cross between a musician's and a marathon runner's. He would rise at seven, take a cold shower, gulp down a quick breakfast and then spend several hours on his compositions. At half past ten he would leave his apartment for the Hamburg Opera, of which he was then musical director. "He runs into the city on foot—it takes three-quarters of an hour."

After several hours of rehearsals with orchestra and singers he would jog back home, "announcing his arrival from the street by whistling his private signal"—the opening bars of Beethoven's Eighth Symphony—which meant that the maid could put lunch on the table. Later, a brief siesta or discussions with opera people, followed by a daily visit to the copyist who transformed his immensely complicated manuscripts into readable scores. If nothing happened to be on at the opera, he might spend the evening making music at home; more often he would be off again at six in order to conduct a performance at the opera, "from which Mahler usually returned in a furious temper, since there was nothing to be accomplished there—'It's an Augean stable that even Hercules couldn't muck out!'"

The breathlessness of the long-distance runner is a theme that recurs as a sinister leitmotiv in German-Jewish history—as though they knew from the first that they had so little time. The young poet Jacobowski, who died at thirty-two in 1900, begins one of his autobiographical poems with the lines:

> *Das Leben hetzt mich durch das Leben,*
> *Es gönnt mir Stille nicht, noch Ruh. . . .*

> Life drives me in a headlong rush through life;
> No stillness does it grant me, and no peace.

The word *hetzt* is difficult to translate since it has no single English equivalent: it means to drive, chase, hunt, persecute. Those who were exposed to the pressures of a German-Jewish childhood usually bore the scars of it for the rest of their lives, though they may afterward have settled in less hectic surroundings. In his essay on Ludwig Wittgenstein, Norman Malcolm recalls what a "formidable strain" it was to go for a stroll with him at Cambridge in 1939; one might as well have been out walking with Mahler: "He would walk in spurts, sometimes coming to a stop while he made some emphatic remark and looking into my eyes with his piercing gaze. Then he would walk rapidly for a few yards, then slow down, then speed up or come to a halt, and so on. And this uncertain ambulation was conjoined with the most exacting conversation."

Often the family resemblance would take even more exasperating forms. I remember from my own childhood the peculiar nervous impatience that made so many refugee intellectuals seem far more out of place in America than they had reason to be. Norman Malcolm, who became one of Wittgenstein's closest friends, admits that the philosopher was always difficult to be with: "a friendly relationship with him was very exacting. He had a tendency to be suspicious of motives and character. Sometimes his judgements were precipitous and in error." Eduard Devrient had written in almost identical words about Mendelssohn: "His irritability, his distrustfulness, even toward his most intimate friends, were sometimes quite incredible."

Mahler, too, was known for his hairtrigger temper. But no one could have been more irascible than Karl Marx, who had a Byron-like reputation for being mad, bad and dangerous to know. To Bakunin, who became his political enemy, he was "immensely malicious, vain, quarrelsome, as intolerant and autocratic as Jehovah, the god of his fathers." Carl Schurz commented that he had never known anyone so provocative and intolerable: "Everyone who disagreed with him was treated with scarcely veiled contempt. He answered all arguments which displeased him with a biting scorn for the pitiable ignorance of those who advanced them. . . ."

Yet evidently there was another side to Marx. His daughter Eleanore ("Tussy") wrote a loving and wholly credible essay refuting the legend of the unapproachable autocrat. It describes him as "a man brimming over with humor and good-humor, whose hearty laugh was infectious and irresistible . . . the kindliest, gentlest, most sympathetic of companions." She remembered him as the bushy-haired "Moor" who jogged her on his shoulders around their small London garden, and as a storyteller of infinite resource who held his children spellbound for months on end with his serial technique of telling bedtime stories.

Marx's disciples, however, were accustomed to seeing this kindliest of father figures suddenly grow furious about the inequities of the modern world. He could speak calmly enough on economic theory, noted the English socialist H. M. Hyndman, but when the conversation turned to the injustice of British policy in Ireland, "the old warrior's brows wrinkled, his small deep-sunk eyes lighted up his heavy brows, the broad, strong nose and face were obviously moved by passion, and he poured out a stream of vigorous denunciation which displayed alike the heat of his temperament, and the marvelous command he possessed over our language." Underlying both the calm and the anger was a boundless messianic faith in the new and higher moral order that lay ahead. It was a matter not just of doing Good Works among the Poor but of preparing for the millennium: as Bernard Shaw once expressed it, "Marx keeps his head like a God. He has discovered the law. . . ." The head itself seemed to come straight out of the Old Testament.

With his fierce eyes and looming forehead, framed by a mass of untrimmed hair and a bushy beard, Marx (according to Hyndman) seemed to combine "the righteous fury of the great seers of his race, with the cold analytical powers of Spinoza and the Jewish doctors."

The never-ending problem of the unfinished volumes of *Das Kapital* involved Marx in an even more compulsive work schedule than that of Freud or Mahler. He could be found at his writing desk from nine in the morning until two or three o'clock the next morning—with time off only for meals and, presumably, bedtime stories. When he worked at the British Museum he would arrive when the library opened at nine and leave only when it closed at seven: to a penniless refugee, the great domed reading room offered the advantages of dependable central heating and comfortable chairs. He would encourage his disciples to study harder with all the insistence of Kafka's mother telling her son to eat, eat. "Marx drove us to the British Museum where he worked every day," recalled Wilhelm Liebknecht. " 'Learn, learn,' was the categorical imperative which he would shout at us often enough, though the message was already conveyed in the example he set us, and in what we could see of his own tremendous labors."

The tendency to think of eminent, graying Jews—particularly bearded ones like Marx and Freud—as biblical prophets is understandable enough: even C. P. Snow, not ordinarily overawed by scientists, could not resist writing of Einstein, "Meeting him in old age was rather like being confronted by the Second Isaiah." The Viennese critic Max Graf described Freud as "a Moses like the one Michelangelo made of stone"—in later years Freud's self-identification with Moses did, in fact, grow more and more pronounced. The disciples of still another "lawgiver," Arnold Schoenberg, looked up to him as a kind of tutelary genius even while he was still in his thirties. "His talk is instruction, his actions are exemplary, his works revelations," wrote Alban Berg in a fervent tribute. "He has in him the teacher, the prophet, the Messiah. . . ." Yet this was the composer who began his most famous book on musical theory with the disarming statement that he had "learned" its contents from his pupils.

It was hardly surprising that the Bible remained a primary reference point for the marginal Jews who had ceased to believe in it: for that matter, the most deliberately messianic figure on the nineteenth-century German horizon was not the bearded Marx but the clean-shaven pagan Richard Wagner, whom Ludwig II of Bavaria habitually addressed as the "Redeemer." But although the

Scriptures furnished precedents for any number of secular prophets and patriarchs, there was nothing in the ancient Jewish tradition to compel them to work so hard at it: the endless hours,
the chronic irritability, the habit of looking too often at one's pocket
watch were all symptoms of a specifically German-Jewish malaise.
Freud, as a young doctor, had heard the classic talmudic doctrine
on this point from an old scholar he met in Hamburg. "The Jew,"
he was told, "is made for enjoyment. . . . The Jew is made for joy
and joy for the Jew." The lesson was lost on Freud, who was
already well on the way to becoming a compulsive worker—soon
to arrive at the stage where "I take no delight in anything else." In
a sense, the extra hours of work were intended to offset the disad-
vantages of being an odd-man-out in a world that would not take
joy for an answer. Discrimination, Freud thought, acted as a spur
rather than a hindrance for gifted people. As he wrote to one of his
students: "The fact that as a Jew it will be more difficult for you
may, as with all of us, have the effect of stimulating your produc-
tivity." He felt that his psychoanalytic theories would have encountered far less resistance had he possessed a more Austrian-
sounding name "like Oberhuber," but he had learned with time, as
he put it, "to develop a little masochism and . . . endure a certain
amount of injustice."

The degree of masochism one had to develop, and the amount of
injustice one could expect to face, varied enormously according to
time, place and circumstance. It would be a mistake to compile the
evidence on this point merely from the antisemitic books and pam-
phlets that poured off the presses in increasing quantities, and to
portray the life of the average German and Austrian Jew as one of
perpetual harassment and discrimination. On the contrary, before
the Nazis, cooperation and mutual understanding were often the
rule rather than the exception, and in virtually every sphere: not
only in business, banking, publishing and the arts, but also where
it counted most, at the personal level. People fell in love, married,
had children: German statistics show that, before World War I, a
third of all "Jewish" marriages were in fact "mixed," or as the
anthropologists would say, exogamous. Germans and Jews attended the same schools, danced at the same Fasching balls,
worked in the same factories, reported for the same newspapers,
acted in each other's plays: they volunteered for the same army
and were duly maimed and killed in the same wars.

The very existence of Jews in Germany and Austria bore witness
to the toleration and forbearance practiced by a least some of their
neighbors. Countless massacres and expulsions had punctuated

the 1,600 years of their common history, yet a few communities had always been willing to "overlook" the disturbing presence of these obstinate dissenters who refused to see the light even when it was offered to them at sword's point. A modus vivendi had been worked out, at least in Germany—Austrian persecution had been far more relentless until the beginning of the nineteenth century—and although a series of stringent edicts had kept them landless until they were legally emancipated, the Jews often spoke of having put down roots in this land. Some elusive quality, wrote the economist and Reichstag deputy Ludwig Bamberger in 1880, "made Germany and all things German particularly attractive for the Jews, and the Jews an especially useful component to the German character."

Nor was it an entirely one-sided love affair. "What a blessing a Jew is among Germans!" exclaimed Friedrich Nietzsche, and the playwright Frank Wedekind suggested that "Jew and non-Jew are the two souls in the breast of mankind, ever at variance and eternally indispensable to each other." (A very German image, this simile of the dual soul: it is Goethe's Faust, after all, who first articulates the great romantic conflict of the divided self: "Two souls live, *ach*, within my breast!") Throughout the century there were men of goodwill on all sides who pleaded for harmony and brotherhood on the basis, no longer as radical as it sounded to many Germans, that all men are created equal. "Sons of Israel!" declared the Viennese Catholic revolutionaries of 1848, "Every noble Christian is your brother. . . ." It was to prove that such words were not idle rhetoric that Else Lasker-Schüler ("Germany's greatest lyric poetess," according to the poet Gottfried Benn) wrote her deeply moving parable of German-Jewish understanding, *Arthur Aronymus*. It begins with a description of the friendship that was formed, over the heads of their congregations, as it were, between a wise old rabbi, her great-grandfather, and Bishop Lavater of Westphalia:

> Every evening, after the two princes had taken their frugal supper, they would meet in a small dining room of "The Golden Half-Moon." This half-moon neither waxed nor waned, exactly like the brotherly bond that unchangingly united these two high priests. They anointed the hours before going to bed with an oil that was pleasing to the Lord; they sought after heavenly gold in sacred discourses, two allies in their quest for God. For in essence they both believed in the only, invisible Lord, the Eternal, King of the World.

The most fortunate among the German Jews could claim that they had never experienced discrimination before the advent of the

Nazis. The novelist Lion Feuchtwanger, who barely managed to escape from the Gestapo, told his fellow exiles in 1943 that the German people were not naturally inclined to Nazism, and that he had known antisemitism neither at school nor at the university. "Despite their best efforts, the Nazis never succeeded in making the Germans antisemitic," he insisted. More recently, when the American biographer of the "Frankfurt School" and the Institute of Social Research, Martin Jay, investigated the background of its most important members—Max Horkheimer, Herbert Marcuse, Friedrich Pollock et al.—he was surprised to learn from Pollock that "all of us, up to the last years before Hitler, had no feeling of insecurity originating from our ethnic descent. Unless we were ready to undergo baptism, certain positions in public service and business were closed to us, but that never bothered us. And under the Weimar republic many of these barriers had been moved away." Similarly, Toni Cassirer, wife of the philosopher Ernst Cassirer, writes in her memoirs that she too, "as the daughter of a respected businessman," had never been troubled by antisemitism. "My brothers and their friends were still young and generally active in artistic occupations; they did not seek jobs in public institutions, and we had never had the experience of being 'measured by a different yardstick.' " Her husband, author of the monumental *Philosophy of Symbolic Forms*, came from the same favored background—he happened to be her cousin. Accordingly he never ceased, even as an émigré, to regard himself as "a German philosopher, torn from the German earth." During his last years, in his American exile, he would tell his students at Yale and Columbia: "This Hitler is an error of history. He does not belong in German history at all. And therefore he will perish."

All of these privileged witnesses, however, came from well-to-do families of the upper middle class, for whom money had always been a talisman against the cruder forms of prejudice. Even for them there were limits as to how far it could smooth their way into German society. Walther Rathenau (son of the millionaire industrialist who founded the giant AEG empire—the German "General Electric" company) made the unhappy discovery that "in the youth of every German Jew there comes the painful moment which he will remember for the rest of his life; when for the first time he becomes fully conscious that he has come into the world as a second-class citizen; that no ability and accomplishment can liberate him from this condition." (Accordingly, Rathenau himself worked very hard to surmount his handicap: he became foreign minister of Germany in 1922, only to be assassinated by a gang of fascist thugs six months later.) At less rarefied levels, the inevitable awakening to the facts of prejudice could come very early in life, often with traumatic results. The poet Ernst Toller remembered such an incident from his childhood in West Prussia during the 1890s:

> I see myself wearing a little, short dress, standing outside our house looking at a cart. It is big, bigger than Marie, as big as a house. Marie is the nurse, and she wears a red coral necklace: round red corals. She is sitting on one of the shafts, rocking to and fro. Then Ilse comes out with her nurse. She runs up to me and we hold hands; for some time we stand hand in hand and look at each other curiously. Ilse's nurse is gossiping with Marie, but suddenly she calls out: "Come away, Ilse! He's a Jew." Ilse drops my hand and runs away. I can't understand what the nurse means, but I begin to cry bitterly. At last the other nurse departs with Ilse, and Marie tries to comfort me, taking me into her arms and showing me her corals; but I don't want the corals, and I break her necklace.

Sometimes, especially in Austria, where prejudice was far more widespread, the encounter with antisemitism could take violent and dangerous forms. The Czech nationalist riots that erupted in Prague in 1897 began with attacks on German institutions and ended with an orgy of looting and window-smashing of shops and homes owned by Jews. Egon Erwin Kisch, the crusading journalist who was to become known as *Der rasende Reporter* (the enraged reporter), remembered how, as a twelve-year-old, he had seen "houses set on fire and property destroyed, the nationalist fury raging through the doors and window-panes, and streets that had been filled with howling mobs and tinkling glass suddenly emptied, and the cavalry clattering by, bugles blowing, sabers flashing. . . ."

This "December storm" was also part of Franz Kafka's private store of childhood reminiscence, afterward to be metamorphosed into fiction. Incidents of this kind tended to reinforce the siege mentality conveyed in Kafka's aphorism, "My prison cell—my fortress." Theoretically there were laws to protect minorities and guarantee their civil rights, but in practice it was never anything less than an age of anxiety. "Once more I screamed at the top of my voice into the world," Kafka jotted into his diary in 1917. "Then they shoved a gag into my mouth. . . ." Thanks to the discoveries of Dr. Freud, one at least had the satisfaction of knowing that this choking sensation was a bona fide neurosis, as honorably acquired as any dueling scar.

"The nobility has a family history; the Jewish bourgeoisie only has a history of neuroses," remarked the novelist Hermann Broch in a letter to his son. "You come from a terribly neurotic family. Your grandfather, manic-depressive and gloomy with touches of genius; your grandmother, a compulsive neurotic of the first rank, but of modest intelligence, power-hungry, obstinate and vain; I could go on for pages about the psychological situation . . . an infernal picture of well-intentioned shabbiness." But parents and grandparents were almost always unfathomable to the German- or Austrian-Jewish intelligentsia: the gulf between father Mahler's small-town grog shop and his son's cosmic *Resurrection* Symphony hardly seemed bridgeable in a single generation. Besides, the normal toils of the Oedipus complex were, for them, entangled in a plexus of secondary anxieties. Fritz Kortner, one of the foremost actors and directors of the twentieth-century German stage, fills a page and a half of his autobiography with a detailed recital of his worries and phobias, beginning with his childhood fear "of being teased as a Jew-boy," and proceeding from there to nineteen other kinds of fear, including stage fright—a formidable collection for any one actor to contend with.

In this assortment of anxieties, antisemitism usually figured not as an active threat but as a dull, throbbing annoyance. Before it was institutionalized by the Nazis it tended to be casual and anonymous—an ugly possibility, never very far beneath the surface, which had a way of rearing its head when least expected. Always it was an imposition in the fullest sense of the word. The young Freud, in a letter to his fiancée, describes a typically nasty little incident that took place on a train between Dresden and Leipzig, when he opened a window in his compartment and became embroiled in an argument with fellow passengers who wanted to keep it closed:

> While the discussion ensued and the man said he was prepared to open the ventilation slip instead of the window, there came a shout from the background: "He's a dirty Jew!"—and with this the whole situation took on a different color. My first opponent also turned antisemitic and declared: "We Christians consider other people, you'd better think less of your precious self," etc., and muttering abuses befitting his education, my second opponent announced that he was going to climb over the seats to show me, etc. Even a year ago I would have been speechless with agitation; but now I am different; I was not the least frightened of that mob, asked the one to keep to himself the empty phrases which inspired no respect in me, and the

other to step up and take what was coming to him. I was quite prepared to kill him, but he did not step up; I was glad I refrained from joining in the abuse, something one must always leave to the others.

It was a ridiculous and puerile state of affairs that could compel young intellectuals with, presumably, better things on their mind, to be prepared at any moment to defend their honor with their fists. Yet it explains why so many Jewish students, particularly among the saber-rattling Austro-Hungarians, turned into champion fencers, winning thirteen gold and three silver medals in foil and saber during the first twenty-odd years of the modern Olympics. These skills were also exercised in the *Mensur*—the classic ear-, nose- and throat-chopping duel with sabers which was a favorite pastime at German universities. Before long, however, the privilege of avenging themselves upon their tormentors in the dueling fraternities was brought to an end by the introduction of a new dueling code, unilaterally declaring Jews to be unworthy of receiving satisfaction from a gentleman. Thus another promising channel for working off their frustrations was closed to them.

Most of the intellectuals thought of themselves, in the first instance, as *people:* perhaps what rankled most was not so much the constant threat of trouble as the necessity of having to appear, willingly or not, as heroes or martyrs for the Jewish cause. Since they had, with rare exceptions, severed their ties to the Jewish tradition, they were not notably well qualified to act as its representatives in any case. Their efforts at assimilation had been intended to help them lead more or less normal lives as musicians, writers, scientists; yet whatever they might produce would instantly be branded as "typically Jewish." Einstein, working in—one would think—the most abstract of disciplines, was bitterly attacked for having introduced "Jewish physics" into German science. Freud was accused, not only by fools but even by C. G. Jung, of purveying "Jewish psychology." Mahler, composing in a supposedly universal language, heard from a critic that his music spoke "with a Jewish accent—*sie jüdelt.*" Even the eminently Protestant and Victorian Mendelssohn was said, by Wilhelm von Lenz, to possess a "Hebraic element," and to have modeled his melodies on synagogue chants—an assertion which, as Berlioz pointed out in *Evenings with the Orchestra,* is sheer rubbish. Each of them at any rate, whether converted or not, ended up in the anomalous position of being regarded as a "representative Jew" by both friends and enemies.

This exasperating circumstance created a curious assortment of bedfellows: nationalists and universalists, rich and poor, left-wing and right-wing, establishment figures and cabaret poets, philosophers and matinée idols—a Marx, a Rathenau, a Karl Kraus, a Schoenberg, a Richard Tauber. There was nothing particularly surprising in this diversity. The Jews as an ethnic group have long held the distinction of being the people who vary most widely among themselves—*untereinander am meisten anders*, in Elias Canetti's phrase. But from the antisemite point of view this very diversity seemed to confirm the existence of a conspiracy to take over the intellectual life of the nation. In Vienna, where the Jews accounted for nearly nine percent of the urban population at the turn of the century, they were heavily represented in literature, the theater, music, journalism and every form of criticism, from feuilleton to concert review. In Berlin, with proportionately only half as many Jews, "the splendor of the Kaiser's empire, its inward and outward wealth, was due in large measure to the Jewish fraction of the population," as the poet Gottfried Benn noted in his autobiography, *Doppelleben* (A Double Life). "The overwhelming stream of stimuli, of artistic, scientific and commercial improvisation which, from 1918 to 1933, put Berlin in a class with Paris, stemmed for the most part from this minority, its international connections, its sensitive restlessness, and above all, its dead-certain instinct for quality." (In 1950, when Benn brought out his memoirs, he thought it propitious to describe the situation in these terms, but in 1933, when Hitler had begun eliminating the Jews from cultural life, Benn had chosen to welcome the Nazis on the grounds that "a lordly race can only grow out of terrible and violent beginnings.")

A development that seemed admirable enough in retrospect appeared far more disturbing and problematic while it was actually taking place. "German cultural life seems to be passing increasingly into Jewish hands," noted the critic Moritz Goldstein in a magazine article that stirred up a major controversy in 1911. "This, however, the Christians had not foreseen or intended when they granted the pariahs in their midst a stake in European civilization. They began to resist; again they began to call us foreigners, to consider us dangerous in the temple of their civilization." All of the Jews' struggles and successes had served merely to create an embarrassing dilemma: "We Jews are administering the spiritual property of a nation which denies us our right and our ability to do so."

Goldstein thought he could understand the anger of the non-Jewish Germans at the presence of so many Jews among the "German poets" of the day. It does not seem to have occurred to him that a civilized nation might welcome a sudden poetry explosion, whatever the source. His instinct—only twenty years premature, as it turned out—was to leave Germany and "to take what gifts I may possess somewhere where people are prepared to use them—if only I knew where." He saw himself fighting on two fronts (another very German image, this "two-front war," which has played such a recurrent and traumatic role in their history). In one direction he faced the fools and super-Teutons who habitually abused anything connected with the Jews. But even more dangerous, he thought, were "those Jews who are completely unaware, who continue to take part in German cultural activities regardless, who pretend and persuade themselves that they are not recognized." Let us not overreach ourselves, was the gist of his argument; as stepchildren we must be on our best behavior, and above all not so numerous or conspicuous as to attract the envy of the "real" Germans.

In discussions of this kind, a sharp dividing line was invariably drawn between German and Jew, as though it were a choice of either-or; the bearded talmudist versus the blond cavalry lieutenant in a spiked helmet. Yet at the very moment Goldstein's essay appeared, the new-born Expressionist movement had already resolved the dilemma with a synthesis that embodied the best of both worlds. Expressionism—broadly speaking the basis of the twentieth-century Renaissance in German art and literature—was a phenomenon so profoundly macaronic that it would be quite impossible to disentangle the German threads from the Jewish. It began as a revolt against what Nietzsche called the "flatness" of Wilhelmine Germany, and as an antidote to the wedding-cake sculptures that the Kaiser insisted on bestowing upon a grateful nation. It was a difficult art that refused to please its audience: dark, unpretty, painfully intense. "Truly it is not beauty and loveliness that are our strength," the sculptor Ernst Barlach had written at the start of his career. "Our power lies rather in the opposite, in ugliness, in demonic passion. . . ." The Expressionists preferred humanity and "the music of feeling" to the most glorious Wagnerian sentiments. Franz Kafka wrote to a friend that "books to make us happy" were no longer what was wanted. "My God, we could be happy even if we had no books, and such books as make us happy we could write ourselves if necessary. But we need books that affect us like a misfortune that pains us very much, like the death of someone whom we have loved more than ourselves. . . a book must be an axe for the frozen sea in us."

The original Expressionists, so-called, were painters like Ernst

Ludwig Kirchner, Emil Nolde and Max Pechstein, who painted the
"ugliest" pictures in Germany. The movement is said to have got
its name around 1910 when a member of an art jury, faced with a
painting by Pechstein, asked the art dealer Paul Cassirer (a cousin
of Ernst Cassirer), "Is that *Impressionismus?*" No, came the answer,
"*Expressionismus!*" At about the same time Expressionism produced its first literary sensation—the poem "Weltende" by Jakob
van Hoddis (the ingeniously renamed Hans Davidsohn), who
foresaw that the world would end, not with a whimper but a
sneeze:

> *Dem Bürger fliegt vom spitzen Kopf der Hut*
> *in allen Lüften hallt es wie Geschrei.*
> *Dachdecker stürzen ab und gehn entzwei*
> *und an den Küsten—liest man—steigt die Flut.*
>
> *Der Sturm ist da, die wilden Meere hüpfen*
> *an Land, um dicke Dämme zu zerdrücken.*
> *Die meisten Menschen haben einen Schnupfen.*
> *Die Eisenbahnen fallen von den Brücken.*
>
> The hat flies off the bourgeois' pointed head,
> The air all round reverberates with cries.
> Tiles fall from roofs and shatter; it is said
> that on the coast the seas are on the rise.
>
> The storm has come, and now the seas enfold
> the land, to crush the dikes and vessels.
> Most people here are suffering from a cold.
> The locomotives tumble off the railway trestles.

These eight lines exercised a now incomprehensible fascination on young German literati of the day. "They transformed us
into other beings, they lifted us out of the dull world of the
bourgeoisie," recalled the poet Johannes R. Becher. "These eight
lines abducted us. We discovered continually new beauties in these
eight lines, we sang them, we hummed them, we murmured them,
whistled them . . . we called them to each other across the street
like passwords." Van Hoddis gave poetry readings in the literary
club known as the Neopathetic Cabaret, founded by Kurt Hiller,
the godfather of Expressionist poetry and easily the best organized
of the Berlin enfants terribles. (Hiller writes in his memoirs that
there was an oral tradition in his family that they were descended
in a direct line from Rabbi Hillel, who lived in Jerusalem at about
the same time as Jesus Christ.) Else Lasker-Schüler, who attended

the readings, noted that van Hoddis would "suddenly flutter up like a raven; an iridescent black head looks moodily over the rampart of the lectern. . . . He speaks the short verses defiantly and proudly; they are so shiny and freshly-minted one could steal them from him. Four-liners—inscriptions; in a state run by poets they would be inscribed in a circle on the silver coins."

There was something strangely familiar in this restless figure who could be seen at any hour of the night strolling briskly through the streets of Berlin. The painter (and poet) Ludwig Meidner, who drew appropriately Expressionist portraits (i.e., very unflattering ones) of all the Expressionist poets, remembered afterward that van Hoddis would leave the literary cafés at midnight in order to lead him on an all-night tramp through the workers' districts in the north of the city. "Van Hoddis marched along and stamped the ground in the middle of the road like a musketeer, for we avoided the sidewalk. At times he would stand stockstill, silent for a moment; then he would laugh and say something funny or else some very wise things, for he was very intelligent. Then he would start off again at his rapid marching pace, for . . . we displayed great stamina on our walks, which would not end even when the sun came up. We were so much in love with the city."

Van Hoddis's literary career lasted only a few years: he was fated to have what one writer calls *ein deutsch-jüdisches Dichterschicksal,* a German-Jewish poet's destiny. In 1914, in the best tradition of earlier German poets like Lenz and Hölderlin, van Hoddis went harmlessly mad. At first he was placed into private care with a schoolmaster's family in Thuringia, where he was known to the local villagers as *der Schnelläufer,* the fast runner. When his mother came for a visit he would, on their walks together, doff his hat to every animal he met. Children threw stones at him. The news that his brother had been killed in the war seemed to leave him quite unaffected. Later he was committed to a mental asylum which—after he had been a patient there for twenty years—duly turned him over to the Gestapo for "deportation" in 1942. He figured as "Number 8" on the delivery list: that is the last anyone knows about the eschatological poet who had foreseen that, in Germany, the end of the world would involve both a cataclysm and a politely stifled cough. In postwar reference books, van Hoddis appears with "date of death unknown"—an uncomfortable phrase, which is also applied to other poets, such as Arno Nadel and Gertrud Kolmar, who simply disappeared into the maelstrom.

Though they had been born into a peaceful world, most of the

Expressionists had terrifying premonitions about the impending descent of man; perhaps that was why van Hoddis doffed his hat to animals rather than people. Franz Kafka looked around him and saw that he was living on murderer's row—the act of writing, fortunately, represented "a leap out of murderer's row." Yet in the distance he could already discern "the alarm trumpets of the void." Else Lasker-Schüler had her own presentiments about the *Weltende* close at hand: "There is a weeping in the world, as though God had died." Alfred Lichtenstein's 1913 poem *Die Dämmerung* (Twilight) focuses on a nightmare vision of two cripples creeping across a field, a poet going mad, a horse stumbling over a woman, a man glued to a window, a piercing scream from a baby carriage. These are typically Expressionist forebodings, drawn from the imagination. The chilling image

> . . . *Am unteren Rand der Viehwagen-Luke*
> *angefroren wie ganz kleine Eiszapfen*
> *die dünnen Finger eines Kindes.*

> Frozen to the lower edge
> of the cattle-car door,
> like very small icicles
> the thin fingers of a child.

was taken from life thirty years later, in the 1940s, by a young poet of the next generation, Lothar Kusche, who actually witnessed the wintry scene he evokes in *Menschen im Güterwagen* (People in a Freight Car). But the Expressionists of 1910 had an uncanny sense of what was awaiting them. They tried to forestall the tragedy with appeals to the brotherhood of man. Franz Werfel begins *Der Weltfreund* (Friend of the World) with the lines, "My only desire, Oh Man, is to be kin to thee!" And Yvan Goll celebrated the opening of the Panama Canal with a broadsheet ode proclaiming, "All that is thine, Earth, will now be called Brother; all water, the bitter and the sweet, the cold stream and the warm springs that burn, will flow together." But it was useless; they were a *génération maudite.* When the war broke out they were nearly all of an age to be sent to the front, where their visions of disaster turned out to have been far more realistic than the operations estimates of the General Staff. Their intuition, however, failed to prevent them from becoming casualties in large numbers. One of the first to be killed was the clairvoyant Lichtenstein, in whose obituary it was written that he had been a "saint" who only needed the slightest wind "to hear the whole world-structure cracking."

The war decimated the ranks of the poets and painters, who died all the more reluctantly because their life's work had just begun. "My entire will to live is contained in my unfinished pictures," wrote the most gifted of the "Blue Riders," Franz Marc, just before he was killed at Verdun in 1916. The poet Georg Trakl committed suicide after harrowing experiences in Poland; the painter Oskar Kokoschka was wounded on the Russian front; Ernst Ludwig Kirchner suffered a nervous breakdown from which he never fully recovered. The survivors returned to Berlin, Munich or Vienna more determined than ever to create a modern humanist Renaissance. "Hell lay behind us," wrote Stefan Zweig in his memoirs. "What was there to frighten us after that! Another world was about to begin." Despite the hard times and the political uncertainty, the ensuing decade is now remembered as the most fascinating and creative moment in German cultural history. Even those who knew nothing about Germany or its literature could recognize from afar that this epoch had that rare and elusive thing called style. Those who actually lived through it, like the Swiss literary critic Walter Muschg, were afterward "unable ever to forget it, and continued to mourn for it like a lost paradise."

The achievements of "Weimar culture" (or rather, "Berlin culture," since that was where most of it was produced) were, like the sufferings of the war, wholly nondenominational. Significantly, the most brilliant piece of 1920s theater, *Threepenny Opera*, was the joint brainchild of a German poet, Bertolt Brecht, and a German-Jewish composer, Kurt Weill, who had succeeded in trapping the *Zeitgeist* in an ingenious arrangement of distorting mirrors. (It set an all-time record for an "opera" by receiving more than 4,000 performances throughout Europe in a single year.) Alban Berg's *Wozzeck*, which caught the pulse beat of the epoch in more menacing harmonies, was the work of an Austrian Catholic, employing the twelve-tone technique discovered by his teacher Schoenberg: the 1925 premiere at the Berlin State Opera that made its composer famous overnight was directed by Erich Kleiber, a Jewish conductor from Vienna who had devoted more than 130 rehearsals to getting it letter-perfect.

The spirit of German and Jewish entente now seemed to be in the ascendant throughout the world of art. In 1920 the Prussian Academy of Arts elected the first Jewish president in its 224-year history, Max Liebermann, a Berlin-born Impressionist who was as celebrated for his quips and anecdotes as for his portraits. But the international avant-garde centered on the composer-writer Herwarth Walden (originally Georg Lewin—the more romantic-sounding name was invented by his sometime wife, Else Lasker-Schüler). Besides publishing the Expressionist magazine *Der Sturm* (not to be confused with the Nazi scandal-sheet, *Der Stürmer*), Walden ran a gallery for such artists as Campendonck, Léger, Chagall, Paul Klee, Kurt Schwitters and Moholy-Nagy. Berlin had become, in the words of its all-powerful theater critic Alfred Kerr, "the most important theater city in the world, and also the first in music"—a distinction it enjoyed in large measure thanks to directors and conductors whom the Nazis were already attacking as "non-Aryans": Max Reinhardt, Leopold Jessner, Max Ophuls, Viktor Barnowsky, Otto Klemperer, Bruno Walter, Leo Blech. Among the city's prominent actors and singers, soon to be banished by Nazi racial laws, were Elisabeth Bergner, Fritzi Massary, Ernst Deutsch, Fritz Kortner, Ernst Ginsberg, Alexander Granach, Conrad Veidt, Peter Lorre, Erna Sack, Alexander Kipnis and Friedrich Schorr. Meanwhile, directors like Josef von Sternberg (*The Blue Angel*), Ernst Lubitsch (*Anna Boleyn*), Billy Wilder (*Emil und die Detektive*) and Fritz Lang ("*M*"; *Metropolis*) were helping create the short-lived golden age of German film: most of them made the transition to Hollywood without waiting for Hitler to force them out.

Literally dozens of writers afterward banned as "Jewish"—though many of them hardly thought of themselves as such—were producing important contributions to German literature. Among the leading dramatists were Carl Sternheim (*The Snob*), Arthur Schnitzler (*La Ronde*), Ernst Toller (*The Machine-Wreckers*), Walter Hasenclever (*The Son*), Ferdinand Bruckner (*Criminals*) and the Hungarian expatriate Ferenc Molnar (*Liliom*); among the novelists, besides Broch and Kafka, Alfred Doeblin (*Berlin Alexanderplatz*), Jakob Wassermann (*The World's Illusion*), Lion Feuchtwanger (*Jew Süss*), Franz Werfel (*The Forty Days of Musa Dagh*), Alfred Neumann (*The Deuce*), Bruno Frank (*Days of the King*), Arnold Zweig (*The Case of Sergeant Grischa*), Ernst Weiss (*Nahar*), Joseph Roth (*Radetzky March*), and Vicki Baum (*Grand Hotel*); among the poets, Ernst Blass, Alfred Mombert, Rudolf Borchardt, Albert Ehrenstein, Martin Gumpert, Walter Mehring, Nelly Sachs, Berthold Viertel, Karl Wolfskehl and Alfred Wolfenstein; among the essayists and critics, Karl Kraus, Alfred Polgar, Maxmilian Harden, Theodor Wolff, Egon Friedell, Theodor Lessing, Kurt Tucholsky, Friedrich Torberg, Walter Benjamin, Ernst Bloch and Felix Salten (who also happened to be the author of *Bambi*).

A century before, Isaac d'Israeli, the father of Benjamin Disraeli, had asserted that he could count all the "Jewish men of genius or talent" on his fingers. "Ten centuries have not produced ten great men." Yet now they seemed to be springing out of the German ground by the score. And the same educated stratum of so-called *Kulturjuden* which produced the gifted poet-sons also constituted the most influential segment of the reading public. Thomas Mann, the North German patrician and Nobel laureate, conceded that there had often been bad blood between him and certain of the Jewish critics; that he had sustained some of "the most poisonously funny" attacks from that quarter, and yet

> Jews "discovered" me, Jews published me and propagated my reputation; they performed my impossible play; it was a Jew, the late S. Lublinski, who wrote of my *Buddenbrooks* (after it had been greeted elsewhere with sour expressions), "This book will grow with time, and will still be read generations from now." And when I go out into the world, and visit cities, it is almost always Jews, not only in Vienna and Berlin, who welcome, shelter, dine and pamper me. . . . It is a fact that simply cannot be denied that, in Germany, whatever is enjoyed only by "genuine Teutons" and aboriginal *Ur*-Germans, but scorned or rejected by the Jews, will never really amount to anything, culturally.

Perhaps, after all, the essential function of the Jews in the German body politic was like that of the irritating grain of sand in the oyster, which causes it to produce the pearl. Historians have been warned not to overemphasize the "importance of the intellectual element in the encounter between Judaism and German culture" (as I am doing here), yet it is precisely this element that confers meaning and purpose to the rest. The fact that a number of German Jews established shoe factories, banks or department stores certainly deserves a chapter in German economic history, but the onward march of the nineteenth-century mercantile spirit was largely the same throughout the Western world, whether the entrepreneur happened to be named R. H. Macy, H. C. Harrod or Hermann Tietz.

What gives the German-Jewish bourgeoisie their special place in history is not their (usually overrated) contribution to the gross national product between 1812 and 1933, but the circumstance that, in an astonishing number of cases, their prosperity was merely a way-station to more idealistic concerns. In accordance with the unwritten rule that sons should, wherever practicable, surpass their fathers—hence the constant, restless need to be doing something—the shoe-factory generation regularly produced and nurtured a brood of scribes, artists, intellectuals. Else Lasker-Schüler was the daughter of an investment banker, Carl Sternheim the son of a banker and newspaper publisher, Walter Benjamin of an antique dealer, Alfred Neumann of a lumber merchant, Stefan Zweig of a textile manufacturer, Franz Kafka of a haberdashery wholesaler, Hermann Broch of a cotton-mill owner; Theodor Lessing and Walter Hasenclever were sons of doctors and grandsons of manufacturers, and so on, in an orderly and predictable procession from the department store into the library, the theater and the concert hall.

Often this pattern involved the sons in a double revolt—against the father's Jewish-bourgeois values, and against the system of obedience training of German society as a whole. Perhaps the process was psychologically easier for those whose fathers had failed in business or had never really brought it to anything—Freud, Schoenberg and Einstein come to mind. The basic pattern, at any rate, applied to nearly all the intellectuals; indeed, it was so pervasive that an anthropologist might be tempted to describe them as a caste or subcaste, like those of India or West Africa—a specialized caste of communicators and problem-solvers who are, as it were, born to be articulate. One thinks of the *griots* of Senegal, or tribes like the Daria Lochar of Rajasthan, who have been musicians and storytellers for generations, and whose skills have endeared them to the people among whom they live: one doesn't persecute singers or tellers of tales.

Had the Germans possessed something of the mental flexibility of the Rajasthanis, they might have accepted their Jews in the same spirit, as the product, not of an "alien race," but of a thousand-year *guruparampara*, the master-to-pupil chain that equipped this scholarly minority with certain communications skills that could now be creatively applied to German problems. For that matter, even the so-called Jewish problem was really a German problem—or rather, the European problem of Germany's isolation from the rest of the world. The average German, unlike the British or French, had no experience of foreigners or foreign ideas. (Hitler, to take a quintessential example, had never been to Paris before he turned up as the city's "conqueror" in 1940.)

If they had seen something of the world beyond their doorstep, particularly if they had traveled in India, the German antisemites might have realized that many of the qualities which they regarded as particularly "Jewish"—the vividness of the body language, the intensity of emotional attachments within the extended family, the exaggerated reverence for writing, learning, exegesis—are also an integral part of life in places like Delhi and Jaipur. Even the famous vaulted nose which provided so much sport for German cartoonists (though according to the anthropological researches of Dr. Maurice Fishberg, its proud possessors are limited to a mere four-teen percent of Jews) is a common enough sight in northern India. Its appearance on Hittite bas reliefs of the second millennium B.C. has given rise to speculation that the bent nose is, in fact, a legacy from ancient Turkey. Be that as it may, it still reappears with stylish consistency among at least some of the important figures of the German-Jewish tradition, notably among musicians—including Mendelssohn, Meyerbeer, Offenbach, Mahler and Schoenberg (though this is not to suggest that "Mahler's nose" should replace what the physiognomists call "Mozart's ear" as the outward sign of musical talent).

At all events, had the German racial theorists of the nineteenth century known more about India, they would not have been quite so prone to regard "Indo-Aryan" as the antithesis of "Jewish." But it was the British who went to India and the Germans who stayed home, reading Indian literature in translations from the Sanskrit, and forming impossibly distorted notions about the "Aryans" who were supposed to have written it. It seems never to have occurred to them that, from the standpoint of physical resemblance as well as social behavior, the "recognizable" Jew was by far the most "Indo-Aryan" type in Europe. Yiddish was an Indo-Aryan lan-guage too, for that matter: it was essentially the medieval High German which the Jews had taken with them in the late Middle Ages, when they escaped persecution in Germany by settling in areas of Poland that had been devastated by Tartar invasions. The German dialect they continued to speak among themselves, writ-ten in Hebrew characters, remained encapsulated in precisely the same way as "Pennsylvania Dutch"—an eighteenth-century Ger-man dialect from the Palatinate which was preserved in one small linguistic enclave in America. By the same token, the traditional beard and kaftan of the Polish Jews, which so offended the young Hitler's sensibilities when he saw them on the streets of Vienna, were nothing else but a medieval German costume that had origi-nated on the Rhine. For the Eastern Jews who migrated westward to Vienna, Breslau or Berlin in increasing numbers during the rail-way age, the move back to German-speaking territory was, in a sense, a cultural homecoming: that was one of the reasons why the transition from Yiddish to German literature proved so easy for many of them.

But even if he wore a Prussian military haircut instead of side-curls, dressed in the latest Berlin fashion, spoke German as mag-nificently as Kortner and wrote it as flawlessly as Heine, the German Jew was not to be allowed, after all, to forget his alien ancestry. Among the Nazis, in fact, such accomplishments would only be dismissed as further proof of "Jewish cunning" and their knack for protective coloration. The more old-fashioned "classical" antisemitism had been directed chiefly against the Jews' insistence on maintaining their own ethnic and religious identity. "Whether they sell pants or write books," the chauvinist historian Theodor Mommsen had written in 1880, "it is their duty to put aside their peculiar ways (*Sonderart*) and, with a determined hand, to remove the obstacles between them and their fellow citizens." Now a new set of obstacles was being erected from the other side. The racism of Hitler and his followers was directed as much against the wholly assimilated Jewish army captain as against his kaftan-wearing cousin from Galicia: ferreting out those who had succeeded in "passing" became something of a Nazi obsession even before they took over the government and were able to write their paranoia into law.

The racial policies of the Third Reich were thus applied with equal ferocity to the orthodox and the assimilated, to bankers and beggars, Nobel laureates, department store clerks and school children; to the president of the Academy, Professor Liebermann, and to the German women's fencing champion, Helene Mayer (popularly known as *die blonde He*), who won two Olympic medals for Germany; to the 100,000 Jewish veterans, many of them wounded or crippled, who had fought for Germany during World War I and had earned their 31,500 iron crosses as bravely as the next man. At the same time, the Nazis proceeded with the willful destruction of everything that had to do with the Weimar Renaissance. During the early years of the regime the world was treated to the unusual spectacle of a whole nation deliberately committing cultural suicide. In the prevailing mindless frenzy to follow-the-*Führer*, the mere possession of intellect became grounds for suspicion, and "Aryans" who persisted in trying to exercise it were denounced in the Nazi press as *weisse Juden* (white Jews). As one popular Nazi jingle expressed it:

> *Intellektueller, du Wort mit dem jüdisch grellen Schein,*
> *Ein rechter deutscher Mann kann nie ein Intellektueller sein!*

> Intellectual—the word sounds so Jewish and shrill;
> A true German man can never be an intellectual!

Nazism from the first had been essentially a revolt of the Know-Nothings, though their ranks were soon swelled by members of the aristocracy: as a cultural revolution it aimed at nothing less than the annihilation of the German intelligentsia. It was as if the early Nazis could hardly wait to get their hands on the machinery of state so that they could begin smashing works of art and burning books. As a matter of fact, one of the party's first official acts, after winning the local elections in Thuringia in 1930, was to order the destruction of the fragile, elegant murals created by Oskar Schlemmer (an artist of impeccably "Aryan" antecedents) for the Bauhaus at Weimar. And within months after taking over the central government of the Reich in 1933 they had succeeded in paralyzing the literary life of the nation, pauperizing its theatrical and musical activities and stripping its museums of all great modern art from Van Gogh and Picasso to Max Beckmann and Paul Klee.

All this was done with an air of triumph and complacency, as well as an utter disregard for any practical consequences. More than 1,100 "non-Aryan" faculty members of universities and technical institutes lost their jobs in the initial wave of persecution. When the Nazi minister of education, Rust, jovially inquired of Professor David Hilbert, mentor of the famous Göttingen Mathematical Institute, how mathematics was faring at Göttingen under the new dispensation, he received the laconic reply: "But Herr Minister, there is no mathematics left at Göttingen!" A traveling exhibition that made the rounds of German schools at the same time displayed Einstein's picture in the form of a "wanted" poster that identified him as an exiled subversive who remained at large and "still unhanged." A postwar German writer, assessing the damage which Nazi policy inflicted on the nation's scientific establishment, described the result in the rueful phrase, *die emigrierte Bombe*.

Altogether, some 360,000 people—slightly more than half of the German-Jewish community—were able to flee Germany so long as the exits remained open; virtually all those who were left behind were annihilated. The refugee intellectuals accounted for only a small fraction of the total, yet they constituted the greatest intellectual migration in history. Included among them were countless non-Jews who chose not to make their peace with Hitler: Heinrich and Thomas Mann, for example, or the playwright and ex-cavalry officer Fritz von Unruh; the poet Max Hermann-Neisse, the Austrian novelist Robert Musil, Erich Maria Remarque (*All Quiet on the Western Front*) and the Bavarian writer Oskar Maria Graf, who had responded to the Nazi burning of the books with an open letter demanding, "Burn my books, too!" They were joined in voluntary exile by musicians like the brothers Fritz and Adolf Busch and the composers Paul Hindemith and Ernst Křenek; by the architects Walter Gropius and Ludwig Mies van der Rohe, and by the painters Max Beckmann, Kurt Schwitters and Paul Klee. Their attitude was summed up by the composer Béla Bartók, who left Hungary for America when he saw the Nazis taking over the lands of the old Hapsburg empire: "If someone stays on here, when he could leave, he can thereby be said to acquiesce tacitly in everything that is happening here."

For understandable motives, some of the minor poets stayed behind to applaud the exodus. "Our wheat is being threshed on the threshing-floor of literature," declared the neo-romantic poet Börries von Münchhausen (appropriately enough, a descendant of the celebrated "Liar-Baron" von Münchhausen). "What does it matter that, in sweeping out the chaff, a few golden grains are lost? Germany, the heart of all nations, is wasteful, like all true hearts; stormy and Siegfried-like beats its pulse." The truth was that virtually the whole harvest had been swept out the door. As Dorothy Thompson informed her American readers, "practically everybody who in world opinion had stood for what was called German culture prior to 1933 is now a refugee." But it was not until after the war that the full extent of the damage became apparent. "German literature is so mutilated that it cannot recognize its own condition," wrote Walter Muschg, who had watched "the destruction of German literature" from a neutral sanctuary in Switzerland. The Nazi years had extinguished a vital spark. "Since then Germany has no longer possessed a great literature. When the terror came to an end it remained silent."

A whole generation of writers had been "buried alive" in the process, their books sent to the pulp mill, their names expunged from the libraries. In exile, if they were not already internationally known like Thomas Mann, they lost their reading public and the possibility of earning a living with their native language: only a few of the younger authors able to switch languages in midstream, like Arthur Koestler, could continue to support themselves by writing. And postwar Germany, for a variety of reasons, was slow to come to terms with its uncomfortable ghosts of the twenties and thirties. What remains is "a literature of the dead," as Muschg pointed out, "or rather of those who died too soon, of those who were disowned and forgotten. There is a great modern German literature, but it lies buried beneath the ruins."

Part of my purpose in writing this book is to give British and American readers some inkling of what was lost in the collapse of the Weimar Renaissance, and how much of it remains forgotten to this day. Those who have not studied the arts of Germany in detail can hardly be expected to grasp the magnitude of the disaster. But it might be illustrative to imagine, for a nightmare moment, that a comparable fate had overtaken the English-speaking world: that schools, universities, libraries and museums had all been duly purged of "undesirables" and their works; that Aldous Huxley had been beaten to death in a prison camp near Oxford; that T. S. Eliot had died in exile in Peru; that the aged Bernard Shaw committed suicide on a ship to South America; that Hemingway and Fitzgerald, as well as Rodgers and Hammerstein, had been compelled to live out their last days in a small community in Guatemala, with Fiorello La Guardia, Harry Hopkins and a few other liberal politicians for company; that George Gershwin had been killed trying to cross the Mexican border; that William Faulkner had learned Spanish in order to teach at a school in Caracas; that Henry Moore had made a new career for himself in Cuba after living underground for a time in London—but that W. H. Auden, Marianne Moore, Louis Armstrong, Aaron Copland and e. e. cummings had been among those rounded up and gassed by the police. With these actors in the principal roles, it sounds like a mad science-fiction plot, absurd and wholly unbelievable. Yet this is what actually happened in my lifetime to the cultural life of Germany, and somehow the world has been able to absorb that fact without paying very much attention, or becoming unduly concerned over its possible implications for the rest of mankind.

But besides material for a tragedy it also contains the makings of an epic, for the most terrifying odyssey of modern times had, at almost every stage and station, its poets and chroniclers who left a soul-shattering record of their struggle to remain human in a murderous world where death, in Paul Celan's bitter line, had become "a master craftsman from Germany"—*der Tod ist ein Meister aus Deutschland*. There was, I am afraid, no satisfying moral conclusion to this epic: as a test of human endurance it was as meaningless as the trial of Kafka's Joseph K. Significantly, one of its first victims was the assassinated Existentialist Theodor Lessing, whose most interesting work, *Geschichte als Sinngebung des Sinnlosen*, concerns the idea that the writing of history is the art of conferring meaning upon events that, in the very nature of things, have no meaning. If one searches for a meaning in the German-Jewish tragedy there is, I fear, only one lesson to be learned: that in the never-ending confrontation between the head and the truncheon, the latter usually wins out, at least in the short run. As the philosopher-poet Salomo Friedländer, who called himself Mynona (*anonym* spelled backward), pointed out at the time, "Any damned fool can put a bullet through the most brilliant brain."

II

FROM THE VERY HEART
OF NATURE

What's past is prologue.
>   —SHAKESPEARE, The Tempest

Origin is the goal.
>   —KARL KRAUS, Worte in Versen

A cholera epidemic had broken out in Italy that year, but Dr. Freud refused to let it spoil his plans for spending several weeks in Rome and Sicily late in the summer of 1910. Before going south, however, he took his two younger sons on a trip to Holland, and August found him at a seaside hotel at Noordwijk on the Dutch coast. He was reading J. L. Motley's *Rise of the Dutch Republic* in order, as he wrote to his Swiss friend and colleague, Carl Gustav Jung, "to discover how something incredibly small can become great through obstinacy and unswerving determination."

Then a telegram arrived to disturb his well-earned rest—a request for an appointment from a distinguished fellow Viennese urgently in need of help. Freud disliked interrupting his holidays on any pretext, but he could hardly refuse to see Gustav Mahler, whose name was a household word in Vienna. A meeting was arranged, though only after several false starts. Mahler's original telegram, sent from the Tyrolean village where he was spending his holidays, was soon followed by another countermanding it, then by a second request and a second cancellation. "Mahler suffered from the *folie de doute* of his obsessional neurosis and repeated this performance three times," reports Freud's pupil and biog-

36

rapher Ernest Jones. Finally, Freud was obliged to remind Mahler that time was running short since he would soon be off to Italy. They got together at last in Leiden on August 26 or 27,* and spent the whole of the afternoon strolling through the old university town while Freud performed a sort of emergency psychoanalysis, condensed into a single one-day session.

"It was as if you would dig a single shaft through a mysterious building," Freud remembered many years later in a letter to the psychoanalyst Theodor Reik. "If I may believe reports, I achieved much with him at that time. . . . In highly interesting expeditions through his life history, we discovered his personal conditions for love. . . . I had plenty of opportunity to admire the capability for psychological understanding of this man of genius." Reik noted that most members of his profession would shake their heads over the unorthodoxy of such a marathon analytic session, "but extraordinary situations and circumstances (as well as extraordinary personalities) demand extraordinary measures."

On the face of it, the marital crisis that had brought Mahler to Freud was a fairly banal and conventional affair. Seven years earlier, as a bachelor of forty-three, he had married Alma Schindler, a Viennese music student nineteen years younger and a head taller than himself. At first she had been content to live in his shadow while he devoted most of his energies to directing both the Vienna Opera and the Vienna Philharmonic Orchestra. But difficulties had arisen after the death of one of their daughters in 1907. Alma had developed a nagging sense that "he, in his fanatical concentration on his own life, had simply overlooked me." Then, at the beginning of this troubled summer, her eyes had been "opened by the impetuous assaults of a youthful lover," and she decided that her life was "utterly unfulfilled." Mahler, as always deeply absorbed in his composing, was finally confronted with the facts when Alma's impetuous lover accidentally addressed a love letter to "Mr." instead of "Mrs." Mahler—the kind of Freudian slip whose mechanism Freud elucidates in his *Psychopathology of Everyday Life.* Mahler, though still unacquainted with Freud's theories, instantly understood that Alma's lover had addressed the letter to him as a way of asking him for her hand in marriage.

Mahler was then in the midst of writing his Tenth Symphony,

---

*Freudian footnote: it is significant, surely, that they should have chosen to meet in Leiden, whose name means "suffering" in German. Mahler had always maintained that his music was the outcome of "my experiences and sufferings." Now he had come to discuss both in Leiden—precisely the sort of "coincidence" which, as Freud had shown, is really arranged by the unconscious. The choice of "Suffering" as a meeting ground was presumably Freud's.

but these alarums brought his work to a standstill. "He realized that he had lived the life of a neurotic and suddenly decided to consult Sigmund Freud," Alma writes. "He gave him an account of his strange states of mind and his anxieties, and Freud apparently calmed him down." Indeed, the session in Leiden produced astonishingly quick results. Freud talked to Mahler about his evident search for a woman resembling his mother: "she was careworn and ailing, and unconsciously you wish your wife to be the same." Alma, fortunately, suffered from a reciprocal fixation: "she loved her father and she can only choose and love a man of his sort. Your age, of which you are so much afraid, is precisely what attracts her. You need not be anxious." (For that matter, it was not a coincidence that Alma, the daughter of a well-known painter, should have rejected her other suitors in order to marry Herr Mahler—which means "painter" in German.) On the train back to Austria, Mahler already felt sufficiently reassured to write a poem telling his wife that all would be well. The translation is Theodor Reik's:

> They melt, the shadows of the night;
> What always tortured me as fright
> Is blown away by power of one word. . . .

It had been, quite apart from its therapeutic results, a remarkably historic meeting of minds. Mahler, at fifty, was at the height of his powers as a composer and conductor; Freud, at fifty-four, was at last achieving international recognition as the discoverer of a new humanist science. What had begun modestly enough as a search for ways of curing the mentally ill had led him, step by step, to a theory of human behavior whose significance went far beyond the boundaries of psychiatry in order to be (as Mahler would have said) "cosmic and inexhaustible like the world and life itself." Freud's discoveries, writes his pupil Abraham Kardiner, "brought into the world a new definition of human fate, because he placed in the hands of man the means with which to alter impediments which were previously considered irremediable. 'You need not be the victim of your own past,' said Freud, 'or of your own environment.' "

Since publishing *The Interpretation of Dreams* at the turn of the century, Freud had taken psychoanalysis even further into related worlds of language, poetry and the visual arts. The year of his meeting with Mahler was also the year in which he published his psychoanalysis of Leonardo da Vinci, the artist whose constitutional reluctance to finish anything had attracted Freud's curiosity. At the same time he was at work on "contributions to the psychology of love" that deal with certain kinds of neuroses arising from men's oedipal need for love-objects that are "mother-surrogates." But as Freud points out, the search for the irreplaceable mother was bound to lead to endless difficulties of the sort that Mahler had encountered:

> We learn through other examples which psychoanalysis has brought to light that the pressing desire in the unconscious for some irreplaceable thing often resolves itself into an endless series in actuality—endless for the very reason that the satisfaction longed for is in spite of all never found in any surrogate. The insatiable questioning which children are given to at a certain age is explicable in this way—they have one single question to ask, the words of which they cannot bring their lips to form; and in the same way, too, the garrulity of many neurotically crippled persons may be explained—what makes them talk is the burden of a secret pressing for disclosure, which in spite of all temptation they never reveal.

Freud, at all events, was ideally prepared to provide the answers when Mahler came to find out where the "irreplaceable thing" was pressing him. Unlike many Viennese, however, he was not very well versed in music: Dr. Jones reports that he went to the opera only on rare occasions, and then only to Mozart or *Carmen*; Dr. Kardiner, moreover, understood Freud to say that the only opera he had ever heard in his life was *Don Giovanni* (a work, incidentally, whose powerfully oedipal symbolism is analyzed in his pupil Otto Rank's most remarkable essay, *Die Don Juan Gestalt*). Either way, it meant that Freud was in no position to judge the importance of what Mahler told him about his work; that the analyst who could write so brilliantly on Michelangelo, Shakespeare and Goethe lacked the musical background for understanding the elements that made Mahler the greatest symphonist of his time. Mahler's earliest childhood reminiscences had a peculiarly poignant relevance to his music as well as his neurosis. As Freud remembered some years after their interview:

> His father, apparently a brutal person, treated his wife very badly, and when Mahler was a young boy there was a specially painful scene between them. It became quite unbearable to the boy, who rushed away from the house. At that moment, however, a hurdy-gurdy in the street was grinding out the popular Viennese air, *O, du lieber Augustin*. In Mahler's opinion the conjunction of high tragedy and light amusement was from then on inextricably fixed in his mind, and the one mood inevitably brought the other with it.

Freud understood Mahler to say that, looking back on this experience, he now realized why his "noblest" musical passages—those inspired by the profoundest emotions—were always "spoiled" by the intrusion of commonplace tunes. But even if Mahler said something of the sort, he must have meant something quite different: certainly he was aware of the juxtaposition of the tragic and the frivolous, the magnificent and the bizarre, which is characteristic of much of his music, but these internal contradictions can hardly be said to "spoil" anything—on the contrary, they account for the interplay of tension and release that can hold an audience spellbound for two hours while listening to a Mahler symphony. It was precisely this polyphony of moods as well as sounds that constituted Mahler's most fascinating contribution to the classical tradition, and which was at the core of this surrealist music designed, as he said, to sound like *ein Strahlenmeer von Tönen*, a radiant sea of sounds.

Once, on a Sunday afternoon in midsummer, he had taken some of his friends to a hilltop from which they could hear a mélange of sounds coming from many directions at once: a male choir, some brass bands, organ grinders and carnival music, all happening simultaneously. "This is polyphony, and that's where I get it from," he told them. "In my earliest childhood in the woods of Iglau I was moved by these sounds and committed them to memory. For it is all the same whether the sounds take this form, or of birds singing, a thunderstorm, the splash of waves or the crackle of a fire. In true polyphony the themes have to meet like this, from many different directions, and must be completely distinct in their rhythmic and melodic contours. . . . the composer merely orders and combines them so that they can sing and sound as a united whole."

There was nothing inconsistent, then, in interrupting a "lofty" melody with a "trivial" tune—this ambivalence constitutes the very essence of Mahler's new harmonic principle: dissonance by collision. Freud himself had shown in another context that such "inconsistency" is merely a hobgoblin of the conscious mind: "We long ago discovered that a thing which in consciousness makes its appearance as two contraries is often in the unconscious a united whole."

It was by means of this multidimensional counterpoint that Mahler achieved the underlying purpose of his music. He told his most intimate friend, Natalie Bauer-Lechner, that "music must always contain a sense of longing, a longing that goes beyond the things of this world." It was as though that nameless longing resolved itself into an endless series of symphonies, whose content was often determined by forces which he did not fully understand.

"There is a second I that works while we sleep," he decided. "It grows and develops and brings forth that which the waking I searched for and desired in vain." Sometimes he thought he could discern a recognizable image in the "mosaic of sounds" that had taken form under his pen:

> This is particularly true [writes Natalie Bauer-Lechner] of the variations of the Andante of the Fourth Symphony, which he says are the first real ones he has ever written. . . . He calls it his most beautiful Andante, indeed the best thing he has done. "There is a divinely gay and deeply melancholy melody that runs through the whole movement, so that you will only laugh and cry when you hear it." He said, too, that it bore the features of St. Ursula, to whom the text of the fourth movement *Heavenly Life* refers. And when I asked him whether he knew anything about the Saint and her legend, he said: "No, otherwise I'm sure I would not have been in the mood, or capable of creating such a definite and splendid picture of her." Once he also called the Andante "the smile of St. Ursula," and said that as he was writing it the face of his mother floated before him as he remembered it from his childhood, deeply marked by sorrow and as though smiling through tears, for she too had suffered without end but had always resolved and forgiven everything with love.

Freud said after their meeting that he had never encountered anyone who understood the principles of psychoanalysis as quickly and intuitively as Mahler did. For that matter he had rarely known anyone whose sensitivities and capacities were so nearly a match for his own. For although they were accustomed to working with very different aspects of the unexpressed and the inexpressible in human life, both were profoundly concerned with what Freud was to call *Das Unbehagen in der Kultur*—literally, the sense of discomfort or uneasiness induced by civilization, though his book was translated into English as *Civilization and Its Discontents*, which is hardly the same thing. Freud's analysis of this *Unbehagen* constitutes one of his most important statements about the world, though he could suggest no lasting solution to the problems it poses. "My courage fails me," he wrote, "at the thought of rising up as a prophet before my fellow men, and I bow to their reproach that I have no consolation to offer them; for at bottom this is what they all demand. . . ." Mahler makes this malaise the underlying theme of his most fascinating scores, including *Das Lied von der Erde* (The Song of the Earth) and the *Kindertotenlieder* (Songs on the Deaths of Children): no composer before or since has ever expressed himself more movingly on what Freud calls "the struggle between Eros and Death, between the instincts of life and the in-

stincts of destruction, as it works itself out in the human species."
The modern composer Karlheinz Stockhausen has written that if a
visitor from a distant star should wish to investigate the nature of
the inhabitants of our earth, he would do well to address himself to
this remarkable music: "In order to discover all that which is most
characteristic of the earthling, to understand his entire range of
passions, from the most angelic to the most animal, to know everything that binds him to the earth and lets him no more than dream
of the other regions of the universe, there would be no richer
source of information than Mahler."

There were many points of resemblance and affinity between
Mahler and Freud, beginning with the fact that both came from
Jewish families who had settled in small towns of what has since
become Czechoslovakia, and both took part in the great migration
to Vienna that swelled the city's population to more than a million
by 1880. Mahler was born in Kalischt, Bohemia, in 1860, but his
parents moved to Iglau in neighboring Moravia three months after
his birth. Freud was born in Freiberg, Moravia, in 1856: seventy-
five years later he wrote that "deep within me, although overlaid,
there continues to live the happy child from Freiberg, the first-born
son of a youthful mother." Ernest Jones, who dedicated a lifetime
to Freud and his work, was convinced that the undaunted courage
which was "Freud's highest quality and his most precious gift"
could have been derived only from "a supreme confidence in his
mother's love."

Freud's mother came from Galicia; she lived to be ninety-five
and was remembered as a lady of immense vitality and impatience
even in her nineties. His father, Jakob Freud, was descended from
a family of Jews who had moved to Moravia from Lithuania, via
Galicia; not an unusual odyssey in the nineteenth century. Freud
"had reason to believe" that his forebears had originally come from
Cologne and had fled east to escape persecution during the four-
teenth or fifteenth century. There were seven younger brothers
and sisters, one of whom died in infancy: when Jakob Freud's
small textile business failed, they went to live in an overcrowded
apartment in Vienna while he struggled to find alternative ways of
earning a living. These were "hard times and not worth remembering," Freud said afterward, but he himself always managed to be
first in his class at school. To encourage him in his studies he was
allotted a small closetlike room of his own, the only private room in
the household. One of his sisters appeared to have musical talent
and began playing the piano, but the sound of it distracted him so

much that he insisted it be removed. No other piano was ever allowed in any of Freud's households for the rest of his life.

With Mahler it was just the reverse: an old piano, the gift of his maternal grandparents, provided him with a bastion against the world. As a small boy he played his way through the local library's entire supply of piano music, from symphonic arrangements to salon pieces. "As soon as I came home from the library, I played over everything that I had brought, stringing the pieces together one after the other, beginning over again each day of the week so as to get the most out of those marvels," he remembered. "I would not leave the piano even to eat. One after another my brothers and sisters were sent after me: Emma, Justi, Alois, 'Gustav you are to come and eat!' In the end my mother came, 'Oh Gustav, do come!' This did not work either, until finally my father's cane got me to the table. I would scarcely have put down my spoon, before I would rush back to sit before the music until evening." It is not difficult to see where Mahler acquired his lifelong habit of neglecting everything but his work.

His father was an irascible man who kept a tavern and ran a distillery; his mother, Maria Hermann, was the daughter of a soapmaker in a nearby town. They had been married against her better judgment and were "as ill-matched as fire and water," as Mahler said. "He was obstinacy personified; she was gentleness itself." Eight of the fourteen children born to this hard-working couple died in childhood: the *Kindertotenlieder* have been interpreted as a kind of belated memorial to his mother's grief. ("I feel sorry for me that I had to write them," he once confessed, "and sorry for the world that someday will have to hear them; they are so terribly sad.") Mahler was the eldest of the surviving children, and from all accounts he dreamed his way through childhood. Since Iglau was a garrison town his earliest musical impressions were of military band music and barrack-room ballads. "When he was a two-year-old his nurse used to leave him in a barracks yard while she enjoyed the company of a soldier friend," reports Bruno Walter, and at the age of four he had learned some two hundred popular tunes by heart. "Whenever he could not be found at home, it was certain that he had gone marching off with some regiment, or else he might be standing on a *Kaffeehaus* table, singing songs for a throng of customers."

Growing up on the edge of a parade ground, Mahler developed a lasting love-hate relationship with the blare of brass bands and the monotonous cadence of the Austro-German military march.

Most of his symphonies have at least one full-blown march movement—a funeral cortège, a mock-triumphal procession or a march to the scaffold. Elsewhere, often in the most lyrical moments, he will launch into a savage parody of the old parade music, the drums lurching drunkenly, the brasses contorted into an agonized grimace. In *Das Lied von der Erde*, for example, when the contralto soloist sings of maidens plucking lotus blossoms in the sunlight, a squadron of winds and percussion suddenly bursts on the scene in a furious cavalry quickstep, provoked by nothing more martial than a reference in the text to "handsome lads on spirited horses." But the musical effect is utterly electrifying.

Long before his encounter with Freud, Mahler had arrived at a Freudian explanation for his lifelong obsession with the sonic materials of his childhood. "In the creative arts," he told the critic Richard Specht, "virtually the only impressions that are fruitful and decisive in the long run are those that occur between the ages of four and eleven, before puberty." And he told Natalie Bauer-Lechner that his entire musical life had been based on what he had heard as a child: "Each day I become more conscious of the degree to which the impressions and the spiritual experiences of that period gave to my future life its form and its content."

He went to Vienna in 1875 to become a student at the Conservatory of Music. By then Sigmund Freud had been a medical student at the University of Vienna for two years, and was about to embark on his first major project in anatomy, a study of the gonadic structure of eels for the Zoological Experiment Station at Trieste. Life at the university had already taught him some unpleasant facts about Austrian antisemitism. He was profoundly angered by "the imputation that I should regard myself as inferior and as not belonging to the people, just because I was a Jew. . . . I could never understand why I ought to be ashamed of my ancestry, or as people were beginning to call it, my 'race.' As to the membership in the [German] ethnic folk-community that was denied me, I relinquished my claims to it without much regret." Afterwards he was satisfied that discrimination at the university had developed his sense of independence: "Because I was a Jew I found myself free of many prejudices which restrict others in the use of the intellect: as a Jew I was prepared to be in the opposition and to renounce agreement with the 'compact majority.' " One indirect result of institutional antisemitism was that he turned from physiology to psychiatry. He had wanted to devote himself to research in anatomy and physiology, but as a Jew his chances for an eventual professorship were negligible, and assistants' salaries were penurious. In 1882 his professor, Ernst Brücke, advised him, in view of his discouraging financial prospects, to abandon his theoretical career. "I followed his advice, left the physiology laboratory and entered the General Hospital as an *aspirant.*"

For Mahler, too, these were difficult years. In 1881, having left the conservatory without the hoped-for Beethoven Prize, he began supporting himself as a conductor in provincial theaters and opera houses. Conducting *Faust* and *Tannhäuser* in places like Laibach (Ljubljana), Olmütz (Olomouc) and Kassel, he often felt "like a noble steed harnessed with oxen to a cart," since the local singers rarely shared his fanatical devotion to music. "Often when I am burning with the fire of enthusiasm and am trying to carry them along with me to greater intensity and style, I suddenly see their stupefied faces smiling at each other knowingly," he wrote to a Viennese friend. "Then my effervescent blood subsides for a time, and I would like to run away for good."

Fortunately there was no shortage of jobs for gifted operatic conductors. He was called to Prague, where he conducted his first command performance for the Austrian emperor; then to Leipzig, as co-conductor with the well-known Artur Nikisch, and in 1888 to Budapest where, as a "young firebrand" of twenty-eight, he became the youngest musical director of a major opera house anywhere in Europe. Working with a lackluster company, he produced a brilliant first season that rescued the Budapest Opera from near bankruptcy. But at the same time he got his first real taste of organized antisemitism. Right-wing Hungarian newspapers rarely missed an opportunity to assail his Jewishness along with his musical innovations; a nationalist deputy denounced him in parliament for running the opera as a Jewish-bourgeois preserve. Though he held out for more than two years, these persistent attacks wore down his resistance. Shortly after conducting a performance of *Don Giovanni* which the visiting Johannes Brahms declared to be the best he had ever heard, Mahler resigned his post and went on to northern Germany as director of the Hamburg Opera. Here, too, his "passion and elemental force" made an instant impression: the critics agreed that with his "demonic" powers and Mephistophelian gaze he could draw superb performances from singers who were ordinarily no better than second-rate. "Whatever else they understood about it is bloody little," was Mahler's wry comment, "but my temperament, *that* they understand, and it carries them along with the music."

His very success as a conductor, however, came into conflict with his career as a composer: audiences wanted to hear him inter-

pret Mozart and Wagner—not Gustav Mahler. From September to
June he led the marathon-running life that absorbed all of his energies in a relentless succession of rehearsals and performances. During a typical Hamburg season he conducted a total of 138 performances, an average of one every two days. Work on his songs and
symphonies had to be deferred to the summer months when the
opera house was closed. As a result he called himself, rather bitterly, a *Sommerkomponist,* a summer composer, only one step removed from a Sunday painter.

All the more intense, therefore, was the creative life he led during his annual retreat to the Austrian Alps, where he would hide
away in some peasant village with only his sister Justi and Natalie
Bauer-Lechner to keep him company. It was at Steinbach on the
Attersee, a lake not far from Salzburg, that he wrote the great
"nature" symphonies of his early years, whose movements bear
such titles as "What the Flowers on the Meadows Tell Me" and
"What the Animals of the Forest Tell Me." Once, when the young
Bruno Walter came for a visit and stopped to admire the mountain
scenery, Mahler told him: "Don't bother to look—I've composed all
this already."

He would have liked to escape from the operatic treadmill and
spend his days outdoors, "roaming over mountains and through
forests, and carrying off my day's bag of sketches in swift raids,"
but he seemed to have little choice except to go on conducting.
After both parents died in 1889, and he had to go into debt to
support his brothers and sisters, he felt more than ever weighed
down by "this endless, complicated apparatus for making money."
Meanwhile he had to subsidize his own music: the concert at which
he introduced his *Resurrection* Symphony to Berlin took in forty-
eight marks at the box office, though it had cost him thousands. No
matter: during the performance people were moved to tears by
"sounds such as no one had ever dreamed of." This symphony,
Mahler said, was intended to sound "as though it were coming
across to us from another world. One is beaten to the ground by
clubs and then lifted to the heights on angels' wings." The climax
of the last movement is reached when the contralto soloist intones
the fervent prayer for which Mahler wrote his own words: *O
glaube, mein Herz, O glaube: es geht dir nichts verloren!* (Believe, my
heart, oh believe; nothing will be lost to you!).

This would have been a propitious time for a visit to Dr. Freud,
for Mahler's neurosis had begun playing psychosomatic tricks on
him. "Last winter," reported Natalie Bauer-Lechner, "he conducted his Second Symphony while suffering from a terrific mi-

graine headache. Normally he cannot bear even to lie down with such a headache, but must walk up and down in order to cope with the pain. And to suffer from it now—what a trick of fate, just at this longed-for hour of his life, when he could at last hear his work and perform it for others. On other occasions when he conducted with a headache the pain would let up as long as he was absorbed in the tension of the performance, but this time the terrible migraine did not leave him for a single minute, so that he hardly dared move on the podium, and conducted with unusual calm. . . . At the end he was barely able to acknowledge the tumultuous, unending applause, and at home he sank to the sofa like a dead man. Half an hour later the attack had passed."

Mahler thought he could recognize his syndrome in a biblical precedent: "What a wonderful image for the creative artist is Jacob, who wrestles with God until he blesses him. Even if the Jews created nothing but this, they would have had to be a magnificent people.—God doesn't want to bless me either; only in a terrible struggle for the creation of my work can I wrest a blessing from him."

He would have liked to find another post, but his agent brought him the disconcerting news that some of the likelier cities "would be happy to have him if he were not Jewish." Antisemitism had been gaining ground throughout the 1890s and, as Mahler wrote to a friend, "everywhere my Jewishness is a stone over which they stumble at the last minute when they want to make a contract with me." Known throughout Germany as the foremost Wagnerian conductor of the day, he was nevertheless excluded from the Bayreuth Wagner Festival by the composer's widow, Cosima Wagner, who was determined not to hire Jews—though that did not prevent her from consulting Mahler on various artistic problems. The Bavarian general, von Perfall, who guided the destinies of the Munich Opera, declared after looking at Mahler's photograph that it was impossible to hire another Jewish-looking conductor since they already had Hermann Levi on the roster. By the time the Munich management had changed its mind, Mahler had made other plans. In reply to their belated offer he sent them a curt telegram: "Have agreed to another offer from those who think less of my nose than of my talent."

For many years Mahler's great ambition had been to become director of the Vienna Opera, but it had been made abundantly clear to him that no non-Catholic would be appointed to such an important public post. Accordingly, he arranged to have himself baptized—a step already foreshadowed by the Second Symphony,

was taken to France in hopes that a specialist there could save his life. Later he was moved to a Viennese sanatorium where, on May 18, he died during a thunderstorm, like Beethoven.

While Mahler lay dying, "virtually every few hours the newspapers published bulletins about his condition; every little improvement, every setback, was reported in detail, as though he were a ruling prince," remembered Katia Mann, who had gone to Venice that spring with her husband, Thomas Mann. They were staying at the magnificent Hôtel des Bains at the Lido, and it was here that Mann's attention was drawn to a Polish family—the girls dressed rather stiffly, and a "charming, beautiful boy of about thirteen," in a sailor suit, whom Mann enjoyed watching on the beach. Later, their holiday was cut short when they learned that the cholera (which had spared Freud in Sicily the previous summer) had now come north to Venice: "Several cases of cholera have broken out; naturally it's being kept secret and hushed up." The result was *Death in Venice,* Mann's finest novella, whose central figure, Gustav von Aschenbach, bears an inescapable resemblance to Gustav Mahler. "The way his death was mourned impressed my husband so much that he actually painted more or less of a portrait of Mahler in the physical description of Aschenbach," Katia Mann explains. And thus began the chain of events that was to transform the image of this immensely athletic and vigorous man into the technicolor travesty-figure of an aging, querulous composer who has nothing to do with his time but pursue a beautiful boy through a decaying city.

Privately, Mann had already made amends for this misappropriation of Mahler's shadow. In September of the previous year he had attended Mahler's last moment of triumph, when he conducted his Eighth Symphony—the *Symphony of a Thousand*—before a Munich audience that included most of the luminaries of the Austro-German musical world. Afterward, in a glowing letter of appreciation, Mann wrote to Mahler that his music "expresses the art of our time in its profoundest and most sacred form." Katia Mann remembers that her husband told her that "Gustav Mahler was the first person he'd ever met who gave him the impression of being a great man."

If happiness, as Freud said, "is the satisfaction of a childhood wish," then Mahler came closest to happiness during his first years at the Vienna Opera, when his childhood fantasies seemed on the verge of being realized. Natalie Bauer-Lechner writes that he never got over the feeling that his appointment was part of a fairy tale. "Once, as we happened to walk past the Opera together, he said,

'To think that I rule here as its chief and monarch—it's just like a dream!' "

By then, dreams in Vienna had become the special province of Sigmund Freud, who had been hard at work unraveling the symbolism of his own and his patients' dream-language. Indeed, the solution to the riddle was already in his grasp. As he proposed half jokingly in a letter to a friend, perhaps one day there would be a marble tablet on the wall of the Bellevue Restaurant on the slopes of the Wienerwald, informing the world that:

> In this House on July 24, 1895, the
> Secret of Dreams was revealed to
> Dr. Sigmund Freud

He had made the transition from neurology to psychoanalysis reluctantly and almost "against my will," but his researches into the etiology of hysteria had already led him to a momentous revelation, "the discovery of the source of the Nile of neuropathology" —namely that human sexuality begins at birth, and that hysteria and neurosis are caused by repressed impulses that have their origin in infancy. "I found myself explaining something from the very heart of nature," he wrote to a friend. "I found myself wrestling with the whole of psychology."

Sexuality, however, and especially infantile sexuality, was still a forbidden subject even in scientific circles. Most of Freud's colleagues reacted like Professor Wilhelm Weygandt who, when psychoanalysis was mentioned at a psychiatric congress, pounded the table with his fist and shouted, "This is not a topic for discussion at a scientific meeting; it is a matter for the police!" Predictably, Freud was ostracized by the Viennese medical profession. At the age of forty, he remembered in later years, "I had reached the peak of loneliness, and had lost all my old friends and hadn't acquired any new ones; no one paid any attention to me, and the only thing that kept me going was a bit of defiance and the beginning of *The Interpretation of Dreams.*"

The book on dreams was published in 1899 but bore the date 1900, as if to signalize the dawn of a psychoanalytic century. The three years of systematic self-analysis that preceded it proved to be Freud's greatest adventure in his exploration of the unconscious. "It is an odyssey of far greater intensity than is recorded in the *Confessions* of St. Augustine," writes Dr. Kardiner, "and much more sincere and modest than those that are contained in the *Confessions* of Rousseau. *The Interpretation of Dreams* is restrained; yet it ranks in intensity with the kind of inner self-encounter and honesty that must have preceded the creation of Kant's *Critique of Pure Reason* and Einstein's general theory of relativity."

In the course of this journey into the self, Freud discovered among other things that his dreams often dealt with the dilemma, not to say *Unbehagen,* of being Jewish in an alien world. One dream in particular took him back to a youthful experience which, as he noted, "still manifests its power in all these emotions and dreams":

> I may have been ten or twelve years old when my father began to take me with him on his walks, and to reveal to me his views about the things of this world in his conversation. In this way he once told me, in order to show into how much better times I had been born than he, the following: "While I was a young man, I was walking one Saturday on the street in the village where you were born; I was handsomely dressed and wore a new fur cap. Along comes a Christian, who knocks my cap into the mud with one blow and shouts, 'Jew, get off the sidewalk.' " "And what did you do?" "I went in the street and picked up the cap," was the answer. That did not seem heroic on the part of the big strong man, who was leading me, a little fellow, by the hand. I contrasted this situation, which did not please me, with another more in harmony with my feelings—the scene in which Hannibal's father, Hamilcar Barka, made his boy swear at the domestic altar to take vengeance on the Romans. Since that time Hannibal has had a place in my phantasies.

Freud adds that not only the "Semitic" warrior Hannibal but also Napoleon's Jewish general, Marshal Masséna, became his boyhood idols: they symbolized the militancy with which he reacted to antisemitism for the rest of his life. For although he regarded himself as a "godless" and unbelieving Jew there was nothing apologetic in his attitude. "I have often felt," he wrote to his fiancée, Martha Bernays, "as though I had inherited all the defiance and all the passions with which our ancestors defended their Temple." His eldest son, Martin, writes in his memoirs of a characteristic confrontation between Freud and some antisemites that occurred in, of all places, Berchtesgaden (later the favorite summer resort of Hitler and his circle). During the summer of 1901 the twelve-year-old Martin and his ten-year-old brother Oliver were fishing from a boat in the lake when a group of men began abusing them for being Jewish. Later, when their father had joined them, a small crowd formed on the shore and shouted more insults. "Father, without the slightest hesitation, jumped out of the boat and, keeping to the middle of the road, marched toward the hostile crowd. . . . They numbered about ten men and all were armed with sticks and umbrellas. The women remained in the background, but cheered on their menfolk with shouts and gestures. In the meantime, father, swinging his stick, charged the hostile crowd, which gave way before him and promptly dispersed, allowing him free passage. This was the last we saw of these unpleasant strangers."

Incidents of this sort made Freud all the more anxious to spare his children the indignities of second-class citizenship. In *The Interpretation of Dreams* he noted that his dream-life revealed a chronic anxiety "about the future of my children who cannot be given a native country of their own, anxiety about bringing them up so that they may have the right of native citizens. . . ." Many Jewish parents with similar concerns chose to have their children baptized, but Freud disliked the idea. When the critic Max Graf told him that he was debating whether to raise his son as a Christian, Freud's comment was: "If you do not let your son grow up as a Jew, you will deprive him of those sources of energy which cannot be replaced by anything else. He will have to struggle as a Jew, and you ought to develop in him all the energy he will need for that struggle. Do not deprive him of that advantage."

Yet for his own children, Freud chose all but total assimilation. They grew up outwardly indistinguishable from their Austrian neighbors: during the summer they wore lederhosen and the rest of the pseudo-peasant paraphernalia that is still considered modish in parts of Austria and Bavaria. Once, again in Berchtesgaden, they met the German empress and three sons of Wilhelm II on a promenade—"dressed very much as we were dressed," writes Martin Freud, "the Empress included, all chatting and talking together very much as we chatted and talked. . . . Had we, I wondered, succeeded in imitating them; or were they imitating us?" Though their mother's grandfather had been the chief rabbi of Hamburg, they were brought up in ignorance of even the most rudimentary Jewish religious customs. Martin recalled that the first time he entered a synagogue—on the occasion of his own wedding—his friends had to tell him "with some vehemence" to put his top hat back on his head.*

---

*Even Hitler knew better, though he was hardly an expert in such matters. A friend of his Viennese vagabond years, a musician named August Kubizek, recalled what happened when he tried to argue Hitler out of his antisemitism: "At the Conservatory there were Jews amongst both teachers and students, and I had never had any trouble with them, and indeed, had made some friends among them. Was not Adolf himself enthusiastic about Gustav Mahler, and was he not fond of the works of Mendelssohn-Bartholdy? . . . I cautiously tried to deflect Adolf from this point of view. His reaction was very strange. 'Come Gustl,' he said, and once again, to save the fare, I had to walk with him. I was astonished when Adolf led me to the Brigittenau Synagogue. We entered. 'Keep your hat on,' Adolf whispered. And indeed, all the men had their heads covered.'"

Clearly it was not an easy time to be Jewish in Vienna, though the dance at the edge of the volcano was still moving at a leisurely waltz tempo. Outwardly at least the Hapsburg capital had not yet lost its romantic charm: people were accustomed to thinking of it, said the essayist Egon Friedell (originally Friedman), as "an enclave of that vanished beauty-in-life to which so many look back with nostalgia." But the Danube monarchy was held together by only the most tenuous of constitutional threads, and behind the storybook façade, Vienna was seething with ethnic animosities and class hatreds. The year of Mahler's appointment to the Vienna Opera, 1897, also witnessed the installation of Karl Lueger as mayor of the city.* Elected after a rabidly antisemitic campaign, he managed to remain in office, using the same propaganda line, until his death in 1910. His antisemitism was conditional, however, and as a jovial "man of the people" he liked to make worthy exceptions: *Wer ein Jud' ist, bestimme ich* (I'm the one who decides who's a Jew around here) was the most famous of his pithy sayings. Mahler, he decided, was a *Jud'* despite his professed Catholicism; hence he was to be barred from conducting the Vienna Philharmonic charity concerts, which were sponsored by the municipal government. In his antipathy to things Jewish, Lueger went so far as to encourage the founding of an "Aryan Theatre of Vienna," which, as a stimulus to "German idealism," offered only plays by non-Jewish authors acted by non-Jewish actors. The reason why this curious enterprise went bankrupt within five years is not far to seek. As Stefan Zweig explains in his memoirs, it was primarily the Jewish bourgeoisie which had taken over from the old aristocracy the task of supporting the city's arts: "They had always loved this city and had entered into its life wholeheartedly, but it was first of all by their love for Viennese art that they felt entitled to full citizenship, and that they had actually become true Viennese. . . . They were the real audience, they filled the theaters and the concerts, they bought the books and the pictures, they visited the exhibitions, and with their more mobile understanding, little hampered by tradition, they were the exponents and champions of all that was new."

Though they constituted less than ten percent of the population, Zweig thought that they "promoted, nourished or even created" some nine-tenths of "what the world celebrated as Viennese culture." His estimate sounds a trifle exaggerated, and in the absence

---

*Freudian footnote: Lueger means "liar" in German. In his case the patronymic appears to have functioned as a form of self-fulfilling prophecy in accordance with the maxim *Nomen est omen*.

of any known quantitative measurement for "culture," would seem impossible to verify. Yet the Jewish (and ex-Jewish) minority undoubtedly produced a vastly disproportionate share of the artists and communicators; the poets, playwrights, composers, novelists, music critics. Among the *Prominenten* at the literary cafés one could meet Peter Altenberg and Hermann Bahr, Richard Beer-Hoffmann and Arthur Schnitzler, Hugo von Hofmannsthal and Leopold von Andrian, Karl Kraus and Felix Salten, Egon Friedell and Theodor Herzl (now remembered as the founder of Zionism, but known to his contemporaries as a feuilletonist and author of a much-discussed play, *The New Ghetto,* which also provided Freud with material for "Hannibal" dreams).

They were as brilliant and articulate a group as has ever been assembled around rival *Kaffeehaus* tables, but the most dazzling talent of them all was Kraus, the anticritic and antijournalist who conducted a forty-year campaign against "the press"—by which he meant more or less all newspapers and magazines except his own gadfly journal, *Die Fackel* (The Torch). With its 922 issues, published from 1899 to 1936—a total of some 24,000 pages—*Die Fackel* must rank as one of the most remarkable achievements in the print media since Diderot's *Encyclopedia.* At first Kraus published both his own work and that of like-minded collaborators, but after a decade he announced with characteristic bravado: "I no longer have contributors. I was jealous of them. They alienated people whom I wanted to antagonize myself." To fill the pages of his one-man magazine, Kraus worked harder than Freud—sixteen to eighteen hours out of every twenty-four. "I work days and nights. That leaves me a lot of free time, to ask the picture in my room whether it likes my work, to ask the clock if it is tired, and the night whether she slept well." He called himself a disturber of the peace, and "fighter, artist, fool." Others have called him "the greatest German satirist and stylist in our time." He wrote against brutality, ignorance, pretentiousness and the abuse of power. Perpetually in opposition, he was the self-appointed guardian of the German language against its abuse and corruption by journalists, copywriters and politicians. But although it was inspiring to see him make war on the strong and the evil, he also turned, at times, on the merely weak or misguided—occasionally, too, on some who were more gifted than himself. First an ex-Jew, then an ex-Catholic, he was a declared enemy of militarism who despised pacifists; a protector of the downtrodden who was not above kicking rival authors when they were down; a champion of justice gifted, as the critic

Willy Haas pointed out, "with a sadist's subtle instinct for wounding the very spot where it hurts most." When not busy at the writing table he could be heard arguing, acting, giving public readings of his own and other people's work (he gave more than 800 one-man readings); always talking, talking. Freud might almost have had Kraus in mind when he analyzed the terrible garrulity of certain neurotics: "What makes them talk is the burden of a secret pressing for disclosure, which in spite of all temptation they never reveal. . . ."

Kraus wrote intelligently about sexual repression, and Freud thought for a time that in the editor of *Die Fackel* he had found a potential ally, since his aims and opinions "partially coincide with mine." No sooner had psychoanalysis achieved a measure of success, however, than Kraus's aphorisms turned predictably venomous:

> Psychoanalysis is the newest Jewish disease; the older people are still suffering from diabetes.

> Psychoanalysis is the very illness whose cure it considers itself to be.

> They reach into our dreams as though they were our pockets.

> According to the latest research, the unconscious appears to be a sort of ghetto for people's thoughts. Apparently many are now homesick for it.

Despite the innuendo, Kraus would not have considered himself antisemitic. It was just that, like so many emancipated Jews, he regarded himself as somehow above the battle; besides, as Haas pointed out, "there was no finer, more complex, more interesting and more vulnerable object for Jewish irony than the Jews themselves."

Among Freud's contemporaries, the writer whose work was most closely attuned to his thinking was Arthur Schnitzler, the leading playwright of fin-de-siècle Vienna. Years after his first delighted encounter with one of Schnitzler's plays, Freud wrote a letter congratulating him on his sixtieth birthday and explaining why, though they had previously corresponded, he had never tried to meet him in person:

> I think I have avoided you from a kind of reluctance to meet my double. . . . whenever I get deeply absorbed in your beautiful creations I invariably seem to find beneath their poetic surface the very

interests and conclusions which I know to be my own. Your deter-
minism as well as your skepticism—what people call pessimism—
your preoccupation with the truths of the unconscious and of the
instinctual drives in man, your dissection of the cultural conventions
of our society, the dwelling of your thoughts on the polarity of love
and death; all this moved me with an uncanny feeling of familiarity.

Schnitzler's candor as an explorer of the psyche, and his eminently un-Victorian treatment of sexual mores, caused him no end
of trouble with the censors. His best-known play, *Reigen (La
Ronde)*, with its chain of interlocking sexual relationships, could
neither be published nor performed when it was completed in
1910; instead he gave away two hundred copies, "privately
printed as a manuscript [*sic*] and not for sale."

La Ronde was the subject of a famous obscenity trial in Berlin as
late as 1922, and although the defense won an acquittal, the case
was only a dress rehearsal for the Nazi suppressions that were
soon to follow. Schnitzler's honesty was not confined to sexual
themes: equally outspoken are some of the things he wrote on the
thorny issue of religious prejudice. The hero of his play *Professor
Bernhardi* is a Jewish hospital director who incurs the wrath of the
Viennese Catholic hierarchy and goes to prison on trumped-up
charges: en route he discovers that his Jewish assistants are quite as
ready to leave him in the lurch as everyone else. Since Schnitzler
himself was a doctor and the son of a doctor, the play has distinctly
autobiographical overtones; so does his best-known novel, *Der Weg
ins Freie* (The Road into the Open), which deals with the psychic
malaise of *Unbehagen* in Viennese society. When one of the book's
aristocratic characters suggests to a Jewish friend that his sensitivity to prejudice might be nothing more than a persecution complex,
the reply is an exasperated *cri de coeur*:

> I want to ask you something, Georg, I want you to search your
> conscience. . . . Do you believe that there is a single Christian on
> earth (even the noblest and most just) who, if his best friend, his
> mistress or his wife happen to be Jewish, would not, in a moment of
> anger or irritation, reproach them with their Jewishness? Not one, I
> assure you. . . . Read the letters of any prominent and otherwise
> intelligent and admirable person, and note the passages in which he
> makes adverse or ironic remarks about contemporaries. Ninety-nine
> times these remarks will make no reference to religion or ethnic de-
> scent. But in the hundredth case, where the person maltreated has
> the misfortune to be Jewish, the writer will not neglect to mention
> this fact. That's how it is, and I can't help you!

Clearly this fictional outburst reflects Schnitzler's own unhappy experience in the matter, though in real life his reaction to prejudice was one of icy disdain. His attitude is summed up in the one-word comment, *"Ekel"* (disgust), with which he records a typical incident in his diary (March 24, 1903): "Lanz was with us this evening. He told us that at the premiere of *Lebendige Stunden* [Lively Hours, his latest play] two people in the gallery were applauding wildly, but when I failed to appear they shouted, 'What's keeping the arrogant Jew?' "

Freud, too, was to become thoroughly familiar with this "Jewish reproach"—the ultimate in *ad hominem* arguments—which cropped up with such tiresome monotony in moments of stress. Even the most distinguished intellectual among his disciples, C. G. Jung, could not resist the temptation of belaboring him with it when he broke away from Freud's too-patriarchal influence in the years preceding World War I. Later, during the crisis of the Hitler years, when the Nazis burned Freud's books and mounted a campaign of vilification against him, Jung was conveniently at hand with the announcement that the time had come when "the difference between Teutonic and Jewish psychology must no longer be obscured."*

A great deal has been written in justification of Jung's statements in the Nazi-sponsored "medical" journal *Zentralblatt für Psychotherapie,* and he has been defended against the "libelous" charge of antisemitism by such persuasive writers as J. B. Priestley, Aniela Jaffé and Laurens van der Post. In her recent biography of Jung, Barbara Hannah claims that nothing could have been further from Jung's mind: ". . . it is mainly, if not entirely, a matter of people *wanting* to believe a rumor." Yet the written record seems to say something quite different, and it should be allowed to speak for itself. In 1934, at a time when the work of Freud and his followers had been banned in Germany, Jung, though a Swiss, wrote an article for "Aryan" psychiatrists purporting to show that Freud's "Jewish psychology" had no relevance to the new German man:

> One cannot, of course, accept that Freud or Adler is a generally valid representative of European mankind. . . . The Jews have this peculiarity in common with women: since they are physically weaker, they have to aim for the gaps in the armor of their adversaries, and on account of this technique, forced on them by centuries of history, the

---

*Jones once asked Freud whether, in fact, psychoanalysis was Jewish in the sense that only a Jew could have discovered it. Freud replied that, on the one hand, it could be said that after all only a Jew actually did, but on the other hand, it might equally be said that there were countless millions of Jews who did not.

Jews themselves are best protected where others are most vulnerable. Since their culture is more than twice as ancient, they are far more conscious of human weaknesses and negative aspects [*Schattenseiten*] than we are, and hence in this respect far less vulnerable. It is also thanks to their experience of ancient culture that it is possible for them to live in benevolent, amiable and tolerant acceptance of their own vices, while we are still too young [*wir sind noch zu jung*] to have no "illusions" about ourselves. Moreover, fate has destined us still to create a culture (which we are in need of), and for that purpose the so-called illusions in the form of one-sided ideals, convictions, plans, etc., are indispensable. . . . The Aryan unconscious . . . contains powers and creative seeds that are still to be fulfilled in the future, and these must not be debased by nursery-romanticism [*Kinderstubenromantik*, Jung's shorthand for Freudian theory]. The still-young Teutonic peoples are thoroughly capable of creating new cultural forms, and this future lies in the darkness of the unconscious of every individual as an energy-laden seed, capable of becoming a mighty flame. The Jew as a relative nomad has never created, and presumably will never create, a cultural form of his own, for all his instincts and talents are dependent on a more or less civilized host people. The Jewish race possesses, in my experience, an unconscious that can bear only a very limited comparison with an Aryan one. . . . The Aryan unconscious has a higher potential than the Jewish; that is both the advantage and disadvantage of a youthfulness not yet far removed from the barbaric. In my view it has been a grave mistake of medical psychology to apply Jewish categories, which are not even valid for all Jews, to Christian Germans and Slavs. In this way the most precious secret of Teutonic man—the deep-rooted creative awareness of his soul [*schöpferisch ahnungsvollen Seelengrund*]—has been explained away as a banal, infantile sump, while my warning voice, over the decades, was suspected of antisemitism. Freud was responsible for this insinuation. He did not know the Teutonic soul, any more than his blind followers in Germany knew it. Has the mighty phenomenon of National Socialism, at which the whole world gazes in astonishment, taught them to know better?

Jung's five-page essay goes on to accuse the Freudians of "complete disregard of all scientific scruple" as well as of "soulless rationalism"; of "poisoning" people with the "infantile-perverse sump of an obscene joke-psychology" (an allusion to Freud's *Jokes and Their Relation to the Unconscious*), and of "debasing" patients by "imputing unnatural filth to their natural cleanliness" (*ihre natürliche Reinlichkeit auf unnatürlichen Schmutz zu verdächtigen*). Perhaps Jung felt that he could overstep the bounds of professional etiquette in this fashion because his article in the *Zentralblatt* was intended as the Parthian shot in his running battle with Freud and his followers. One wonders, however, how a psychologist capable of drawing such fine distinctions was also able to make such drastic generalizations. When he was questioned about some of them at the time, his reaction was: "Why this ridiculous touchiness when anybody dares to say anything about the psychological difference between Jews and Christians? Every child knows that differences exist."

In 1934, however, every child also knew that the Nazis had begun persecuting and even killing people on account of these "differences," and some adults, at least, thought it unsporting of Jung to attack Freud with the "Jewish reproach" at a time when the *Zentralblatt* (coeditors, Dr. Jung and Dr. M. H. Göring, a cousin of Hermann Göring) would not have accorded Dr. Freud the right of rebuttal. Jung's remarks, at any rate, are indicative of the mental climate of the 1930s, and of the ease with which eminent men like Jung and Heidegger could align their thinking with this "mighty phenomenon" of Nazism. After the war, Jung explained that he had gone on working for Dr. Göring's *Gesellschaft für Psychotherapie* for seven years out of loyalty to his German colleagues, and "for the sake of suffering humanity, doctors, and—last but not least— science and civilization."

But it is precisely this claim to "science" in a man who could write of an "Aryan" versus a "Jewish" psychology that presents the most puzzling aspect of the case. Barbara Hannah, forty years after the fact, declares that Jung had merely been "emphasizing the importance of realizing the great differences that exist not only between the Jewish and Aryan races but between *all* races and *all* nations." She seems unaware, to begin with, that only in the Nazi vocabulary were "Aryans" a race, and synonymous with Teutons. Insofar as the term "Aryan" had any scientific meaning, it referred to a language group, the Indo-European, and not an ethnological category. The philologist Friedrich Max Müller, who gave it currency in the late nineteenth century, was careful to specify that by Aryans he meant "neither blood nor bones nor hair nor skull; I mean simply those who speak an Aryan language"—i.e., Hindus, Persians, Spaniards and Russians as well as Greeks, Romans and Germans. "To me an ethnologist who speaks of Aryan race, Aryan blood, Aryan eyes and hair, is as great a sinner as a linguist who speaks of a dolichocephalic dictionary or a brachycephalic grammar."

Jung, with his enormous erudition, was perfectly aware that he was using Nazi jargon, even if his biographers are not. But, to do him justice, he had a lifelong weakness for sweeping generalizations about the "collective psyches" of whole nations: a typical example is his analysis of America after a short visit to the United States, together with Freud, in September 1909. "American culture really is a bottomless abyss," he decided. "The men have become a flock of sheep and the women play the ravening wolves—within the family circle, of course. I ask myself whether such conditions have ever existed in the world before. I really don't think they have." It is, I think, on this level of profundity that one should interpret Jung's remarks about the Jewish psyche.*

In one respect, at least, Jung's remarks about his former friend were demonstrably correct: Freud did not know the Teutonic soul. Despite his many years as a psychoanalyst, Freud still harbored misconceptions about the German psyche—if, indeed, there was such a thing. In 1930 he told the American ambassador to Berlin, W. C. Bullitt: "A nation that produced Goethe could not possibly go to the bad." (It seems, for once, to have been a genuinely non-Freudian coincidence that his remark to W. C. Bullitt should sound like a paraphrase of W. C. Fields's famous dictum, "No man who hates dogs and children can be all bad.")

By that time Freud had become something of an international culture hero. After World War I (which wiped out his savings but added the death-instinct to his arsenal of impulses) his theories had taken the avant-garde by storm: with the Expressionists and Surrealists, Franz Kafka, Tristan Tzara, Max Ernst, Picasso et al., "Freudian" and "Freudianism" entered the vocabulary of art. Those who were lucky enough to know him personally, like Stefan Zweig and Thomas Mann, came to consult him as a sort of Delphic oracle. Zweig writes that a conversation with Freud constituted one of his greatest intellectual satisfactions: "While one learned, one marveled; it was plain that one's every word was fully comprehended by this magnificent, unprejudiced person whom no admission startled, no statement excited, and whose impulse to

---

*One could also, of course, attempt a Freudian depth-analysis. Curiously enough, Jung's equation of Jews and women bears out a point that Freud had made in a footnote to a paper written some twenty-five years earlier: "The castration complex is the deepest unconscious root of antisemitism; for even in the nursery little boys hear that a Jew has something cut off his penis—a piece of his penis, they think—and this gives them the right to despise Jews. And there is no stronger unconscious root for the sense of superiority over women. . . . what is common to Jews and women is their relation to the castration complex." If this seems farfetched, it may be recalled that, during the years when the Nazi extermination machinery was in full operation, many boys' lives literally depended on whether or not they were circumcised. During the round-ups that preceded deportation, sons of mixed parentage *(Mischlinge)* were delivered to the gas chamber if they were *"mosaisch beschnitten"* (i.e., circumcised), but allowed to go free if they were not.

make others see and feel clearly had long since become an instinctive life impulse." His impact on the small, tough, unimpressionable world of the European intellectuals was all the more profound because many of his readers understood instantly what he was driving at: far from making unexpected revelations, he was merely giving form and expression to something inchoate but already dimly perceived, which needed only a shift in perspective to be recognized. André Gide provides a glimpse of this process when he records his first encounter with Freud, in his diary for February 4, 1922:

> "Here is something that, I fear, will bring grist to your mill," [Jacques] Rivière said to me the other day, speaking of Freud's little book on sexual development. I should say!

And it occurs to Gide that for the past ten or fifteen years he has been practicing "Freudianism" without being aware of it. Without quite knowing how or why, an obscure Viennese crank psychiatrist had become a major landmark on the twentieth-century horizon. Thomas Mann speaks of Schopenhauer, Ibsen and Freud; others of Dostoyevsky, Nietzsche and Freud, or of Bergson, Freud and Einstein. The doctor himself also thinks in threes, but claims for himself an even older line of succession: his work, he writes, has delivered the third and most devastating blow to the ancient, narcissistic view of man as the center of the universe and the prime object of creation. First there had been the cosmological blow aimed at it by Copernicus; then the biological blow delivered by Darwin to man's notion of a gulf between himself and the animal kingdom; now the psychological blow to man's presumption of the supremacy of reason in his own soul.

In Weimar Germany, thanks to a magnificent prose style that is still held up as a model of its kind, Freud received the nation's most coveted literary award, the Goethe Prize of the city of Frankfurt. There was, it seemed, only one city that displayed not the slightest interest in Freud. In the 1920s psychiatrists who had come all the way from America to study with the discoverer of psychoanalysis were surprised to be told by the Viennese, "Professor Freud? Never heard the name." When Freud heard about this from Kardiner he was much amused. "You see," he said, "a prophet is never known in his own country."

His seventieth birthday, in 1926, which brought him a spate of congratulations from around the world, was studiously ignored by the academic world of Vienna. But this official neglect was due to something more than indifference: even before 1933 Freud had become a politically controversial figure. Later, when Hitler came to power in neighboring Germany, Freud was regarded as a potential embarrassment by an Austrian government which was at pains to give the Nazis no cause for offense. By 1936 things had reached the point where Viennese newspapers were forbidden to mention the fact that Freud was being honored on his eightieth birthday—by, among others, some two hundred writers and artists headed by Romain Rolland, H. G. Wells, Virginia Woolf and Thomas Mann, who came from Switzerland to deliver his birthday address in person. "The idea of the future," Mann said, "is the one I associate most instinctively with Freud's name."

In Berlin, meanwhile, Freud's books had been publicly burned on the Opernplatz "on account of their soul-destroying overemphasis of the sex-drive" (*seelenzerfasernde Überschätzung des Trieblebens*) as the official speaker declared. Freud was unperturbed. "What progress we are making!" he remarked with a smile. "In the Middle Ages they would have burnt me; nowadays they are content with burning my books." Ernest Jones comments that even that much progress was to prove illusory: ten years later they would have burned his body as well. Indeed, four of Freud's aged sisters were afterward deported and killed in the Holocaust.

Freud's fatalist attitude toward the Nazis was reinforced by the knowledge that he himself was slowly dying of cancer of the mouth. In *Das Unbehagen in der Kultur* of 1930 he had issued an ominous warning about the "aggressive cruelty" that was latent in mankind, merely lying in wait for some suitable provocation: "In circumstances that favor it, when those forces in the mind which ordinarily inhibit it cease to operate, it also manifests itself spontaneously and reveals men as savage beasts to whom the thought of sparing their own kind is alien. . . . Civilized society is perpetually menaced with disintegration through this primary hostility of men towards one another." But although he could see the menace far more clearly than most, he refused to heed his friends' advice to seek safety in Switzerland or France. "I don't believe there is any danger here," he wrote to his most influential supporter, Marie Bonaparte, a princess of Greece and Denmark, "and if it should come I am firmly resolved to await it here. If they kill me—good. It is one kind of death like another. But probably that is only cheap boasting."

Shortly after the *Anschluss* of March 11, 1938—when the "nation that produced Goethe" annexed the nation that produced Mozart—Freud's home in the Berggasse was invaded by a gang of Storm Troopers who helped themselves to whatever money was in the house, including 6,000 Austrian schillings (then about $840) which belonged to the Psychoanalytic Association. "They were debating their prospects of continuing their career of petty burglary," writes Jones, who came to Freud's aid shortly after the incident, "when a frail and gaunt figure appeared in the doorway. It was Freud, aroused by the disturbance. He had a way of frowning with blazing eyes that any Old Testament prophet might have envied, and the effect produced by this lowering mien completed the visitors' discomfiture. Saying they would call another day, they hastily took their departure."

As they left, reports Prince Hubertus zu Löwenstein in his memoirs, Freud's daughter Anna noticed that her father was laughing aloud. "Why did you laugh?" she asked. "It wasn't that funny." "It was," Freud said. "I've been a doctor for fifty years, but I never got 6,000 schillings for a visit to an old, sick man."

In June 1938, thanks to the intervention of Marie Bonaparte (who paid the Nazis a ransom of 250,000 Austrian schillings), of W. C. Bullitt (then American ambassador to France) and of the British Home Secretary, Sir Samuel Hoare, Freud and the members of his immediate family received permission to leave Vienna for London. Before his departure, the Gestapo forced him to sign a certificate declaring that he had been well treated by the authorities. Freud complied, but added a sentence of his own in an advertising copywriter style that would have delighted Karl Kraus: *Ich kann die Gestapo jedermann auf das beste empfehlen*—"I can heartily recommend the Gestapo to anyone."

In London, where he was soon settled in a comfortable house near Primrose Hill, he wrote to a friend that his feeling of triumph on being liberated was mitigated by sorrow, "for in spite of everything I still greatly loved the prison from which I have been released." His escape had been enthusiastically reported in the British press, and he was besieged by well-wishers and autograph hunters: "For the first time and late in life I have experienced what it is to be famous." Despite his failing health he worked as unremittingly as ever. It was only here in England that he could publish *Moses and Monotheism*, which had been banned by the censors even in pre-Hitler Austria. It was clear to him that he was close to death: "My world is again what it was before—a little island of pain floating in a sea of indifference," he wrote to Marie Bonaparte in the spring of 1939. When the war broke out he was certain that it would mean the end of Hitler, but when a speaker on the BBC declared that this was to be the last war, Freud said wearily, "Anyhow, it is *my* last war."

Stefan Zweig, who had moved to London four years earlier, writes of having visited Freud during these last months of his life:

On his desk lay the large folio pages of his manuscripts which, at eighty-three, he wrote with the old legible rounded script, every day, as clear in his mind as in his best period and equally tireless; his strong will had risen superior to everything, illness, age, exile, and for the first time the kindness of his being which had been dammed during long years of struggle flowed freely from him. Age had only made him mellower, the trials he endured more forbearing. . . . It was my first experience of a true sage, exalted beyond himself, to whom neither pain nor death longer counted as a personal experience but as a super-personal matter of observation and contemplation; his dying was no less a moral feat than his life. Freud already then suffered greatly from the illness that was soon to take him from us. One could see that it was a strain for him to speak with his artificial palate and one was almost apologetic for every word that he granted because articulation cost him exertion. But he would not let one go; it was the pride of his spirit of steel to manifest to his friends that his will remained more potent than vulgar bodily torments. His mouth distorted by pain, he wrote at his desk until the last days, and even when pain tortured his sleep at night—the wonderfully sound, healthy sleep which had been the prime source of his strength for eighty years—he denied himself sleeping potions and any narcotic. He did not wish the lucidity of his mind to be dulled for a single hour. . . . The struggle of this strongest will, this most penetrating mind of our time against destruction became increasingly cruel; only when he himself realized clearly—he, to whom clarity always had been the highest quality of thinking—that he would not be able to continue to write, to function, like a Roman hero he permitted the doctor to end his pain. It was the noble end of a noble life, a death memorable even among the hecatombs of that murderous time.

This time it was not Thomas Mann who took possession of the dead man's shadow for a novella about decaying London; something in Freud's toughness of character would have resisted that, in any case. But the arts were not unrepresented at his deathbed. "Once, on one of my last visits," Zweig writes, "I took Salvador Dali with me, in my opinion the most gifted painter of the younger generation, who revered Freud immensely and, while I talked with Freud, he worked at a sketch. I dared not show it to Freud, because, clairvoyantly, Dali had already incorporated death in the picture." It was Zweig, and Ernest Jones, who spoke at the funeral, but the eulogy that was best remembered was W. H. Auden's tribute to this man who had changed the world "simply by looking back

with no false regrets/ All that he did was to remember/ Like the old
and be honest like children":

> . . . about him at the very end were still
> Those he had studied, the nervous and the nights,
> And shades that still waited to enter
> The bright circle of his recognition
>
> Turned elsewhere with their disappointment as he
> Was taken away from his old interest
> To go back to the earth in London,
> An important Jew who died in exile.
>
> Only Hate was happy, hoping to augment
> His practice now, and his shabby clientèle
> Who think they can be cured by killing
> And covering the gardens with ashes.
>
> . . . over a grave
> The household of Impulse mourns one dearly loved.
> Sad is Eros, builder of cities,
> And weeping anarchic Aphrodite.

III

TURN TOWARD THE LIGHT
FOR A MOMENT

A book is their fatherland, their possession,
their ruler, their fortune and misfortune. . . . From
here they cannot be driven out.
— HEINRICH HEINE, Ludwig Börne

The three men were related: Karl Wolfskehl, the symbolist poet, was a second cousin of Theodor Lessing, the essayist and philosopher, and both of them, in turn, were cousins of the playwright Carl Sternheim. Literary talent could thus be said to have run in the family. Besides, other ramifications of the family tree provided connections to Heinrich Heine and to Paul Heyse (the first German poet to win the Nobel Prize for literature, in 1910), to the Bernays of Hamburg, one of whom— Martha Bernays—married Sigmund Freud; to the art historian Max J. Friedländer, who became director of the Kaiser Friedrich Museum in Berlin, and to Philipp Spitta, the biographer of J. S. Bach. They belonged to that stratum of "privileged" Jews who had risen to prominence and prosperity as merchants and bankers to the princely houses of western Germany. Wolfskehl, who took particular pride in his ancestry, traced it back (on the grounds of a family tradition) to the Jewish physician Calonymos, who saved the life of the emperor Otto II during a battle with the Saracens in A.D. 982, and whom Otto brought back with him from Italy to Mainz. (An even earlier ancestor, Moses ben Calonymus the Elder, a resident of Lucca in the ninth century, had introduced kabalistic studies to Europe.) The famous thousand-year-old rosebush which interlaces its branches with one of the windows of the Hildesheim cathedral had its roots no more firmly embedded in German soil than Wolfskehl's persistent and durable forebears. When, as an old man, he was driven from Germany by the Nazis, he addressed an understandably bitter poem *An die Deutschen,* pointing out that he was leaving with a heavy heart because, among other things, "a thousand years go with me" into exile:

> *Euer Wandel war der meine*
> *Eins mit euch auf Hieb und Stich. . . .*

"Your ways were my ways, I was with you through thick and thin; indissoluble, the bonds that united us. . . . A German province bore me, German bread was my nourishment; the Rhenish grape fermented in my blood for a thousand years." Something in this legacy, at any rate, sufficed to turn Wolfskehl into a neo-medieval poet, attracted to folklore, magic and mysticism—one of the "last romantics" who chose for their theme the traditional values of bygone epochs in order, as Yeats once said, to "liberate the arts from 'their age' and from life, and leave them more and more free to lose themselves in beauty."

Wolfskehl in his later years struck the philosopher Erich Kahler as "the truest and most palpable personification of a visionary—and also of the Eternal Jew." But as a young man, before World War I, he was a bon vivant among the poets; a passionate collector of books and experiences, a lover of wine, women and music, and the uncrowned king of the Munich "Latin Quarter" known as Schwabing. The painter and stage designer Emil Preetorius remembered afterward that Wolfskehl constituted the "very center and glory of everything" that made Schwabing the artistic mecca of art-nouveau (alias *Jugendstil)* Germany. "From early morning till late at night Wolfskehl's apartment was the favorite meeting place to find color and mental stimulation. It was a curious environment, filled to overflowing with art as well as odds and ends, with objects of every sort of provenance, valuable or worthless, serious or scurrilous, yet united by a secret significance they had for their owner. And to this confusing jumble was added an inexhaustible selection of the most beautiful and rarest books of all epochs."

It was the household of a well-to-do and thoroughly civilized young man. Both his parents came from banking families: his father, in addition to being a banker, was also leader of the Liberal party in Darmstadt for more than thirty years, and for much of that time vice-president of the upper chamber of the Hessian state legislature. There were three Wolfskehl children, and their several fates were typical of their generation. Karl, the eldest—born in

Darmstadt in 1869—was to die as an exile in New Zealand. His sister Margaret married Baron von Preuschen, a captain and future general in the German army; his brother Eduard, a leading figure in the German Red Cross during World War I, was killed in a concentration camp during World War II.

Karl Wolfskehl felt that he had been born to be a poet, and wrote that he had "led a poet's life even as a boy." At school he specialized in Germanic philology and wrote his doctor's thesis on Teutonic myth. At twenty-three, while still a student at the University of Giessen, he met the symbolist poet Stefan George, only a year older than himself but vastly superior in his knowledge of the world: George had already been to Pre-Raphaelite London, as well as to Paris, where he had been befriended by Mallarmé. From the moment they met, Wolfskehl wrote, "I knew where I belonged, and who would serve as my model." He was to become the most loyal, if not the most intimate, of George's numerous and often absurdly sycophantic disciples: their friendship was the only one in the circle to last from the 1890s until George's death in 1933.

Stefan George emerges, in retrospect, as a sort of Wagner without music. To Wolfskehl and the others he was nothing less than the high priest of a new religion of art, the bearer of a new dispensation, whose poetry managed to combine the loftiest attributes of Mallarmé, Swinburne and d'Annunzio (all of whom George translated into German). His genius as a poet was matched by the immensity of his ego. "I as one am as much as they are as many," he said, quite unjustly, of his "circle," most of whom worshiped the ground the *Meister* walked on. He had "the innate kingliness of a self-possessed soul," as Hugo von Hofmannsthal expressed it, and the young Wolfskehl approached him with the diffidence of the wanderer who "stands and pleads" in his early poem, *At the Ancient Waters*:

> *Lasst mich baden*
> *Im quell der ruhe*
> *Der eure heilige burg bespült.*
> *Bleiben will ich mit euch.*

> Let me bathe
> in the spring of quiet
> that moats your holy castle.
> I would remain with thee.

But Wolfskehl lacked self-confidence only in George's company. His friends knew him as a cheerful giant who loved to talk and recite poetry—a walking encyclopedia who could always supply a missing quotation or an apposite pagan myth. One of his contemporaries, Ludwig Curtius, recalled that when he first met Wolfskehl he hardly knew what to make of this long-haired, chaotic figure whose wild gestures always threatened to sweep the teacups off the table. He would recite poetry while stalking up and down in rooms that seemed much too small for him: "In an unchecked flood of speech, he would recite first from a medieval poet, go from there to an Indian one, then change to Sappho, explain some verses of the *Iliad*, and toss in some remarks about Dostoyevsky, and whilst I was mulling these over, he had already arrived at Mallarmé, only to praise Stefan George at the end, and to talk scornfully about the times in which we lived—it was difficult to discern the center of gravity around which this superabundance was governed and arranged." Some of his listeners thought it downright farcical when he recited the Old Testament poetry of his mystery play *Saul*, with all the characters speaking in a Darmstadt accent. But George, too, came from the provinces, and no one laughed when he declaimed his poetry in a regional accent.

Wolfskehl married Hanna de Haan, the daughter of an orchestra conductor, and their elegant home in Munich became renowned for its hospitality. "It was more like a court than a household," Erich Kahler remembered, "for it was the center of the city's intellectual life. . . . From morning to night people came and went, seeking his counsel, his opinions, his assistance, or simply because they wanted to be stimulated by his restless inspiration." He was always available, for literary advice, for Bohemian parties or carnival pranks, for concerts, outings and café conversations. No one knew where he found the time to read the countless books from which he quoted, and which he mined for his translations and anthologies. "It was understandable," Ludwig Curtius writes, "that he should appear on the street only when he was walking hurriedly in double time, his coat half-unbuttoned, and that his personality had in it something of a giant bird of passage, always about to take flight for another hemisphere. But it would be wrong to think of him as a typically nervous modern man, always driven by lack of time. . . . He gave himself with immense delight to every attractive landscape, work of art or company; he loved the Oktoberfest in Munich as much as the baths of Caracalla."

One room in the Wolfskehl apartment was permanently set aside for Stefan George's use whenever he came to the city, and it was here that the *Meister* would hold his private audiences with hopeful young poets (women had no claims upon his attention). But the circle of the Munich *Kosmiker*, so called, was too riven with jealousies and disagreements, particularly on the "Jewish question," to remain together for very long. They were, from the beginning, an ill-assorted group of disciples, and—as with the Wagnerites—the result was a certain sense of discomfort felt by one group of his admirers at the presence of the other. A number of prominent Georgeans, including Wolfskehl and the critic Friedrich Gundolf, came from Jewish backgrounds, but some of the others—notably the irrationalist philosophers Alfred Schuler and Ludwig Klages—were self-proclaimed "Aryans" and vociferous antisemites. At first George tried to maintain an uneasy truce between the two camps. "Jews make the best leaders," he once confided to a friend. "They are very gifted in the distribution and conversion of values. Of course they cannot experience things as elementally as we do. They are a different people, in any case. I shall never allow them to become the majority in my circle."

All of the *Kosmiker* shared George's penchant for pre-Christian mythology, but it was Wolfskehl, the only serious scholar in the circle, who called their attention to Johann Jakob Bachofen's writings on pagan symbolism and the significance of matriarchal patterns in ancient culture. Schuler, an intellectual jack-of-all-trades, assembled half-digested bits of Bachofen into a "philosophy" of sorts that condemned everything Jewish and Christian (the one as the offspring of the other) and advocated a return to the golden age of ancient paganism. As the symbol of his creed, Schuler chose the *Hakenkreuz*, or swastika, the ancient wheel of the sun which had once been in use throughout Asia—even (though he was unaware of it) in certain synagogues of biblical times. The very sight of the emblem in the design of a porcelain coffee pot, reports one of his friends, was enough to send him into a sort of trance, during which he could only stammer, "Swastika, swastika!"

The swastika in its original context was a great primitive symbol representing, among other things, the sexual union of God-father with Earth-mother—a symbolism that was still dimly understood during the Middle Ages; a swastika on the miter of St. Thomas à Becket, for example, bore the inscription, "Hail to thee, earth, O mother of man. May you thrive in God's embrace. Overflow with fruit for man's benefit." Since the swastika is a schematic yet recognizable representation of two human figures in coitus, it acts as a powerful stimulus on deep layers of the psyche, according to the psychoanalyst Wilhelm Reich—"a stimulus that proves to be that much more powerful the more dissatisfied, the more burning with sexual desire, a person is."

At Schuler's behest, Stefan George changed the cover signet of the group's literary journal, *Blaetter für die Kunst*, from a Greek amphora to the swastika. But Schuler was not satisfied with a purely ornamental victory. The swastika was to signalize a great cataclysm in which a Nero-like force would bring about cosmic revolution: "We throw fire into the night, a copper fury, so that everything bleeds and boils from the city to the village to the charcoal-burner's hut." His hooked cross would sweep away the hated Judeo-Christian ethic, for the Christian cross was merely a "castrated swastika" on which, he said, devout dupes "come to a sticky end like flies on flypaper." As for the Jews, their God was really Moloch, the Canaanite idol who devoured children. For two thousand years, Schuler wrote, the Jew had "blotted out the hot, beating, foaming, dreaming mother-heart" and had blocked all access to the Earth-mother, so that "the heart of earth has become hell for Christians." The solution was to "murder the father before he devours your child, your soul, and thus ye will release the primal skein, the fire-wheel of a hundred spokes"—i.e., the swastika. It was a vague but excitingly nihilist doctrine for which Schuler, reciting in unrhymed verse or delivering impromptu harangues, could usually drum up an attentive audience. He never succeeded in reducing his ideas to a coherent system, but before his death in 1923 he managed to pass them on to the small nationalist-irrationalist circle which met at the Munich home of Elsa and Hugo Bruckmann, and which included an unemployed ex-soldier named Adolf Hitler.

Long before that, however, the Stefan George circle had split apart on the issue of antisemitism. It was Ludwig Klages who tried to force the *Meister* to sever connections with Wolfskehl and Gundolf. *"Was bindet Sie an Juda?"* (What ties you to the Jews?) was Klages's insolent question, to which George replied by letter: "You would regard certain of the people with whom I associate as abominable; I could mention some of your acquaintances whom I regard as far more abominable." Klages could never forgive him for tolerating the intolerable: more than thirty years later, in 1940, he was moved to write a vengeful essay suggesting that George himself could not have been of pure "Aryan" blood, since he was so suspiciously fond of Jews.

> Whatever George achieved in the way of literary success, he achieved through Jews. Jewish is the publisher, Bondi, who issued his books, his *Blaetter* and his writings; in Jewish hands were the bookshops and art galleries in which the *Blaetter* were sold. . . . The Jewish artist Thomas Theodor Heine provided the cover drawings for the first volumes; Jewish professors—I shall name here only Dessoir, Simmel,

Kantorowicz—were his heralds and followers; he liked to have his portrait painted by Jews and half-Jews; Jewish or half-Jewish houses provided him with temporary quarters in the cities he visited when he wanted to promote his work; it was primarily Jews who celebrated his birthday in foreign newspapers, and it is still Jewish intellectuals who, beyond the German borders, try to prevent his laurels from withering too soon.

This curious diatribe sounds like a parody of Thomas Mann's essay on the making of his own literary reputation (see p. 28), but Klages could not have known Mann's article, which was not published until after the novelist's death.

Wolfskehl, the innocent cause of the rift among the *Kosmiker*, was not left entirely unscathed by the episode. Early in 1904 Schuler sent a soldier to his house with a black-bordered envelope containing a "declaration of war." Wolfskehl (who was half blind even as a young man) took his and Klages's threats seriously enough to acquire a pistol, with which he then accidentally shot himself in the leg. But the pleasure of Stefan George's company outweighed the occupational hazards of belonging to his wild-eyed circle of fabulists and myth-spinners. It was through George's example, Wolfskehl wrote, that "the world received meaning; one knew why one existed and to what end." Technically, too, he learned from George "this new poetic language" which reflected, perhaps even determined, the "posture, gesture and standards of the whole epoch." Yet at the same time he prided himself on having given as well as received: *Euch dank ich mein* Wissen: *mir danket den* Weg! (To you I owe my *knowledge*; to me you owe the *way*!). He had, indeed, learned to cultivate his own distinctive vintage—Hellenic, and slightly archaic to the taste—within Stefan George's extensive domains, and could be found determinedly treading his own harvest with the bottoms of his trousers rolled:

> *Ich will euch stampfen hochgeschürzten beins*
> *Quellt über, gischt im kelternden gewitter,*
> *Ertränkt und schwängert heilige fluten weins*
> *Mich Heilige Mitte!*

> I shall trample you, barefoot with high-tucked leg;
> Gush up and foam in the wine-press tempest.
> Drown and fructify me in holy floods of wine,
> O sacred center!

Wolfskehl's *heilige mitte*—the "sacred center"—was the *Mittelmeer*, the wine-dark Mediterranean that had been the navel of the ancient world. Like so many of the earlier German poets he kept

returning to Italy, Goethe's "land where the lemons grow." Yet he
remained as fascinated as ever with Nordic saga and the beginnings of Germanic literature. One of his more extraordinary works
is a small anthology of "the earliest German poetry," preserved,
often by accident, in various manuscripts of the eighth to the four-
teenth centuries and translated by him into modern German. It
includes Christian prayers as well as pagan charms and bless-
ings—a verse for addressing a swarm of bees, for example, so that
they will buzz their way into the waiting hive, and similarly ef-
ficacious rhymes for dealing with horses, dogs, wounds and wild
boar. Another of his discoveries—or rather, rediscoveries—was the
oldest German cradle song:

> *Sleep my darling, quickly sleep*
> *and cease thy crying.*
> *Triwa defends you against*
> *the choking wolf;*
> *Sleep till the morrow*
> *favorite little son.*
> *Ostara will bring the child*
> *sweet honey eggs;*
> *Hera will break for the child*
> *flowers, blue and red.*
> *Zanfana will send small*
> *white lambs tomorrow,*
> *And the one-eyed Lord will*
> *soon give thee spears.*

Wotan, of course, was the one-eyed Lord of German antiquity.
The others—Triwa, Ostara, Hera, Zanfana—are pagan goddesses:
in tenth-century Christian Germany they were evidently still called
upon to watch over sleeping infants. This is the only song of its
kind and furnishes unique, if fragmentary, evidence of the survival
of the old gods in medieval Germany. What made it particularly
fascinating to Wolfskehl, the conscious heir of a thousand-year
Jewish tradition, was that the tenth-century manuscript on which
it was preserved is in the handwriting of someone more accustomed to writing in Hebrew, and apparently just learning to write
German, for he replaced some of the Gothic letters with Hebrew
characters, and added Hebrew comments to the song. The manuscript—a slip of vellum cut from a larger sheet—was found in the
1850s, pasted into the binding of a medieval book. Its original
discoverer, a baptized Jewish scholar from Vienna named Georg
Zappert, had also recognized its importance. The fact that both he
and the manuscript had a "Jewish connection," however, was suf-

ficient to brand the discovery as a fraud. Zappert was vilified in the press and charged with forgery: unable to prove his innocence, his reputation destroyed, he shot himself. It was not until seventy years later that Wolfskehl, reopening the case, was able to show that Zappert had been an honest man after all, and that—"miracle upon miracles"—the survival of the oldest German cradle song also illustrated the ancient bond that existed between the two highly literate and poetic peoples whose representative he had always felt himself to be.

"In contrast to many important Jewish intellectuals," writes Ludwig Curtius, Wolfskehl "did not suffer from his Judaism, nor did he harbor some secret resentment, but rather he cherished it as one of the sources of his religious-poetic character." After World War I, when he had lost his inherited fortune and earned his livelihood as a writer of prose, he produced several essays on aspects of the German-Jewish tradition. He was deeply convinced that "Jews and Germans—how they belong together; neither can exist without the other!" And as antisemitic agitation against the Jews grew steadily more strident he tried his best to make German readers come to terms with the reality, not of the "Jewish question," but of *das jüdische Geheimnis,* the ancient mystery that he saw reflected in their existence:

> Are the Jewish people a race or a kind of religion or an accidental mixture of some kind; a nation, a tribe, a congregation? Did Judaism perish or does it continue to exist; when was its antiquity, when will its transcendent stage begin? Is the age of prophecy, this extraordinary novelty for the world, something new for the Jews? Every thesis misses the point, every statement one can make is uncertain and glides off the ungraspable reality. Even the most basic questions are unanswerable—mystic, moral or pragmatic. Is the Jewish people at home here, or in exile; is it loyal or subversive, chosen or proscribed? The divine was always in dispute with this people, and always present in it: what a condition, what a movement! Countless its ways, but the goal in darkness. Immense its influence on the alien world; infinite its loneliness.

Wolfskehl wrote passionately on art, drama and music; on language and philology, on magic, masks and talismans; on Molière, on Heine, on obscure poetry. "Every poem is an ascent, a beating of wings, and a wondering and a knowing, all at the same time," he remarks in his notes on a rare volume of German Baroque verse, "Poetry-in-Spite-of-Nightingales." He translated Spanish Hebrew poetry, and the medieval Latin lyrics of the Archipoeta, the prince of wandering goliard poets; he produced a new singing translation of Mozart's *The Marriage of Figaro* and of sundry Italian arias and songs; he made a collection of poetry on the subject of wine and wine-drinking; he wrote a German version of Charles de Coster's Franco-Flemish *Ulenspiegel*. These accomplishments are the work of a man with an insatiable appetite for reading. His love of books, the meaning of books, the pleasure of collecting books, are themes that recur as a persistent *basso ostinato*. Life amid treasured books, he said, created a "gently erotic atmosphere" akin to living in a harem both polygamous and peaceful, like the paradise that Mohammed promised the faithful: "Many women thou hast, and peace in the house." He wrote a book for bibliophiles on the care and appreciation of old books in which, among other things, he advised them not to rush into leather bindings. "A cover of simple boards, gray and unassuming as it may be, encloses books of the seventeenth and eighteenth century more snugly, more appropriately, more authentically, than any Morocco binding, no matter how ostentatious, from some pampered biblio-snobbish library on this or the other side of the ocean." His own bibliomania seemed to him almost an inherited rather than an acquired characteristic. "For three thousand years The Book has meant for every Jew the very reason, center and compass of his existence. . . . Always and again, from journey or from repose, he must return to the book, his divine book."

With so many interests, Wolfskehl seemed overextended and too multifaceted to suit Stefan George, who would have liked him to lead a much more tightly focused life. "The conversations with Karl," he wrote to Gundolf in 1905, "despite all his abundance and charm, were often quite irritating; it is as though one were gazing at a marvelous landscape while the earth moved under one's feet. He always embraces the clouds, and one can prophesy an Ixion fate for his.spirit." George, no less than Wolfskehl, was well versed in Greek mythology, and he must have chosen his classical precedent with care. Ixion is the mythological king who makes love to a cloud (cunningly shaped into Hera's form by Zeus) and is punished by being scourged and bound to a fiery wheel that rolls ceaselessly through the sky. His name, which is derived from the Greek for mistletoe, indicates that Ixion is a variant of the ancient "oak king" whose sacramental role was to marry the Moon Goddess, then to be scourged and emasculated so that his blood and sperm would fructify the land, crucified against a tree, and ritually eaten by those whose harvest he had ensured. In the deeper Freudian sense at least, Wolfskehl did suffer Ixion's fate—he was racked on the fiery "wheel of the sun" which the Nazis had appropriated, and carried, if not ceaselessly through the sky, then to the ends of the earth, as far as New Zealand. Symbolically he was crucified on the swastika exactly like the human victim in John Heartfield's famous photomontage of 1934, derived from a medieval sculpture in which a man (perhaps an "oak king") is broken on the wheel. If this seems merely coincidental, it may be recalled that the Nazis themselves deliberately revived the symbolism of the sun-wheel. In their *Sonnenwend* (solstice) festivals they rolled flaming swastikas downhill at night, in imitation of the pagan custom of rolling fiery wheels downhill to dramatize the fact that the sun, having reached its zenith, must now decline again until the winter solstice.

Ironically, it was Wolfskehl's magnificent collection of books that saved him from the final indignities of the "pagan solution" to which his brother was to fall victim. When the Nazis came to power he was able to sell his library of 30,000 rare books to the publisher Salman Schocken in exchange for a small annuity: it enabled him to live, frugally enough, first in Italy, then in the antipodes for the last fifteen years of his life. He was sixty-three when, on the day after the Reichstag fire, he quietly slipped across the Swiss border carrying only a small suitcase with a few of his most essential books: he was never to own much more than that again. But material possessions were the least of what he was forced to leave behind. "I have lost *everything*," he wrote to Preetorius after fourteen years in exile. "I have lost my native land; do you know what that means for a poet? . . . I have lost the cities where I worked and where I made an impression for a whole lifespan. . . . I have had to become my own world, my own mental space, the cradle of words."

The poetry he wrote under the pressure of political events has something in it of William Blake's innocence and experience—an echo, perhaps, of the primitive bee-blessing and wound-healing poems that also figured in Blake's literary lineage. His first book of exile, *Die Stimme spricht* (The Voice Speaks) appeared in 1936 and (according to its English translators, Ernst Morwitz and Carol North Valhope) was "carried in the baggage of German Jews to the four corners of the earth":

> *A seed is dug under*
> *In the world—somewhere*
> *Who waits for its growing,*
> *His days promise fair.*

During the last ten years before his death in 1948, everything he wrote was *in signo Hiob*—under the sign of Job: "I am, I live, I experience Job." One of the poems of the cycle *Job, or the Four Mirrors,* dictated when he was totally blind, begins with the lines (in Peter Dronke's translation):

> *If you knew what I know*
> *Your laughter would sound low.*
> *Low as the stifled moans*
> *Over tombstones. . . .*

From the day his ship left Europe he had "recognized, experienced, expressed, cried out, sung out" the fate of the exiled Jew, and yet he felt more than ever *Mithüter des deutschen Geistes*—one of the guardians of the German spirit. Efforts were made to bring him back to Germany after the war, when he was in his mid-seventies, but he declined, politely, painfully, petulantly. "My native land has completely forgotten that a German poet named Karl Wolfskehl still exists," he complained. For the last of Stefan George's paladins, it was intolerable that Munich, "the city that once called me its favorite son," should have filed him away among the missing and nameless. To have returned to Munich as a briefly resurrected Lazarus was not Wolfskehl's style: better to die as Job in New Zealand.

In 1930, while he was still living in Munich, Wolfskehl received a letter from his distant cousin Theodor Lessing, then research professor of philosophy in Hanover, whom he had known briefly during the early years of the George circle. Lessing wanted Wolfskehl's opinion of his book *Europe and Asia,* a new edition of which had just come off the press, but he was also in a mood to talk about old times:

> We have traveled our entire lives in separate paths, but now, at my age, it often seems to me as if *you* had known and possessed very early what I in my way, on difficult paths with many a wrong turning, have only reached quite recently. Yours was the greater fortune, of taking part as the planet with the widest orbit in a solar choir; I suppose I was only a meteor that sometimes traversed your cosmos, and it is to these encounters that our common memories and sympathies are confined.

Wolfskehl hoped that they might have a chance to renew their acquaintance, but in fact they never saw each other again during the two years that remained before Hitler made Germany untenable for both of them. And although Wolfskehl wrote nostalgically enough about their earlier meetings, he also recalled that "we never really knew what to make of each other," and wondered whether "it would really be different now if we met face to face." Lessing, who was three years younger than Wolfskehl (he was born in 1872), had a far more difficult and prickly personality: he was born to be a critic and reformer rather than a poet, though he, too, had published several volumes of poetry. Beside the towering Wolfskehl, described by Lessing as "a handsome, masculine Assyrian prince" who bore the mark of his ancient nobility upon his brow, Lessing himself cut an unprepossessing figure. Small, sickly, with a perpetual stoop, he had, as a boy, been beaten so hard with his father's riding crop in an effort to make him "stand up straight" that one of the muscles in his back had been injured, and "never again in my life was I able to straighten my back without a paroxysm of pain."

Theodor Lessing revenged himself on his father by writing a brilliant and utterly honest autobiography, *Einmal und nie wieder* (Once and Never Again), which has been compared to the *Confessions* of Rousseau. In it he recounts the intellectual and emotional adventures of an ugly duckling son growing up in an atmosphere of almost unrelieved oppression from which he was eventually able to escape. Lessing had read Freud by the time he wrote his memoirs in 1925, but he thought his own experiences contradicted the theory of the Oedipus complex. "However conscientiously I try to reconstruct my childhood: my aversion to my mother was just as primal and instinctive as my hatred of my father." Lessing's account is both a fascinating document of self-analysis and a detailed indictment of the whole authoritarian system of education that prevailed in Germany. From the very beginning, his life as the son of a well-known physician—the *kleine Herr Doktor*—was hedged about with prohibitions. "Countless people came every day. One had to be 'well behaved.' One had to 'shake hands.' One had to 'make one's bow' [*Diener machen*, i.e., click one's heels and bow from the waist]. At last I could return to the nursery, where I crept into my corner. . . . Father and mother came into the nursery to scold, to reprimand, to prohibit—then to leave again. Thank God! We were entrusted to the servants."

Half the year he was habitually in bed—with whooping cough, or diphtheria, scarlet fever, measles, scurvy and much else. School was a progressive agony of suffering, boredom and misunderstanding. The teachers took no interest in children outside the classroom. "They were Prussian officials, lieutenants of the Army Reserve, loyal to the Kaiser and intensely patriotic. They were passionately attached to their status, and terribly rank-conscious. . . . They were men who were forever trying to prove their manhood. . . . Again and again I stood before authoritarians who were like my father. All had preconceptions. All made demands. All demanded admiration, or at least obedience. And the defenseless boy shuddered before these unattainable giants."

One teacher taught arithmetic with a system whereby the last boys to solve the day's quota of problems were teased and booed by the whole class. "All those who had done the work correctly were allowed to charge up to those who didn't know the answers and show their contempt by 'squeaking.' That meant pointing at the dunces with their index-fingers and calling out, while rubbing the fingers against each other, '*Ätsch, zipp, zipp!*' This was regarded as the highest disgrace." Other teachers beat him as unmercifully as his father—for his persistently illegible penmanship, among other things. His Latin professor "liked nothing better than to step before the class in his reserve lieutenant's uniform, and to win Caesar's victories 'tactically and strategically' all over again. . . . He addressed us in the third person, in the manner of Frederick the Great: 'What, he doesn't know that? He *must* know that! . . . Let him sit down!' " The upshot was, Lessing adds, that "I had to sacrifice my youth to the task of surviving my school, my parents and my upbringing." To complicate matters, he was one of the few Jewish boys in the school, though at first he was not even aware of that fact:

> At home we never talked about Judaism. Jewish customs were no longer observed in our family. A rather puzzling problem arose, therefore, when I became conscious, relatively late, that unlike the others I was not a Christian. The teasing of Jewish children was not really meant to be mean. The word "Jew" for the boys of Hanover was just an ordinary epithet like "fool" or "moron." People were always calling each other names, and I did likewise. In my primary school there were two other Jewish boys, Süssapfel and Ransahoff. Süssapfel was always the first in his class; Ransahoff was very retarded, and always being knocked about. Children are very cruel, and I also teased poor Ransahoff till one day, when I called him "Jew," he answered, "You're one yourself." I said indignantly, "It's not true," but I did go to my mother and inquire what a Jew was. She laughed and gave me an evasive answer. But once, on the street, she showed me a man wearing a kaftan and said, "There goes a Jew." I gathered from her remark that we weren't "real" Jews. But the word itself took on a sinister meaning for me. Since I had childishly absorbed all the patriotic and religious prejudices of the school, and there was nothing to counterbalance them at home, I became convinced that being Jewish was something evil. "The Jews crucified our Lord." At the age of nine I already felt that I was somehow included in the

general aversion to Jews. The boys had a silly teasing-rhyme: *Jude, Jude Itzig, mach dich nicht so witzig* [Jew, Jew Bunny, don't try to be so funny—or something of the sort]. As soon as it was sung I felt ashamed, and this sensitivity was soon discerned by the others. When I entered a classroom, some of the more aggressive boys would sing: *Jude, Jude Itzig, mach dich nicht so witzig!* Whereupon I would shout back, "What makes you think *you're* so funny?"

Lessing writes that his education would have ended in disaster had it not been for two saving relationships. There was the elderly spinster who nursed him through his worst illness—"without her I would not have lived"—and encouraged his first attempts at poetry. And there was the adolescent friend who shared his last years in secondary school, and who became his inseparable companion, "blood brother" and co-conspirator. Both of them dreamed of becoming philosophers and changing the awful world in which they lived; they wrote poetry and made literary discoveries together, paid exploratory visits to the theater, went for hikes in the countryside and, to their parents' dismay, became known in their neighborhood as Damon and Pythias, alias "Schiller and Goethe." They were complementary opposites—"the more delicate one with black hair and an ivory-pale complexion; the more robust one with blond hair and ruddy cheeks." They spent hours trying to define their differences: one was "fiery," the other "passionate"; one sanguine, the other choleric; one a "flying soul," the other a "brooding soul."

Years later, Lessing wrote that when he looked back on those years he was "transfixed by a bright ray of joy" because this friendship had opened up the whole of nature to him. "My native land, the North-German heath, the mighty North Sea, the clouds that wandered above our Gothic spires toward Denmark, the pitch-pines on the craggy cliffs and the storm that plays through their branches, our beech forest, our ghostly moors, our wide sky, our austere landscape—it was through the friend of my youth that they first entered my vocabulary." Against the intensity of this friendship, parents, teachers—"my prison wardens"—and even the opinion of contemporaries, were powerless to prevail. Both friends were convinced that the other was a genius: that the coming age would one day bear the other's name. Moreover, at the age of sixteen, "we had already mentally completed our doctoral dissertations and carried them with us in our heads"—both of them, indeed, ultimately went on to write high-flown works of philosophy based on remarkably similar hypotheses. Lessing's bears the title

Der Untergang der Erde am Geist (The Decline of the World Through Intellect); his friend's, *Der Geist als Widersacher der Seele* (The Intellect as Adversary of the Soul). Both, as it happens, belong to that species of pretentious "philosophy" so much in vogue in early twentieth-century Germany, Spengler's *Decline of the West* being the best-known example of the genre. It tends to pursue a constant zigzag course between the sublime and the ridiculous—a strange game of generalizations, intuitions and racial misconceptions that bears no recognizable relationship to reality. It was Lessing who first arrived at the formula that "the intellect is the parasite of the life-force," the very theme which was to become a lifetime obsession in his friend's anti-intellectual, antiliterary and above all, antisemitic writings. For, as luck would have it, the young man who played Damon to Lessing's Pythias happened to be the selfsame Ludwig Klages who, a few years later, was to declare open war on Wolfskehl and to denounce Stefan George for his ties to *Juda*.

Klages had inherited his instinctive antisemitism from his father, a former army sergeant, but soon discovered ways of rationalizing it: the Teuton, he told Lessing, is the "idealist," whereas the Jew is the "materialist." To overcome this handicap and to escape the destructive influence of the Semitic spirit, Lessing was to engage in "the struggle of the nobler self against his inborn racial soul." Though he did his best, their friendship was doomed to come to a painful end once both of them had left Hanover to attend separate universities. Lessing, having studied both philosophy and medicine, came to Munich in 1895 to find Klages already deeply involved with the *Kosmiker*, particularly with Alfred Schuler, who figures in Lessing's memoirs as "a curious mixture of charlatan and genius, of braggart and fanatic." Schuler's neo-pagan hedonism, Lessing decided, was the outgrowth of his "primitive and feminine homosexuality," which was attracted only by masculine strength—"of young soldiers and sailors, boxers and wrestlers, muscular workers in work clothes and heavy-chested peasants in mountaineer's costume." Though Schuler, Klages and the *Kosmiker* talked a great deal about the life-force, Lessing felt they were wholly out of touch with it. "They deified the oceanlike immensity of life, but they hid themselves away behind walls and dams, in towers and behind locked doors." Not only the disciples but Stefan George himself—a "technician of aesthetic-pretentious snobbery"—failed to impress the brash and irritable Lessing, who had decided to cast his lot with the social critics and "enlighteners" rather than the myth-makers. Relations with Klages, already under a severe strain, reached the breaking point in 1899, when Lessing fell in love with the aristocratic girl who was to become his first wife, Maria Stach von Goltzheim, and brought her to Munich to live with him. Their final, cruel scene was a meeting in Klages's apartment that ended with the words, "You are a disgusting, pushy Jew!"

Lessing once described his career as "the honest struggle of a man who has been beaten into a cripple in his youth." But it was not just the riding crop that had injured him; for years he remained traumatized by the boyhood friendship that had taught his "nobler self" to despise his Jewish origins. He was to become an influential essayist, critic and teacher of philosophy, yet years were to elapse before he could recognize in himself the symptoms of a neurosis which he went on to describe in a classic collection of case histories, *Der jüdische Selbsthass* (Jewish Self-Hatred). Only then did he discover the phenomenon of the self-fulfilling prophecy: "To turn a man into a dog, one has only to say to him often enough, 'You dog!' " In the normal course of events, Lessing was instinctively on the side of the victim. In his memoirs, for example, he describes the terrible moment when, as a student at the Pathological Institute of Munich, he had to witness the delivery of the corpses of five children who had died that day of malnutrition. "Bollinger, the pathologist, had no word of indignation, and the assistants and students gazed at the little bodies with their impudent cold eyes, while I was choked by a sobbing in my throat as if they had been my own children. I clenched my fists in my pockets and swore, in order to master my anger, that someday I would avenge the deaths of these children on the society to which I still belonged." Yet, much as he hated injustice, he was somehow unable to feel much compassion toward the Jews: he had, as the saying went, "swallowed the stick with which he was beaten"—or what the psychoanalysts would term "identification with the aggressor."

Among his best-known literary satires was a vitriolic and wholly unprovoked attack on the critic Samuel Lublinski, who had earned Thomas Mann's undying gratitude with his timely and perceptive praise of *Buddenbrooks* but who had overreached himself by writing a self-important survey of modern literature. Lublinski offered an attractive target of opportunity, but Lessing's attack was laced with gratuitous expressions of *Selbsthass*—as when he pokes fun at the portly critic for having "a little synagogue of a figure on short, unsteady legs, with a stomach that extends like an apse into the outer world." In the polemics that followed, Thomas Mann pointed out that people who live in glass houses should not throw stones. But Lessing, at the time, seemed to think that the pain he had suffered gave him the right to inflict it on others. His account of a journey he made among the Jews of Poland hardly bothers to conceal the traditional German (and German-Jewish) ill will toward the Yiddish-speaking *Ostjuden*. Someone took him to a prayer meeting of Hasidim, a Jewish sect which shared the American Holy Rollers' penchant for movement and passion in prayer. Despite his supposed preference for "life" over "intellect," Lessing was shocked to the very soles of his German patent-leather boots:

> Everyone cried, shouted, sang, gesticulated. . . . An earsplitting song, like a single plaint, echoed through the room. The general ecstasy grew steadily more insane, more rapturous. Crying, nasal sounds, convulsive jerks, general excitement and movement. . . . I almost shuddered with fear of this kind of prayer. I became ill. . . . I had the feeling of being among madmen. I pushed my way to the door by force and ran outside.

It came to him at last that self-hatred, even in this relatively harmless form, was potentially as self-destructive as Otto Weininger's suicidal psychosis. He purged himself of it by writing a series of essays on prominent Jewish antisemites, including Weininger, and an analysis of the guilt-displacing mechanism that underlies all race hatred: "When I bring suffering into another human being's life by interfering with it, I justify my action by blaming the character of the *other*." Moreover, injustice to the Jews had been sanctioned by generations of precedent: it had become "justified injustice." They themselves had come to believe the negative stereotypes created by the process he called *die Verhässlichung des Verhassten*, the "uglification" of what one wants to hate. Remembering his own experience, he adds wistfully that the poison becomes even stronger when a secret feeling of sympathy has to be anesthetized and destroyed: "One can observe this in cases where a love or a friendship is turned to hatred and persecution."

Lessing reasoned that the most prominent Jew-haters of Germany were motivated by a lust for power: antisemitism was merely a stepping-stone to world conquest. In any event, the Jews would never be able to do anything right so far as the rest of the world was concerned: "We were told, you are parasites on alien soil, so we left our homes. We were told, you are nothing but middlemen, so we raised our children as farmers and peasants. We were told, you are cowardly weaklings, so we went into battle and produced the toughest soldiers. . . . But when we insisted on maintaining ourselves as a distinct people, we were told: have you still not learned that preserving your distinctiveness is treason against the universalist, pan-human spirit of mankind?" Perhaps even the traditional argument in defense of the German Jews—that they had contributed so many musicians, poets, scientists to German culture—ought to be interpreted as a disaster signal rather than a cause for rejoicing because this was Jewish treasure that was being squandered. "Perhaps this brilliance was only the phosphorescent shimmer of a dying body; perhaps it was only the brief flickering of a European bonfire in which our nobility immolated itself."

Lessing's work, in all its diversity, contains a fascinating mixture of prophecy and fallacy, of vision and nearsightedness. He never lost his suspicion of what, in the title of one of his books, he calls *Accursed Culture*. Though he had come to terms with his Jewishness, he continued to berate the literati, professors and "rootless intellectuals," alias *Luftmenschen* (air people), of whom he himself was such a remarkable example. The idea of *Geist* (intellect), on which both he and Klages blamed so many of the world's ills, was only their way of describing the confinements and frustrations of the superego: a more careful reading of Freud on this point might have resolved many of his most nagging problems. But Lessing maintained a contemptuous attitude toward Freud's theories— perhaps, after all, because he really cherished his painfully acquired neuroses, and would not have relinquished them on any account. One wonders what Freud would have made of the recurring dream that plagued Lessing in middle age: "My father comes and scolds me for not having succeeded in anything. The tyrannical Dörries and other teachers from my school come to tell me that I am useless for intellectual work. And always I wake up with the same feeling of insecurity: 'Now you are old, and still haven't accomplished anything!' "

Actually, Lessing had achieved a good deal of success despite the psychological odds against him. Though his first marriage ended in divorce, the second brought him domestic tranquility. After his appointment to the philosophical faculty of the Technical Institute in Hanover, he became a prominent figure in many of the progressive movements of pre-1914 Germany—adult education, social welfare, women's rights, law reform, "the reform of clothing," and several others, including the first Association Against Unnecessary Noise, founded by him in 1908. The antinoise campaign seems to have been closest to his heart. "It grew so quickly," he notes with pardonable pride, "that soon I had to maintain an office with two secretaries. The various forms of disturbing noise, such as the piano-playing plague, the automobile plague, bell-ringing nuisance, carpet-beating plague, faulty road-construction noise, etc., had all to be combated individually. The journal of the association, *Der Antirüpel* (The Anti-Boor), which I wrote entirely myself, has become a great rarity."

When the war broke out, he tried to lead a pacifist revolt among German "thinkers" and was rudely disillusioned. But the book he wrote during the war, *Geschichte als Sinngebung des Sinnlosen* (History—or How to Make Sense out of Nonsense), as well as a gentle trilogy on animals and flowers, earned him an international reputation as a cultural philosopher during the postwar years. Despite the progressive measures introduced by the Weimar Republic he managed to remain perpetually at odds with the authorities. In 1924 he tried, unsuccessfully, to induce the city of Hanover to declare a "day of general repentance and prayer" to mark the execution of a notorious "Werewolf," Friedrich Haarmann, who had been convicted of the murder of twenty-seven boys and young men. In Lessing's view, the whole of society shared in the murderer's guilt, since it had permitted the creation of soul-destroying "new deserts" in the city slums. The following year he wrote a sarcastic essay against the nomination of Field Marshal von Hindenburg as president of the republic. Hindenburg would serve only as a figurehead, and a dangerous one, Lessing argued. The ex-general had just promised an audience of students that soon they would be able to avenge Germany's defeat: "And you, my dear graduating class, will one day occupy Paris as the victorious conquerors, the way your fathers did!" Lessing foresaw that this "venerable nullity" would serve as a façade for worse to come. "People might say, better a zero than a Nero," he concluded. "Unfortunately, history shows that behind every zero lurks a future Nero."

A storm of patriotic indignation greeted Lessing's prophetic essay. This time he had gone too far: any man—and a Jew at that—who would insult the venerable Hindenburg was clearly an enemy of the people. There were riots in the classroom when he tried to lecture, and he received anonymous threats against his life. Mass meetings were held by students and faculty members to demand his expulsion from the institute. When the ministry of education refused to oblige, 1,500 students walked out in protest. In the ensuing "compromise," Lessing was relieved of his teaching duties and given a "research" assignment instead. To avoid further incidents, he moved his second wife and their daughter to a village on the outskirts of Hanover, and it was here that he wrote the remarkable autobiography whose underlying assumption is that "human life, in contrast to the rest of nature, is incurably tragic."

In 1933, shortly after Hitler was appointed chancellor by President Hindenburg, Lessing and his family—after yet another attack by hooligans—fled to Czechoslovakia. The day after their escape, Storm Troopers broke into his house and destroyed his library. In Prague he delivered a public lecture on "Germany and Her Jews":

> So we Jews are leaving our native land. Are there no armies with us? No! It is not like that. With us are the armies of the fathers, Abraham, Jacob, Moses. And with us, too, are the German guardian spirits. Leaving Germany with us are all those who have a place in our hearts—and who, perhaps, would have no other place in this world if not in us: Goethe and his worldly, wise humanity; Schubert with his consoling song; Dürer the steadfast, child-like painter; Hölderlin, with his Elysian joy. . . .

"He stood on the podium, an old, stooped man, speaking his 'final prayer' concerning life and art, thinking and emotion," reported a member of the audience. "It was not a scholarly lecture: a deeply sensitive human being told us in simple words about a world that had reverted to the Middle Ages and was turning humans into beasts. This recital caused the already broken man to age still more visibly. Silently, their heads bowed in shame, his listeners left the hall."

Lessing rented part of a house in Marienbad, not far from the Czech border with Germany, and began working on a new book. In a letter he described his shock at hearing a radio broadcast from Germany in which the minister of propaganda, Dr. Goebbels, denounced him as the Jew who had called Hindenburg a wholesale murderer, "and I heard how the masses roared out, 'Hang him!'" Shortly afterward he learned that a price of 80,000 marks had been placed on his head. On the evening of August 30, 1933, as he was sitting at his desk on the first floor of the Villa Edelweiss, Lessing was hit in the head by two bullets fired through an open window: he died in the local hospital at one o'clock the next morning. The assassins, Eckert and Daubner, were members of the local Nazi party. They escaped to Germany and received promotions. In the Nazi newspapers there was general rejoicing at the death of "the ill-famed professor," but the *Manchester Guardian*, perhaps with unconscious irony, called him a "patriot" in its obituary: "He was always zealous for the harmonising of German life and Jewish life, for he saw no reason why a Jew should not live a full German life and be a credit to his country, and always strove to live up to that ideal himself."

In his autobiography, Lessing has little to say about his other literary cousin, Carl Sternheim, the satiric playwright—six years his junior—who was regarded as Germany's Molière. But he recounts a conversation he had with Sternheim's father (Lessing's first cousin) about his son's flourishing literary career. When Lessing praised the younger man's talent and the success he was having in the German theater, the elder Sternheim replied rather sourly: "I can't approve of my son's art; it doesn't appeal to me. I demand from true art that it edify and bestow joy. I am an idealist." Lessing comments that Carl Sternheim's art had "never seemed more delightful or true to life" than at that moment when the baffled bourgeois father was grumbling about his son's heresies.

Most of the characters in Sternheim's plays, as a matter of fact, talk precisely like this disgruntled idealist of a father—a language of lofty impulses, interlarded at frequent intervals with more pragmatic considerations and the necessities of everyday life. Sternheim had an infallible ear for the idiom of the company boardroom, the romantic novel, the parade ground and the railway timetable, and sometimes he manages to telescope them all into a single dialogue, so that the whole of German bourgeois culture passes smartly in review. A typical Sternheim love scene, for example (in this case from *Die Kassette*—The Strongbox), has the newlywed wife dreaming of Wagnerian passion; the husband mentally totting up the value of the legacy with which he hopes to feather their nest:

FANNY: I must have lost my locket.
KRULL: The golden one with my picture?
FANNY: This morning in the coupé I felt it upon my breasts. *(She shakes herself.)*
KRULL: That would be it!
FANNY: Can you reach it?
KRULL *(feels)*: I have it. *(He brings it up.)* Sweet woman; my sweet darling!
FANNY: Heinrich!
KRULL *(after a moment)*: What do you think she's worth?
FANNY: Fifty-, sixty-thousand at least.
KRULL: I also thought sixty thousand. *(He kisses her.)* My sweet darling!

Sternheim grouped together a series of his comedies, most of them written before World War I, under the ironic title, *Aus dem bürgerlichen Heldenleben* (From the Heroic Life of the Bourgeoisie). The astonishing thing about them is that they are entirely impervious to the metaphysical maundering that inspired Richard Strauss's *Heldenleben* and marred the work of so many fashionable writers of the day, including Lessing and Wolfskehl. Sternheim had always refused to truckle to the symbolists, and his innate distaste for clichés preserved him from the "cosmic" generalizations of the George circle. As an author he was nothing if not surgically precise: one of his favorite targets was the language of circumlocution, the "metaphors and idylls" with which the age liked to camouflage its greedy and murderous intentions. Among the dramatists of prewar Germany, Sternheim stands out as the one utterly dry-eyed observer of an otherwise weepy and sentimental epoch.

As a child he had enjoyed the benefits of a sort of comic-opera upbringing that nurtured his instincts as a satirist: not for him the dark Freudian labyrinths of Lessing's domestic tragedy. Born in Hanover (a stone's throw from the Lessings) in 1878, he was the child of a *mésalliance* between the scion of a banking family and a dancer from the Hanover ballet. In his autobiography Sternheim remembered his mother as a "dazzlingly beautiful" woman—so beautiful, indeed, that during her dancing days, on the way to Australia for a ballet tour, King Kalakaua of Hawaii offered her his crown and kingdom if she would become his wife. She chose instead to marry Herr Sternheim and raise an organ-pipe family of six children born at regular yearly intervals. Like Sebastian Bach she came from a Saxon-Lutheran family: "Once when a piece by Bach was being played, she remarked that Bach was her uncle, and when my father objected, 'But Marie, the man has been dead for a hundred years,' she replied with unshakable conviction: 'So much the worse for him!' "

Sternheim described his childhood as a happy time in a positively "exemplary" household—"one lived prosperously and wished the same for one's neighbor, the city, the nation. In Germany at that time . . . no one thought beyond the frontier. An Austrian or a Frenchman, if he appeared at all, was the equivalent of what we now imagine a Greenlander to be: something exorbitant, beyond the secure and recognized boundaries of everyday reality." In this family it was the mother who administered the discipline, "for while my father was incapable of harming a fly, my mother was always ready with a box on the ear for the children and the servants." The father, who doubled as a newspaper publisher, could be counted on for a stream of suggestions for the improvement of everything under the sun—"for the whole of creation, from the head of state to the milkman. He was not satisfied unless his children could go to bed at night secure in the knowledge that Papa had set the tottering world to rights again." He also played the piano, teaching them operatic arias by Weber, Lortzing, Offenbach. His idea of eurhythmic exercises was to have the six children sit on a row of chairs and, as he played, to jump up on cue and sing didactic ditties of his own composition:

> *Politik—Polizei,*
> *Geht mir weg alle zwei!*
> *Polizei—Politik*
> *Ja, die hab ich nicht lieb.*

> Politics or Police—
> Kindly leave me in peace!
> Police or Politics—
> No, with me they don't mix.

With the decline of the family's banking fortune in the 1880s they moved to Berlin, the burgeoning capital of the new Hohenzollern Reich and a city that Sternheim learned to detest: "Its ideal is the uncertain, the unfinished, the variable. . . . It is a bottomless puddle in which every certainty is drowned and transformed." Still, there were the pleasures of seeing la belle Otero and Cléo de Mérode at the Wintergarten, and countless other performances in theaters and music halls. He saw the kaiser appear on the palace balcony, heard magnificent concerts at the Philharmonic, and fell in love with some of the most beautiful young ladies of Berlin's *jeunesse dorée*. Since his best friend, Walter Simon, was the son of one of the city's leading financiers and grandson of the founder of the *Frankfurter Zeitung*, still the most important newspaper in Germany, Sternheim's memoirs afford a rare glimpse of life in the uppermost stratum of German-Jewish society:

The Simon household exceeded the comfortably bourgeois circumstances of my own house and fulfilled all the requirements of what was regarded as cosmopolitan culture at the end of the nineteenth century. With the help of her social secretary, Fräulein von Holz, Frau Therese Simon filled her salon with leading personalities from many different fields. Here I became acquainted with virtually all the political leaders of the period when Prince Hohenlohe served as Reich Chancellor. At the same time, thanks to the hostess's passion for music I got to know the whole repertoire of classical German chamber music. Once a week she played trios with the famous violinist Joseph Joachim and the cellist Robert von Mendelssohn.

In this environment, Sternheim inevitably turned into something of a snob: he kept an account with the best tailor in town, learned the racing studbook by heart, played exquisite social tennis and danced at the most fashionable cotillions. When he went into the army for the obligatory year, it was not as a foot-slogging grenadier but as a cavalryman with the aristocratic Sixth Regiment of Cuirassiers, whose officers were members of the oldest Prussian nobility. Sternheim was fascinated by the type: "After I had become acquainted with the world of high finance, the Rothschilds, Schwabachs, Mendelssohns, Bleichröders, Friedländer-Fulds, and the way they lived in their town houses and country châteaux, I became absorbed for a time in the German *ancienne noblesse*, and soon knew as much about their character, connections and family histories as I already did about horse-racing and the army."

He attended seven different German universities, including Munich and Heidelberg, dabbling in law, philosophy, literature and art history, but it is reliably reported that his books remained on the shelves, their pages uncut. His first wife, whom he married in 1900, was the daughter of a wine-grower on the Rhine. But it was his second marriage, in 1907, to the heiress Thea Bauer, that catapulted him into the life of a *grand seigneur* for which he was so well equipped temperamentally. To "erect a visible memorial to our love" they built a thirty-room château in the style of Louis XVI in the suburbs of Munich. It had a small private theater where Sternheim could stage trial performances of the comedies he had begun to write. Much to everyone's amazement these bizarre plays also proved immensely successful on public stages: in 1911, with the appearance of *Die Hose* (The Pants—or rather, since it refers to an article of women's lingerie, The Underpants, alias Bloomers) its bourgeois-gentilhomme author suddenly emerged as the major new figure of the German theater. *Die Hose* represented a giant "Expressionist" step in the direction of what is now known as the Theater of the Absurd. As Sternheim described it laconically, "in my play a bourgeois woman lost her panties; of nothing but the banal affair did one speak in bald German on the stage."

His triumphs were not to be won without a running battle with the censors and the upholders of public decency. In Berlin the chief of police prohibited performances of *Die Hose* until its title had been changed to the enigmatic *Der Riese* (The Giant). And there were riots in the theater during the next two Sternheim premieres, *Don Juan* and *Die Kassette*. He himself was delighted by the fuss: "Never before had three works by the same playwright provoked such rebellion among ordinarily lamblike and pious audiences."

The "Expressionism" that created such a scandal in the theater had little in common with the dramatic exaggeration of the Expressionist poets. Sternheim's distortions, which give his comedies a strange marionettelike stiffness, have to do with a speeding-up of reality that compresses the bald-faced truth about his characters. "The essence of the German bourgeois," he explained, "is broken out of its setting, tersely, simply, brutally. His psychic motor reveals itself on the surface. The craven purpose of widespread hypocrisy is unveiled." Critics remarked that Sternheim's characters spoke as though the devil had got hold of their tongue and was forcing them to reveal their deepest secrets while they thought they were talking commonplaces. Sometimes, too, it is Sternheim himself who stands there, stripped of his moral underpinnings and seized by an exhibitionist compulsion to confess his own bourgeois weaknesses. The hero of his comedy *The Snob* bears an unmistakable resemblance to its author, not only in the meticulousness with which he ties his cravat, but also in the swiftness of his ascent into the upper class. And when the Snob tells his newly acquired aristocratic wife about his family, he does not fail to mention that when his mother was a young girl, "King Kalakaua fell hopelessly in love with her in Honolulu." Sometimes in passing one also glimpses the tops of other icebergs:

THEOBALD	(*husband of the lady who has lost* Die Hose): Are you a barber, Sir?
MANDELSTAM:	My name is Mandelstam.
THEOBALD:	A Semite?
MANDELSTAM:	But no . . .
THEOBALD:	Turn toward the light for a moment.
MANDELSTAM:	With one *m*, "—stam."
THEOBALD:	I'm a German. I don't make much noise about the Jewish thing, but prefer the Red Sea between them and me.
MANDELSTAM:	Precisely my opinion.

Despite his habit of cutting too close to the bone, Sternheim—"with one *m*"—won a vast and appreciative audience among the very burghers whose lives he was dissecting with such clinical detachment. As a result he became more nouveau riche than ever. In his memoirs he remarks quite proudly, like one of his more pedantic characters, that success in the theater "brought me a large annual income so that from now on I could contribute my full share to the conduct of our life." The Sternheims spent vast sums of money buying paintings for their new château, but no one could say that they threw it away like parvenus. In Munich one day, as he was passing the window of an art gallery, Sternheim had taken fancy to a painting by a little-known Dutchman, recently deceased, whose work he then proceeded to acquire, first one or two pictures at a time, then in wholesale lots. "In Amsterdam," he writes, "in the attic of the home of Van Gogh's sister-in-law, Frau Cohen-Gottschalk, I had the extraordinary opportunity of finding fifty of the immortal painter's beautiful canvases, their surfaces still stuck together, and I was able to buy half a dozen."

Only as a collector of books did he fail to live up to the standards established by his more knowledgeable cousin, Wolfskehl. To fill the shelves of his library, built in the style of Louis XV, he and his wife motored through France, "collecting the best known and most valuable works of Louis' and the following century in Morocco or calf bindings . . . augmented in Germany by an almost complete collection of first editions of the German classics." He himself, by general consensus, had already joined their ranks: as the critic Willy Haas pointed out, his comedies were "classics" not only in the usual sense, "but because they belong to the great classical tradition of European comedy—the line of Molière, Beaumarchais, Congreve and Sheridan. He created comic roles like no other German author before him."

Sternheim was far from modest about his accomplishments. He liked to think that "just as in music there are the three B's—Bach, Beethoven and Brahms—in literature there are the three S's: Shakespeare, Schiller and Sternheim." Many of his admirers complained about his increasing arrogance: in later years, reported Klaus Mann, no one dared go near him because he insisted on insulting everybody he came into contact with—critics, directors, publishers, hotel porters, tailors, actors, doctors, politicians. Apart from Van Gogh, Gauguin and his own comedies, nothing ever quite suited him—like his father, he had an inexhaustible supply of suggestions as to how the world should be improved. He sent Max Reinhardt a telegram proposing that he give up directing plays (Reinhardt's productions of his comedies were the most important of his career) and go off to Argentina with a troupe of trained seals. His fellow playwright Carl Zuckmayer described him as "a cross between a business magnate and a Belgian marquis, who loved to assume the tone and attitude of a Prussian *Junker*." But the critic Franz Blei, who worked for Sternheim on the magazine *Hyperion*,

wrote that behind the arrogant mask there was "another Sternheim: naïve, insecure, uninformed, timid, homeless. The ur-
bane-insolent style was only a façade." The problem was, as
Sternheim was perfectly aware, that "my nervous system had
never been too steady in the saddle—even while I was still at
school our family doctor had often been called in to help." With the
years he became so overwrought and cantankerous that he was
forced to spend long periods in mental clinics recovering his
equilibrium.

The atmosphere in Germany became too tense for him as early as
1912, when he sold the Bavarian château and built another at La
Hulpe, near Brussels. There the war caught up with him: as a
German national his property was confiscated when Belgium was
liberated at the end of the war, though his sympathies lay with the
Belgians. He had already written *1913*, a comedy banned by the
wartime censors, which exposed the social injustice that had led to
the war—it drilled to the root of the diseased imperial tooth as
unerringly and painfully as the kaiser's dentist.* After the armistice,
Sternheim was the first writer to declare unequivocally, in prose,
that "all of Germany without distinction between classes and persons bore an equal responsibility for having brought about the war,
for both the highest and the lowest classes participated in an insatiable capitalism that was devoid of any ideals. The general contempt for things of the spirit in Germany I regard as a collective
guilt."

The prose of Sternheim's hectoring essays and short stories was
just as hard-edged and idiosyncratic as the language of his plays.
Robert Musil, himself one of the great prose stylists, admired "the
extraordinary discipline, the coldness, the geometry, the sobriety
of this poet—a dry, clean manner of thinking. This is a man who
loves to saw hardwood logs rather than cut fodder for literary
cattle." Even Franz Kafka, the most exigent of critics, thought that
Sternheim's "very popular and very repugnant" stories were in-
trinsically important, and not only because Sternheim had passed
on to the impecunious Kafka the 800 marks he received for the
Fontane Prize of 1915.

But Sternheim never recovered his literary momentum after the

---

*The kaiser's dentist, Dr. Schramm, also happened to be my first dentist. I received
my earliest dental treatments staring at the kaiser's signed photograph, which hung
on Schramm's wall. Thus, though the kaiser abdicated more than a decade before I
was born, I was enabled to have the exquisitely painful Wilhelmine associations
normally enjoyed only by people twice my age.

war: he seems to have missed the formal structure of Wilhelmine Germany, which had provided so many rewarding targets for his kind of satire. His comedies had already portrayed the nasty petty-bourgeois stratum that produced Hitler, and he had long since prophesied, with uncanny accuracy, how the Nazis would speak once they mounted the rostrum. One of the characters in *1913*, for example, declares in strident patriotic tones: "Suddenly, through the greatness of your thought, a fatherland stood before us of which we had known only dark intimations. The fire of your Will created a future national destiny that transports us not only as human beings but as *Men!*" Yet not even Sternheim could have foreseen the dire consequences of a Germany actually governed by people who thought this way. This man Hitler, he told Klaus Mann, was an utterly negligible nullity. "Who is he, after all? A minor character from a comedy by Carl Sternheim; a farcical night watchman who suddenly goes mad and imagines he could play the principal role. . . ."

In 1927 the Sternheims were divorced; three years later he married Pamela Wedekind, daughter of the playwright Frank Wedekind, but this third marriage, too, ended in divorce. After living in Switzerland for a time he committed the error of returning to Belgium, and that was where, in 1940, for the second time in his life, the invading German armies caught up with him. He died there two years later, in a precarious exile, still under a nurse's care after years of intermittent mental illness. His last message to Thea Bauer ends with the words: "But beyond all this be assured that I—though in the best of humor—have had enough of life, and await my end as the greatest of earthly privileges." Fortunately he did not live to see his son Karlhans hanged for anti-Nazi activities, or his daughter, the stage designer Thea Sternheim, tortured by the Gestapo for her part in the French Resistance and imprisoned in Ravensbruck for eighteen months prior to the Liberation. He had, however, seen the Nazis ban his work in 1933 and, after occupying the Lowlands, the invaders had taken care to destroy all existing stocks of his last book, *Prewar Europe in the Parable of My Life*, which had been published in Amsterdam in 1936. The unfinished manuscript of a sequel is also said to have been destroyed when the Germans marched into Brussels. Still, Sternheim believed that he might one day have the last laugh. "This ridiculous epoch will be swallowed up," he insisted. "Nothing will be left but the brilliant description I've written of it."

IV

AN ANGEL AT THE GATE

Denn ich liebe dich am meisten!
Mehr als jene Griechengöttin,
Mehr als jene Fee des Nordens,
Lieb' ich dich, du tote Jüdin!

For I love you more than all the others!
More than any Grecian goddess,
More than any Nordic fairy,
It is you, dead Jewish woman, that I love!
—HEINRICH HEINE, Atta Troll

It was said of Else Lasker-Schüler that she was "gifted like the stars" and that she "consisted only of soul, pure loving soul"—though Karl Kraus noted rather more sourly that she struck him as a combination of "archangel and fishwife." Had her work not been caught in the conflagration that devastated German literature, it might now be known the world over. As it is, only a handful of people are familiar with her poetry, but those who know it well speak of it in superlatives. Kraus himself was the first to call her "the greatest lyric poet of modern Germany." That was at the time of World War I. Forty years later the poet Gottfried Benn reminded a German public that had almost forgotten her name that she was "the greatest lyric poetess that Germany ever possessed." More recently, the critic Hans W. Cohn suggested that she was "perhaps the greatest poet the Jews have ever had"—and not just in Germany.

The poet Erich Mühsam touched on the underlying sources of her strength when he described Lasker-Schüler in his memoirs as a "genius of untamed eruptivity" whose poetry "glowed with the fire of oriental fantasy." She had the ability, moreover, to inspire affection in the most diverse kinds of audiences. "I love your verses so much," the young playwright Ernst Toller wrote to her from a Bavarian prison. "Sometimes I read them to fellow prisoners, workers from the great cities, farmhands. . . . They have been moved, and made happy by your verses."

Not everyone, of course, was made equally happy. A Hamburg judge who had to rule on her poetry in a copyright case declared that it conveyed "the feeling of utter unintelligibility" and consisted only "of words, words that, at least *prima facie,* contain no significant meaning." Perhaps it was something in the fastidious legal mind that strained at her verbal exuberance. Franz Kafka, admittedly a very different sort of jurist, decided that he "couldn't stand" her poetry because it was "empty and artificial." Her prose essays also irritated him. He wrote to Felice Bauer that they seemed to be the product of "the indiscriminate spasms of the brain of an overexcitable urbanite." As usual, however, Kafka was not quite sure of his ground. "Perhaps I am making a fundamental mistake; there are many people who love her: Werfel, for instance, speaks of her only with enthusiasm. Yes, things are going badly for her, her second husband has left her, as far as I know, and here too they have taken up a collection for her; I had to give five crowns without having felt the slightest compassion for her."*

People were always taking up collections for Lasker-Schüler since she was so obviously one of the more deserving poor. But it was not easy to help her: if she were given a large sum of money she would, in a day or two, have given it all away to people even needier than herself. As a result she lived most of her life in absurdly threadbare circumstances. Even at the height of her fame she led a gypsy existence in furnished rooms and Bohemian cafés—partly, one gathers, as a sort of protest against the terrible neatness, order and affluence to which others aspired. Though she complained about having been "born to suffer," she was also very proud of the fact: it would have been difficult for her to live any other way. "I sit on the throne of my ruin," she boasted in 1906 in a letter to Richard Dehmel, the author of *Verklärte Nacht.* Having no worldly possessions meant that she was "always free as a bird—

---

*She, on the other hand, later confessed to a great admiration for this "Kaffka [sic] who died so young."

not free in the manner of the feminists with their heavy footsteps," as she told her English friend Jethro Bithell. "I am like a Cinderella who can only fit into her own shoe."

In her own domain of lyric poetry she considered herself "a reigning prince, not some commoner from nowhere," and she meant her claim to royalty to be taken seriously. She dressed the part of an oriental potentate and signed herself, "Jussuf, Prince of Thebes" or "Tino of Bagdad." She once described her father, Arthur Schüler, as the most uninhibited (ausgelassenste) human being she had ever known, but it was she herself who was the most untrammeled of the German poets. She was proud of having "a soul and—not an intellect, but a heart and a beehive"; her stupidities, she said, were far more valuable than her grains of wisdom. Like Gertrude Stein she was past mistress of the run-on sentence, and one of the great pioneers of the aesthetic movement which, for want of a better name, has come to be known as "letting it all hang out."

The critic Willy Haas, who fell in love with her when he was twenty and she was twice his age, remembered her as a "completely fantastic figure, covered with jangling colored bracelets, earrings, necklaces and little chains, dressed in a long white burnous, daggers dangling from her belt." And Gottfried Benn, with whom she exchanged poems and conducted a brief affair, recalled that whenever she crossed the street, "the whole world would stop and stare after her: extravagantly wide skirts or trousers, impossible blouses and jackets, neck and arms draped with conspicuously fake jewelry, chains, earrings, pinchbeck rings on her fingers, and since she was continually brushing her hair out of her face, these (I must say) servant-girl rings were always prominently the focus of attention." But he remembered her, too, as a woman of mysterious fascination, "slim as a boy, her pitch-black hair cut short (still very unusual at that time) and large, restless coal-black eyes with an elusive, inexplicable gaze."

The Berlin Establishment, on the whole, considered her an impossible person. Count Kessler (who was quite willing to be charmed by such women writers as Virginia Woolf and Vita Sackville-West) confided to his diary in 1919 that "for four years I have tried to avoid this beastly person," and when she finally caught up with him at a party given by her publisher, Paul Cassirer, "I said how-do-you-do and took my leave." Yet much as they would have liked to banish her to the fringes of Bohemia, there was no denying the extraordinary power of her verse. Benn was not alone in admiring her work as, "in its perfection, the most complete fusion of the Jewish and the German." In 1902, when she published her first slim volume, the Catholic poet Peter Hille introduced her to the literary world as *"the* Jewish poetess . . . her creative spirit a black diamond . . . the black swan of Israel."

She herself was aware that much of her strength as a poet derived from the Jewish tradition, and unlike many of her colleagues among the *Grenzjuden* she was wholly unashamed of the fact. "It is a wonderful thing to be Jewish," she wrote, "if one has never avoided it for the sake of a shortcut to some goal; if one has remained true to it and united with it, immersed in the Jordan, without being led astray by some outward and insignificant motive." Yet her Judaism was neither conventional nor dogmatic: there was ample room in it for the Madonna and for Jesus, whom she called *der Gottesjude von Nazareth*. Often she addressed herself directly to God, though most of her early religious poems question rather than affirm his existence. Walter Hasenclever—a very different sort of poet, though from a similar background—was, I believe, the first to suggest that the human concept of God *(Gottesbegriff)* had undergone such sweeping changes that it was now "the task of the poets to formulate it anew for our time." Else Lasker-Schüler devoted herself to this Blakean task more assiduously than any of her contemporaries. She formulated her personal concept of God as a variant of Walter Benjamin's never-ending question. *Gott, wo bist du?*—"God, where are you?"—she asks, in an allusion to an old German children's game of hide-and-seek, *Kuckuck, wo bist du?*:

> Ich möchte nah an deinem Herzen lauschen,
> Mit deiner fernsten Nähe mich vertauschen. . . .

> I want to listen closely at your heart,
> In your remotest nearness find my counterpart.

This is a child's question, though susceptible of endless variations in prose as well as poetry. "We want to explore, to dig for God, until we strike upon him," she writes impatiently in one of her Berlin essays. Toward the end of her life she compared herself to an astronomer "who is the only one to know that a certain precious star is hidden behind a cloud, but cannot discern it with the naked eye." Among the best of her early poems is the *Gebet* (Prayer) that depicts her fervent longing for the possibility of God:

> Ich suche allerlanden eine Stadt
> Die einen Engel vor der Pforte hat.
> Ich trage seinen grossen Flügel
> Gebrochen schwer am Schulterblatt
> Und in der Stirne seinen Stern als Siegel. . . .

> I seek a city throughout all the world's estate
> that has an angel standing at the gate.
> It is his pinion that I carry, broken,
> upon my shoulder blade, a cumbrous weight;
> and on my brow, his star as seal and token.

The lilt and assonance of her verse are (for me, at any rate) quite impossible to convey in translation. But even this brief strophe provides a characteristic example of the supreme self-assurance with which she coined new words that sounded as though they had always existed. "Did the word *allerlanden* [in all lands] even exist before she created it?" asks the Swiss critic Max Rychner. "Not that I know of, but now it is here and belongs in the dictionary. Not only the language of today but also the spirit of centuries is content to accept and welcome this word. . . . In her work there are verses that the stars helped to write."

Lasker-Schüler's poetry exerted its greatest influence during the decade before World War I, when it was widely imitated by the young Expressionists trying to break out of the academic mold. Her prose, too, had an impact on German literature comparable to that of Gertrude Stein on American fiction, and for many of the same reasons: it was fluent, informal and sometimes befuddling, studded with seeming irrelevancies, yet so concerned with the communication of essentials as to be impervious to the niceties of grammar and punctuation. From Lasker-Schüler, as from Stein, one could learn that prose is architecture and not interior decoration. She liked to say, *Ich schwärme für die Wahrheit*—"I'm mad about the truth"—but her truths were visionary and psychological. In her essays, fact and fantasy usually become inextricably entangled; that was her ingenious way of coping with a complexity of personal experience that could be interpreted on so many levels:

> My heart, indeed, has always played a principal role in my life. When I was very young I saw it, to my mother's great alarm, hanging dark red at the doorpost of my playroom for seconds at a time. . . .

She wrote often and lovingly of her family and her childhood— stories, fables, essays, plays and poems that constitute a literary landscape of not quite Yoknapatawpha dimensions. Her origins were in the Rhineland. She was born much earlier than she liked to admit—on February 11, 1869, in Elberfeld, "where my dear parents performed so many good deeds." Elberfeld was an industrial city on the Wupper River, which even then was thoroughly polluted: "In the Wupper the workers always rinsed the colored cotton and it was on that account, I gathered, that the dear river always shimmered like black milk that had gone sour." Her madcap father, the most uninhibited person she ever met, figures in her stories as an architect who filled the city with his towers. In point of fact he was a merchant banker who financed building projects. To the local press he was known as "the Till Eulenspiegel of Elberfeld." Not the least of his eccentricities was that he always took his daughter's side in her inevitable battle with the then prevailing system of education. Arthur Schüler was the son of a businessman with twenty-three children, and the grandson of a prominent rabbi: his family, like the Wolfskehls, had lived in Germany for generations, though Else also had the inescapable Spanish ancestor. "I am from *Rheinland*," she wrote to Jethro Bithell in her confident mixture of English and German, "my *herrliche* mother half *Spanierin*; my Ur-grandfather my good father's Grandfather was *Oberrabiner von Rheinland* and *Westfalen*."

The Schülers had three boys and three girls, but in Else's memoirs the other children were wholly eclipsed by their *herrliche* (glorious) mother, who was to figure in her daughter's poetry as the embodiment of human love and understanding. She gave Else her first treasure, a collection of sample buttons from a button factory, blue, green, purple, red, yellow, white and black, with which she was content to play for hours: "The child must be left alone to play with her buttons." Among the games she and her mother liked to play together was something they called *Einwortsag-en* (Saying a Word):

> My mother would shout, importantly, "chocolate," and I would shout back a word that rhymed with it. My mother: "ink" and I: "think." "Paul"—"call." Until my brother, who was much older than I and whose brusqueness impressed me which is probably why I called him "man," would interfere, and for the word *hoch* choose the clumsy rhyme *Koch*, and I almost choked from the muffled sound of this mismating, yes, became absolutely beside myself, and fell from my anxious mother's knee onto the carpet. I was two years old. At four, to help my governess pass the time I learned how to write. I painted a scarf around the neck of each letter because it was winter and they were freezing. As a five-year-old I wrote my best poems; my mother always found the slips of paper with the scribbles on them which fell from the pockets of my clothes when I took out the favorite buttons of my button collection.

There was no question, certainly, that Else's family belonged to the people of the book. Yet she detested going to school, where the teachers were stern and exigent. When the dreaded Direktor visited the class to check up on his pupils, "the arithmetic problems that I had finally begun to master all fell back into my stomach, and I swallowed and sobbed *(schluckte und schluchzte)* and was sent to stand in the corner. In those days my heart was still a freshly ripened cherry, but that was just the trouble, school always made me feel the stone." Then one day, according to her memoirs, she was relieved of the necessity of going to school. Else's mother, who had gone for a walk on the hill adjoining their house, was caught in a sudden thunderstorm. When she failed to return in time for supper, Else's father and the older children went to look for her:

> O, it was so sad—bad enough when a child is lost—but now, as in this case—a Mama. . . . My father cried bitterly with open eyes, as infants do. I tried not to look at him so that I wouldn't have to laugh. It was lightning the whole time, and then thundering afterward as if to intimidate us! I climbed up to our tower, from where I could look out on all sides. All of a sudden I saw my dear, dear Mama come down the hill looking very sad, so sad that my hand cannot describe it, I would have to take my heart out of my breast and teach it to write. But my heart constricted itself into a single drop of blood that knew no danger, and I sprang across the wooden battlements of our tower so as to reach my melancholy mother all the sooner: instead I was caught in the outstretched canopy of our tower window and lay there as securely as in my mother's arms.

The volunteer fire brigade brought a long ladder, and her brother, who belonged to the brigade, "carried me on his broad shoulders from rung to rung, from space to space—it shuddered like that through my body—down the long alarming ladder. Then suddenly I had St. Vitus' dance." Her uncle the doctor ascribed her illness to the shock she had suffered, but Else knew that it had been caused "by the first pain in my life which even the most beautiful home was powerless to prevent." At any rate, there were compensations: " 'Going to school is now out of the question,' said my uncle the doctor and what was more he said it in a very authoritative voice."

The fact that as a teen-ager she was tutored at home rather than drilled at school may have had something to do with the subsequent anarchy of her syntax, which still occasions raised eyebrows among grammarians of the strict observance. Her editors complained that she always needed someone to put the commas in for her. Yet the German language, in her hands, was something marvelously elastic and allusive. She had no compunctions about creating new words or combinations that would look interesting to the eye or sound intriguing to the ear: *Veilchenhimmel* (a sky full of violets), *Ringelrangelhaaren* (a tomboy's wild locks), *frischfreifroh-*

frohlocken (rejoicing in freedom and fresh air), *strickpicknadelspitze Augen* (darting eyes that are as sharply focused as the points of knitting needles)—to take a few typical examples from just one of her poems, an ode to puppy-love called *Schulzeit.*

When her mother died in 1890, "the moon broke in twain." Even as an old woman, Lasker-Schüler could write: "On my table the candle / burns for my mother throughout the night. . . ." Her father lived until 1897; three years earlier she had married Dr. Berthold Lasker, a Berlin physician (and brother of the international chess master, Emanuel Lasker). In one of her autobiographical fables she explains that as a girl she had been frightened by a giant snake* that someone had concealed in her room, and "ever since I have had an aversion to sneaking and intrigue. That is why I decided . . . to marry a kind of stone marten that is in the habit of killing snakes." Then, as soon as "the last snake had been disposed of," the marriage broke up: they were divorced before the turn of the century. At the same time she turned her back on bourgeois convention and began living the life of the Berlin *Bohème,* a transformation she compared to a "festive reception of spring" after having led "a duteous life." She fell into love and out again as easily as George Sand. But it seems that, like Teilhard de Chardin, she came to see physical love as the one tactile, graspable manifestation of divine love. Since God had created man in his own image, there was no cause to "despise this ancient likeness of God, the corporeal, the covering of the soul." It was time, she thought, "to experience summer from body to body in all its extravagant forms."

Her friend Jethro Bithell divided the women writers of Germany into two camps, "the naughty girls and good girls," with Else Lasker-Schüler as the dividing summit: "she is not flagrantly naughty but she would be terribly shocked if she were classed as one of the good girls." For a time at least she managed to burn her candle at both ends in the fashion then prevailing among liberated poetesses. In 1898 she fell in love with someone who, she said, was both Greek and a prince, and bore the improbable name of Alcibiades de Rouan. He became the father of her son Paul, or rather Paulchen (little Paul)—"my precious child who was also my younger brother." Born in 1899, he proved to be an infinite source of poetic inspiration as well as maternal concern.

---

*Freud, in an early paper on *The Anxiety-Neurosis,* writes of "the fear of snakes, thunderstorms, darkness" in that order: "what makes these experiences significant and their retention in memory of long duration is indeed simply the anxiety, which both originally and subsequently thus found a means of expression."

> . . . Und wundersüss küsst der Maienwind
> Als duftender Gottesbote mein Kind.

The May wind, wondrously fragrant and mild,
Comes as God's messenger to kiss my child.

It was the existence of this child, moreover, that led her to ponder seriously the question of something beyond material reality. Before Paul's birth she had "always lain listening to the thunder of my heart," but now—

> . . . Nun aber wandle ich um meines Kindes
> Goldgedichtete Glieder
> Und suche Gott.

But now I circle closely round my child's
gold-composed limbs
and search for God.

Styx, her first book of poems, appeared in 1902 with a dedication to Paulchen. In prose, too, she was to write of mother-love as the great transforming and liberating experience: "The eternal fire of love that unites mother and child even before the birth of the child, and even beyond earthly life, is the wick of the living light that unites every mother to her child, binds her unconsciously to the delicate form of the child still growing in the profoundest inner spaces of her body. Love on love produces: light. Those who love—know. Those who love are illuminated and never again blind."

These were the years in which Lasker-Schüler joined the circle of artists and utopians around the poet whom she was to canonize as "St. Peter Hille" in a series of prose sketches whose nearest counterpart, I'm afraid, is Khalil Gibran's *The Prophet*. Erich Mühsam, a member of the same group for a time, described Hille as a genius "with the dreamy eyes of a child" who personified "the art of living for the inspiration of the moment, with a timeless devotion to the world and mankind, and compassion for all those who suffer in their struggle for knowledge and happiness." Hille and his friends formed part of the *Grün Deutschland* (Green Germany) movement, which advocated radical reforms in the political and moral premises of life in the Wilhelmine Reich: they were antimilitarists, socialists, humanists, anarchists, feminists. Most of them met every Friday night at a literary club, in the Kleiststrasse, known as *Die Kommenden* (The Coming Ones), which had been founded by the poet Ludwig Jacobowski. Mühsam remembered it as the place "where leading spirits contended for a favored spot on Parnassus." Both Hille and Lasker-Schüler appeared there regularly, reading their poetry to audiences consisting of prominent scholars and philosophers as well as the young poets of Berlin. Dr. Rudolf Steiner was in charge of the proceedings, but as Mühsam explains, no single literary movement prevailed. "One could hardly talk about a 'younger generation' as such. The leading poets of the Naturalist generation were still very much among us, most of them not yet forty. . . . Ibsen remained a controversial figure in literary circles; as yet Strindberg's importance was recognized only by a very few; Frank Wedekind was admired only by a tiny, mad minority who were laughingly dismissed by the rest as hypermoderns."

Amid this welter of styles, Lasker-Schüler's poetry struck a new and altogether personal note. When Karl Kraus first published some of it in *Die Fackel* he called her the "strongest and most indomitable figure in modern German literature." He was especially taken by the love lyric, *Ein alter Tibetteppich* (An Old Tibetan Carpet), whose very title begins the elaborate shuttlecock of word-play that runs through the entire poem. "It belongs," wrote the crotchety Kraus, "among the most enchanting and the most moving poems I have ever read":

> *Deine Seele, die die meine liebet,*
> *Ist verwirkt mit ihr im Teppichtibet*
>
> *Strahl in Strahl, verliebte Farben*
> *Sterne, die sich himmellang umwarben.*
>
> *Unsere Füsse ruhen auf der Kostbarkeit*
> *Maschentausendabertausendweit.*
>
> *Süsser Lamasohn auf Moschuspflanzenthron*
> *Wie lange küsst dein Mund den meinen wohl*
> *Und Wang die Wange buntgeknüpfte Zeiten schon?*

With its deep-pile texture of puns, metaphors and double meanings, the *Tibetteppich* is virtually untranslatable. As Kraus pointed out, there are few poems in which "sense and sound, word and picture, language and spirit are so tightly interwoven." Only on the premise that anything is better than nothing have I ventured an attempt at a rhyming translation:

> Your soul, which yearns so lovingly for mine
> Does here with me in carpet-Tibet intertwine.
> Thread upon thread, enamored colors steeped in passion's dye
> And stars pursuing their infinitude of courtship through the sky.

Our feet caress the carpet weaver's treasured pride.
Knottedthousanduponknottedthousand-wide.

Dearest lama-son upon your muskplant throne
How long will our mouths be kissing yet
And your cheeks flush bright-woven life against my own?

Among other things this is a *poème-à-clef*, for apparently there actually was a *Lamasohn* in her life—at least, someone she called by that name. All her friends received nicknames which she deemed more suitable than those they already had. Richard Dehmel became the Great Caliph, Karl Kraus the Dalai Lama, Franz Werfel the Prince of Prague, Jethro Bithell the Earl of Manchester, Martin Buber Herr von Zion, Gottfried Benn "The Nibelung" or "The Barbarian." Generically all the people she liked were *Indianer*, that is, American Indians. Bithell thought all this was just her playful way of teasing or idealizing the literati of her circle, but another of her friends, Wieland Herzfelde, has suggested that her penchant for titles and disguises should be interpreted as a protest against the rigidities of Wilhelmine society—that far from being a form of escapism it was basically a "democratic impulse."

During the years before World War I, Lasker-Schüler, or rather Prince Yussuf, was usually to be found at a table in the Café des Westens on the corner of Kurfürstendamm and the Joachimsthalerstrasse — better known as the "Café Grössenwahn" (Megalomania) because so many of its customers suffered from delusions of grandeur. The café, she wrote, "is our stock exchange; this is where one has to go, to conduct one's affairs. All the playwrights, painters, poets and many proles who want to gawk, ladies with giant hats, men with monocles, sober people, drunks; purple-powdered faces; boys, too, who powder their faces. . . ." This literary meeting-place was Yussuf's throne room, an island of emotional security in "this city of haste and people being trampled underfoot." Though at one point she was so poor that she owned only a single blouse, made from a man's shirt, which she had to wear and wash every day, no one minded her shabbiness at the Grössenwahn, where she could hold court among her admirers and engage in endless literary discussion with her peers—including not only the Berlin literati but such visitors as Chagall, Marinetti and Kokoschka. "I am sick of the café," she decided after a decade of this life:

but that doesn't mean that I shall bid it farewell for all time, or take off in a gypsy wagon. On the contrary, I shall go on spending a lot of my time there. Yesterday the doors were constantly opening and shutting as though in a bazaar, though not all the goods are genuine: imitation poets, counterfeit word-smithing, borrowed ideas, unmotivated cigarette smoke. . . . Why are people so attracted to the café? Every evening a dead man is brought to one of the upper rooms; his spirit cannot find rest. Why remain in Berlin for that matter, in this cold, unedifying city? Berlin is an indestructible clock, it keeps watch on time, we always know what time of art it is. And I would much prefer to sleep the time away.

She had married again, though not more successfully than the first time. Her husband was the composer-writer-art-critic Georg Lewin, for whom she devised the more romantic, forest-murmuring name, Herwarth Walden. Their friend, the young physician-novelist Alfred Doeblin, remembered it as a stormy and difficult marriage: "Walden, with his talent for discovering things, had recognized the immense gifts of this young woman, but he was less certain, it seems to me, in his understanding of her temperament. I witnessed some explosive scenes between them. She was passionate and headstrong." Their marriage was handicapped from the first by Paulchen and chronic insolvency. The actress Tilla Durieux, wife of Paul Cassirer (who published the first collected edition of Lasker-Schüler), writes in her memoirs that "this couple, with their unbelievably spoiled son, were to be found at the Café des Westens from noon to late at night. . . . They seemed to live on nothing but coffee, which the hunchbacked headwaiter would let them have on credit, or for which some generous guest would foot the bill. Meanwhile the child would sneak off to the platters in the kitchen and help himself to whatever he liked when no one was looking." To keep afloat, they would levy periodic tribute on friends and admirers. In one of her letters Lasker-Schüler claims that she was not above stealing the carpets from the hallways of friends' apartment houses. Herwath Walden eventually became a successful avant-garde publisher with his Expressionist magazine *Der Sturm*, which published some of Lasker-Schüler's finest poetry. By 1911, however, their marriage had come unstuck. "I know you and you know me," she wrote to him. "We cannot surprise each other any more, and I can only live on wonder. Think of something to astonish me, please!" To Richard Dehmel she confided a more mundane reason: "Herwarth Walden has fallen in love with an idiotic lady with locks and long, timid pearl earrings, and I'm divorced."

She had come to doubt that marriage was an honest institution. "It's the *filles de joie* I admire," she told Bithell. "They carry no secret thong in their pockets with which to catch those who are free. I would throw my lasso every time, but only for fun. . . . I might commit bigamy from sheer egotism if I were in the mood for it, but we would only say beautiful things to each other."

She was over forty now, though pretending to be thirty-three. (For years, the birth date she gave on her wedding license, 1876, was accepted by all the literary reference works.) She fell in love again—with Gottfried Benn, among others, who was seventeen years younger. Their relationship was predictably short-lived. As she wrote to the painter Franz Marc, for him "it is already extinguished in his heart, like a Bengal light, a fiery wheel*—it simply rolled over me." She realized that the situation was hopeless because there were now so many more beautiful women in the world. "I am so ugly otherwise I would write you quite differently," she wrote to him. ". . . Perhaps you feel only pity; that shames me."

One of the more significant men in her life was the Russian revolutionary Johannes Holzman, whom she called Senna Hoy (his first name spelled backward). Editor of an anarchist newspaper in Berlin, he was arrested and imprisoned while on a visit to czarist Russia. Lasker-Schüler made the long journey to St. Petersburg in November 1913 to negotiate with the authorities for his release. But the prisoner's health had already been ruined by the treatment he received from the Secret Police, and the German embassy in St. Petersburg declined to facilitate the return to Germany of a known anarchist. Lasker-Schüler came back empty-handed and Senna Hoy died in the prison ward of a hospital near Moscow in 1914. Her tribute to his memory is a group of her most ecstatic love songs and elegies. The last in the series moves to the mournful cadence of the dying fall:

> Seit du begraben liegst auf dem Hügel
> Ist die Erde süss
>
> Wo ich hingehe nun auf Zehen,
> Wandele ich über reine Wege,
>
> O deines Blutes Rosen
> Durchtränken sanft den Tod.
>
> Ich habe keine Furcht mehr
> Vor dem Sterben. . . .

---

*She could not have known, in 1912, that thirty years later her "Barbarian" would prove to be, if only for a time, an outspoken admirer of the Nazis and their "fiery wheel."

Now that you lie buried on the hill
The earth is sweet.

Wherever now I walk on tiptoe
I wander over pure paths.

O the roses of your blood
gently saturate death.

No more am I afraid
of dying.

World War I, which descended on the *vie de Bohème* like the blade of a gigantic guillotine, was to provide innumerable occasions for threnodies of this sort. The literary cafés were quickly decimated as the young poets and painters were sent off to die in the trenches. Prince Yussuf's friend and adviser, the "Blue Rider" Franz Marc, was killed on the Western front after sending her a memorable series of postcards illustrated with the blue and red animals of his cubist imagination. He was, she wrote, "a great biblical figure to whom clung the scent of Eden. He cast a blue shadow over the landscape. He was the one who could still understand the animals when they spoke; and he transfigured their souls. . . . Strong angels have carried his giant body to God, who holds his blue soul, a radiant banner, in his hand. . . . Never did I see any painter who painted with such divine seriousness or as gently as he." In her elegy for Franz Marc she envisaged him as a splendid Blue Rider descending from the mountains to the plain:

> *Durch die Strassen von München hebt er sein biblisches Haupt*
> *Im hellen Rahmen des Himmels.*
> *Trost im stillenden Mandelauge,*
> *Donner sein Herz. . . .*

> Through the streets of Munich he lifts his biblical head
> In the bright frame of the sky.
> Comfort in the calming almond eye,
> His heart thunder.

George Trakl, the Austrian Expressionist poet whom she had befriended in Berlin shortly before the war, committed suicide after a series of harrowing experiences as a medical corpsman on the Russian front. She had a vision of him in her furnished room on the night of his death.

> *Sein Schatten weilte unbegreiflich*
> *Auf dem Abend meines Zimmers*

concludes one of the poems she wrote in his memory: "His shadow lingered inexplicably / upon the evening of my room." But when she tried to console Trakl's sister, then living in Berlin, she was embarrassed to find that Frau Langen was an ardent antisemite who made no secret of the fact that she thought "all Jews should be deported to Asia." Lasker-Schüler felt deeply offended. "This is impertinent and cruel, particularly just now when thousands of Jews are giving their lives, among them great artists," she wrote to the friend who had brought her together with Trakl, Ludwig von Ficker. Though appalled by the woman's prejudice she was anything but intimidated. "This woman with whom I sat through the whole night does not have the right to insult me. . . . I am a Jew. Thank God!" But she also felt compelled to add that "there is no one who is more international than I; I love *all* people who carry God's house or God's spirit [*Gotteshaus oder Gotteshauch*] to the heights."

Incidents of this sort served as a reminder that it was not easy to be Jewish in Germany even if one had no complexes about it. She had published her magnificent *Hebräische Balladen* (they were not, of course, written in Hebrew, a language she never learned) and many other poems and essays on biblical and Jewish themes. Yet the great majority of German Jews declined to accept this eccentric lady as their representative poet. She, in turn, had little use for them. "I hate the Jews," she wrote petulantly to Martin Buber, "because they disregard my voice, because their ears have grown shut and because they prefer listening to cretins and jargon. They eat too much; they should go hungry. . . . Are you angry?" Buber was not angry. He enjoyed the I-Thou of this correspondence with a master of the art of epistolary complaint. Very patiently and gently he pointed out to her that one could "love the Jews with anger and yearning," and that it was a pity she felt so aggrieved by them. "I think one ought to be more concerned with how one hears the world than how one is heard *by* it, and he who no longer worries how the world hears him will, when he looks up, catch sight of God listening at his window."

Except when she felt cross about her royalty statements, Lasker-Schüler did not, in fact, pay much attention to the size of her readership. She had invented a language that was comprehensible to a small circle of initiates. "I don't even want the public to read my books, just a few people and if only my dead dear Mama could have read them." During the twenties there were times when she was astonishingly well supplied with publishers and readers: "I now write a great deal for the newspapers, and the

Berlin *Tageblatt* pays me well. It is so comical when one receives money for things that one weaves with one's heart." Still, she continued to "live on air, which tastes good once you have learned to open it like an oyster," and went on writing at café tables and in furnished rooms: "I am as harried as if hostile tribes were after me, and I am so tired that I have to tie myself to the chair to finish my work. But it has to be done."

In postwar Berlin the literary rendezvous had moved to the Romanisches Café near the Kaiser Wilhelm Memorial Church, and there had been other profound changes: Expressionism had given way to Dadaism, George Grosz and a new insolence in the arts; the Berlin theater was on its way to becoming the best in the world; the Jazz Age had come to the Kurfürstendamm and the film studios in the suburbs. Most of these developments left Lasker-Schüler unmoved: in her stories and sketches she wrote of her youth and of the friends she had lost in the war. If the old Berlin had been a disquieting place in which to work, the postwar city was even more so: "This vast Berlin, in the evenings always illuminated and during the day beflagged with people—it would be beautiful if everything in a human being were settled and clear. I am always full of restlessness and apprehension."

It was not only the war dead who were missing from the postwar cafés. Some of her friends had taken part in the abortive Bavarian revolution at the end of the war, and had been killed or imprisoned in the ensuing "White Terror." Lasker-Schüler had never taken any interest in party politics, but her sympathies were with the oppressed, and in the rambling polemic which she wrote in 1925 as an indictment of her publishers, *Ich räume auf!* (i.e., I Settle Accounts!), she also took up the matter of the poets who had "offered their bodies for the sake of justice," and whom she called her "martyr-friends":

> Two of them, Gustav Landauer, the St. James, and Leviné [another murdered radical], who was like an archangel, became victims of their own ballad of salvation. They tore the mighty red ticker out of the former's chest, and in a prison yard they drilled holes through the gentle star the latter wore at his forehead. And two other poets have been languishing in prison for years. But why should that be? And why does no one liberate them—from Bavaria's fortress? Erich Mühsam and Ernst Toller. These four men of love, who despised all outward pomp and who loved their neighbor more than themselves, these are our kings. Whatever criticism might be made of them, their honest, bloodstained poetry will be respected for all time. It was their death sentence. A poet can sooner create a world than build a state.

Under other circumstances, Lasker-Schüler might have worked as tirelessly for Mühsam and Toller as she had to obtain the release of Senna Hoy. But during these years she devoted most of her energies to her son Paul, who was to contract pulmonary tuberculosis in 1926. The nineteen-year-old Paulchen had been with Toller the day he was arrested by the Munich police: he was a gifted art student who had made a promising start as an illustrator and had begun leading a Bohemian life of his own. (An anonymous patron—now known to have been the philosopher Ludwig Wittgenstein—had enabled his mother to send him to one of the first progressive schools in Germany.) Franz Marc and other prominent friends had expressed astonishment at the boy's talent. As she wrote to a relative in Chicago in her inimitable English: "Mr Albert Professor Einstein had telled me verry interessant America, he likes my Paul verry much." When he was hospitalized in the third-class ward of a Munich clinic in 1926, his mother tried desperately to drum up enough money to send him to the Magic Mountain: "All the doctors are of the opinion that he'll be well again in a year and a half." Friends helped her send him to a sanatorium near Lugano, then to a clinic in Davos. In the spring of 1927, since he seemed to be improving, she took him to Berlin, where she managed to rent a sculptor's studio large enough for them both. But Paulchen was dying. For weeks she remained at his bedside day and night. "Think of it," she wrote to one of her *Indianer*. "I am filled with a great sadness, sadder than sadness. . . . To see my poor boy always feverish, now for almost two years together. Please do not try to console me. I pray sometimes for God to perform a miracle or to punish me in his stead or if it should please Him, to save us both." When her son died in December 1927, she wrote the most austere and painful of her elegies:

> *Immer wirst du mir*
> *Im scheidenden Jahre sterben, mein Kind,*
>
> *Wenn das Laub zerfliesst*
> *Und die Zweige schmal werden.*
>
> *Mit den roten Rosen*
> *Hast du den Tod bitter gekostet. . . .*

> Always, for me, will you
> die with the parting year, my child,
>
> When the leaves dissolve
> And the branches grow slender
>
> With the red roses
> You have tasted death bitterly.

For her remaining years in Germany, Lasker-Schüler moved to a hotel room. Now that she had little need of them, the prizes and stipends came pouring in. In 1931 she received an award of 1,000 marks from the Prussian Academy of Arts, which she promptly distributed among "three women artists who are ill and must absolutely have the chance to recover at the seaside next spring." Her own requirements were more Spartan than ever: "I feed myself, I don't need much—only the cinema, my daily dessert." She gave poetry readings in Holland, France, Belgium and Czechoslovakia, appearing on stage not in her oriental costume but "in a faultless tuxedo and with her brushed hair parted at the side, erect and almost awe-inspiring on the podium." She was invited to read her ballads on the Frankfurt radio and there were patrons who commissioned her to paint some of her strange, visionary pictures for them, but despite her success she was frequently plunged into periods of black depression: "I am forever sad and dark and I no longer believe in the blue miracle."

Meanwhile she was at work on *Arthur Aronymus, the Story of My Father*—the finest of her short stories and one of the most extraordinary pieces of writing in the whole of German literature. The language is disarmingly simple; the style alternately nebulous and lucid. She deals with her theme—the possibility of brotherly love between German Christians and German Jews—in a breathless stream of consciousness that seems born of the desire to tell everything in a single outpouring before some malign spirit can interrupt the narrative. Among the principal characters are her father as a young boy, her great-grandfather the old rabbi and the young Catholic priest who saves a small Jewish community in the Rhineland from a sudden recrudescence of witch-hunting and antisemitism. On the surface it is only a family remembrance of things past, yet she accomplishes the remarkable feat of compressing the essence of a five-hundred-year history into a single short story—the Jews in the Germany of the Middle Ages, in the days of their emancipation, and in Arthur Schüler's lifetime: everything happens simultaneously, as though Mr Albert Professor Einstein had taught her about the curvature of space-time. The story supposedly takes place in the nineteenth century. Yet what is one to make of the guest who sits down at her grandfather's Passover meal and of whom she notes in passing that he "was murdered a few years ago in Saragossa in the synagogue while praying"—when, as her readers were well aware, there had been no synagogue in Saragossa since the expulsion of the Jews from Spain in 1492. Certain of her grandfather's tales also belong to another time stratum: when he mentions "Jewish children strung up like Christmas confectionery," the narrative looks back to the sixteenth century or ahead to the Hitler era. It concludes, however, with a great interdenominational Passover agape: His Grace the Bishop of Paderborn, whose pastoral letter has brought the bigots to their senses, has come to celebrate the feast with Else's grandfather and his Bach-like family of twenty-three children:

> With a genial gesture His Grace nodded assent to the words of the wise father, my father's father, and both gentlemen concurred that "with a little love it really is possible for Jews and Christians to break bread together in harmony"—"even if it is unleavened bread that is being offered," concluded the mother of my father who is now also with God, Arthur Aronymus.

Else Lasker-Schüler was sixty-three when *Arthur Aronymus* was published as a novella in 1932. That year she received the Kleist Prize, one of the highest distinctions that could be bestowed on a German poet. She had turned the story into a play and it was to be staged at Christmas 1932, but the times were no longer propitious and the production had to be canceled. Instead, Adolf Hitler mounted a triumphal torchlight parade of Storm Troopers when he took over as Reich Chancellor in January 1933. Lasker-Schüler had already been beaten up several times by Storm Troopers after giving poetry readings: in 1931 she had received injuries on the arms and ankle during a scuffle on the Nollendorfplatz at which, as she complained to the Prussian minister of culture, "fists exploded like grenades." Now, however, the "city of haste and people being trampled underfoot" had been turned over entirely to the Storm Troopers, and there was no longer anyone in the government to whom she could appeal for protection. In April 1933 she was again attacked and knocked to the ground in front of her modest hotel. A friend recalled that this time she was terribly frightened. She had made no preparations for escape. Bruised and bleeding, without money or a suitcase, she fled to Switzerland, where she had several friends. Since none of them happened to be available when she arrived in Zurich, she spent the first six nights sleeping in a park until she was arrested as a vagrant and her case attracted public attention.

It was regarded as a scandal that the winner of the Kleist Prize, whose poetry appeared in the best anthologies beside that of Goethe and Schiller, should have to sleep at the lakeside like a common tramp. A number of Swiss Jews came to her aid, and she received a residence permit from the police that enabled her to rent a room and resume her work, first in Zurich, then in Ascona. Fortunately she was accustomed to living on next to nothing: "I take a daily dose of four francs like drops of medicine," she wrote to a Zurich businessman who sent her a monthly stipend. But although she had no compunction about asking wealthy people for help, she was determined not to cut a pathetic figure. "Pity," she decided, "would only make me seem all the poorer." She had hopes that as a resident alien she would be allowed to play a modest role on the Swiss literary scene. Twice she was invited to read her poetry on the Swiss radio; a Zurich publisher signed up one of her books, and the Zurich Schauspielhaus announced its intention of staging the banished *Arthur Aronymus*. She was very conscious of her good fortune, "now that the world bleeds," in being able to live unmolested in her "moon-cell" in Switzerland: "I think constantly of those who are being tortured in the concentration camps, and am almost ashamed of my complaints." Indeed, her old friend Erich Mühsam had been one of the first to be tortured and killed in a Nazi camp. Ernst Toller, the only one of her four "martyr-friends" to remain alive, had found refuge in England and was helping to organize the literary resistance to Nazism. Through Klaus Mann, then editor of the Amsterdam émigré magazine *Die Sammlung*, to which they all contributed, she sent word to Toller and to Heinrich Mann how much she "admired their lives" in exile.

Lasker-Schüler was to outlive not only Mühsam, who was nine years her junior, but also Toller, twenty-four years younger than herself. Their three lives were never closely interwoven at the personal level, yet her instincts were not mistaken when she identified herself publicly with these two poets whose works were so very different from her own. It was their common search for "a city with an angel at the gate" that justified their status as "kings" in her book of martyrs (and warrants their inclusion in this chapter). They were politically *engagé*, though unwilling to submit to the discipline of party membership; she was emphatically nonpolitical, yet considered herself a *Parteimensch*—in the sense of "a woman of definite opinions" rather than a person with a party mentality. "What else could one be," she once wrote to Bithell, "particularly if one enjoys doing battle and is descended from the Maccabees?"

She was very fond of *wilde Juden,* among whom she counted herself, and that was one of the reasons she felt a special affinity for Mühsam and Toller, each of whom was a "wild Jew" in his own fashion. Mühsam's political ideal was summed up in the title of his essay, *Die Befreiung der Gesellschaft vom Staat* (The Liberation of

Society from the State). He could be heard preaching this messianic doctrine in the literary cafés of Munich, though people rarely
took him seriously. Much of his "revolutionary" poetry sounds, in
fact, like Lasker-Schüler transposed into a more proletarian mode:

> . . . Ich weiss von allem Leid
> fühl alle Scham
> und möchte helfen aller Kreatur.
> Der Liebe such ich aus dem Hass die Spur,
> Dem Menschenglück den Weg aus Not und Gram. . . .
>
> Doch keiner war noch, der mein Wort verstand,
> und keiner, der die Hand ergriffen hat.
> Ich weiss vom Leide nur, fühl nur die Scham,—
> Und kann doch selber nicht Erlöser sein,
> wie jener Jesus, der die ganze Pein
> der Welt auf seine schwachen Schultern nahm.

I know of all suffering, feel all pain, and seek to help all of creation. I
want to find a path whereby love can escape from hatred; I want to
lead humanity out of misery and need. . . . Yet there is no one who
understands my words, and none to seize my hand. I only know of
suffering, can only feel the pain! I cannot myself be the redeemer,
like that Jesus who took the whole of the world's suffering upon his
slender shoulders.

Mühsam means "arduous" in German, and something in his
style was eminently suited to the name:* though he could write
devastating satires and comic verse, his serious writing is often
laborious in its earnestness, as though he were spelling out a message for an audience by which he felt himself misunderstood. Toller, too, lived up to his name like a character in a Restoration
comedy. Toll means crazy, often in a positive sense—ganz toll being
the equivalent of "absolutely fantastic!" Ein Toller is a wild man,
extravagant, prodigal, impulsive. The impetuous Toller was all of
these things, which is why he spent five of his first thirty years in
prison. Yet Lasker-Schüler remembered that "Ernst Toller was
above all things a loving human being":

His heart dreamed so often of twilight. His eyes were like hazelnuts
that have just peeped out of their shells. His hair exuded the scent of
heather. He loved forests and gardens; he traveled to the towns in
which his friends had grown up in order to see the fields they had

*He himself must have regarded the name not only as a rich source for puns but as a
kind of self-fulfilling prophecy. A friend quotes him as saying to a psychoanalyst
who proposed to probe the etiology of his neuroses: "Ich lasse mir aber meine
mühsam erworbenen Hemmungen nicht nehmen"; i.e., I refuse to let you take
away the neuroses that I have acquired so laboriously (in such a mühsam fashion).

known at home. . . . I loved Ernst Toller very much in life, and in death as the image of someone whom one will always love. For life and death go hand in hand.

Perhaps what was most remarkable about these poets was that they brought to Germany something which had been part of the English literary tradition for over a century—William Blake's conception of the poet as visionary and social revolutionary whose allegiance was "to the slave grinding at the mill, and the captive in chains, & the poor in prison. . . ." Mühsam's "Liberation of Society from the State" was nothing other than Blake's "Striving with Systems to Deliver Individuals from Those Systems." Toller's radicalism sprang from the same sources as Blake's cry of compassion: "Is this a holy thing to see/ in a rich and fruitful land,/ Babes reduc'd to misery,/ Fed with cold and usurous hand?" Lasker-Schüler, too, had summed up her politics in the sentence: "I think about the poor, pale children who never see the sunshine." And she believed with Blake that the poet's allies were "all the gentle Souls who guide the great Wine-Press of Love."*

Mühsam thought of himself as a realist, though his friends all describe him as a "good-natured and shaggy" romantic. He confessed to being a revolutionary by temperament. Even as a schoolboy he had "resisted the influences that sought to impose themselves on me," and this *esprit de contradiction* had determined the course of his life because it endowed him with a fatal weakness for lost causes. He was the son of a pharmacist, born in Berlin in 1878 but raised in Lübeck, the home of Thomas and Heinrich Mann.† His education followed the familiar pattern of more or less continuous conflict with an authoritarian school system. In one of his autobiographical sketches he gives a telegraphic account of his childhood, as though he could hardly bring himself to write about it: "Uncomprehending teachers; nobody who might have understood the peculiarities of this child, hence rebelliousness, laziness, preoccupation with other things. Early attempts at writing poetry, encouraged neither at school nor at home; on the contrary, seen as

---

*Blake also knew, well before Einstein, that "Energy is the only life."

†It was also the birthplace of the free-thinking Countess Reventlow, Wolfskehl's inamorata, who was later to become a close friend of Mühsam's in Munich. Around the turn of the century the burgomaster of Lübeck was heard to complain of this embarrassing brood: Thomas Mann and his *Buddenbrooks*, Heinrich Mann with *Professor Unrat* (to become better known as *The Blue Angel*), the countess with her illegitimate child and Mühsam the anarchist poet. "And they all have to be from Lübeck! What do you suppose the people in the rest of the German Reich must think of us?"

distraction from school and thus as attempt to evade duty; poetry had to be written in secret."

As a student in the Lübeck Gymnasium he sent the text of a speech given by the Direktor, together with appropriate comments, to the local Social Democratic newspaper, and was expelled from school as a radical and a troublemaker. He became a pharmacist's apprentice and then an assistant in a pharmacy, but it occurred to him, while working in Berlin, that he had no vocation to be anything but a poet. For a time he, too, belonged to the group around "St. Peter" Hille and the "New Society" of the brothers Hart, who wanted to create a "great commune of humanity, happiness, beauty, art and a new religious spirit of dedication." Gustav Land-auer, another member of the circle, soon converted him to a more militant kind of Utopian Socialism. One of Mühsam's first published essays was an article for Karl Kraus's *Die Fackel* in which he de-scribed the young Berlin Bohemians and their ideas. A Bohemian, he explained—he was, of course, writing mainly about himself—"is a person who has despaired of ever establishing contact with the great majority of his fellow human beings. This great despair is the underlying reason for his wanting to be an artist, and on that account he goes into life to experiment with chance, to play catch-ball with the accidents of the moment, and to unite himself to the eternity that is always with us."

Mühsam's Bohemians—as opposed to Henri Murger's *La Bohème*—were not really antisocial; it was "the compulsive way in which conventions are drilled into people" that alienated them from the rest of mankind. Their skeptical attitude toward the world, and "their negative view of all conventional values" was combined with "a great social longing for an ideal civilization." These Bohemians, in fact, would have liked to live like early Chris-tians, and their tracts bear a more than glancing resemblance to the hippie pronunciamentos of the 1960s. By the same token, there was no love lost between the Utopians and the Communists. In 1906—well over a decade before the Russian Revolution, when the Bolsheviks were able to test their theories in practice for the first time—Mühsam prophesied in *Die Fackel* that a state built on Com-munist principles would produce "such a regime of bureaucrats and officials that the present Prussian State would be a veritable holiday camp by comparison." He himself could see no advantage in a system where "Father State will function as the only employer, the sole monopolistic exploiter." Later he was to coin the term *Bismarxism* for the rigidities of Communist-authoritarian thinking. Immediately after the Russian Revolution he supported the Communists for a time, thinking they might have begun to move toward his kind of Socialism, but the party found him unamenable to discipline and denounced him as a *"Kaffeehaus* poet."

Indeed, Mühsam's natural habitat was the literary café, where he was to be found at all hours improvising nonsense rhymes and the Spoonerist couplets *(Schüttelreime)* for which he became famous:

> *Man wollte sie zu zwanzig Dingen*
> *In einem Haus zu Danzig zwingen.*

They wanted to force her to do twenty things in a house at Danzig.

There were also long, satirical ballads that Mühsam wrote for his café repertoire, and love lyrics in which he celebrated the newly emerging sexual mores of the twentieth century:

> *Als ich dich fragte: Darf ich Sie beschützen?*
> *Da sagtest du: Mein Herr, Sie sind trivial.*
> *Als ich dich fragte: Kann ich Ihnen nützen?*
> *Da sagtest du: Vielleicht ein andres Mal.*
> *Als ich dich bat: Ein Kuss, mein Kind, zum Lohne!*
> *Da sagtest du: Mein Gott, was ist ein Kuss?*
> *Als ich befahl: Komm mit mir, wo ich wohne!*
> *Da sagtest du: Na, endlich ein Entschluss!*

> And when I asked: how may I serve you?
> You said, Monsieur, you're being trivial.
> And when I asked: do I deserve you?
> You thought the question unconvivial.
> And when I pleaded for a fond embrace
> You laughed at me with some derision.
> But when I said: let's go to my place!
> You said: at last a real decision!

Mühsam would recite his poems and then pass the hat, since most of the time he had no other source of income. "Nothing was sacred to this rebel," reported one chronicler of the Berlin scene. "There was no word in the German language which he would not turn inside out for a *Schüttelreim,* and there was no well-to-do patron of the café from whom he would fail to extract a thaler as a tribute to his art." The humorist Roda Roda remembered him as a desperately thin little man with wild hair and a full red beard—"A solidly decent fellow, whom I liked a lot. I used to play chess with him." But Mühsam would rather talk about politics than art, and Roda Roda regarded him as an "incurable crank" politically. "Once I invited him to dinner, together with one of his like-minded friends. At the same time I invited three young officers of the feudal Berlin *Franz-Regiment*; they came, as I had requested, in civilian clothes. I seated them at the table; each anarchist between two aristocrats. It was a memorable occasion. After the first bewilderment they got along perfectly well, and they parted company with assurances of mutual respect."

Mühsam's way of life was even more minimalist than Lasker-Schüler's. He slept in a barn in the suburbs or relied on friends with apartments in the city to put him up. Richard, the hunchback headwaiter at the Café des Westens, is said to have been the one who subsidized the first of his pamphlet "pages for humanity." The Heidelberg philosopher Gustav Radbruch recalls in his memoirs that while he was living in Berlin at the beginning of the century, Mühsam was "periodically without a place to live. He would spend his nights at the Café des Westens and then, almost every morning, would knock on my door at six o'clock in order to get some sleep. Once he arrived coatless, having given his overcoat to a freezing beggar. . . ."

In 1907 the thirty-year-old poet set out for Paris via Switzerland, where he spent some time with the exiled Russian revolutionaries at Ascona before wandering across the Alps on foot, stopping at the Simplon for three days to discuss theology with the Cistercian monks who kept a hospice for travelers at the top of the pass. He had already come to the realization that wanderlust was an *Unbehagen* of the modern soul:

> *Weiter, weiter, unermüdlich!*
> *Westlich, östlich; nördlich, südlich.*
> *Suche, Seele, suche! . . .*
>
> *Mit dem Fahrschein bahnbehördlich*
> *westlich, östlich; südlich, nördlich.*
> *Suche, Seele, suche!*
> *Siehst dein Glück vorübertreiben*
> *hinter Schnellzugsfensterscheiben.*
> *Fluche, Seele, fluche!*

> Onward, onward without rest
> to the north, east, south, west!
> Seek, soul, seek! . . .
>
> With your ticket sallying forth
> to the west, east, south, north.
> Seek, soul, seek!
> See your life flash by in pain
> from the window of a midnight train.
> Shriek, soul, shriek!

In Paris he fell in easily with the artists and poets who frequented the Café du Dôme in Montparnasse, among them Picasso, Paul Fort and Jules Pascin. The satirical weekly *L'Assiette au beurre* published some of his pieces. He spent his nights at the Lapin Agile, the most creative of the Montmartre cabarets, which, as he afterward remembered it, was always crowded with poets, singers, pretty girls. "In this cabaret no distinction was made between performers and audience; there were no program schedules or contracts: people simply wanted to be sure that their art was seen and heard, and to discover what other people were creating that was new." When he returned to Germany the following year he summed up his impressions with the phrase, *Paris lebt—Berlin funktioniert* (Paris lives, Berlin functions).

Munich seemed to offer a more congenial atmosphere for a man of his talents, and for a decade he became a prominent member of the Schwabing literary set—though as one of its members recalled, "he never had any money because he gave away everything he had." To readers of the Munich weekly *Simplicissimus* he was already known as the author of some of the most sardonic ballads of the day. His poem *Idyll,* for example—first published in *Simplicissimus* in February 1906—opens with a cheerfully macabre vision of a lynch victim:

> *Ein alter Leichnam hängt*
> *an einem Telegraphenmast.*
> *Nach seinen Schlenkerbeinen fasst*
> *   —ob er sie fängt?—*
> *ein ausgespreizter Eichenast. . . .*

> An aging corpse
> hangs from a telegraph pole.
> Toward his dangling legs reaches
>   —can it catch them?—
> the outspread branch of an oak.

Mühsam produced scores of such poems as well as "vegetarian hymns," a rhyming calendar for the underprivileged, workmen's ballads, songs to sing to a barrel organ, social satires, a *Psychology of the Erbtante* (the aunt from whom one expects to inherit money) and the numerous essays about ways of improving the world with which he filled the pages of his one-man "Journal for Humanity" with the curiously accusative title, *Kain.* The playwright Frank Wedekind, his boon companion of the Torggelstube (a wine bar adjoining the Munich Hofbräuhaus) once warned

Mühsam that his political fixation was dangerously at odds with his literary gift. "You're like a bareback rider standing on two horses that are headed in different directions," Wedekind told him. "They will tear your legs apart." Mühsam disagreed. "If I let one of them go," he said, "I'll lose my balance and break my neck."

Although Mühsam had written love lyrics in praise of plain girls with bowlegs and frizzy hair, he married the very pretty Kreszentia—Zensl, for short—whom friends described as an "arch-Bavarian peasant girl." She was immensely devoted to him, and he to her. "Erich was the most attentive husband you can imagine," she wrote to his sister three years after his murder. "Besides, he was always so terribly proud of me—'My wife does everything herself!' . . . He filled out my life, far beyond his death. I know that people do not simply die; everyone leaves a faint shadow behind. But Erich, he stands beside me, he walks beside me, he remains with me. When I dream, I have never yet dreamed that Erich is dead."

In his prewar essays, Mühsam repeatedly attacked the militarism which was considered the very foundation of Wilhelmine Germany, and which had produced the heel-clicking cult of the officer class that Nietzsche once characterized as "Obedience and Long Legs." Mühsam tried to show his readers that armies were both dangerous and immoral. "Special prerogatives for the military encourage people's enthusiasm for war," he wrote. "One has to work against that. It is with children that the 'patriots' begin their work. The antimilitarists should also start with children. They have to be taught that war is murder. They have to be imbued with an aversion and hatred for murder. . . ." Besides, the garrison state was uneconomical. "Hundreds of thousands of young men otherwise capable of doing work or having families are torn from their normal occupations and dressed in comically colored gear in which everyone looks alike, decked out in shiny buttons, tin headgear and numbered badges on their shoulders."

When the war broke out, Mühsam's "small, squeaky voice" was drowned out by the cheering and the marching songs. Though he went on agitating for pacifist solutions, the government did not consider him sufficiently dangerous to be sent to jail. Only when he refused to be conscripted into the *vaterländische Hilfsdienst* (Patriotic Auxiliary Service) was he finally imprisoned as a conscientious objector. Then, after years of isolation from the mainstream of German events, he suddenly found himself— distinctly out of his depth—at the center of a real, as opposed to a literary, revolution. On November 7 and 8, 1918, the leader of the

Independent Socialists in Bavaria, Kurt Eisner, persuaded the Munich army garrison to support him in declaring a Bavarian republic. The last of the Wittelsbach kings had already departed: without a shot having been fired, Bavaria was transformed from a kingdom into a "Free State" and acquired a provisional government. Eisner was a gifted statesman and orator, but his rise to power as prime minister was something of a fluke: he was a Berlin Jewish intellectual who had been working in Munich for a decade and had acquired a small following among the voters of the moderate Left. He hoped to change Germany by kindness, and when he took office he declared that he was "certain that we can find the way toward a new freedom . . . without the use of force."

Among the most prominent figures to participate in Eisner's government were Gustav Landauer, Ernst Toller and Erich Mühsam—all of them Jewish intellectuals, and not one of them with so much as a Bavarian accent. It was not only the right-wing establishment that recoiled from this unheard-of state of affairs. Franz Kafka, looking on from the sidelines, wrote to Max Brod a year after the revolution that the Jews had overreached themselves: "They have always tried to push Germany into things which it might have accepted slowly and in its own fashion, but which it was bound to reject because they came from outsiders." Kafka had reached this conclusion after listening to the German guests at a hotel where he was staying: "They don't forgive the Jewish Socialists and Communists a single thing; they drown them during the soup and quarter them while carving the roast."*

After three months in office, Eisner was assassinated in the street on his way to the opening of the Bavarian Provincial Assembly (where, in fact, he intended to deliver his resignation speech). His murderer was Count Arco Valley, a young man who felt stigmatized by the fact that his mother was Jewish, and who wanted to prove to his Teutonic friends in the Thule Club that (as the club's founder, Rudolf von Sebottendorf, expressed it) "even a half-Jew was capable of a heroic deed." Eisner's death was followed by a short civil war in which the hastily organized *Räterepublik*—the "Republic of Soldiers' and Workers' Councils"—was liquidated by

---

*The German Right always accused the German Socialists and Communists of being "terrorists," though in 1918 even such radical leaders as Rosa Luxemburg were outspoken opponents of violence. Socialism, she wrote, did not need to "destroy its own illusions with bloody acts of violence." She also pointed out that her critics on the Right were "the very people who sent one and a half million German men and youths to the slaughter without blinking an eyelid, who supported with all the means at their disposal for four years the greatest blood-letting humanity has ever experienced—they now scream hoarsely about 'terror'. . . ."

200,000 freebooting soldiers of the so-called *Freikorps*, the forerunners of Hitler's Storm Troops.

Leading figures of the *Räterepublik* who were left alive after the "White Terror" were given long prison sentences by a military tribunal that charged them with treason. Mühsam received a fifteen-year sentence of which he was to serve six years before being amnestied—most of them at the notorious fortress prison of Niederschönenfeld, where the lives of political prisoners were made as miserable as possible. Mühsam was repeatedly singled out for special punishment—for writing the "subversive" poetry that was discovered in his cell, for having insulted a Bavarian minister or for minor infractions of the prison regulations. Once he drew special punishment for calling the health authorities' attention to the fact that a fellow prisoner needed psychiatric treatment. "For this," Toller recalled in his memoirs, "Mühsam was punished with seven weeks' solitary confinement. 'It will give Mühsam an opportunity to decide whether it is worth while to try and gain leadership by interfering in the affairs of other prisoners,' the report read."

Though he became deaf in one ear and developed heart trouble as a result of his experiences, Mühsam continued writing poems and plays whenever he was permitted the use of writing materials. Since his first brushes with the law he had been perfectly aware that with his wild hair and rabbinical beard, he was to be made to pay for more than purely political crimes. His poem *Das Verhör* (The Interrogation) touches on this point with a delicacy reminiscent of Carl Sternheim:

> *Sie heissen? fragte mich der Direktor.*
> *Ich nannte den Namen.*
> *Geboren?*
> *Ja!*
> *Wann, meine ich.*
> *Ich nannte das Datum.*
> *Religion?*
> *Geht Sie nichts an.*
> *Schreiben Sie also: mosaisch!—Der Beamte schrieb. . . .*

> Your name? the Director asked me.
> I told him the name.
> Born?
> Yes!
> When, I mean.
> I named the date.
> Religion?

Doesn't concern you.
Very well, write: Jewish!—the clerk wrote it down.

When he was paroled in December 1924—Lasker-Schüler and
Kurt Tucholsky were among the influential writers who had cam-
paigned for his release—his arrival in Berlin drew such a large
crowd to the railway station that the police felt justified in breaking
up the welcoming party with rubber truncheons. After what he
called the "Kaspar Hauser adventure of my return among people,"
he devoted himself to helping others whom he considered unjustly
imprisoned. A lecture tour was organized for him, and he spoke of
his prison experiences on behalf of the Communist-sponsored *Rote
Hilfe*, the "Red Assistance" for political prisoners. But he resigned
from the organization when it became apparent that *Rote Hilfe* ignored the plight of anarchist prisoners in the Soviet Union. The call
for an amnesty, Mühsam insisted, "must not fall silent at the borders of Russia."

Since the existing political parties failed to come up to his expectations, he fell back on publishing a small, eccentric magazine of
his own, *Fanal*, while at the same time writing comic verse in *Berlinerisch* dialect for one of the local weeklies. He had not lost his
touch, and he was still being asked to recite his poetry on all possible occasions. "Young people loved him," writes the critic Alfred
Kantorowicz. "They crowded around him, asking him to recite his
verses—especially the memorable song of the *Revoluzzer im
Zivilstand Lampenputzer* (the revolutionary who cleans lamps for a
living). He could be very cheerful. He was not fanatical, not doc-
trinaire, not 'always in the right.' " The young writer Günter
Dallmann remembered him "not only on account of his bushy
beard, as an infinitely good and gentle prophet—though he could
also grow very angry about injustice. . . ." Indeed, much of
Mühsam's poetry is deliberately prophetic and biblical in its allusions:

> . . . *Ein Jude zog aus Nazareth*
> *Die Armen glücklich zu machen.*

"A Jew came from Nazareth/ that the poor might be happy," run
the concluding lines of one of his most messianic poems. His vision
of Moses, too, is based on what the philosopher Ernst Bloch was to
call *das Prinzip Hoffnung*, the Hope Principle—*Des Menschen Himmel
ist allein sein Hoffen* (man's sole heaven is his ability to hope). In the
poem *Vermächtnis* (Legacy) Mühsam went so far as to employ the
symbolism of the Eucharist to describe his own impending Passion:

Bald wird vielleicht uns das Henkerbrot
in den Keller gereicht.
Dann segne das Blut, das dem Leibe entrinnt!

Soon, perhaps, the hangman's bread
will be passed to us in the cellar.
Then bless this blood that from the body flows!

In March 1933 Mühsam was caught in the Nazi roundup of left-wing intellectuals following the Reichstag fire. Klaus Mann reports that friends had urged him to leave Berlin, and had provided him with a third-class ticket to Prague. While he was packing up his books and papers, an acquaintance who was also wanted by the Gestapo came to him for help. "The young man told later how Mühsam behaved that afternoon. In his bearded, Christ-like face, his eyes shone. 'Would you go if you could?' he asked. And as the lad nodded, he drew a ticket from his pocket—the third-class ticket to Prague which was to have helped him to save his life that night. The lad did not ask many questions. From Mühsam's house he ran straight to the station." Early the next morning the poet was arrested by Storm Troopers.

He was fifty-five at the time of his imprisonment. For seventeen months he was subjected to a crescendo of beatings and tortures in a succession of concentration camps: Sonnenburg, Brandenburg and Oranienburg. On the day of his arrival in Sonnenburg they began by smashing his glasses, knocking out his teeth and tearing out bunches of his hair. He was stood against a wall, blindfolded and told he was going to be shot. Mühsam tore off the blindfold and shouted at the firing squad: "I want to see the dogs who are going to shoot me!" But it turned out to be only one of the mock executions with which the guards amused themselves. A fellow prisoner who escaped to Prague wrote a detailed account of what he had seen of the way Mühsam was treated in Brandenburg. Besides the routine beatings which were administered to almost all the prisoners there were scenes of public humiliation reserved especially for Mühsam. "On October 12, 1933, Mühsam was pushed into the courtyard where we prisoners had to form a ring around him. The section leader, SS-man Schmidt, gave the following speech: 'Look at this miserable specimen, this target in a shooting gallery! These are your leaders! This is Erich Mühsam of the Munich *Räterepublik!* Mühsam is that you?'—'Yes, that is who I am,' Mühsam said.—'See, this *Judenschwein* is even proud of it!' Schmidt cried, and punched Mühsam in the face with such terrific force that he fell to the ground."

In November Mühsam requested the authorities' permission to write a letter to his wife. Shortly afterward an SS-man called him aside and demanded: "Mühsam, give me your hand!" When the poet refused, the SS-man reached out and broke both of Mühsam's thumbs: "There, now you can write to your wife!" By now, according to several eyewitness reports, he had been beaten nearly blind and deaf. On November 11 (the fifteenth anniversary of the Armistice) he was seized by several guards and publicly beaten with a rifle butt until he collapsed. "One could hear only a single groan. Mühsam never cried. Even when both his thumbs were broken he uttered only a stifled groan." He recovered from this beating, too, though his ears had been beaten to a pulp and "he was in terrible condition. From his right ear, which bled continuously, hung a giant blister of blood and pus."

At Oranienburg, the camp to which he was transferred in February 1934, the guards devised ever more ingenious ways of torturing their prisoner. The Gestapo had discovered a chimpanzee at the home of a scientist who had been arrested. They brought it to the concentration camp and loosed it on Mühsam. The ape was supposed to bite the poet, but it seemed capable of distinguishing friend from foe: it threw its arms around Mühsam's neck, hugging and kissing the prisoner, who "spoke kind words to him." When they saw that their plan had misfired the guards tortured the animal in Mühsam's presence and then killed it. And yet in spite of everything, when one of his friends was about to be moved to another camp, Mühsam told him, by way of farewell: "Have faith, humanity will triumph!"

He was aware that they were trying to goad him into suicide—as many other prisoners had been goaded—but he was determined not to cooperate. Finally, on July 9, 1934, he was called to the camp's headquarters and bluntly told: "We'll give you forty-eight hours to kill yourself, and if you don't we'll help you along." He had already survived a number of such threats, but this time he was convinced they were in earnest. "If you hear that I have taken my own life, don't believe it," he told his friends among the prisoners. "I shall not do this work. I am not my own executioner; I shall leave that to others." That night he was called out of the barracks and failed to return. The next morning his scarred, beaten body was discovered hanging from a beam in the latrine. But it was clear that the rope had been knotted by a specialist and not by the near-blind Mühsam, who had difficulty tying his shoelaces. The position and condition of the body also indicated that the poet had, in fact, been murdered during the night.

Only a handful of people dared to attend Mühsam's funeral in Berlin-Dahlem on July 16. His wife, Zensl, who had done everything in her power to get him released, was not among them. She had already arranged with the press attaché at the Czech Embassy to smuggle her husband's papers out of Germany by diplomatic pouch, and now she followed them to Prague, where she took refuge with one of their Czech friends.* Mühsam had always regarded his unpublished diaries as the most important of his writings. According to their friend Erich Wollenberg, Mühsam had warned his wife at their last meeting: "You must promise me, Zensl, never to visit Russia so long as Stalin rules. Guard my diaries like the apple of your eye, and never allow my papers to fall into the hands of the Communists. That would be worse than my death!" The International *Rote Hilfe* for political prisoners, however, persuaded Zensl Mühsam to visit Moscow in 1935, and the following spring she concluded a contract with the Soviet government giving the Moscow Literary Institute exclusive rights to her husband's literary estate. She arranged to have the manuscripts delivered to the Soviet Embassy in Prague.

As soon as they were safely in Soviet hands and her signature was affixed to the contract, Zensl Mühsam was arrested in Moscow, charged with being a "Trotzkyist agent." Apparently she had been tricked into surrendering her husband's manuscripts so that, in the words of one knowledgeable observer, his "anarchist criticism of the Communists could be rendered harmless for the future." In point of fact, Mühsam's literary legacy has never been made public: his papers continue to repose behind locked doors at the Gorki Institute for World Literature in Moscow.

His widow, meanwhile, was to spend most of the next twenty years in Soviet prisons and labor camps. Margarete Buber-Neumann, a German writer imprisoned on much the same charges, afterward remembered meeting her in a Moscow prison cell. "Zensl Mühsam was about sixty. She wore her gray hair in a plait around her head, she was slender and tall, and moved like a young woman. She never complained about her cruel fate. Her calm superiority was remarkable. In her conversation she always came back to, 'Erich said even then . . .' or 'If Erich were still alive. . . .' "

Unlike Lasker-Schüler's ex-husband, Herwarth Walden, who emigrated to Russia only to vanish into the Gulag without a trace,

---

*The attaché, Camill Hoffmann, was himself a surrealist poet of note. He was arrested by the Germans after the occupation of Czechoslovakia, and later killed in a concentration camp.

Zensl Mühsam survived her imprisonment and, though mentally disoriented, was repatriated to East Germany at the age of seventy-two, seven years before her death in 1962. Whether her husband's writings are ever to be disinterred remains an unanswered question: there are known to be 12,540 pages of material in the microfilm copies which the Moscow Institute deposited with the East Berlin Academy of Arts, but these, too, continue to be kept under lock and key. (Actually, the Moscow Institute's contract for publication—or rather, nonpublication—rights appears to be legally invalid, since the co-executor of Mühsam's will, then living in America, never consented to the arrangement.)

Ernst Toller, who spent nearly five years in the same Bavarian prison, came away with a picture of Mühsam as "a man of rare integrity and great courage." Yet they were in no sense allies or co-conspirators, even in literary matters. Toller's plays were written in the stylized Expressionist idiom that Mühsam considered unnecessarily sophisticated: "The Expressionist stammer," he wrote, "fulfills the bourgeois' need for modernity but not the proletarian's need for an art that will illuminate his experience of life." Toller belonged to the avant-garde but he was never really a Bohemian, and his radicalism was more literary than political. Like Eisner, he would have preferred Germany to reform itself through kindness. Ilya Ehrenburg, who knew him not only in Berlin but also in Paris, Moscow and London, remembered Toller as a man divided against himself who had "chosen a path that is at variance with the stuff of which he is made." Ehrenburg waxes quite lyrical on the subject: Toller seemed to have been "made for meditation, for producing tender lyrics, yet from early youth he chose the strenuous path of action, of struggle." Others noticed the contradiction and accused Toller of being an actor; of having a theatrical temperament. W. H. Auden described him as "one who is egotistical and brave." Certainly his career was complicated by the fact that he became a very successful playwright and that he was strikingly good-looking (no one had ever said this of Mühsam). To Ehrenburg "he looked like an Italian, gay and melancholy, like the perpetually unlucky heroes of Neo-Realist films."

Toller's fondness for a life of action was probably a belated reaction to an overprotected childhood. Toller's mother was forever fussing over him. Lasker-Schüler recalled that, long after he had become a well-known playwright, "his refined and delicate mother wrote to me, always with worries about Ernst who had been so 'defiant' even as a boy. But between the lines of her letters glowed the pride of her loving heart. Her son's soul was pure, and beloved by God."

Toller came from Samotchin, a small market town in what was then Prussian Posen and has since reverted to being the Polish province of Poznan. His father was a shopkeeper and town councilor, but as Toller explains in his memoirs, it was his mother who was in charge of things: "Mother is always working; she is working when I wake up in the morning. She works in the shop, in the granary, she does the housekeeping, she gives food to the poor and invites beggars to the midday meal, and when the farm-hand goes to the fields to plough and sow it is to her he comes for supplies." In this family, too, there was the almost inevitable Spanish ancestor, a paternal great-grandfather "of Spanish extraction" who had owned a large estate in West Prussia.

Yet Toller's memoirs are anything but a nostalgic remembrance of a lost childhood paradise, à la Lasker-Schüler. If his autobiography, *Eine Jugend in Deutschland*, now seems the most important of his books, it is precisely because it renders an almost wholly honest and unvarnished account of his emotional experiences as a young German Jew. This was a subject with which none of the *Grenzjuden* authors were wholly at ease, partly because they felt an open discussion would only make matters worse, and partly because they were too proud to admit how badly their feelings had been hurt. Toller, however, was determined to let the chips fall where they might. Born in 1893, he was not yet forty when he wrote his autobiography (which was called *I was a German* in Edward Crankshaw's English translation), and many of the events he relates were still fresh in his memory. His first encounter with antisemitism—"Come away, Ilse! He's a Jew!"—must have occurred when he was only three or four years old. It is virtually the first thing he tells us about himself in this extraordinary book, which reads like the classic German *Bildungsroman* (the young idealist's initiation into the world of realities) translated from fiction into a far more bizarre and unimaginable realm of fact. When Toller as a grammar-school boy hears from a friend that "it was the Jews killed our Saviour on the cross," he secretly prays to an image of Christ: "Please, dear Saviour, forgive me for letting the Jews kill you dead." Later he makes the discovery that he could safely "pass" by blending into the general environment: "I am blissfully happy. I am not a Jew any more, and I have a Christmas verse to learn; nobody will ever be able to call 'Dirty Jew!' after me again. . . ." Yet the problem continued to plague him, and he returns to the subject in the closing pages of his book:

I thought of my own childhood, of my misery when the other children shouted "Dirty Jew!" at me, of my childish appeal to the picture of Christ; of my terrible joy when I realised that nobody would recognise me for a Jew; of the first day of the War and my passionate longing to prove that I was a real German by offering my life to my country. . . . And wasn't the German language my language, the language in which I felt and thought and spoke, a part of my very being?

But wasn't I also a Jew? . . . I had denied my own mother, and I was ashamed. It is an indictment of society at large that a child should have thus been driven to deception.

But was I an alien because of all this? Is blood to be the only test? Does nothing else count at all? I was born and brought up in Germany; I had breathed the air of Germany and its spirit had moulded mine; as a German writer I had helped to preserve the purity of the German language. How much of me was German, how much Jewish? I could not have said.

All over Europe an infatuated nationalism and ridiculous pride was raging—had I too to participate in the madness of this epoch . . .? The words "I am proud to be a German" or "I am proud to be a Jew" sounded ineffably stupid to me. As well say, "I am proud to have brown eyes." . . . Pride and love are not the same thing, and if I were asked where I belonged I should answer that a Jewish mother had borne me, that Germany had nourished me, that Europe had formed me, that my home was the earth, and the world my fatherland.

Like Mühsam, Toller began his career with a minor local scandal that was indicative of future patterns of protest. A half-mad orphan boy, Julius, had been allowed to die of convulsions at the Samotchin railway station because for six and a half hours no one would send for a doctor or come to his aid. "When the police were informed of his condition their attitude was that it was nothing to do with them, since he was lying in the territory of the Prussian State Railway." Toller wrote an indignant article about the incident for a local newspaper and was saved from legal prosecution by the offended burgomaster only by the fact that his father happened to be a member of the town council. Toller began his university studies in Germany but went on to the University of Grenoble, supposedly to learn something about French civilization. Instead he spent much of his time drinking beer with the German Student Union: "We deprecated the smuttiness of the French, and preened ourselves on being pioneers of a loftier culture. To bring the evening to a close we would open the window and sing *Deutschland, Deutschland, über alles, über alles in der Welt* at the top of our voices. The townsfolk would gather in the square below and listen to our songs, and shake their heads and laugh." He was still in France when the war broke out in August 1914, but managed to slip across the border at the last moment in order to enlist in the German army. In his patriotic enthusiasm he volunteered for front-line duty, first in the artillery, then in the more hazardous infantry. It was during his thirteen months in the trenches that he experienced the change of heart which he was afterward to dramatize in his play *Die Wandlung*, known in English as *Transfiguration*. In his autobiography, too, he describes his gradual awakening to the reality of war as the turning point of his life:

> One night we heard a cry, the cry of one in excruciating pain; then all was quiet again. Someone in his death agony we thought. But an hour later the cry came again. It never ceased the whole night. Nor the following night. Naked and inarticulate the cry persisted. We could not tell whether it came from the throat of a German or a Frenchman. It existed in its own right, an agonised indictment of heaven and earth. We thrust our fingers into our ears to stop its moan; but it was no good: the cry cut like a drill into our heads, dragging minutes into hours, hours into years. We withered and grew old between those cries.
>
> Later we learned that it was one of our own men hanging on the wire. Nobody could do anything for him; two men had already tried to save him, only to be shot themselves. We prayed desperately for his death. He took so long about it, and if he went on much longer we should go mad. But on the third day his cries were stopped by death.

Toller saw innumerable men killed, maimed or shell-shocked during the fighting. But for a long time he "saw the dead without really seeing them" and without feeling personally involved. Then one day, as he stood in a trench cutting into the earth, the point of his pick got stuck:

> . . . and I heaved and pulled it out with a jerk. With it came a slimy, shapeless bundle, and when I bent down to look I saw that wound round my pick were human entrails. A dead man was buried there.
>
> A—dead—man.
>
> What made me pause then? Why did those three words so startle me? They closed upon my brain like a vice; they choked my throat and chilled my heart. Three words, like any other three words.
>
> A dead man—I tried to thrust the words out of my mind; what was there about them that they should so overwhelm me?
>
> A—dead—man—
>
> And suddenly, like light in darkness, the real truth broke in upon me; the simple fact of Man, which I had forgotten, which had lain deep buried and out of sight; the idea of community, of unity.

A dead man.
Not a dead Frenchman.
Not a dead German.
A dead man.
   . . . it was only then that I realised, at last, that all these dead men, Frenchmen and Germans, were brothers, and I was the brother of them all.

By the time Toller was invalided out of the army in 1916 he had become an ardent pacifist, convinced that "there was no rhyme or reason in all this slaughtering and devastation." He returned to his studies, first in Munich, then Heidelberg, as part of a university class consisting largely of sick or crippled veterans. Obsessed with the suffering he had witnessed, he organized a student group that made a public appeal for an end to the fighting, with the result that he was threatened with arrest for "treason to the Fatherland." Driven out of Heidelberg, he joined the Independent Socialists led by Kurt Eisner and Gustav Landauer, whom he helped organize a "peace strike" among Munich munitions workers in January 1918. Some of his poetry about the horrors of war from the hospital scenes of his play *Die Wandlung* was distributed to the workers in leaflet form. He was reconscripted and sent to a military prison for his part in the strike. Later he was briefly committed to an insane asylum for having been mad enough to demand "peace without annexations or indemnities." At the time, though their armies were on the verge of defeat in the West, the Germans on the home front were still under the impression that they were, in fact, winning the war. In the treaty of Brest-Litovsk of March 1918, Russia had ceded to Germany nearly a third of her farmland, thirty-four percent of her population and half of her industrial holdings. To demand "peace without annexations" was tantamount to forgoing the enormous spoils that Germany had already won in three years of fighting on foreign soil. It was only when the Western front collapsed that these Eastern conquests proved to be wholly illusory.

During the bloodless Munich revolution of November 1918, when Kurt Eisner was elected president of the "Bavarian Free State" by the Workers' and Soldiers' Councils, Toller was elected his deputy. After Eisner's assassination three months later he emerged, at twenty-five, as one of the moderate leaders of the Republic of Councils. But with the beginning of open warfare against the *Räterepublik*, Toller was faced with another crisis of conscience. "I hated force, and had vowed to suffer from force rather than employ it myself. Was I to break this vow now that

Revolution had come? I had to break it. The workers had put their trust in me and made me their leader, and I was responsible to them. If I refused to defend them now, if I called on them to renounce force of arms, would I not be betraying that trust?" In the Imperial Army he had risen to the rank of corporal. Now suddenly he found himself in command of the entire "armed forces" of the hard-pressed republic. A "White" offensive was being launched against Munich. At Dachau, just north of the city, Toller mustered 2,000 men loyal to the republic and fought his first and only pitched battle with the Whites:

> The enemy's fire increased. My men wavered and demanded support from the artillery. But I refused to bring the heavy guns into it and went forward with a handful of volunteers. The others followed. We came up with the main body and stormed Dachau. As the fight developed the workers from the Dachau munitions factory attacked the Whites from the rear. The women among them were even more determined than the men. They disarmed the troops and drove them out of the town. The White Commander escaped on a railway engine. . . . We took prisoner five officers and thirty-six men, and occupied the town.

When General von Epp's *Freikorps* units entered Munich in April 1919, they avenged themselves on the "Red Army" by the wholesale slaughter of prisoners and civilians. Landauer, the minister of education in the republic (who had written important books on Shakespeare, Hölderlin and Milton), was shot, beaten and trampled to death by a gang of soldiers in the courtyard of Stadelheim Prison. Baron von Gagern, the officer who commenced the killing by hitting Landauer in the face with his riding crop, was later acquitted: only the soldier who stole the dead man's watch was sentenced to a few weeks in prison. Toller heard from a prisoner who had witnessed the killing that Landauer's final words to his murderers had been: "Kill me, then! To think that you are human!"

Toller, who would certainly have been accorded the same treatment, managed to remain in hiding until a semblance of order was restored in Munich. He was arrested in a friend's apartment, tried for high treason, and sentenced to five years' "fortress arrest," of which he had to serve all but the last day.* His account of his first

---

*By comparison, Adolf Hitler, who received an identical sentence for leading the Beerhall Putsch in 1923, had to serve only nine months of his five-year term. He was assigned private quarters in Landsberg Castle where, accompanied by a valet, he lived under hotel-like conditions. He, too, put his prison time to literary use: the result was *Mein Kampf.*

prison interrogation is not without the familiar Sternheim-like dialogue:

"What is your religion?"
"I have none."
He turned to a stenographer:
"Put down 'Jew, non-professing.'. . ."

Toller proved an even more refractory prisoner than Mühsam. During a single year, by his own count, he spent 149 days in solitary confinement, was deprived of writing materials on 243 days, of his bed on 14 days, of exercise on 70 days, of visitors on 168 days and of parcels on 217; he spent 8 days in the dark cell and was forbidden any food on 24 days. Yet he made the most of his writing materials when he did have permission to use them. He wrote poetry and plays that won him an enormous following in the outside world, and corresponded with many of the leading writers of the day, including Fritz von Unruh, Theodor Lessing, Stefan Zweig, Henri Barbusse, Romain Rolland—and Lasker-Schüler. At one point his admirers succeeded in electing him a member of the Bavarian parliament *in absentia*. Even so, the prison authorities continued to treat him with the special harshness reserved for political prisoners of the Left. When a pair of swallows nested in his cell, Toller wrote a series of poems about "all that I saw and heard and felt and thought" as he watched these visitors "from holy fields of Africa." The authorities discovered the manuscript and confiscated it as subversive propaganda. And when the birds returned the following year, their nest was destroyed by the warders on the grounds that "stables are the proper place for swallows to build in." The swallows redoubled their efforts, building nests in several locations simultaneously. All six were torn down by the guards: "The struggle lasted for seven weeks, a glorious and heroic struggle between the united forces of Bavarian law and order and two tiny birds. . . . After that the swallows built no more. In the evening they would fly into a cell and spend the night huddled close together. One evening the male swallow came alone; the female was dead." Toller, the ex-soldier, came to see the symbolic significance of these events. The destruction of nests, he said, was "a thumbnail sketch of war." He succeeded in smuggling his *Swallow Book* out of prison on small slips of paper sewn into the lining of a departing prisoner's jacket; it was to become known as his finest book of poetry.

Meanwhile, the plays he was writing in prison were produced by many of the most important German theaters, including Max

Reinhardt's Grosses Schauspielhaus in Berlin. *Masse Mensch* (Masses and Man) deals with his personal dilemma as a nonviolent idealist caught up in a violent tide of revolution. In *Die Maschinenstürmer* (The Machine-Wreckers) the English Luddite movement provided him with a tragic test case for the possibilities of achieving social justice through violence. *Hinkemann* (published in English both as *Broken Brow* and as *Hinkemann*) is an antiwar morality play whose central figure is a much-abused veteran who has been mutilated the same way as the hero of Hemingway's *The Sun Also Rises,* and for the same allegorical reason: "He did me in, and another fellow did him in. But who did us all in? All of us: one soul in one body." It was a hell of a way to be wounded.

By the time Toller was released from prison (he was discharged a day early to protect him from the Nazi assassins said to be waiting at the gate) he had become the most famous German playwright of the 1920s. Else Lasker-Schüler remembered his arrival in Berlin as one of the happiest events of 1924: "We all hurried to the Grosse Saal in Berlin, as devoutly as if we were going to church, to greet him and hear him after six years of confinement." Her heart beat faster when she saw him on the podium dressed in the simplest of jackets: "He looked a little like Senna Hoy, that splendid son of kings." She was very grateful to him because "he had always written me so lovingly from prison, as if I were the prisoner and he in freedom." And she never forgot the "final chord" of the speech he gave that day: "If men were able to feel only a tenth of the pain suffered by their neighbor, there would soon be no more injustice and no more hate on earth."

Toller had lost faith in political parties and was no longer certain as to the role he should play in the real world. "Poets may dream in verses and write dramas,/ But statecraft is the business of hard men," declares one of his characters in the prologue to *The Machine-Wreckers.* Like Mühsam, however, he was now more sensitive than ever to the crimes and injustices that were being committed in German prisons and asylums. His 1927 book, *Justizerlebnisse* (Experiences of Justice), exposed the sadism of prison wardens and the one-sidedness of Bavarian justice. The hero of his next play, *Hoppla, wir leben!* (in English, *Hoppla! Such Is Life*), falls victim to the same repressive system of "law and order" and is finally driven to suicide:

KARL THOMAS: Nobody hears, nobody hears. Nobody. We speak and do not hear one another. . . . We hate and do not see one another. . . . We love and do not know one another. We murder but are unaware of one an-

other. . . . Everything to no purpose! Go on riding on
your merry-go-rounds! Dance, laugh, weep, beget.
Enjoy yourselves! *I* jump off. . . .
(Karl Thomas tears a strip of bedsheet, gets on to stool, fastens the strip to the
door-hook.)

Black Out

Hoppla, wir leben! took the Berlin theater world by storm when
Erwin Piscator inaugurated his Theater am Nollendorfplatz with a
brilliant production of the play in 1927. Toller had become an international celebrity: literary critics spoke of him as the great revolutionary dramatist of Expressionism, as the foremost modern expo-
nent of the "moralizing theater" of Schiller and Lessing. Some of
his friends felt that it was not easy for him to adjust to his new
situation. "Theatrical successes, fame, women, money, more action, but no sleep," reported Klaus Mann. "Writers' congresses,
meetings, premieres, more women, more successes, but also de-
feats (What's happening to my talent? Am I slipping?). . . ." Like
Ehrenburg, Mann perceived Toller as something of a dual personality: helpful and egocentric, honest and rhetorical, often cheerful
but with ominous manic-depressive tendencies. Count Kessler met
the playwright at a dinner party (he was always meeting everybody at dinner parties) and noted in his diary that Toller "is
hyper-excitable and touchy to a degree, speaks softly and stares at
his interlocutor with glowing eyes."

Toller happened to be on a lecture tour of Switzerland when the
Nazis took over, or he would certainly have shared Mühsam's fate.
He exchanged his Zurich-Berlin ticket for a Zurich-London ticket
and took up temporary residence in England, where he had several
publishers and many admirers. After a year in Britain he wrote that
"the land of Shakespeare and Shelley" had become a second home
to him. He rented a house in Hampstead and married a young
German actress, Christiane Grautoff, who had refused important
film offers in the Reich in order to follow him into exile. His energies as a writer were now directed toward awakening Europe to the
dangers of Nazism. "They can kill the mind for a time and they can
kill it in any one land. But across the border they are impotent;
across the border the power of the word can save itself and harbour
itself. . . ." He wrote more plays, gave lectures, contributed articles
and poems to the anti-Nazi press, now exiled to Prague, Paris and
Amsterdam. Together with Lion Feuchtwanger he established the
German émigré branch of the International P.E.N. Club, on whose
behalf he spoke against Nazism not only in Western Europe but
also at the 1934 Writers' Conference in Moscow—the last before

Stalin terminated all vestiges of an East-West dialogue—where he shared the limelight with Maxim Gorky and André Malraux.

Beyond the borders of Germany, Hitler was still regarded as a great enigma, and spokesmen against Nazism were not always welcomed even in Britain. The London *Morning Post*, for example, attacked Toller as "one of those Germans who have not stayed to examine the Third Reich. . . . It is partly to the meddling, muddling hoe of such visionaries as Herr Toller that we owe the present state of Central Europe."* When he was invited to Dublin to address the Irish Labour League, the Irish government, under pressure from the Germans, advised him to stay away. Toller was infuriated by the apparent indifference to Nazism that he encountered everywhere. He told Ehrenburg, in London, that Europe was in for a winter longer than Moscow's—"a winter for the next ten or twelve years. There are people with strong roots, they'll endure. But the others are being killed by the frost, one by one."

He visited Spain after the outbreak of the Civil War and decided that something must be done about the starving children he saw everywhere. On a fund-raising tour of England and the United States he collected more than a million dollars to feed needy children on both sides of the battlefront. But things were not going as well with his work or his marriage. His wife left him early in 1939, while they were in New York for the production of his newest play, *Pastor Hall,* in which he paid tribute to Erich Mühsam and other victims of the concentration camps.

Prince Hubertus zu Löwenstein, then one of the leaders of the German exile colony in America, writes in his memoirs that he was struck by Toller's mood of depression when they met in April 1939, though at the same time he observed that Toller "had progressed more and more towards a spiritual, even a religious concept of Man." Stephen Spender, one of the co-translators of *Pastor Hall,* recalls in his autobiography that at their last dinner together, Toller, "rather surprisingly, fished a silver brooch out of his pocket and presented it to Inez," Spender's wife. He failed to understand the finality of Toller's symbolic gesture, but he noted that the playwright was strangely fascinating, "with his large brown eyes like a doe's, and his pale skin like an American Indian's." At about this time, Klaus Mann accompanied Toller on a trip to Washington to attend a luncheon at which President and Mrs. Roosevelt received a group of prominent émigré writers. Though Toller had

---

*This line of argument has often been used to justify various aspects of Nazism. It is summed up perfectly in the title of one of Franz Werfel's early short stories: *Not the Murderer, the Murdered Is Guilty.*

been lively and interested in everything when they went sightseeing with Dorothy Thompson afterward, he complained to Mann about his incessant insomnia: "It is terrible when one can't sleep; it is absolutely terrible."

They traveled back to New York in a Pullman car, and as Mann recalled, "at breakfast, in a cafeteria, he was very depressed again; he had not slept at all during the night." Not long afterward Toller telephoned his friend Ludwig Marcuse, a refugee writer newly arrived in New York, to say that he was in desperate need of company and no longer in a state to be left alone. Marcuse and his wife spent several days trying to help him. Toller painted his situation in the darkest colors: "His wife . . . had left him. His good fortune had deserted him. He could no longer work. His boat was sinking." The Hitler-Stalin pact was in the offing, and the dreary prospect added to his apprehensions. They went for a long walk along the Hudson River; Toller remarked that he wished he could be a better writer. One evening their conversation touched on suicide: Toller declared himself vehemently opposed to it. In his room at the Mayflower Hotel the next day (May 22, 1939), after his secretary had gone out for lunch, Toller stepped into the bathroom and hanged himself with the cord of his dressing gown. He left no suicide note, but none was necessary: it had been written more than a dozen years earlier for Karl Thomas's farewell in *Hoppla, wir leben!*—"I jump off. . . . *Black Out.*"

In its obituary notice, the *Times* of London called the forty-five-year-old poet "a generous-hearted idealist, a passionate believer in human dignity, and a Utopian champion of those whom he believed to be downtrodden and oppressed." Lasker-Schüler, hearing of his death in her own exile, dedicated to Toller the poem *Herbst* (Autumn) which, as she said, "I want to lay in his hand like a lovely flower":

> . . . *Ich will dir viel viel Liebe sagen*
> *Wenn auch schon kühle Winde wehen,*
> *In Wirbeln sich um Bäume drehen,*
> *Um Herzen, die in ihren Wiegen lagen.*

> I want to tell you of my great, great love
> Though the cold winds have begun to blow,
> Swirling in eddies round the trees,
> Around hearts that lay in their cradles.

Lasker-Schüler had lived in Switzerland until a month before Toller's death, when she had left Europe to settle in Palestine. Switzerland had proved to be only the most problematic of sanctuaries, for here, too, the Jews were unwelcome, and the lucky few who had succeeded in obtaining a residence permit were expected to remain as inconspicuous as possible. Public opinion was not favorably inclined toward German refugees because Nazi propaganda had persuaded many of the Swiss that "the Jews had brought antisemitism upon themselves." Moreover, the director of the Swiss police, Heinrich Rothmund, had established such an excellent working relationship with the Gestapo that it was at his suggestion that the German police introduced the large red "J" which was stamped in the Jewish refugees' passports and identity cards, thus enabling the Swiss frontier police to distinguish desirable from undesirable Germans at a glance. Switzerland, Rothmund assured the Gestapo, "can use these Jews just as little as Germany can."

Lasker-Schüler was one of the very few émigré writers to receive permission not only to reside in Switzerland but to publish her work there: virtually all the others were turned down because the Association of Swiss Authors, which had to rule on each application, was determined to protect itself against alien competition. As an elderly lyric poetess, Lasker-Schüler seemed to offer no particular threat to anyone's livelihood. Yet difficulties arose in 1936 when the Zurich Schauspielhaus staged the premiere of her "great peace-play, from the home of my dead people," *Arthur Aronymus*. The actors and most of the audience loved the play; they were "swept off their feet" by this extraordinary vision of brotherly love between German Christians and Jews, with the bishop's culminating benediction: "I bestow a blessing upon this ancient people, Israel!" As Franz Werfel wrote to her in a glowing letter of appreciation:

> Your *Arthur Aronymus* is a wholly wonderful work. Once again the unique genius that lives and works in you has succeeded in resolving what is currently the most perilous, delicate, inexpressible problem. . . . Every character, even the most minor, has such depth and truthfulness that one can only be amazed. . . . It is the most Jewish and at the same time the most naïve work of art that one could imagine. . . . Ironically enough, it is also the most *German* work that I know. None of the so-called "national poets" of today could write anything even remotely as close to the true nature of Germany and its people. . . .

Werfel also tried to console her for the difficulties she was experiencing at that moment. She was to consider herself as having been "specially marked out by God" for some as yet indiscernible purpose. "For that you have to pay with your destiny. God could help you only if he were to abandon you. But you are more than a poetess; you are a soul for whom he must have some special intention beyond the here and now."

Things had already reached the point, however, where a "peace-play" with a message of brotherly love could be regarded as a political provocation. *Arthur Aronymus,* previously banned in Germany, was permitted to run for only two performances in Zurich because there were complaints in the press that it was a "tendentious" piece of anti-Nazi propaganda which could not be tolerated in a neutral nation.* "The director was threatened," Lasker-Schüler explained to a friend. "He *had* to stop giving the play because there are forty-two Jews in it." Not long afterward, she herself was once more kicked and beaten during an incident in a post office. She tried to defend her play against its critics in a long letter to the leading Zurich newspaper: though not published at the time, a copy was found among her papers after the war. Almost incidentally, it contains her most definitive statement about the art of poetry and her own intuitive relationship to it:

> The critics have overestimated me. I am only a poetess—or rather, poems occur in me; they compose themselves in me.† A poet, in any case, *never* has intentions when he writes poetry. He merely experiences the necessity of writing it. . . . The more attentively he listens to his angel, the more willingly he surrenders to it, the more valuable and profound is his poetry. This is the condition that people have called "inspiration."
>
> A poet happens to be a plantlike creature. He resembles the fruit tree that produces blossoms in the spring. The tree doesn't consider whether someone will rest in its shade during the summer, or pick its cherries—or might hang himself from one of its branches.
>
> I, too, never tried to achieve any particular purpose in my writing, either in my play or the rest of my nineteen books; I aimed neither for pain nor joy, neither for political nor unpolitical effects. And I am surprised to find myself suddenly being charged with having had worldly motives. Poetry creates itself within the poet! He cannot decide to write anything, cannot even select the material for his poetry the way one chooses silk for a dress. The poem grows within the poet; the finished poem, whether tart as a nut or sweet as a pomegranate, falls into his lap as a ripe pear falls from a tree into the grass. . . . Why have they attacked my white play, and me in my play?

---

*Swiss "neutralists" insisted that "the struggle between National-Socialism and the Emigration" must not be "fought out on Swiss soil"—as though it were a battle between two nations in which a neutral should not take sides. This scrupulousness did not prevent them, however, from materially aiding the German side.

†Mahler, too, had declared: "I don't compose; I *am* composed."

Thirty years earlier she had said that, above all, she wanted "to be playful and like a child." Now she was still too childlike to understand the realities of the Swiss situation: that a large and increasingly influential number of Swiss-Germans were only too anxious to accommodate their neighbors to the north. The Swiss borders were being closed to Jewish refugees: it had been decided that the traditional Swiss right of political asylum did not apply to Jews because they were not "politically" persecuted. With the help of private humanitarian organizations, several thousands of Jewish refugees did manage to survive the war in Swiss internment camps. But many other thousands who had escaped the Gestapo dragnet and actually succeeded in reaching Swiss soil were turned back—some directly to the Gestapo, others to the Vichy-French police, who then delivered them to the Germans for deportation.* The prevailing attitude was summed up for the Swiss Patriotic Association by Dr. Eugen Bircher, an influential member of parliament, colonel in the Swiss army and inventor of "Bircher Müssli" breakfast food: "These emigrants will spread their poison among us. . . . These people will bring us political body lice which we cannot use."

Lasker-Schüler, who had, as she put it, "learned to say 'thank you' in the emigration," would have liked to escape this atmosphere but was uncertain where to go next. In 1937 she had paid an exploratory visit to Palestine and had written an ecstatic account of her travels, *Das Hebräerland*, for a Swiss publisher. Yet she saw no possibility of earning a living there, and "Else Lasker-Schüler cannot live on laurel leaves." Two years later, when she emigrated to Palestine after all, she was suddenly terrified at the thought of having to stay in this Near East which she had so often evoked in the Arabian Nights of her imagination. She was a German poetess and she needed the sound of German in her ears. "I *must*, I want to come back," she wrote in despair to a Swiss friend in August 1939,

---

*The official figure of 10,000 *Zurückweisungen*, i.e., people actually handed back by the police between 1942 and 1945, tells only part of the story. Countless others were rejected at places other than the border. James Joyce, who had lived in neutral Switzerland during World War I, was almost refused entry during World War II because it was thought that he was Jewish. Only when the creator of Leopold Bloom could show that *"je ne suis pas juif de Judée mais aryen d'Erin"* did he receive the ticket of admission that entitled him to sanctuary in Switzerland a second time. Joyce, who died in Zurich in 1941, was thus enabled to participate in the great literary tradition of death in Switzerland—*Der Tod in der Schweiz*—which had been initiated by Georg Büchner and Rainer-Maria Rilke, and to which Stefan George, Robert Musil, Alfred Mombert, Hermann Hesse, Alfred Neumann, Thomas Mann and Erich Maria Remarque also subscribed. As F. Scott Fitzgerald had written some years before: "Switzerland is a land where few things begin, but many things end."

but the war forced her to stay on. She was seventy, though she would admit to only sixty-three and had tried to persuade the Swiss that she was in her fifties. Time, in any event, had always been as relative to Lasker-Schüler as to Dr. Einstein:

> Jesus of Nazareth is of God's age like eternity. Moses was ten thousand years old when Pharaoh's daughter found him in the basket. . . . What do you make of me? I am David and perform Samson-deeds, I am Jacob and interpret the dreams of kine and wheat. . . . Thus time is thrown into disorder in the human past. Today I am a poetess and I ask you to excuse that my poetry has not turned out to be a colored map of my mind, printed in lilac, green and red. You accept my confessions as a de luxe gift, for I am very lavish, that lies in my star system. I am not even worried about dropping some of the moons of my planet. My chaos, too—no man can get along without chaos—is a special case.

There was too much chaos in the British-mandated Palestine of the 1940s. The Jerusalem of her fantasies was not this harsh, indifferent city where she was compelled to live on a charity allowance of less than twenty pounds a month, in a furnished room so small that there was not even room for a bed, only a reclining chair in which she used to sleep. One of her friends has testified that the Prince of Thebes did her own laundry and cooked her own frugal meals in this tiny room, "in which the spiders wove the curtains, and where, with sooty fingers, she wrote her last play, *Ich und Ich* (I and I), on a cramped table that also held a smoky kerosene cooker." It says much for her state of mind that in this play she depicted one of her two selves as a scarecrow, the other as a poetess. In real life there was constant friction with her uncomprehending landlady, who regarded her tenant as just another cranky old lady. "It is too hard for me among the people here," Lasker-Schüler wrote at the age of seventy-four. "Even King David would have moved on." She showed herself all the more grateful to the happy few who remembered her from Germany. There was a professor in Haifa who "thinks I am a prophet—yet actually I'm a street urchin. Thus is one misjudged—!" She was delighted to read her poetry to any group that would pay her a three-pound fee: it was a way of reminding people of her continued existence, for "It's years now that I live, forgotten, in my poems"—*Längst lebe ich vergessen—im Gedicht.*

Still in the habit of thinking first about people more unfortunate than herself, she drew up a ten-point program for improving the city of Jerusalem. It begins with a proposal for day-care centers for poor children, both Jewish and Arab: "I believe that only compassion can strengthen the holy city of Jerusalem." She was concerned about the signs of misery everywhere, whether it was the overloaded donkeys or the lack of drinking water for the poor. "So long as there is one hungry child, God will dispense with all synagogues," she insisted. "I believe, in all modesty, that I am speaking in God's name." She had long since decided, too, that "the Arabs are our brothers in heart."

The critic Werner Kraft remembered her as a difficult and eccentric old woman who loved nothing better than to sit in a Jerusalem café talking to anyone who would listen—"profundities, metaphors, banalities, occasionally indiscretions, about her landlady, who took on demonic dimensions, about people she had known during her life who had died long ago but about whom she talked as though they were still alive—Maria Moissi and Max Reinhardt, Franz Marc, her husband, her son; she spoke of Karl Kraus, of the war, of God, of Stefan George who had been beautiful as a fallen angel though with one shoulder that hung lower than the other, and of her hundred-year-old uncle . . . and always, in between, she kept saying that she wanted to leave, for London, or Zurich. . . ."

She complained, with good reason, that no one paid any attention to her as she sat "lonely at the window of the Café Imperial." It made her feel that she was being treated as a "stepsister" by the very people "for whom I have fought since childhood." Still, she consoled herself with the thought that, "after all, I'm not Jewish for the Jews' sake, but for God." When there was no one else to talk to she was visited by angels. "The other day I was so sad that no one invited me. Then I heard God say, 'I'll invite you.' I sat at a large table, next to me sat the Angel Gabriel and, with the hand of my mother, passed me a fiery dish; it was the plum pudding we always had at home."

The habit of writing great poetry dies hard. She went on writing it, almost automatically, throughout the last years of her life. When she was seventy-two she still spent six to eight hours a day at her typewriter—"so you see I'm not lazing about." It was poetry without malice or an exile's bitterness: indeed, her last book, *Mein blaues Klavier*, published in Palestine during the war, is dedicated "to my unforgettable friends in the cities of Germany and to those who, like me, have been banished and are now scattered throughout the world." There are signs of mortal weariness in these last poems— the "Blue Piano" of the title is depicted as an instrument that has fallen silent "since the world became brutal," and whose keyboard is broken: *Nun tanzen die Ratten im Geklirr* (now rats are dancing amid the clatter). Still, her last volume, like her first, contains some of the finest love songs in the German language. *Ein Liebeslied*, for example, concludes with the lines:

> *Komm zu mir in der Nacht auf Siebensternenschuhen*
> *Und Liebe eingehüllt spät in mein Zelt.*
> *Es steigen Monde aus verstaubten Himmelstruhen.*
>
> *Wir wollen wie zwei seltene Tiere liebesruhen*
> *Im hohen Rohre hinter dieser Welt.*

Wear seven-star boots and come to me in the night
garbed in love, late to my tent.
The moons will rise from dusty cabinets of light.

And we shall rest our love like rare beasts tired of flight
In the high reeds where the world is spent.

Else Lasker-Schüler was not quite seventy-six when she died on January 22, 1945, after collapsing of a heart attack in one of the streets of Jerusalem. She was buried on the Mount of Olives, but the exact location of her grave is now unknown, her tombstone having been uprooted when the Old City fell to the Jordanians in 1948. Her friends record that during her last years, despite her familiarity with angels, there were moments when she was beset by terrible doubts. Once, in her anxiety, she went to a German rabbi whose synagogue she had often attended. "Here we are in private," she said to him. "Tell me, do you believe in God?" But in her poetry she now spoke only of certainties. Picking a last flower by the wayside, she met "an angel who had come to sew me a dress in which to be buried"—*Es kam ein Engel, mir ein Totenkleid zu nähen.* Whatever her private anxieties may have been, her public voice was one of perfect composure when she announced, in *Ich weiss* (I Know), that it would soon be time for her departure: "I set my foot quietly upon the path that leads to the eternal home"—*Ich setze leise meinen Fuss/ Auf den Pfad zum ewigen Heime.* And in the last line of *Ich und Ich*, the "Poetess" cries in a transport of delight: "I am so happy, I am so happy—*God is* here!" Actually she had no need to seek reassurance on this point: she had known all her life that poets were vouchsafed a special state of grace, and that an angel stood waiting at the gate: "The prophets were poets; poetry is the flower of truth . . . poetry makes its bed next to God."

LES INDÉSIRABLES

*"Your presence in the class is disruptive
and affects the other students!"*
—A teacher at the Luitpoldgymnasium, Munich,
to Albert Einstein in 1894

Shortly after the Nazi takeover in 1933, the Prussian Academy of Arts and its sister institution, the Academy of Sciences, lost a number of their best-known and, from the new government's point of view, most dangerous and undesirable members. Among them was the physicist, Professor Albert Einstein, whose hobby was music, and the composer, Professor Arnold Schoenberg, who dabbled in the mathematics of mystic numbers.

Neither of them, as it happened, was Prussian by birth, though each had received Prussian citizenship upon his appointment to a place of honor in the Academy. Schoenberg, born in Vienna in 1874, carried a Czech passport, by virtue of the fact that his parents had come from Bratislava; Einstein, born at Ulm, southern Germany, in 1879, had become a naturalized Swiss citizen in 1901 and carried a Swiss passport.* Neither expressed any particular regret, therefore, at having to sever connections with the Berlin Establishment. Even so, their leave-taking proved to be something of a traumatic experience for both of them.

---

*Einstein had never placed much reliance in his Prussian citizenship, such as it was. "Today in Germany I am called a German man of science and in England I am represented as a Swiss Jew," he told the *Times* of London in 1920. "If I come to be regarded as a *bête noire* the description will be reversed, and I shall become a Swiss Jew for the Germans and a German for the English."

On March 1, 1933—the day after the Berlin fire department had extinguished the Reichstag fire—the Academy of Arts held a formal session in its headquarters near the Brandenburg Gate, only a stone's throw from the gutted shell of the Reichstag building. The day had come, announced the Academy's president, Max von Schillings, to destroy the "Jewish influence" at the Academy. Professor Schoenberg rose to say that he never stayed where he wasn't wanted, and walked out.

Until that moment, Berlin had been the undisputed capital of musical Europe, and Schoenberg, who taught the master class in composition given by the Academy, held the most important musical post in Germany. At the time of his fiftieth birthday, in 1924, he had been widely hailed as "the greatest musician of modern times." From the Nazi point of view, however, he was a cultural Bolshevik who had tried to subvert "the Germanic element of the triad" in order to destroy the cultural heritage of the nation.

It was not until May that Schoenberg received notice of his "suspension" from the Academy, and it was several more months before he was formally expelled "in accordance with the Law for the Reconstitution of the Government Service"—i.e., the first of the Nazi directives banning "non-Aryans" from public posts. By then, however, he had fled to Paris with his wife and their year-old-daughter. There, as a symbolic gesture—and with Marc Chagall as his witness—he formally adopted the Jewish faith which he had supposedly abandoned as a boy, at the time of his conversion to Christianity.

Later that year he went to America in the vanguard of the exodus of great composers that was to shift the musical balance of power from Europe to the United States—with Schoenberg, Stravinsky and Milhaud as leading representatives of the California émigré colony, and Bartók, Hindemith and Rachmaninoff on the East Coast.

Professor Einstein happened to be already in America, visiting the California Institute of Technology in Pasadena, when Hitler became chancellor of the Reich. Had he been in Berlin his life would have been in danger, for he had long been pictured in the Nazi press as one of the leaders of the "Jewish world conspiracy." Reports of the wave of beatings and murders that was sweeping the New Germany persuaded him not to return to Berlin. So long as he had the choice, he told an American interviewer, "I shall live only in a country where civil liberty, tolerance and equality of all citizens before the law prevail."

On their journey back to Europe on the Belgian liner *Belgenland* at the end of March, he and his wife went ashore at Antwerp rather than continue on to Hamburg, and they accepted an invitation to remain in Belgium for the time being. While on the high seas they had heard the news that their house on the outskirts of Berlin had been broken into by a gang of armed Nazis "searching for weapons." Now he formally renounced both his Prussian citizenship and his membership in the Prussian Academy, where moves were already afoot to have him expelled. In the ensuing exchange of letters he was accused of being an "atrocity monger" whose "activities as an agitator in foreign countries" had made him unworthy of belonging to that venerable institution whose members had, *seit alten Zeiten* (since the good old days), "regarded themselves as intimately bound to the Prussian state, and emphasized its patriotic ideals." Almost as an afterthought, he was then expelled from the Bavarian Academy of Sciences as well.

At about the same time he learned that his picture was being circulated in Germany as part of a "rogues' gallery" propaganda campaign depicting prominent enemies of the Fatherland. Later there were reports that Fehme, a Nazi terror organization, had put a price of fifty thousand marks on his head. He might have disregarded these threats had they not coincided with the news of Theodor Lessing's assassination at his writing desk in Marienbad. To protect their distinguished guest—who happened to be a close friend of the queen of the Belgians—the Belgian police assigned two detectives to watch the house where he was staying for the summer, at a seaside village near Ostend. When an old friend from Prague, the physicist Philipp Frank, arrived at the Einsteins' villa unannounced, he was pounced on by the detectives, who, as he later wrote, "threw themselves at me and seized me" before the flustered Mrs. Einstein could reassure them that he was not the expected assassin.

These alarums ultimately persuaded Einstein to leave for England and, shortly afterward, for the United States. He had always been an ardent believer in pacifism and nonviolence, and he was distinctly out of his depth in this unwanted role as a target character in an Eric Ambler thriller. Though puzzled by the importance that the Nazis had assigned him as "the leader of the opposing party throughout the world," he also felt rather flattered at having been chosen as the *bête noire* of the Nazi movement. "I have been promoted to an 'evil monster' in Germany, and all my money has been taken from me," he reported cheerfully in a letter to a fellow refugee, Max Born, who was to win a Nobel Prize in physics in 1954.

Einstein was inclined to dismiss Nazism as a "state of psychic distemper in the masses," and he infuriated them by saying so in public. They, in turn, regarded this tousle-haired professor as the very embodiment of the German Jew, the totem of everything they hated about his kind. Shortly before the outbreak of the war, Hitler's ideological deputy, Alfred Rosenberg, delivered a speech demanding that "the Albert Einsteins" and other representative Jews be deported "to a wild island with a deadly climate . . . from where there is no return, from where there is but one exit—death." In so doing he was, in effect, serving notice on the whole of European Jewry as to the fate that was being prepared for them by the Third Reich.

It was no accident, noted the *New Statesman* in London, that the "Nazi lads" were venting their spleen against this "Charlie Chaplin with the brow of Shakespeare." He personified all the things they detested—"intellectualist, individualist, supernationalist, pacifist, inky, plump"—hence it was "unthinkable that the nasty lads should not kick Albert."

Indeed, both Einstein the menace to "Aryan physics" and Schoenberg the perverter of "Ayran music" were exceptionally well qualified for the role of whipping boy and bogeyman on the puppet stage of Nazi propaganda. Einstein had spent much of his professional career devising and defending a system of physics which by its very name, the "theory of relativity," seemed an affront to the certainties of German science. His life as a professor in Berlin, even after he had won the Nobel Prize in 1921, had been disrupted by countless incidents involving fascists and assorted cranks, roused to a now incomprehensible pitch of fury by the idea that time is not a fixed and immutable dimension. His situation in Berlin, he once remarked, was "like that of a man who is lying in a beautiful bed, tortured by bedbugs." In the end, he came away convinced that "the tyranny of the ignoramuses is insurmountable and assured for all time."

Schoenberg had spent most of his adult life formulating an almost equally esoteric theory—his so-called "method of composing with twelve tones related only to one another," better known as the twelve-tone technique. Though by no means as complex as relativity, it seemed to be comprehensible to just as few people. Yet Schoenberg, like Einstein, was not at all averse to working in an atmosphere of intellectual isolation. He seemed to take a certain quixotic pleasure in his own unpopularity, as though it confirmed the importance of his mission. During World War I when, at forty-three, he was briefly drafted into the Austrian army, a fellow soldier asked him whether he really was Arnold Schoenberg, the controversial modernist about whom so much had been written in the newspapers. Schoenberg thought for a moment and then conceded that he was the man. "But see here," he added. "Somebody had to be it, but nobody wanted to be, so I agreed to give myself for the purpose."

Earlier in the century, Schoenberg's music had precipitated a memorable series of Viennese concert-hall scandals. In 1905, at the premiere of his tone poem *Pelleas und Melisande,* the audience was "seized by a kind of madness" and made a rush for the doors in the middle of the piece. The same wild scene was repeated at the first performance of his First String Quartet two years later, when one particularly waggish listener led the way out through the emergency exit.* In 1908 there was a riot at the premiere of the Second String Quartet, with its mysterious, free-floating last movement in which a soprano soloist goes soaring off into a cantilena that seems to defy the musical laws of gravity. The words are by Stefan George:

> *I feel the air of other planets. . . .*
> *I dissolve into tones, circling, wreathing. . . .*
> *I feel as if I were swimming beyond the farthest cloud*
>   *in a sea of crystalline fire.*

At the unaccustomed sound of a soprano singing in a string quartet, a critic noted, "part of the audience first giggled, then laughed and became restless; some shouted to the performers to stop. . . . Marie Gutheil-Schoder, the soprano, stood on the podium exposed to the fury of this scene and went on singing in tears. Afterward the noise-makers demanded that the hall be aired out so that the walls would be worthy of receiving Beethoven's *Harp* Quartet, which was next on the program."

Most of the music critics had a field day depicting Schoenberg as a "fanatic of nihilism and disintegration." Even the Wagnerian *Pelleas* was "one long-drawn-out wrong note." His Chamber Symphony, opus 9, was nicknamed the Chamber-of-Horrors Symphony. His Three Piano Pieces, opus 11, were the subject of a devastating review by the Berlin critic Walter Dahms: "First a child taps the piano aimlessly, then a drunk smashes the keys like mad,

---

*Gustav Mahler was in the audience that night, loudly applauding Schoenberg's Quartet. Someone came up and stood next to him, ostentatiously hissing and whistling. Mahler turned on him furiously: "How can you presume to hiss when I'm applauding!" "I also hiss at your *Dreck*-symphonies" was the reply. Mahler: "I could tell that just by looking at your face!"

and at the end someone seats his —— on the keyboard." When Schoenberg came to Berlin, Dahms proposed taking up a collection to send him back where he came from: "Your antimusical impertinence contaminates the public taste for art." It was only a short step from there to the Nazi critics' view of Schoenberg as the leading representative of the *jüdische Zersetzungsgeist* in music—this terrible "Jewish tactic" supposedly intended to "destroy the cultural values of the host nation" in order to impose a new set of degenerate Jewish standards.

The tumult and the shouting at Schoenberg's concerts thus bore a more than superficial resemblance to the "exclamations and uproar" that greeted Einstein's defense of his theory of relativity at a meeting of the German Association of Scientists and Doctors in 1920. It seemed odd at the time that such abstract and apolitical exercises as music and physics should be capable of arousing such violent human passions. Einstein remarked that he couldn't see what all the fuss was about. "When Copernicus dethroned the earth from its position as the focal point of creation, the excitement was understandable," he told Count Harry Kessler. But relativity should produce no real change in humanity's view of things: "It is a theory which harmonizes with every reasonable outlook or philosophy and does not interfere with anybody being an idealist or materialist, pragmatist or whatever else he likes." Schoenberg, too, was surprised to find himself arraigned as a disturber of the peace. "I could never understand what I had done to make them so malicious, so violent and so aggressive," he wrote in later years. "I am still certain that I never took anything from them which was theirs."

Yet that was precisely the point at issue. In proposing a new approach to physics and tonality they may, after all, have robbed the German public of something it regarded as essential to its well-being—the categorical absolute that dinner's at seven and all's right with the world. The outcry over Einstein and Schoenberg was somehow central to the whole question of the German-Jewish intellectuals as the inveterate troublemakers and askers of questions—the so-called *Querulanten*—in German society. Every society, of course, has a certain intellectual inertia that accounts for the phenomenon known as the Nonacceptance of the Unfamiliar. It was in twentieth-century Germany, however, that the urge to cling to *das alte Wahre,* the old home truths, came to assume increasingly desperate and paranoid forms. It created, among other things, a vast literature of disenlightenment in which quacks of one sort or another taught that modern science, music and art were part of a giant plot to befuddle the upright German mind. Einstein's theory, argued the spokesmen of the association calling itself the *Antirelativistische GmbH* (Anti-Relativity Society), was first and foremost an offense against sound common sense.

"Think of it," wrote the pseudo-scientist Bruno Thüring in his exposé of *Einstein's Attempt to Overthrow Physics*, "now instead of one universally and eternally valid geometry, there could be many possible geometries; yes, theoretically as many geometries as one likes!" It was clear that if the Jews were allowed to continue in this fashion, the ground would soon be quaking under German feet.

In one of the essays he wrote during his years of exile in England, the émigré sociologist Karl Mannheim pointed out that "socially induced stupidity" is a common defensive reaction in certain authoritarian societies that are "set in their thought-ways; they do not advance towards new knowledge, much in the way in which old people refuse to learn." And old people tend to be immobile in their thinking, "not because they are biologically unable to learn new things, but because their claim to authority would be weakened if they conceded that they are not omniscient." Here was the root of the difficulty. Consciously or not, Einstein and Schoenberg represented an element of instability in a society preoccupied with the quest for *eine gesicherte Stellung*, an assured position, as secure as a job in the post office. With Einstein, or so it seemed at the time, the Absolute had once again become problematic and negotiable. In that sense, the theory of relativity was not only incomprehensible but also subversive. As Bruno Thüring summed up, "the Jewish plot to relativize all concepts and values must lead to chaos."

Surely it was not just a coincidence that, over and over again, it was the Jews who were chipping away at the foundations of German certitude. Whatever their politics or métier, if there was one connecting thread that ran from Heine and Marx to Freud, Schoenberg and Einstein, it was their indifference to revealed truth and secular authority. Nor was it only the hard-core Teutonists who had noticed the pattern: the word *Nörgler* (malcontent) meant the same thing in both German and Yiddish. "Wherever there was agitation," noted the novelist Jakob Wassermann, "wherever social demands were made, the Jews were in the front line. . . . Jews were the Jacobins of our epoch."

Needless to say, there were many Jews who tried to redress the balance by becoming more German than the kaiser. But the more original minds among them agreed with Kant that, with the Age of Reason, modern history had entered *das eigentliche Zeitalter der*

Kritik, the age of criticism par excellence, and they were determined to make the most of the opportunities it offered. Freud suggested that if one wanted to espouse new ideas or unpopular causes it was actually helpful to be Jewish—i.e., to have been born beyond the pale. In his own case, he said, it was "not entirely a matter of chance that the first advocate of psychoanalysis was a Jew. To profess belief in a new theory called for a certain degree of readiness to accept a position of solitary opposition—a position with which no one is more familiar than a Jew."

By the same token, Franz Boas wrote in his memoirs of the "unforgettable moment" in his youth when he first became aware that he had "the right to doubt what the past has transmitted to us," and when he suddenly felt free to challenge the implicit authority of the German and Jewish traditions to which he had been expected to conform. His life's work as an anthropologist was to center precisely on this problem of the psychological origins of tradition: "In fact my whole outlook upon social life is determined by the question: How can we recognize the shackles that tradition has laid upon us? For when we recognize them we are also able to break them."

In Einstein's case the "position of solitary opposition" had begun during his first years at school, in circumstances not unlike those that prevailed at Theodor Lessing's repressive Gymnasium of hard knocks. He was a late developer as a child—at the age of nine he was still unable to speak fluently—and afterward he remembered having hated the "convict atmosphere" and the "self-opinionated tone and customs" of the schools which he had to attend in Munich. In the lower grades the teachers "had the character of sergeants," while those "later in the Gymnasium were of the nature of lieutenants." (Indeed, many of his teachers were probably reserve lieutenants in the Bavarian army.)

As a consequence Einstein did badly in everything except mathematics, and eventually received his discharge with the remark that stands at the head of this chapter regarding his adverse effect on class discipline. Einstein's father had run a small electrical factory in Munich for a time, and when it failed he tried to launch a similar venture in Italy, again without success. At fifteen Einstein followed him to Milan, where as a token of his newfound freedom from compulsion, he renounced both his German citizenship and his membership in the Jewish community. To prepare for entry in the ETH—the Swiss Federal Polytechnic Institute in Zurich—he then spent a year at a Swiss cantonal school in Aarau. In those far more relaxed and democratic surroundings, he decided that he wanted to study physics rather than mathematics. But during his five years at the ETH he was obliged to teach himself most of what he wanted to know, since physics was taught by rote from obsolete textbooks. These were difficult years, for he had already recognized the shackles that tradition had laid upon theoretical physics, and his position as a student was that of a barely tolerated troublemaker. "He has no one who would support him and for a time he was nearly starving," wrote his classmate Friedrich Adler in 1909. "During his student days he was treated with contempt by the professors of the Polytechnic; they denied him the use of the library, and he was not capable of getting along with these people. Finally he found a job with the Patent Office in Bern but continued his theoretical work. . . . Now the situation is that on the one hand the professors have feelings of remorse because of their earlier behavior toward him and on the other hand one feels the scandal that such a man should sit in a Patent Office."

Yet it was as a twenty-five-year-old patent examiner in the spring of 1905 that he produced four extraordinary contributions to the literature of physics—his Ph.D. thesis on the determination of the size of molecules; his revolutionary paper on light quanta and the law of the photoelectric effect (for which he was to win the Nobel Prize sixteen years later); his paper on Brownian motion, which, as he said, "convinced the skeptics . . . of the reality of atoms," and finally the famous paper "On the Electrodynamics of Moving Bodies," which introduced the Special Theory of Relativity.

It was to be followed by more than a dozen other papers before Einstein left Bern to accept a professorship at the University of Zurich: among them was the historic exposition of relativity in the *Jahrbuch der Radioaktivität* for 1907 which contains, for the first time, the elegantly cosmic equation, $E=mc^2$. With its sequel, the General Theory of 1916, it represented, so to speak, a quantum leap into a new dimension of theoretical physics. If Einstein had not created the theory of relativity when he did, wrote C. P. Snow in 1972, "no one else would have done so, perhaps not until now, perhaps not for generations."

Einstein himself ascribed his achievement to the circumstance that he had always looked at the world through the eyes of a late developer. "Sometimes I ask myself," he wrote, "how it came about that I happened to be the one to discover the theory of relativity. The reason is, I think, that the normal adult never stops to think about space and time. Whatever thinking he may do about these things he will already have done as a small child. I, on the other hand, was so slow to develop that I only began thinking about space and time when I was already grown up. Naturally I then went more deeply into the problem than an ordinary child." Besides, his education had taught him to be, as he said, *eigenwillig, aber bescheiden* (self-willed but diffident). It had left him, too, with "a positively fanatical desire to be a free spirit, as well as with the impression that the state has a way of systematically lying to its youth." The result was an ingrained "distrust of every form of authority" that remained a prominent feature of his public personality, inducing him to stick out his tongue at press photographers, university professors and government officials with ungrudging impartiality. As one of his professors at the ETH told him during his first years in Zurich: "You are an intelligent lad, Einstein; a thoroughly intelligent lad. But you have one great defect: no one can tell you anything!"

Schoenberg, too, was largely self-taught—as a composer, painter and writer of Expressionist poetry and prose. His father, a shopkeeper who had come to Vienna from Bratislava, died poor when Arnold was sixteen. To support himself he left school and worked for several years, not very willingly, as an underpaid clerk in a small Vienna bank. Like Einstein he had taken violin lessons as a boy, and afterward taught himself how to play the cello. "One learns only what one knows anyhow," he liked to say. His first compositions were songs and duets, or string arrangements of operatic arias and the music he heard at band concerts. Then in 1894 he composed a fledgling string quartet which four of his friends performed for a distinguished teacher, Joseph Labor. When the first movement came to an end, remembered his friend Josef Bach, "Labor said very quietly, 'You have to become a musician.' All the objections—that he couldn't play the piano, that he was entirely self-taught—failed to shake Labor's conviction. Schoenberg became a musician."

He found a job as conductor of a metalworkers' choral society and hired himself out as an arranger of operettas and popular songs, turning out over six thousand pages of commercial orchestrations. This mountain of hack work interfered with more serious projects, but it taught him how to put his musical thoughts on paper with the fluency of a court stenographer.

His first major works—the tone poem *Verklärte Nacht* (Transfigured Night) and the *Gurrelieder* song cycle—were sufficiently close to the Brahms-Wagner tradition to earn him the reputation of being the most promising of the younger Viennese composers. The English critic Ernest Newman, who was to be anything but an admirer of the later Schoenberg, described the *Gurrelieder* as "the finest musical love poem since *Tristan*." Richard Strauss recommended him for a teaching post; Gustav Mahler provided a stipend to solve his most pressing financial problems. Yet Schoenberg was steadily moving toward that point of no return which he came to call "the emancipation of dissonance." By 1908 he had broken with the traditional principles of harmony, abandoning the use of key signatures and "tonal centers." Music critics promptly christened the new style "atonality," though Schoenberg and his followers would have preferred "undetermined tonality" or "floating tonality." It was, at any rate, ideally attuned to the darker currents of the early Freudian era: Expressionism, psychoanalysis and the Blue Rider school of painting.

Schoenberg's early operas foreshadow the German Expressionist films of the *Caligari* decade: most of the leading characters are dream figures that have just graduated from the Freudian Unconscious. In his 1909 monodrama *Erwartung* (Expectation), a solitary woman holds the stage for half an hour with only the moon and her lover's corpse for company. Schoenberg himself called it an *Angsttraum*, a nightmare, or more literally, a "fear dream." *Die Glückliche Hand* (The Hand of Fortune, 1913) presents a succession of dreamlike sequences about the temptations of a modern artist. Its autobiographical libretto was written by Schoenberg himself with the same painful honesty and deliberate clumsiness that characterized the pictures he was painting at the time—a series of Expressionist portraits and sketches which, as he was proud to record, were "highly praised by experts in the field." The most revealing of these curious canvases is the 1911 self-portrait in which his back is turned to the viewer and the world. "In your pictures I see a *great* deal," commented his friend Vassily Kandinsky. "This is what I foretold in my books as *fantasy in the hardest material.*"

But the culminating point of Schoenberg's prewar Expressionist style is the eerie pointillism of his 1912 song-cycle *Pierrot Lunaire*. This time it is the classic figure of Pierrot who stands in the inevitable moonlight, by the gallows tree, dreaming of Columbine, the Madonna, and his ancient home in Bergamo. The texts are "thrice seven poems" by the Belgian symbolist Albert Giraud, exquisitely rendered into German by Otto Erich Hartleben. Underscored by changing combinations of chamber instruments, they are not so much sung as declaimed in a sort of recitative that Schoenberg called *Sprechstimme*, a singsong incantation in "absolutely exact rhythm," compounded of bits of speech, fragments of song, long glissando sighs, groans, whispers. The cumulative effect is breathtaking. *"Pierrot Lunaire,"* writes the Berlin critic H. H. Stuck-enschmidt, "is one of the representative works of the twentieth century, as much as Pablo Picasso's *Man with the Guitar* or James Joyce's *Ulysses."*

World War I broke out just as Schoenberg arrived at the next phase of his harmonic evolution. Though too old for the trenches, he was twice conscripted for garrison duty between 1915 and 1917, with the result that he felt compelled to abandon his sketches for an oratorio, *Die Jakobsleiter* (Jacob's Ladder), with its allegorical "ladders" of chromatic melody. This immensely serious and dif-ficult score was intended to show, as he explained to a friend, "how the man of today, who has passed through materialism, socialism, anarchy; who has been an atheist, but has still preserved a remnant of ancient beliefs (in the form of superstition)—how this modern man struggles with God and finally arrives at the point of God and becoming religious. And learning to pray!"

It was while he was at work on the *Jakobsleiter* that he confided to his former pupil, Anton von Webern, that he was "on the way to an altogether new thing"—the twelve-tone technique with its "law" of structural tonality, in which a basic, nonrepetitive series of twelve notes determines the architecture of the entire piece. Its purpose was nothing less than the creation of a new harmonic system to take the place of classical harmony and to "break the barriers of a past aesthetic." Schoenberg saw it, not so much as a revolution, but as the logical outgrowth of the entire development of music from Bach to Brahms. It was, therefore, a product of the Austro-German classical tradition: hence his remark to one of his pupils that in formulating "the law" of twelve-tone music, "I have discovered something which will guarantee the supremacy of German music for the next hundred years."

In time Schoenberg was to develop his mastery of twelve-tone polyphony to the point where he could extrapolate an entire opera from the various inversions and permutations of a single twelve-note row. Composing in this fashion, he insisted, was not nearly as artificial or forbidding as most people believed. "It is primarily a method demanding logical order and organization. . . ." What mattered was not the technique but the result—a new sound, *ein neuer Klang.* "A new sound is an unintentionally discovered sym-bol which proclaims the new man who utters it," he declared in his *Harmonielehre,* the theory of harmony.

The twelve-tone system made such an impact on modern music that it was soon being compared to the theory of relativity. Actu-ally, the method owed something to magic squares and mystic numbers, but Schoenberg had the sense to realize that it was light-years removed from the complexities of space-time. "A problematic relationship between the science of mathematics as expressed by Einstein and the science of music as developed by myself has been suggested," he wrote. "There may be a relationship between the two fields of endeavor, but I have no idea what it is. . . ."

Indeed, if there was common ground between them, it lay not in the more obvious area of mathematics but in the remarkably parallel sweep of their extracurricular interests. Both were modern Renaissance men, dabbling in the arts, sciences, politics and practical invention. Einstein patented a camera; Schoenberg invented a music typewriter. Schoenberg made modern arrangements of Baroque composers. Einstein played Bach, Biber, Tartini and Corelli—he had an aversion to the Romantics and no ear for anything modern: "I feel uncomfortable listening to Beethoven. . . . Give me Bach rather, then more Bach."* Both men often wrote on subjects having nothing whatever to do with their fields of specialization, and the breadth of their interests is apparent from even a brief sampling of the titles listed in Einstein's bibliography and Schoenberg's *oeuvre* catalogue:

Peace Treaties	Education and World Peace
My War Psychosis and That of Others	Why War?
Advertising Language	The Meaning of American Citizenship
	Aphorisms
Aphorisms	Appeal for Jewish Unity
Notes on Jewish Politics	The Problem of Today and Tomorrow
Zeitwende (Turn of Time)	Greeting to George Bernard Shaw
The Singularity of Johann Strauss	Gandhi's Statesmanship

---

*Einstein's violin playing, though the subject of many a jest, is not to be confused with Jack Benny's. He was proficient enough to play in charity concerts, and he was not above announcing to a lecture audience: "It will perhaps be pleasant and more understandable if instead of making a speech I play a piece for you on my violin"—whereupon, writes Philipp Frank, he played a sonata by Mozart "in his simple, precise and doubly moving manner." Those who heard him as a young man speak of the "Hellenic beauty, mischievous grace and clarity of line" of his playing. In Aarau, he appeared as soloist with the school orchestra. "Say, do you count while you play?" a classmate asked him. Einstein's reply, "Oh no, never; it's in my blood," recalls Leibnitz's remark: *Musik ist die Lust der Menschenseele, welche zählt, ohne zu wissen, dass sie zählt* (Music is that pleasure of the human soul which arises from counting without one's being aware that one is counting).

On: Spanish Tennis
Why do we make it so difficult
   to our children and especially
   to our babies?
Sketches for a Highway
Stylistic Gems of My Lying
   Enemies
Against the Specialist
Streetcar Ticket: Letter to the
   management of the Berlin
   Streetcar Company with
   carefully worked-out
   sketches for a streetcar
   transfer

Some Thoughts Concerning
   Education

Let Us Save Liberty
Why Do They Hate the Jews?
A Message to Intellectuals
Conditions in Germany

Schoenberg once remarked that "everything I write bears a certain inner resemblance to me," and even this short list—his, needless to add, is the left-hand column—suggests the outlines of his difficult personality: restless, inventive, didactic, fussy about details. An artist who will go to the trouble of telling a streetcar company how to run its affairs is an artist whom nothing will ever satisfy. The singularity of Arnold Schoenberg arose from precisely this sense of *Unbehagen* with art and the world, with public transportation, traditional harmony, world politics, advertising copy. His chronic discontent turned him into something of an exile even while he was still on home ground. Toward the end of his life he compared his career to "falling into an ocean of boiling water; and as I couldn't swim and knew no other way out I struggled with my arms and legs as best I could."

One thing he could do supremely well: teach others how to write music. He loved teaching so much that, as Alban Berg noted, it formed "an inseparable part of his art." Outsiders usually assumed that he taught atonality and forced his pupils to adopt his style but, on the contrary, he taught no particular style and refrained from assigning any sort of routine exercises. "He advocates neither the use of old nor of new methods," testified Anton von Webern. "He says, 'What good is it to teach solutions to everyday problems? That way a student only learns the techniques he should not employ if he wants to become a creative artist.' " In his later years as a professor at UCLA, recalls the American composer John Cage, Schoenberg taught like a Zen master. "During a counterpoint class . . . Schoenberg sent everybody to the blackboard. We were to solve a particular problem he had given and to turn around when finished so that he could check on the correctness of the solution. I did as directed. He said, 'That's good. Now find another solution.' I did. He said, 'Another.' Again I found one. Again he said, 'Another.' And so on. Finally, I said, 'There are no more solutions.' He said, 'What is the principle underlying all of the solutions?' "

Einstein had used essentially the same sort of teaching method. Schools, he was convinced, were intended to produce "human beings, not merely mental machines." As a professor at Zurich University he would lecture ad lib from a single slip of paper, the size of a visiting card, on which he had jotted the main points he wanted to cover. Usually only a handful of students attended his lectures, and they were encouraged to interrupt and ask questions whenever they felt uncertain about a point—an almost unheard-of procedure at any European university. Afterward he and his students would sit together in a nearby café and discuss the new theoretical physics until closing time—the absurdly early *Polizeistunde* that still inhibits the nightlife of the Swiss. Sometimes, therefore, they were obliged to continue their discussions in Einstein's apartment until the small hours of the morning. One of his Swiss students, Hans Tanner, remembered that "it was Einstein's greatness as a scientist that he was able to approach every problem without being bound by traditional prejudices about it—not because he enjoyed criticism for its own sake, but because he had a deeply personal need to understand everything, and to see clearly."

When Max Brod (Kafka's friend and biographer) attended Einstein's classes at the German University of Prague in 1911, what struck him most was the young professor's habit of changing his point of view in mid-discussion, sometimes switching to a diametrically opposed standpoint in order to view the problem from a wholly new perspective. "He seemed to take real pleasure in trying out, with indefatigable energy, all the various scientific approaches to any given subject. He never tied himself down to only one point of view: teaching with humor and virtuosity, he would never detour around an ambiguity or a heterodoxy, yet he was always very sure of himself and retained his creative grasp." What set him apart from most of his colleagues was his willingness to be wrong. As Einstein himself wrote to a fellow physicist in 1911, "I have to discard almost every idea that occurs to me."

It was ironic that both of these incorrigible antiauthoritarians should end up with professorships in that most status-conscious of cultural institutions, the Prussian Academy. Einstein certainly had his doubts about accepting the call to Berlin in 1914: he was put off by the cold, unfriendly manner of the German professors, whom he had gone to such lengths to escape as an adolescent, and who had now, perforce, become his esteemed colleagues. "These cool blond people make me feel uneasy," he confessed. "They have no psychological comprehension of others. Everything must be explained very explicitly." But Berlin, with its Kaiser Wilhelm Institute, was the headquarters of German science, and at the time of his appointment it was said, not altogether facetiously, that of the dozen men in the world who really understood relativity, eight lived in Berlin. His professorship, moreover, involved no academic responsibilities, and left him free to devote all of his energies to theoretical speculation. Count Harry Kessler once asked Einstein, at a Berlin dinner party, what problems he was working on at the moment, and the reply was, "I am engaged in thinking." Einstein went on to explain the advantages of this unusual way of spending one's time, and Kessler was struck by "the ironical *(narquois)* trait in Einstein's expression, the *Pierrot Lunaire* quality, the smiling and pain-ridden skepticism that plays about his eyes. . . ."

The move to Berlin also represented a homecoming of sorts: it precipitated a divorce from his first wife, Milena Marcic, who had been a fellow student at the ETH, and brought him back together with his childhood playmate, Elsa Einstein, the quiet cousin who was to become his second wife. As the daughter of a prosperous businessman who had moved from Munich to Berlin, she contrived to surround her husband with all the bourgeois comforts of a well-ordered existence. There were paintings on the wall and carpets on the floor of their Berlin apartment, but Einstein seemed curiously out of place in this setting—a friend said it was as though he were "a Bohemian guest in a middle-class home."

Meanwhile, life in Berlin had exposed him to attitudes and prejudices he claimed not to have encountered before. "When I came to Germany," he wrote in 1929, "I discovered for the first time that I was a Jew, and I owe this discovery more to Gentiles than Jews. . . . I saw worthy Jews basely caricatured, and the sight made my heart bleed. I saw how schools, comic papers, and innumerable other forces of the Gentile majority undermined the confidence even of the best of my fellow Jews. . . ." His position of solitary opposition became still more isolated after the outbreak of World War I, since most of the German Jews joined the rush to the colors, leaving Einstein and a few fellow pacifists as a minority within a minority. While ninety-three leading German scientists, from Paul Ehrlich to Max Planck, signed a manifesto supporting Germany's "defensive" invasion of Belgium, Einstein succeeded in obtaining only one other signature for an antiwar manifesto that he and Georg Nicolai, professor of physiology, circulated among the professors of the University of Berlin. In March 1915 he wrote a letter to the French pacifist leader, Romain Rolland, openly condemning the war: "Must later centuries say of our century that Europe, after three hundred years of active cultural effort, had gone no further than from religious mania to nationalist mania? Even the scientists of the warring nations are behaving as though eight months ago their brains had been amputated. . . ."

Einstein's pacifism during the war years earned him the lasting hatred of the German jingoists and accounted for much of the controversy that surrounded his work in the 1920s. By then Sir Arthur Eddington had achieved experimental confirmation of relativity by observing and measuring the "Einstein deflection" of starlight near the sun, as predicted by the Relativity Theory, during the eclipse of 1919. The ensuing publicity had made him a household word, and Einstein found himself far too famous for comfort. "Like the man in the fairy tale who turned everything he touched into gold—so with me everything turns into a fuss in the newspapers," he wrote to Max Born in 1920. In Berlin the fuss was fueled by a group of *völkisch* nationalists who held a mass meeting at the Philharmonic auditorium to denounce Einstein's "Bolshevist" physics—"in the last analysis one cannot blame workers for being taken in by Marx, when German professors allow themselves to be misled by Einstein." During the meeting, the audience became aware that Einstein himself was an amused spectator, loudly applauding the speakers from a seat in one of the boxes. But the anti-Einstein movement was not entirely a laughing matter. It involved a bizarre chain of reasoning whose convolutions were neatly summarized in one of Kurt Tucholsky's articles in *Die Weltbühne*: "Our time needs the Absolute! Down with Einstein! We have to penetrate to the inner cause of things! *Heil!* Hurrah! Down with him! Kick him!"

By 1922 the agitation had reached such a pitch that Einstein was forced to call off a public lecture because, as he wrote to Max Planck, "I am supposed to be one of the people whom the *völkisch* side is planning to assassinate." He thought the trouble stemmed from the fact that "my name has been mentioned too often in the newspapers, and the rabble has been roused against me." Under the circumstances he proposed to take a trip and wait for the storm to blow over: "Please look on this with a sense of humor, as I'm doing."

It was also in 1922 that Schoenberg had his first head-on collision

Gustav Mahler

Sigmund Freud

Karl Wolfskehl

Hessiche Landes und Hochschulbibliothek, Darmstadt

Theodor Lessing

Carl Sternheim

Else Lasker-Schüler

Ernst Toller in prison, c. 1920

The poet Peter Hille (left) with Erich Mühsam

Albert Einstein

Ullstein Bilderdienst

Arnold Schoenberg in St. Petersburg, 1912

Franz Kafka

Kurt Tucholsky

Kurt Tucholsky Archiv, Rottach-Egern

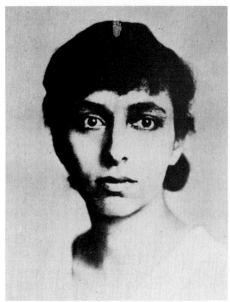

Gertrud Kolmar

Walter Benjamin

Alfred Doeblin as a German army surgeon during World War I

Hermann Broch

with postwar antisemitism. That summer he had gone to Mattsee, near Salzburg, for a working holiday à la Mahler, and had been refused accommodation because, as the polite phrase had it, Jews were *unerwünscht* (undesired). "I had to break off my first working summer in five years, leave the place where I had sought to find peace in which to work; afterward I was unable to regain any peace of mind. . . ." Like Einstein he had left Judaism many years before and, again like Einstein, had acquired a wife and two children who were at least nominally Christian. (Mathilde von Zemlinsky, his first wife, was the sister of the conductor Alexander von Zemlinsky, one of his oldest supporters.) Now he, too, was forcibly reminded of his residual Jewishness. "The lesson that has been forced on me this year, and which I shall never forget, is that I am not a German, not a European, indeed scarcely even a human being (at least the Europeans prefer the least of their race to me), but that I am a Jew."

Vassily Kandinsky, who had helped establish the Bauhaus School of Design in Weimar, wrote to him in the spring of 1923 proposing that Schoenberg join the faculty. But the composer was given to understand that Jews, on the whole, were also *unerwünscht* at the Bauhaus, although an exception would be made in his case. Schoenberg's reply was an impassioned protest against what he regarded as the height of effrontery—this rising tide of intolerance whose ultimate consequences he could foresee only too clearly:

> . . . when I walk along the street and each person looks at me to see whether I'm a Jew or a Christian, I can't very well tell each of them that I'm the one that Kandinsky and some others make an exception of, although of course that man Hitler is not of their opinion. And then even this benevolent view of me wouldn't be much use to me, even if I were, like blind beggars, to write it on a piece of cardboard and hang it round my neck for everyone to read. . . .
>
> I ask: Why do people say that the Jews are like what their black-marketeers are like?
>
> Do people also say that the Aryans are like their worst elements? Why is an Aryan judged by Goethe, Schopenhauer and so forth? Why don't people say the Jews are like Mahler, Altenberg, Schoenberg and many others?
>
> . . . And yet you join in that sort of thing and "reject me as a Jew." Did I ever offer myself to you? Do you think that someone like myself lets himself be rejected! Do you think that a man who knows his own value grants anyone the right to criticize even his most trivial qualities? Who might it be, anyway, who could have such a right?
>
> . . . How can a Kandinsky approve of my being insulted; how can

he associate himself with politics that aim at bringing about the possibility of excluding me from my natural sphere of action; how can he refrain from combating a view of the world whose aim is St. Bartholomew's nights in the darkness of which no one will be able to read the little placard saying that I'm exempt!

. . . But what is antisemitism to lead to if not to acts of violence? Is it so difficult to imagine that? You are perhaps satisfied with depriving Jews of their civil rights. Then certainly Einstein, Mahler, I and many others will have been got rid of. But one thing is certain: they will not be able to exterminate those much tougher elements thanks to whose endurance Jewry has maintained itself unaided against the whole of mankind for twenty centuries. . . .

Schoenberg ultimately patched up his quarrel with Kandinsky, but it was the Prussian Academy and not the Bauhaus that offered him a professorship. In Vienna, meanwhile, the atonalists had made little headway. Their Society for Private Performances, founded after the war to encourage modern music of all kinds, had managed to attract only two hundred regular subscribers—just one ten-thousandth, according to Schoenberg's rueful calculations, of the city's population. After the death of his first wife he had married Gertrud Kolisch, sister of the violinist Rudolf Kolisch, and his fiftieth birthday—September 13, 1924—was celebrated with a serenade at the Town Hall, a message from the mayor, and a special issue of the magazine *Musikblätter des Anbruch*. Yet the State Academy of Music still resisted appointing an atonalist to its faculty, and when the Berlin offer came he was not at all sorry to leave Vienna. "I want to depart just as unnoticed as I always was when I lived here," he told one of the newspapers. In his new post he was expected to teach only six months of the year, leaving him free to spend long holidays in Switzerland and Spain. "At least, after years of neglect, again a beginning," he wrote to Webern after moving to Berlin in 1926. There were special concerts in his honor, performances of his operas in several German cities, invitations to lecture abroad and guest-conducting appearances in London, Paris, Barcelona.

The seven years in Berlin were a time for testing the wings of twelve-tone music. He applied "the law" to such traditional forms as the scherzo, the rondo, the gigue. In the *Variations for Orchestra*, introduced by Wilhelm Furtwängler and the Berlin Philharmonic in 1928, he gave a brilliant demonstration of the Bach-like ease with which he could devise twelve-tone solutions to the most complex problems of counterpoint. For another group of twelve-tone experiments, the *Six Pieces for Male Chorus*, he wrote free-wheeling texts

of his own in lieu of the pious chorale verses used by his predecessors. The results are sometimes very funny, notably the piece that
begins: "Someone helps you into the world—God bless you!
Someone digs a grave for you—Rest in peace! They patch up your
wounds at the hospital—Get well!" And the moral of the chorus:
"Go on, try to deny that you, too, belong—you're not alone!" As a
group they constitute one of the earliest avant-garde efforts to
"sing it like it is" without poetic elaboration; in fact, without any
real attempt at literary style. Yet in spite of their apparent
formlessness "the law" was very much on Schoenberg's mind
when he wrote them:

> *If it happens the way one expects it,*
> *that is in order; one can understand that.*
> *But if it happens otherwise, it is a miracle.*
>
> *And yet, just reflect:*
> *the fact that it always happens the same way,*
> *that, surely, is the miracle*
> *which you should find incomprehensible.*
> *The fact that there is a law*
> *which all things obey*
> *as you do your Lord;*
> *and which orders things*
> *as your Lord orders you:*
> *This is what you should recognize as a miracle!*
> *The fact that one rebels*
> *is self-evident and banal.*

At the same time he began writing both text and music for *Moses
und Aron,* an immense biblical opera embodying "the central tenets
of my thinking" on many aspects of art and philosophy. Musically
the entire score grows out of a single twelve-tone row that assumes
an endless multiplicity of shapes, including some of the most pro-
tean fugues and canons in the history of music. Dramatically it
focuses on the conflict between matter and spirit; the Golden Calf
versus the Tables of the Law. Moses perceives "the inexpressible,
many-sided idea" of God but cannot convey his vision to Aaron
and the people: his laborious *Sprechstimme* role provides a stark
contrast to Aaron's fluent singing part. In the end, when Moses
destroys the Golden Calf, it has become the symbol of his power-
lessness "to enclose the boundless in a finite image."

Only two acts of *Moses* were completed before the Nazis drove
Schoenberg from Berlin. Afterward, as with the *Jakobsleiter,* he
never again "found the right mood" for finishing the score. But
posthumous productions have shown that the existing acts can

stand by themselves as an evening-filling experience—one of the most complex and demanding operas in the modern repertoire.

Schoenberg and his family arrived in America in October 1933, and he spent his first winter teaching composition at the Malkin Conservatory, a small private music school with branches in Boston and New York. But the New England climate aggravated the asthma from which he had been suffering for several years, and after one serious attack he was persuaded to move to southern California. Here, too, in the midst of the Depression, it was not easy even for "probably the greatest of contemporary German composers" (as he was billed in Los Angeles) to find ways of earning a living. When his initial lectures at the University of Southern California failed to attract more than a handful of students he was moved to wonder, in his still rather tentative English, "What have the people and the society of Los Angeles taken of the advantage offered by Schoenberg?" He wrote to the conductor Hermann Scherchen, in Switzerland, that as a teacher he was more dissatisfied than ever. "Unfortunately, my students are so inadequately prepared that my work is as much a waste of time as if Einstein were having to teach mathematics at a secondary school."

Still, life in Los Angeles had its compensations. The smog had not yet settled in over the city, and Schoenberg was enchanted by what he saw: "It is Switzerland, the Riviera, the Vienna Woods, the desert, the Salzburg region, Spain, Italy—all together in one place. And withal, hardly a day without sun." Besides, in the words of another Viennese refugee, the satirist Alfred Polgar: "If you have fallen on hard times, you will have better hard times in California. . . . You can live here in more comfortably straitened circumstances than anywhere else."

After Schoenberg was appointed professor of music at UCLA in 1936 he soon became adjusted to the syncopated rhythm of this life in the sun: despite his continental manner and ineradicable accent, he became Americanized in his own fashion even before receiving U. S. citizenship in 1941. He moved to a suburban house in Brentwood Park where, as Darius Milhaud discovered, he was "surrounded by the happy din made by his two little boys [Rudolf and Adam, both born in America], whom even the gentleness of their mother and sister is powerless to subdue." He took up do-it-yourself carpentry and built his own furniture. Tennis had always been his favorite form of recreation: when George Gershwin came to Hollywood to compose songs for the movies, they often played together on Gershwin's court. Perhaps partly on that account, Schoenberg grew to like Gershwin's music, which was so very different from his own—yet it "expressed musical ideas and they were new." The last thing Gershwin painted before his sudden death in 1937 was an affectionate portrait of Schoenberg, not in his tennis persona but wearing the sterner mien of prophet and lawgiver.

Most of his new neighbors, in fact, found him a rather daunting personality. "He could be as churlish as he could be charming," wrote the conductor Otto Klemperer, a sometime pupil with whom the composer was not always on the best of terms. Klemperer noted that Schoenberg only liked to play tennis and Ping-Pong against opponents who would let him win, and by the same token he would get very annoyed with people who were less than enthusiastic about his music.

On the other hand, kindred spirits among the exiles found him extremely funny when he wanted to be, especially during the happy evenings at Brentwood Park when Schoenberg gave readings from Karl Kraus in an appropriately jaunty Viennese accent. As more and more refugees arrived in Los Angeles, there were reunions with such old friends and distinguished contemporaries as Alma Mahler and Franz Werfel, Thomas Mann, Bertolt Brecht, Theodor Adorno and Hanns Eisler. Yet these were not celebrities on tour; they were people who had been forced to flee for their lives. And although they themselves had found refuge, they had to endure the tragedy of standing by helplessly while a civilization was being destroyed in Europe—a civilization in large part of their own making. "It is so sad," Schoenberg wrote to the conductor Alfred Hertz in 1938, "that all these people with the finest musical culture of Europe are being driven out and must spend the last years of their lives in grief, sorrow and need."

Like most émigré intellectuals, Schoenberg was alternately fascinated and repelled by such distinctive American phenomena as radio commercials and soap operas. He quoted advertising slogans in letters to his friends, and lectured a newly arrived son-in-law on how to behave if he landed a job with an American corporation. He had taken a close look at the organization man, and concluded that American business mores demanded some of the skills of a Florentine courtier: "Above all . . . keep differences of opinion to yourself. Obsequiousness is unnecessary and is regarded as tiresome. But everything must be said in a friendly way, *smiling*"—here Schoenberg used the English word—"always smiling."

Though he lived next door to Hollywood, Schoenberg never worked in the movie industry. He was offered a chance to do so only once—when Irving Thalberg, "the last tycoon," heard *Ver-*

klärte Nacht on the radio and decided to ask Schoenberg to compose a score for his next film, *The Good Earth*. The émigré screen writer, Salka Viertel, who brought Schoenberg to Thalberg's office, remembered the scene in her autobiography, *The Kindness of Strangers*:

> I still see him before me, leaning forward in his chair, both hands clasped over the handle of the umbrella, his burning, genius's eyes on Thalberg, who, standing behind his desk, was explaining why he wanted a great composer for the scoring of *The Good Earth*. When he came to: "Last Sunday when I heard the lovely music you have written . . ." Schoenberg interrupted sharply: "I don't write 'lovely' music."

When Thalberg proceeded to describe the "Chinese" score he had in mind, Schoenberg ventured the opinion that conventional film music was terrible, meaningless and inexpressive. He would accept the assignment only if he were given complete control of the sound, including the spoken words: he would write out the speaking parts in pitch and key, as in *Pierrot Lunaire*, and personally rehearse the performance with the actors. Thalberg, though taken aback, "did not move a muscle of his face," and confined himself to pointing out that the director also wanted to handle the actors himself. "He could do that after they have studied their lines with me," Schoenberg assured him. Predictably, nothing came of the project, particularly since Schoenberg demanded "an absolute guarantee that nothing will be changed in my score." But Salka Viertel recalled that when she discussed the episode with Schoenberg a few days later, he told her: *"Komponieren heisst einen Blick in die Zukunft des Themas werfen"* (To compose means to cast a glance into the future of the theme), and she confesses: "I was very moved by these words."

In Vienna and Berlin, Schoenberg had gone out of his way to avoid having to teach beginners. At UCLA, however, most of the students in his composition classes knew only the rudiments of music and had no intention of becoming professional composers. Schoenberg decided to make a virtue of necessity by developing new techniques for the education of amateurs. "Just as almost anyone can be trained to draw, paint, write an essay or deliver a lecture," he reasoned, "it must also be possible to make people with even less than mediocre gifts use the means of musical composition in a sensitive manner." Learning how to compose, he felt, was the best way of training young amateurs "to help them understand music better, to obtain that pleasure which is inherent in the art."

As an educational experience, studying music with Schoenberg was, indeed, rather like taking freshman physics with Enrico Fermi—as it happens, we did both at the University of Chicago in the late 1940s. I remember the excitement of hearing Schoenberg lecture at Chicago in 1946, when he was already past seventy—a gnomelike figure whose wispy voice filled us with awe and admiration. I realized then, for the first time, that his much maligned twelve-tone method was neither a kabalistic formula nor an aesthetic straitjacket, but rather, an outgrowth of the Bach tradition, and the key to a vast range of new possibilities in music. At the same time he was giving a magnificent demonstration of how best to perform the cultural function that Karl Mannheim had assigned to the refugee intellectual—"to serve as a living interpreter between different cultures and so create living communication between different worlds which so far have been kept apart."

Albert Einstein and his wife had also arrived in America in October 1933, but there was no need for him to teach undergraduates for a living. His arrangement with the newly founded Institute for Advanced Study in Princeton left him, even more than before, completely free to engage in thinking. Life in Princeton suited him so perfectly that it seemed as though he had been "exiled into paradise." Soon he was back at work on the elusive Unified Field Theory which was to remain the focal point of his scientific thinking for the rest of his life. The outward sign of his adjustment to America was the cotton sweatshirt that he liked to wear on all except the most formal occasions. There were, of course, periodic appearances that called for a jacket: dinner with the Roosevelts at the White House; speeches on behalf of refugee organizations; charity concerts; a trip to Harvard University to collect an honorary doctorate together with Thomas Mann (it was rumored that FDR, an influential alumnus, had personally recommended them both). He, who had never really felt at home in any country, was delighted to be living in America, in Princeton, in his wooden house at No. 112 Mercer Street, within walking distance of his cluttered office at the institute. "I have settled down splendidly here," he wrote to Max Born in 1937. "I hibernate like a bear in its cave, and really feel more at home than ever before in all my varied existence."

Yet even in his cave there was no way he could avoid further entanglement in the affairs of the outer world. He was mystified though not entirely displeased at being celebrated in the press as a sort of modern saint-*cum*-enfant-terrible; at least it was a change from bomb threats. "I really can't understand why I have been made into a kind of idol," he wrote to Mrs. Born. "I supposed it is just as incomprehensible as why an avalanche should be triggered off by *one particular* particle of dust, and why it should take a certain course." He had also become, if not the leader of the "Jewish opposition" pictured by Nazi propaganda, then at any rate the representative Jewish refugee, symbol and rallying point for the intellectual emigration from Hitler's Europe.

As a physicist, his obstinate refusal to accept the indeterminacy principle of quantum mechanics—his insistence that "God does not play dice with the world"—had long since isolated him from the mainstream of theoretical physics. It was on account of his name, therefore, and not because of the work he was doing at the time, that Einstein was asked by his worried colleagues, Leo Szilard and Eugene Wigner, to sign the famous letter alerting Roosevelt to the dangers and potentialities of atomic energy. Research into atomic fission in Berlin was known to be well advanced, and it seemed reasonable to suppose that the Germans would be the first to build an atomic bomb (indeed, they were ultimately prevented from doing so only because the Nazis had decimated the German scientific establishment). Altogether, Einstein signed three warning letters to the president, which helped prepare the ground for the Manhattan Project.

Afterward he himself was the first to recognize the terrible irony of his role in this affair: that he, who had been a pacifist for so long, should have encouraged the development of the most destructive weapon in the history of mankind. It was, he admitted, his "one great mistake." In point of fact he played no part in the research that led to the production of the bomb: though $E=mc^2$ was at the heart of the matter, he was not privy to the secrets of the Manhattan Project. It has been suggested that his background as a pacifist-socialist-internationalist would have disqualified him as a "security risk" on the project. But the U. S. Navy's Bureau of Ordnance had no compunctions about consulting him for more than three years on the theoretical physics of conventional high explosives. At any event, when he heard of the impending completion of the bomb, in April 1945, he supported Szilard's belated and futile attempt to persuade the government not to employ the bomb against Japan. In the Einstein biography that Banesh Hoffmann wrote in collaboration with the professor's secretary, Helen Dukas, there is a sobering glimpse of him on August 6, 1945, the day the bomb exploded over Hiroshima:

> Einstein's secretary heard the news on the radio. When Einstein came down from his bedroom for afternoon tea she told him. And he said,

"*Oh weh,*" which is a cry of despair whose depth is not conveyed by the translation "Alas."

Toward the end of his life Einstein was still at work on the problem that Schoenberg's Moses had failed to solve: to enclose the boundless in a finite image. He was engaged, as he wrote to Born, "in a rather daring attempt to get to a unified physics, after trying vainly so many times before." It was to be a "mighty leap forward in our thinking," but he could not be certain of success; it was as though he were fated to see the promised land—or rather, the unified field—from afar, and yet be barred from entering it with any theory capable of proof. "The calculation difficulties are so great that I will be biting the dust before I myself can be fully convinced of it," he wrote to Born in the course of a series of letters on the problem:

> You believe in the God who plays dice, and I in complete law and order in a world which objectively exists, and which I, in a wildly speculative way, am trying to capture. I firmly *believe,* but I hope that someone will discover a more realistic way, or rather a more tangible basis than it has been my lot to find.

Two other subjects remained of overriding concern during his last years: the cause of world peace and the fate of the Jews who had survived the Holocaust. With the defeat of the Axis powers he returned to his earlier dream of a world without war or violence, united under a world government that would outlaw the use of weapons of mass destruction. "We scientists," he wrote, "whose tragic destiny it has been to help make the methods of annihilation ever more gruesome and more effective, must consider it our solemn and transcendent duty to do all in our power in preventing these weapons from being used for the brutal purpose for which they were intended."

Since the early 1920s he had dreamed, too, of a Jewish homeland in Palestine, although "my awareness of the essential nature of Judaism resists the idea of a Jewish state with borders, an army, and a measure of temporal power no matter how modest. I am afraid of the inner damage Judaism will sustain—especially from the development of a narrow nationalism within our own ranks. . . ." When the state of Israel was established in 1948 it fell short of being the peaceable kingdom he had wanted it to be, where the Jews would live "side by side with our brother the Arab" in something like Mozartean harmony. No matter: it was a beginning, and Einstein was filled with "joy and admiration" for what had been accomplished. Now, as he said in a fund-raising broadcast, the most urgent priority was to rescue "our endangered brethren, dispersed in many lands, by uniting them in Israel." Peace with the Arabs would follow in due course, "for we *want* peace and we realize that our future development depends on peace."

When he himself was offered the presidency of Israel in 1952, after the death of Chaim Weizmann, Einstein declined politely on the grounds that he lacked "both the natural aptitude and the experience to deal properly with people" in a political context. He regretted his decision all the more because, as he said, "my relationship to the Jewish people has become my strongest human bond, ever since I became fully aware of our precarious situation among the nations of the world." It was a remarkable avowal from a man who had, by his own account, "discovered for the first time that I was a Jew" when he was in his midthirties.

Einstein died in Princeton, at the age of seventy-six, in 1955. Schoenberg had died five years earlier, in Brentwood Park, also at the age of seventy-six. The Judaism which he, too, had only rediscovered under the pressure of political events, had come to be an increasingly dominant element in his work and thought. His sense of solidarity with the Jews found its most powerful expression in his last dramatic score, *A Survivor from Warsaw*, which presents a terrifying scene from the massacre of Polish Jews under the Nazi occupation—a brief, flickering vision, like the sudden opening of the doors to an inferno. Schoenberg wrote the text himself, in English, grimly noting on the cover of the score that it was "based partly upon reports which I have received directly or indirectly." Musically it is one of his most extraordinary works: the climax of his twelve-tone Expressionism and the fulfillment of his *Angsttraum* premonitions of forty years before. If the twelve-tone method had created nothing else, it would have been justified by this one achievement—the only great musical work of art to come out of the crucible of Jewish experience in the Holocaust. Certainly no other harmonic idiom could have done justice to the subject.

Schoenberg had never been robust, and after 1944 he was often ill: "First I had diabetes, then I suffered increasingly from asthma. Then came attacks of dizziness, fainting and disturbed vision." During one long illness his heart stopped beating and he actually experienced "clinical death" before being revived by an injection into the heart. "I have risen from real death," he wrote to Stuckenschmidt, "and now feel very well." He had lived long enough to see his "law" vindicated, for the twelve-tone method had proved to be the point of departure for the whole of modern music in the postwar years. Even his old rival Stravinsky was to adopt the "serial" technique for the most important music of his old age.

In the last year of his life Schoenberg wrote a group of "psalms, prayers and other talks with and about God." Only one of these was set to music before his death. "The text is like a summation of everything that Schoenberg created, and of everything he suffered," wrote his pupil Winfried Zillig. "And it is of a mysterious significance that at the words, 'And still I pray,' death took the pen from the composer's hand."

> *. . . Und trotzdem bete ich, wie alles Lebende*
> *betet, trotzdem erbitte ich Gnaden und Wunder;*
> *Erfüllungen . . .*

> And yet I pray, as everything living
> prays, and yet I ask miracles and grace;
> Fulfillments . . .

VI

TRIALS AND TRIBULATIONS

> *. . . My people, provided that I have one.*
> —FRANZ KAFKA, Letters

T wo young men from Berlin on a visit to Prague, Kurt Tucholsky and Kurt Szafranski, made Franz Kafka's acquaintance in September 1911. Kafka was twenty-eight and still virtually unknown as a writer, except for a few prose pieces that had appeared in Sternheim's avant-garde magazine *Hyperion*. Tucholsky, at twenty-one, was just setting out to be a writer. He had published one or two essays and was on the verge of producing a whimsical modern love story, *Rheinsberg*, for which Szafranski drew an elegant set of illustrations, and which was to become an instant best-seller.

Max Brod, at whose home they met Kafka, later recalled that they resembled a pair of journeymen artisans, and that they had brought him a cardboard model of a Czech village complete with cows, geese and goose-girls. Kafka, who was intrigued by these visitors, listened carefully to the way they spoke their native dialect and made a note in his diary about "this aspirated *Berlinerisch* in which the voice seems to require breathing spaces consisting of the sound *nich*." Tucholsky impressed him as "an entirely consistent person of twenty-one"—

From the controlled and powerful swing of his walking-stick that gives a youthful lift to his shoulders to the deliberate delight in and contempt for his own literary works. Wants to be a defense lawyer, sees only a few obstacles and at the same time how they may be overcome: his clear voice that after the manly sound of the first half-hour of talk pretends to become revealingly girlish—doubt of his own

capacity to pose, which, however, he hopes to get with more experience of the world—fear, finally, of changing into a melancholic, as he
has seen in older Berlin Jews of his type, in any event for the time
being he sees no sign of this. He will marry soon.

It was not surprising that Kafka should have known so much
about Tucholsky after a single encounter; he was the kind of gifted
listener to whom people always confessed everything that was on
their mind. Besides, he felt a distinct affinity for this Berliner: "Yesterday evening, on the way home, if I had observed myself from
the outside I should have taken myself for Tucholsky. . . ."
Though they did not look alike, their lives seemed to run in parallel
channels. Both were the sons of Jewish businessmen who had
worked their way up from the lower rungs of the social ladder;
both had experienced the requisite conflicts with parents and
teachers, but had survived the exigencies of an educational process
that Tucholsky once described in a thumbnail report: "German: a
ridiculous dismembering of the classics, fatuous essays, sloppily
and unintelligibly corrected. . . . History: a senseless, incoherent
compilation of dynastic dates. . . . Geography: tributaries, government districts, names of cities. Latin: learned by rote; I never
got to the point of being able to read a Latin author. Greek: see
Latin. French: indescribable."
Kafka, too, had often thought it over, "and then I always have to
say that my education has done me great harm in some ways."
Still, one learns when one needs a way out, and both had learned
at all costs, going on to university to study law—Kafka had become
Doctor of Jurisprudence in 1906, while Tucholsky was not to attain
that eminence until 1914. Since they wanted to be writers, not
lawyers, neither of them practiced law, but they remained very
much preoccupied with the idea of justice, or rather with the problem of injustice in a world ruled by brute force and an insufferable
bureaucracy. One of Kafka's services to German literature was that
he wrote of the plight of the humiliated and oppressed in a system
of authority which, as K. says in *The Trial*, "not only employs
corrupt warders, stupid Inspectors, and Examining Magistrates of
whom the best that can be said is that they recognize their own
limitations, but also has at its disposal a judicial hierarchy of high,
indeed of the highest rank, with an indispensable and numerous
retinue of servants, clerks, police, and other assistants, perhaps
even hangmen, I do not shrink from that word." Tucholsky did not
shrink from it either: he wrote a long series of hectoring essays and
Villon-like *Lieder* on the subject of capital punishment and law

reform. His protest-ballad *Das Gesetz* (The Law) calls on the members of parliament who "sit in the Reichstag and fiddle away at new laws" to begin by tempering justice with mercy:

> *Wach auf, wach auf, Barmherzigkeit!*
> *Ein neuer Ton—eine neue Zeit!*

> Wake up, wake up; we need compassion!
> A new tone, a new time—a new fashion!

Thanks to their legal training, both Kafka and Tucholsky were thoroughly versed in Officialese, the harsh, bureaucratic language of the military and the ministries, which had been employed as an instrument of oppression since the days of Frederick the Great. It is a special third-person language, rigorous and impersonal, that allows a judge to communicate with the accused across a total vacuum of emotion. Kafka mimics this voice of authority in *The Trial*, *The Castle*, *The Penal Colony*, where it is spoken by wardens, inspectors, lawyers and the assorted hypocrites whom he satirizes as part of his generalized critique of pure cant. Translators often have trouble rendering its implacability into English. "Perhaps it strikes you that I talk almost like a jurist?" says the painter Titorelli to the accused, K. "It's my long association with the gentlemen of the Court that has made me grow like that. I have many advantages from it, of course, but I'm losing a great deal of my élan as an artist."

Tucholsky could see Officialese gradually spreading out and engulfing the private sector. "Why is it," he asked, "that the very civilians who have suffered so much under the rule of the bureaucrats are so busy copying them? . . . Every moving company sends out letters that sound like army orders. The recipient is cudgeled with curt phrases until reels the mind. . . ." He supposed that even love letters would soon be written in this idiom:

1. My inclination toward you unchanged.
2. Rendezvous tonight at 1930 Hours, second exit of Zoo.
3. Clothing requirements: green dress, green hat, brown shoes. Carrying of umbrella is recommended.
4. Evening meal at Gambrinus, 2010 Hours.
5. Tenderness may be anticipated at my apartment afterwards.

(Signed) Bosch, Head Book-keeper

Tucholsky believed almost to the bitter end that there was hope for Germany and the world; despite his incessant criticism, his position was essentially that of a Berlin optimist. Kafka, in the depths of his pessimism, believed that there was "plenty of hope, an infinite amount of hope . . . but not for us." The result was a curious blend of rebelliousness and resignation. As Elias Canetti says about *The Castle*: "No author ever wrote a clearer attack on subjection to the superior, whether one views the latter as a higher power or as a merely terrestrial one. For all sovereignty has here become one, and is shown to be abominable." Walter Benjamin, on the other hand, quotes from the last sentence of *The Trial*—"It was as if he meant the shame of it to outlive him"—to support his thesis that "shame is Kafka's strongest gesture."

Kafka himself, in his diaries and letters, kept a painfully detailed account of the shame and embarrassment that beset his existence at every turn. Even in the presence of people who were friendly toward him his attitude was "always respectful and embarrassed"; he had a way of feeling "so very small while they all stood around me like giants." When he listened to himself talking to Franz Blei, a critic who was one of his staunchest admirers, "it sounded like the whimpering of a young cat." To his fiancée, Felice Bauer, he admitted quite candidly that "fear, next to indifference, is the basic feeling I have toward people." One has the impression that if all the self-reproaches were to be deleted from his correspondence there would be nothing left of it. "I fear that no single member of your family will be pleased with me," wrote the prospective bridegroom in 1913, "that nothing I will do will seem right to them, that even what I write in my first letter won't be to their liking." But Walter Benjamin points out that "shame is not only shame in the presence of others, but can also be shame one feels for them":

> Kafka's shame, then, is no more personal than the life and thought which govern it and which he has described thus: "He does not live for the sake of his own life, he does not think for the sake of his own thought. He feels as though he were living and thinking under the constraint of a family. . . . Because of this unknown family . . . he cannot be released." We do not know the make-up of this unknown family, which is composed of human beings and animals. But this much is clear: it is this family that forces Kafka to move cosmic ages in his writings. Doing this family's bidding, he moves the mass of historical happenings as Sisyphus rolled the stone.

Albert Camus (who loved Kafka) interpreted the myth of Sisyphus to mean that there is no fate which cannot be overcome by scorn. Kafka's achievement is not that he repressed his shame but that he summoned up the immense reserves of strength needed to bring it into the open; to produce the definitive portrait of the Kafka who lives in all of us, crying to get out. This one small

German-Jewish writer from Prague grappled with the phenomenon of *Angst*, discovered it to be a primordial as well as universal
experience, and defeated it in the very act of becoming its victim—
"the *Angst* of which I have spoken so often, but *Angst* expanded to
include everything, *Angst* of the largest as of the smallest, convul-
sive *Angst* before the enunciation of a word. . . ." This victory
demanded far greater courage than the conventional heroism then
being urged on Kafka's Europe (in Berlin, the kaiser could be seen
on Sunday parades wearing a golden helmet that glittered in the
sun). It involved the rock-hard core of work and self-discipline
that, paradoxically, so often characterizes the career of consump-
tive artists like Kafka and Chopin, each of whom was said to be
"dying all his life." Schumann once wrote of Chopin that his music
reminded him of "cannon buried in flowers." By the same token,
Kafka's will was no less iron for being wreathed in anxieties. "I
make of my reproach and laughter a drumbeat sounding into the
world beyond," he wrote at the beginning of his diaries.*

He was conscious of possessing a stabilizing purpose that kept
him functioning as a writer, for "I too have my center of gravity
inside me from birth," though at times it turned to lead and "sticks
in the body like a musket ball." The imagery he uses for his state of
mind is always of wounds and injuries—"the world and I are tearing my body apart in an insoluble conflict"—and yet the writing is
marvelously intact and all of a piece. His books, as Alfred Doeblin
remarked, could only have been written by "a very deep, free,
clairvoyant human being, a wholly integrated person." Kurt
Tucholsky, too, came to see them as the product of a writer with a
unique ferocity of will:

> Of Tamerlane it is said that he once had his prisoners cemented
> together to make a wall, a shrieking wall, that slowly twitched into
> silence. This work is something like that. A god transforms a world,
> puts it together anew, a heart appears in the heavens and beats but
> does not shine, a fetish moves, an apparatus becomes alive only
> because it is there and the question "why?" is pointless, almost as
> pointless as in the real world. All the pieces are there but they are
> seen as a patient shortly before the operation sees the surgeon's in-
> struments: sharply in focus, very clearly, very materially—but behind
> the gleaming pieces there is something else; *Angst* shrieks from the
> pores of the material, the operating table stands there mercilessly;
> have pity! says the sick man to the table as well. It is so alien and yet

---

*"What is a poet?" asks Kierkegaard in the opening sentence of *Either/Or*. "An
unhappy man who in his heart harbors a deep anguish, but whose lips are so
fashioned that the moans and cries which pass over them are transformed into
ravishing music."

somehow allied to him. Kafka's is the kind of will that is possessed by founders of sects and religions—he has written books, a few, unattainable books that can never be exhausted by the reading of them. Had the Creator willed it otherwise, and had Kafka been born in Asia, millions would hang on his words and meditate on them their whole life long.

When Kafka writes, in one of his innumerable confessions, "I am nothing but literature and can and want to be nothing else," he comes close to defining the center of gravity that has helped him "remain upright" over the years. Writing is "a form of prayer" for him, and at the same time a sort of talisman against evil: his diaries mention "the strange, mysterious, perhaps dangerous, perhaps saving comfort that there is in writing."* It served as his sanctuary, at any rate, and as a therapy for the tensions that were always threatening to "rend me asunder." The image he used for his social situation was that of "a circus rider on two horses" (which Wedekind had applied to Mühsam), or more frighteningly, of a human bridge suspended between two cliffs: "I was stiff and cold. I was a bridge, I lay over an abyss; my toes buried deep on one side, my hands on the other. I had fastened my teeth in crumbling clay. The tails of my coat fluttered at my sides. Far below brawled the icy trout stream. . . ." The bridge holds only until it is tested by a mountaineer who jabs him with his iron-pointed stick and jumps on his back. He turns to look at his tormentor, "and before I had fully turned I was already falling, I fell, and in a moment I was ripped apart and impaled on the sharp stones that had always gazed up at me so peacefully out of the rushing waters."

This brief parable is nothing but a capsule history of the Czech Jews, at first balanced precariously between cultures and afterward flung into the abyss. Kafka was only too conscious of the anomalies of their position in Bohemia while it remained a crown land of the Hapsburg monarchy. Living among Czechs, they were nonetheless wholly committed to German culture—speaking German, reading Schiller and Goethe, gave them a sense of belonging to "a sort of noblesse." Hence, most of the 30,000 Jews of Prague were caught between the rising tide of Czech nationalism and the increasingly strident Teutonism of the *völkisch* Germans, with whom they had little in common besides the language, though they

---

*Kafka's ideas on this point are foreshadowed by the medieval Jewish belief in the magic properties of certain texts that, when worn as an amulet, would protect the wearer "in all his two hundred and forty-eight organs against imprisonment and against the two-edged sword," ward off misfortune, and "rescue him from evil men and evil speech."

jointly supported such institutions as the "German" University and the "German" Opera House of Prague. When Czech nationalist mobs went on the rampage, as they did every few years, they made no distinction between German and Jewish enterprises; indeed, anti-German (i.e., anti-Hapsburg) riots usually culminated in a cry of "Hang the Jews!" Inevitably they were the odd man out, resented as much by the Czechs, who executed a Jew on trumped-up charges of "ritual murder" as late as 1899, as by the Sudeten Germans, who displayed signs in their village pubs declaring, CZECHS, JEWS AND DOGS NOT ALLOWED.*

Kafka, whose writing struck the critics as possessing "something fundamentally German," never became reconciled to the fact that he and other German-Jewish writers had, as it were, acquired the language secondhand. Once, in a bitter mood of self-reproach, he wrote to Max Brod that Jewish writers had "usurped" this alien language; had, indeed, "stolen" instead of earned it. Their position reflected "the terrible inner dilemma of this generation," which he described by combining the cliff-hanging bridge with the insect image of *Metamorphosis*: most of the Jews who became German writers did so because they wanted to escape from Judaism— usually with the vague acquiescence of their fathers—"but with their little hind legs they remained stuck to the Judaism of their fathers and with their forelegs they could find no new ground." Another image also occurred to him: German-Jewish writers had created "a gypsy literature that had stolen the German child from its cradle and trained it, in a great hurry, to perform any which way because someone had to dance on the tightrope."

In the same letter, Kafka asserted that writing is not a cure for despair, and he came to the terrible and prophetic conclusion that German writing by Jewish authors had been only a temporary expedient, "as though for someone writing his last will and testament, just before he hangs himself."

Yet there were days when he could see the whole process of cultural assimilation as a much funnier and more enjoyable experience. In his happiest treatment of the subject, *A Report to an Academy*, a guest speaker lectures a scientific body on "the life I formerly led as an ape." It was a great honor to be permitted to acculturate, aided by good advice and accompanied by orchestral

---

*Canetti has pointed out that Kafka was hounded by this unflattering equation. He humbles himself before his fiancée "more deeply than any dog"; the condemned man of *In the Penal Colony* resembles a submissive dog that has only to be whistled for when it is time for the execution, and there are K.'s final words when the executioners thrust the knife into his heart: " 'Like a dog!' he said; it was as if he meant the shame of it to outlive him."

music, "yet essentially alone." Fortunately the task was accomplished despite concerted criticism from "ten thousand windbags who vent themselves concerning me in the newspapers, saying: my ape nature is not yet quite under control":

> I could never have achieved what I have done had I been stubbornly set on clinging to my origins, to the remembrances of my youth. In fact, to give up being stubborn was the supreme command I laid upon myself; free ape as I was, I submitted myself to that yoke. In revenge, however, my memory of the past has closed the door against me more and more. . . . I felt more comfortable in the world of men and fitted it better; the strong wind that blew after me out of my past began to slacken; today it is only a gentle puff of air that plays around my heels. . . .
>
> And so I learned things, gentlemen. Ah, one learns when one has to; one learns when one needs a way out; one learns at all costs. One stands over oneself with a whip; one flays oneself at the slightest opposition. My ape nature fled out of me, head over heels and away.

There is no question that the former ape has a considerable talent for assimilation: "With an effort which up till now has never been repeated I managed to reach the cultural level of an average European." What is not certain, either from his account or Kafka's, is whether he can expect to be accepted in his new role; whether "the way of humanity" will be opened to him. Kafka seemed rather dubious about the chances of an uninvited guest being welcomed into an alien culture. K., the land surveyor in *The Castle*, is baffled in all his efforts to obtain even the most tenuous legitimacy for his stay in the village. "Can I pay you a visit one day?" K. asks the schoolteacher. "I live in Swan Street at the butcher's," is the reply. "That was assuredly more of a statement than an invitation, but K. said, 'Right, I'll come.' "

Kafka's sense of belonging to the uninvited was constantly being reinforced by encounters in real life that would have wounded even a less vulnerable ego. The reminders usually came when he least expected them. "In the park on a bench with some little girls; we called it a girls' bench and defended it against some boys. Polish Jews. The children called them Itzig and didn't want to sit down on the bench right after them."* In November 1920, when

---

*I know a former German Jew, now in a prominent American government post, who owes his life to a casual insult of this kind. In 1933, when he was fourteen, a Gymnasium teacher forbade him to go swimming with the rest of his class because his presence would "pollute the water." The boy demanded of his parents to be allowed to emigrate then and there; he could not go on living in a country where his mere presence could pollute a swimming pool. The father understood, and bought his son a ticket to New York.

antisemitic violence erupted in the streets of Prague, Kafka was quietly in the midst of it: "The whole afternoon I am in the streets and bathe in Jew-hatred. Just now I heard someone call the Jews *Prašivé plemeno* [a mangy race]." German-speaking passersby were being beaten up in the streets; Jewish archives were ransacked and burned; a bonfire of Hebrew manuscripts raged all day outside one of the medieval synagogues in the former ghetto. But the sight of mounted police breaking up a screaming mob filled Kafka with shame at "always having to live under protection." His reactions to such crises were complicated by that ever recurring anxiety, "the absence of any firm Jewish ground beneath my feet"—as well as by an oedipal aversion to people like his father, "Jewish businessmen who are German one day, Czech the next." He could never identify with their lukewarm Judaism, which was devoid of the mysticism that attracted him to "the dark complexity of Judaism." In one of his letters to Felice Bauer he recalled "how as a boy I almost suffocated from the terrible boredom and pointlessness of the hours in the synagogue; these were the rehearsals staged by hell for my later office life."

Kafka's father had committed the cardinal error of having become a success in the wholesale haberdashery business; his son, of course, thought it was nothing, or at any rate only a source of constant irritation if one was expected to be "endlessly grateful":

> It is unpleasant to listen to Father talk with incessant insinuations about the good fortune of people today and especially of his children, about the sufferings he had to endure as a youth. No one denies that for years, as a result of insufficient winter clothing, he had open sores on his legs, that he often went hungry, that when he was only ten he had to push a cart through the villages, even in winter and very early in the morning—but, and this is something he will not understand, these facts, taken together with the further fact that I have not gone through all this, by no means lead to the conclusion that I have been happier than he.

Kafka once wrote a hundred-page letter to his father—never delivered—in which he tried to tell the whole truth about their unhappy relationship and "why I maintain I am afraid of you." Among other things it was the father's sheer physical bulk and unremitting energy, his "will-to-live, to do business, to conquer" that intimidated the son. Tall and broad-shouldered, Hermann Kafka had come to Prague from southern Bohemia, where his father was a small-town butcher. He married the daughter of a brewer, Julie Löwy, who also came from provincial Bohemia.

Franz, born on July 3, 1883, was their eldest child, and there were three sisters: Elli, Valli and Ottla. It was from his mother that Kafka inherited, as he said, "obstinacy, sensitivity, a sense of justice, restlessness"—as well as what Willy Haas calls "his very long, noble, olive-skinned Arabian prince's face." The Löwys were a bookish family: in an autobiographical sketch, Frau Kafka described her grandfather as "a very Jewish learned man," who neglected practical affairs in order to study the Talmud. Several of his grandchildren, however, had successful careers in business and the professions; Kafka's "Madrid Uncle," Alfred Löwy, became the much decorated director-general of the Spanish railways.

Although Kafka preferred his mother's company, both parents made him chronically uncomfortable. "I have always looked upon my parents as persecutors," he told Felice. "All parents want to do is drag one down to them, back to the old days from which one longs to free oneself and escape; they do it out of love, of course, and that's what makes it so horrible." He realized the absurdity of demanding too much of one's parents, yet his comments sound as though he expected them to be perfect. Taking their heroic leap into affluence for granted, he saw only their defects—while "on the other hand their good qualities seem a hundred thousand times smaller than they are in reality."

There is a curious and significant remark in his diaries—curious in that it comes from one of the great prose stylists of German literature—that he had not loved his mother as she deserved because "the German language" had prevented it: "The Jewish mother is no 'Mutter,' to call her 'Mutter' makes her a little comic (not to herself because we are in Germany). . . . [under Hapsburg rule, the German-speaking inhabitants of the Austrian empire still regarded themselves part of cultural, if not political, "Germany."] Mama would be a better name if only one didn't image 'Mutter' behind it."

It was the backswing of the pendulum. Kafka, the archetype of the educated son of assimilated parents, came to feel an acute nostalgia for the older, more securely Jewish world of the *stettl* or the ghetto where, as he supposed, mothers must have been warmer and more protective. "If one had allowed me to be whatever I liked," he wrote toward the end of his life, "then I would have wanted to be a little East European Jewish boy. . . ." At first he knew of this world only by hearsay and what little he had read of it in German books. But when a Yiddish theater troupe came to Prague in 1911 he was instantly captivated by what they showed him of the spirit of Polish ghetto life—"people who are Jews in an especially pure form because they live only in the religion, but live in it without effort, understanding, or distress."

He had never seen Jews who were so light on their feet: they danced "with their hands on their earlocks in delight" and bounced into the air with exuberance. This was a far cry from the bourgeois stuffiness he had known at home. Some of the Yiddish actors "made my cheeks tremble" with their "talmudic melody of minute questions, adjurations, or explanations. The air moves into a pipe and takes the pipe along, and a great screw, proud in its entirety, humble in its turns, twists from small, distant beginnings in the direction of the one who is questioned."

Kafka made friends with one of the actors, Jizchak Löwy (who was unrelated to his mother's family), discovered several Yiddish authors who were "great" and even "sublime," and fell in love with one of the actresses. It was a revelation for him to hear Löwy's tales of the Hasidim, and of the parties at which they discoursed merrily on the Talmud. "If the entertainment runs down or if someone does not take part, they make up for it by singing." Kafka heard stories of wonder-rabbis, village matzo-baking associations and of angels who accompany pious men on their way home from the synagogue on Friday evenings. Löwy's account of the death of his wise old grandfather made a particularly deep impression and was duly recorded in the diaries:

> The bed was set up in the middle of the room, the candlesticks were borrowed from friends and relatives, the room therefore full of the light and smoke of the candles. Some forty men stood around his bed all day to receive inspiration from the death of a pious man. He was conscious until the end and at the right moment, his hand on his breast, he began to repeat the death prayers. During his suffering and after his death the grandmother, who was with the women gathered in the next room, wept incessantly, but while he was dying she was completely calm because it is a commandment to ease the death of the dying man as much as one can. "With his own prayers he passed away." He was much envied for this death that followed so pious a life.

Kafka's encounter with the Yiddish theater prompted him to study Hebrew and to take an active interest in Jewish affairs. It was not as though he could return to the traditional forms of Judaism, but there were times when his own writing seemed to be developing into "a new secret doctrine, a kabala." The angel that appeared to him in his room in 1914 was not at all like one of Lasker-Schüler's unambiguous angels but rather like one of Kierkegaard's, for whom the external was the internal and the internal the external. It wore bluish-violet robes girt with a belt of gold cord and it floated toward him on shining silk wings. Kafka lowered his eyes, expecting it to speak to him. "When I raised them again the angel was still there, it is true, hanging rather far off under the ceiling . . . but it was no living angel, only a painted wooden figurehead off the prow of some ship, one of the kind that hangs from the ceiling in sailors' taverns, nothing more." As usual with Kafka it was a case of both Either and Or. He stuck a candle into the hilt of its sword and "sat late into the night under the angel's faint flame."

Erich Heller has pointed out that Kafka knew two things at once, "and both with equal assurance: that there *is* no God, and that there *must* be God." It was a question he approached with a mind unclouded by current or conventional opinion. Haas, Werfel and several other writers once invited him to a Spiritualist séance in the basement of a Prague café. Kafka participated in the table-tipping but was unimpressed: "That the sun rises tomorrow is a miracle; that a table moves after you have maltreated it for so long is not a miracle."*

Many of the people who knew him well suspected, as did Haas, that Kafka might be "an Old Testament saint" in disguise. Even the young Bible-tract missionary who tried to interest him in Christian salvation decided, after talking with him for an hour and a half, that he was "close to grace" as it was. But the diaries indicate that his prospects for grace fluctuated with his moods. There were despondent days when "the secret raven" flapped about his head and he wondered whether in heaven he would be "permitted to be as despairing there as I am here." At other times "life calls again" and he would write in his diary: "It is entirely conceivable that life's splendour lies in wait about each one of us in all its fullness, but veiled from view, deep down, invisible, far off." This sense of imminent glory was another direct inheritance from the Talmudists, for whom (as Walter Benjamin put it) "every second of time was the strait gate through which the Messiah might enter."

As a sort of modern saint, secretly at work on a new *Commentarius super Apocalypsum*, Kafka must have seemed strangely out of place in the offices of the "Workers' Accident Insurance Institute

---

*Cf. Schoenberg's chorus on the same theme (p. 177, above), and Blake's *Vision of the Last Judgment*: " 'What,' it will be Questioned, 'When the Sun rises, do you not see a round disk of fire somewhat like a Guinea?' O no, no, I see an Innumerable company of the Heavenly host crying 'Holy, Holy, Holy is the Lord God Almighty.' "

for the Kingdom of Bohemia, in Prague," where he was employed as a junior executive. Yet the head of his department remembered him afterward as a model of probity whose "devotion to duty was exemplary," who had not a single enemy at the institute (though he was one of only two Jews on the staff) and whose work was highly regarded despite the fact that "Franz Kafka attacked every question from the opposite end of that from which everyone else generally did"—a comment that recalls the analytical method of Professor Einstein, whose private lectures on relativity, given at the home of a Prague art patron, were attended by Kafka and his friends.

Kafka himself said that the job at the institute was "unbearable" because it prevented him from writing his books. Still, the time he spent at his desk was by no means wasted. Max Brod testifies that most of what Kafka knew of life and the world was derived from his day-to-day experiences at the office—"from coming into contact with workmen suffering under injustice, and having to deal with the long-drawn-out process of official work, and from the stagnating life of files." Only a writer versed in modern bureaucratic routine could have produced *The Trial* and *The Castle*. Kafka's duties included writing accident reports and making recommendations for improving the safety of industrial machinery: "By turning back the spindle according to Schrader's patent and flattening it in a gentle slope right up to the cutters, clogging up the cutter block will be avoided. . . ."

Readers of *In the Penal Colony* will recognize this device, which was intended to prevent a milling machine operator from cutting off his fingers, as the forerunner of the infernal apparatus that inscribes a condemned prisoner's sentence on his back with needles before torturing him to death: "As soon as the man is strapped down, the Bed is set in motion. It quivers in minute, very rapid vibrations, both from side to side and up and down. You will have seen similar apparatus in hospitals. . . ." It is only when the Harrow starts to write on his back that the recalcitrant prisoner learns what sentence has been passed on him: before that, as the presiding officer explains, "there would be no point in telling him. He'll learn it on his body."

> "But surely he knows that he has been sentenced?"
> "Not that either," said the officer. . . .
> "No," said the explorer wiping his forehead, "then he can't know either whether his defense was effective?"
> "He has had no chance of putting up a defense," said the officer.

When it was first published, in 1920, Kurt Tucholsky described this story as a masterpiece—the most remarkable German novella since Kleist's *Michael Kolhaas*. He was uneasily aware that it had some special relevance to the age in which they were living. In its "ruthless objectivity and the crystalline clarity of its language" it dissected the great totalitarian dream of unchecked power and the possibility of inflicting limitless torture on defenseless human beings. The officer in charge, who describes the machine with such cool professionalism, is not primarily brutal "but something worse, amoral":

> The officer is certainly no sadist. And when, after the sixth hour of torturing an ever-weakening prisoner, he feasts on his signs of suffering, that is only an indication of boundless, slavish obedience before that which he calls justice but which is actually power. And here this power has no limits. To exercise unlimited power! . . . Kafka has dreamed and structured this limitlessness. And the only impediments to this system of institutionalized torture are also dreamlike. It is not, as one might imagine, a whole society, or the public sense of order, or the state, that rises against this torment in protest and indignation—no, the machine's parts fail to function properly, and the colony's new commandant, a modernist compared to his predecessor, fails to support the machine-officer and his torture duties as energetically as the old one, though he, too, goes on tolerating this work. . . . All this is told with such extraordinary coolness and lack of involvement. The writer has time to depict very, very tiny details, just as in real life or in a dream one may remember a torn fingernail or a flower petal on a carpet as the significant feature of some catastrophic experience. And so the machine does its work before the visitor's agitated eyes, and the needles write and write.

The death sentence that Kafka experienced on his own body was tuberculosis. There is reason to think that it may have been an elaborate psychosomatic stratagem for escaping from the office routine and the other aggravations of life in Prague. He coughed blood for the first time in August 1917—and Brod noted in his diary that Kafka had insisted his illness was "psychic, just like something to save him from marriage. He calls it his final defeat. And yet he has been sleeping well since." In a letter to his publisher, Kurt Wolff, Kafka wrote that he had "provoked" this disease for many years, and now it was "almost a relief" to have it out in the open. He was sent to the mountains to be cured, but each time he broke off the treatment to return to Prague. "I am spiritually ill," he told his Czech translator, Milena Jesenská, with whom he fell in love in 1920. "The disease of the lungs is only the river of my spiritual disease rising above its banks."

For the last six or seven years of his life he played a cat-and-mouse game with his illness, reminding himself periodically to "immerse yourself in your suffering." He told Milena not to laugh at the operatic tenor who lies on stage mortally wounded and sings an interminable aria; his, Kafka's, last aria would take years to sing. He had begun to enjoy "the independence conferred by the proximity of death." It was clear to him now that he had systematically destroyed himself over the years, "like a slowly widening breach in a dam, a purposeful action." He used his new leisure to sit in judgment on himself, acting at the same time as both prosecutor and defense attorney. Some of his briefs bear the imprint of Kierkegaard, whom he had read very attentively, and "who bears me out like a friend":

> While I was still contented I wanted to be discontented, and with all the means that my time and tradition gave me, plunged into discontent—and then wanted to turn back again. Thus I have always been discontented, even with my contentment.

Dr. Freud, the specialist in civilization and its discontents, might have found a cure for Kafka's complaint, but like all true hypochondriacs the patient instinctively avoided the only treatment that offered any hope of success. "The therapeutic part of psychoanalysis," he decided, "is a hopeless error." He preferred the ambiguities, even the "sweetness" of being ill, which seemed to heighten his perceptions as a writer. A man in his condition, he wrote, might need one hand to ward off despair, but with the other "he can note down what he sees among the ruins, for he sees different (and more) things than do the others; after all, dead as he is in his own lifetime, he is the real survivor."

He now led what he called his maneuver-life, sleeping in the afternoon and writing at night—*The Castle, First Sorrow, A Little Woman, A Hunger Artist*. He himself had become something of a hunger artist, a vegetarian and food faddist with a growing aversion to eating. His friend Albert Ehrenstein, a Viennese Expressionist poet who was to die in New York many years later, came to the conclusion that Kafka's life was "one long drawn-out suicide" in protest against the multiple tyrannies of father, family, office, Prague; and that he killed himself by self-deprivation of every kind. He would always break off his engagements and love affairs before they led to anything; his vegetarianism was equally directed "against the flesh"; he published only a few of his short stories but none of his novels, thereby forestalling any possibility of literary success; "he was against alcohol, ecstasy and self-indulgence—as a matter of principle and cleanliness he abstained from the fatness of feeling." Moreover, once his illness had become acute his abstemiousness prevented him from getting well. "Parents, sisters, friends, doctors, tried to introduce some meat and eggs into his diet, but it was never enough, especially as Kafka overdid his attempts to harden his body by sleeping in unheated rooms."

Milena Jesenská, who knew another side of Kafka, wrote that he was not really against life as such, "only against *this kind of life.*" He rejected every kind of "heroism" as a lie; it was his purity, his clairvoyance, that had turned him into an ascetic: "He is absolutely incapable of lying, just as he is incapable of drinking too much. He is without the slightest sanctuary, without shelter. That is why he is vulnerable to everything from which we are protected. He is like a naked man among people wearing clothes."

Kafka was to make one last attempt to escape from Prague and to let himself be "caught up in the current of life." For seven or eight years he had been hatching plans for moving to Berlin, whose "invigorating effect" he had experienced in the course of several short visits. "As a city Berlin is so much better than Vienna, that decaying mammoth village," he wrote in 1914. "I do want to go to Berlin, Berlin does me good in every way." But events had conspired to keep him at home: "Prague won't let go . . . this little mother has talons." At last an opportunity presented itself. During the summer of 1923 he visited a holiday camp at Müritz, on the Baltic, which was run by the Berlin "Jewish People's Home." He fell in love with a nineteen-year-old member of the staff, Dora Dymant, "a wonderful creature" with whom he went to live in Berlin in the autumn of that year. It was "a madly daring deed" and a thoroughly novel experience, for although he had been engaged to two girls he had never lived with a woman before. Dora surprised him by making him happy, a sensation to which he was unaccustomed. They found an apartment in a quiet suburb: "my street is the last half-urban one; behind it the landscape dissolves into gardens and villas, the abundant gardens. On warm evenings the scent in the air is stronger than I have known it anywhere else."

Berlin was then in the midst of its postwar cultural resurgence, but Kafka saw little of it. In the center of the city, among the crowds of the Potsdamer Platz or the Kurfürstendamm, "I lose a large part of my capacity to breathe," and he took care to remain in the suburbs, away from the "terrifying and pedagogic pressure of Berlin proper." He had chosen an unfortunate moment to move to

Berlin. Germany was in the grip of runaway inflation which reached its peak in November 1923, when one U.S. dollar was worth 4.2 billion paper marks. Though the currency was eventually stabilized, it was the Jews who were blamed for the inflation: shortly after Kafka's arrival, hooligans attacked Jewish residents in the poorer districts of the city. "How I trembled before the slogans on the walls, and how I still tremble now, almost daily. . . ." In previous years Berlin had struck him as a city that offered "an easy life, great opportunities, pleasant diversions, etc.," but now he was so short of money that he could not even afford to buy a newspaper: "I know much less of the world than I did in Prague."

In any case it was too late now for all the things he wanted to do—learn to be a gardener, for example, with a view to emigrating to Palestine. "For the practical instruction I am too weak, for the theoretical too restless." He would have liked to marry Dora Dymant, and he wrote a letter to her pious, Hasidic father in Poland, explaining that although he was not a practicing Jew, he was a "repentant one, seeking conversion," and hoped to be considered worthy of marrying into the family. As Max Brod remembered,

> The father set off with the letter to consult the man he honored most, whose authority counted more than anything else for him, to the "Gerer Rebbe." The rabbi read the letter, put it on one side, and said nothing more than the single syllable, "No." Gave no further explanation. He never used to give explanations. The miracle-working rabbi's "No" was justified by Franz's death, which followed soon afterwards. . . .

It was Brod himself who brought Kafka back to Prague in March 1925. Within a month he was taken to a Vienna clinic where doctors discovered that he had tuberculosis of the larynx. He spent the last weeks of his life at a sanatorium in Kierling, where Dora Dymant and a Hungarian friend, Dr. Robert Klopstock, were constantly with him. Though scarcely able to speak, he was at work on his last manuscripts—and on proofs of *A Hunger Artist*—until the day of his death, June 3, 1924. As he felt himself suffocating he asked Klopstock for an injection of morphine: "Kill me, or else you are a murderer!"

Kurt Tucholsky wrote in *Die Weltbühne* that Kafka would become world famous now that he was dead and his novels were being published posthumously: *der einzige Kafka* (K. the unique) had written "the clearest and most beautiful" modern German prose; "We can read, marvel and give thanks." By then, Tucholsky was already a well-known author. His tributes to Kafka reflect an uncom-

fortable awareness that, while his own lightweight books were
selling by the tens of thousands, Kafka's work—"every word precious, weighty, wholly remote from this world, the work of a
sage"—was still largely unknown.

Tucholsky's art was anything but remote from this world; it belonged to what proponents of the New Functionalism called
Zeitkunst—art-for-now as opposed to the romantic aesthetic, my-
time-will-yet-come. He himself was a key figure in the Weimar
Renaissance, and though he preferred to spend much of his time
on the outside looking in, his twenty-five hundred articles,
sketches and poems constitute a sort of Froissart's Chronicle of
Berlin culture. He wrote constantly, and unlike Kafka he never
held anything back; his "diaries" were the essays and squibs he
wrote for the influential weekly *Die Weltbühne,* which published so
much of his work that he invented four pseudonyms—Ignaz
Wrobel, Peter Panter, Theobald Tiger, Kaspar Hauser—to avoid
repeating his byline on page after page of the same issue.

"What had begun as a game ended as gay schizophrenia,"
Tucholsky explained. Each of the alter egos—"we are five fingers
on one hand"—possessed a distinct and recognizable personality.
Wrobel, close-shaven but with a blue chin, had red hair, wore
glasses and tended toward a vinegarish Weltanschauung: his specialty was politics and other bad news. Panter was literary, theatrical and funny: "agile, round as a ball, a little man." Tiger signed
the cabaret poetry: "he sang only in verse, and slept if there was
none." Kaspar Hauser, who signed many of the more personal
essays, was the namesake of the nineteenth-century German mystery man whose youth had been spent in solitary confinement and
thereafter looked at the works of mankind through the eyes of a
child: "he saw the world and did not understand it." The four
pseudonyms also provided a smokescreen for the real Tucholsky, a
shy, rather retiring writer who preferred to stay out of the
limelight. In an "Interview with Himself" published in 1919, it is
the garrulous Panter who sits in for his creator: " 'Herr Panter will
see you now!' said the butler. . . . There sat the master massively at
his desk; a man who could almost be called obese; he displayed a
cultivated Caesar profile, marred only by a double chin. . . . In his
bright, beady eyes lay an air of richly satisfied contentment."

These appearances were deceiving. Tucholsky was never satisfied either with himself or with the state of the world. He had
begun writing professionally in 1912, shortly after his meeting with
Kafka, whose influence is clearly visible in one of his earliest essays, an article about an exhibition of photographs of workers'

hands mutilated in industrial accidents. Even in these prewar pieces he aligned himself with the protest poets and the young reformers, writing against police controls, military *Komman-dogewalt,* film censorship (an issue even in 1913) and the sexual double standard. Then the war interrupted his career. He served first as a conscript in an ordnance battalion, later as a headquarters sergeant in Latvian Courland and on the Rumanian front. He returned to Berlin after the armistice with a "belly full of the bitterest gall" against the military mentality that had been responsible for the slaughter. Wartime censorship had prevented him from publishing his views of a system that had "some people dying in the mud while the others praised them for it."

During the first year after the war he vented his anger and frustration in a brilliant series of articles about warmongers, the officer corps and the Prussian society of "lords and underlings." Walking past the former Army War Academy in the Dorotheenstrasse, where the daily casualty lists had been posted during the war, he noticed that the brown granite slabs were flecked with white, and it occurred to him that the color of the spots should have been blood-red. "Every time I pass the War Academy . . . I say to myself quietly: promise yourself; make a solemn vow. Work. Try. Tell the people. Free them from the nationalist madness. You with your small powers. You owe it to the dead. The spots cry out. Do you hear them? They cry: *Nie wieder Krieg!* No more war!"

He declared a war against war *(Krieg dem Kriege)* and directed his heaviest fire against those who, after four years of fighting, had still not come to realize that "blood is blood and there is no such thing as holy murder." Germany could only become civilized, he wrote, if it were to abolish its traditional system of military training, the exaggerated respect for authority and "the penchant for standing in rank and file." The herd instinct cultivated by the Reichswehr during the war had transformed decent people into killers and wild men: "hence the incomprehensible brutality of Germans 'in the service' which contrasts so strangely with their good-naturedness in private."* To counteract this passionate love

---

*During World War II the Prussian aristocrat Ursula von Kardorff noted in her diary, in connection with the murder and deportation of the last Berlin Jews: "What hideous aspect of evil manifests itself here, and why does it show itself particularly among our people? Through what transformation has it become possible to make such devils of a group of people who are, on the average, good-natured and warm-hearted? It all takes place in a coldly bureaucratic atmosphere in which individuals are difficult to discern; each is like a tick that has burrowed into the body politic and has suddenly become part of it." See Ursula von Kardorff: *Berliner Aufzeichnungen, 1942–45* (Munich, 1962); the entry for March 3, 1943.

of authority *(diese tiefe Liebe zur Macht)* people would have to learn to speak softly to one another, and not as officer to enlisted man. As Theobald Tiger expressed it in one of his catchier cabaret chansons, "No more conscription, no more soldiers, no more potentates with monocles; no more medals, no more lining up for parades, no more reserve officers!"

> Keine *Wehrpflicht!* Keine *Soldaten!*
> Keine *Monokel-Potentaten!*
> Keine *Orden!* Keine *Spaliere!*
> Keine *Reserveoffiziere!*

He hoped, too, that the newly established republic would finally put a stop to that infernal military band music:

> *Lass endlich schweigen, O Republik,*
> *Militärmusik! Militärmusik!*

These were by no means unconventional sentiments in 1918, for they were shared by the great majority of the young German writers and artists who had managed to survive the war. The Dadaist movement that took Berlin by storm as soon as the shooting stopped was, in essence, nothing but the long-delayed artists' revolt against the rigidities of German "normalcy."* One of the founders of the movement, Walter Mehring, explained afterward that he and his fellow Dadaists had wanted "to make a laughing stock of the humbug of authority." Mehring, an ex-artilleryman, and George Grosz, formerly of the infantry, helped make Sunday, December 7, 1918, a day that will live in art history by staging a "Dada Matinee" at the Tribune Theater in Berlin-Charlottenburg at which the chief attraction was a race between a sewing machine (operated by Grosz) and a typewriter (played by Mehring), accompanied by an obbligato dialogue:

GROSZ: Schnurre, schnurre basselurre. . . .

MEHRING: Tacktacktack! Bumsti! Ping, ping!

GROSZ: Tülitetüt; Lüttitü! O, sole mio! Old man's river [sic]; Mississippi. . . .

IN UNISON: Eiapopeia! Tandaradei! Hipp, hipp Dada . . . Dada-capo!

*Walter Benjamin realized, in retrospect, that Dadaism served an important aesthetic function. "The revolutionary strength of Dadaism lay in testing art for its authenticity. You made still-lifes out of tickets, spools of cotton, cigarette stubs, and mixed them with pictorial elements. You put a frame round the whole thing. And in this way you said to the public: look, your picture frame destroys time; the smallest authentic fragment of everyday life says more than painting. Just as a murderer's bloody fingerprint on a page says more than the words printed on it."

Not long afterward, Grosz told Count Kessler (who had saved him from a firing squad during the war by having him declared mad instead of mutinous) that he wanted to become the German Hogarth, "deliberately realistic and didactic; to preach, improve and reform." This attitude endeared him to Tucholsky, who described him in *Die Weltbühne* as a brother-in-arms, the greatest of Dadaists: "He alone is Sturm und Drang, outcry, mockery and—how rare—revolution." The resurrected German army took umbrage at Grosz's portfolio of military caricatures, *Gott mit uns* (the words "God with Us" were embossed on army belt buckles) and had him haled into court for attempting to undermine the nation's fighting spirit *(den Wehrgedanken in Deutschland zu vernichten).* Tucholsky assured his readers that no one had ever portrayed the army more truthfully—top sergeants, surgeons, medical orderlies, boozing generals, bordello-visiting lieutenants, *Freikorps* officers—"We are happy to look at these drawings, compare them to a certain kind of soldier and say, amicably but firmly, 'Yes, that's how you look.' "

In the ensuing "Dada Trial," Grosz was found guilty and sentenced to a fine of three hundred marks; his publisher Wieland Herzfelde, to six hundred marks. (Neither, incidentally, was Jewish so there were no antisemitic overtones to the affair.) Grosz failed to take the lesson to heart: in 1924 he received a six-thousand-mark fine for "attacks on public morality" in the *Ecce Homo* series, and four years later there was another trial involving his lithograph of the crucified Christ wearing gas mask and army boots, entitled *Maul halten und weiterdienen* (Shut up and continue carrying out your orders). The court was uncertain as to how this caption was to be interpreted. Did Grosz mean to imply that in time of war, Christ's only message to the troops was to go on fighting? No, Tucholsky was obliged to explain in *Die Weltbühne*, it was the state that had spoken these words to people who were driven into the war, even under the sign of the cross. "They issue orders in Christ's name, *Maul halten und weiterdienen,* and He himself is forced to obey them . . . this Christ has been betrayed by his own church."

Grosz remained in Berlin just long enough to draw some of the most important pictures of the epoch, and to provide the backdrops for Erwin Piscator's memorable production of *The Good Soldier Schweik*. With his unusually fine sense of timing he emigrated to America in June 1932, and thus avoided being sent to a concentration camp as a subverter of fighting spirits for the next war. Mehring, meanwhile, achieved a certain local eminence with his poems and cabaret ditties, performed in such Berlin cabarets as Friedrich Holländer's *Bunte Bühne* (Motley Stage), Trude Hesterberg's *Kleinkunsttheater* (Theater of the Minor Arts) and Max Reinhardt's *Schall und Rauch* (Sound and Smoke), of which he was artistic director from 1919 to 1921. Some of his best poems were published in the famous *Dada Almanac* of 1920, and it was thanks to the Dada influence that he created an entirely new genre of cabaret *lied*—"a wild chase of impressions in free rhythm," as Tucholsky described them, "which have the same effect as though you were driving quickly past a wall full of posters":

> *Berlin, dein Tänzer ist der Tod—*
> *Foxtrott und Jazz—*
> *Die Republik amüsiert sich königlich—*
> *Vergiss mein nicht zum ersten Mai*
> *Als alle Knospen sprangen!*

> Berlin, your dancer is death—
> Foxtrot and jazz—
> The republic amuses itself royally—
> Forget me not on the first of May
> When all the flowers were budding!

The last line is a quotation from one of Heinrich Heine's most romantic poems, as though to confirm Grosz's assertion that Mehring was Heine and François Villon rolled into one. Mehring was a native-born Berliner, the son of a Jewish newspaper editor, who had studied art history before becoming a cabaret poet. Tucholsky said that he was "the first to see Berlin just as the world had always seen Paris," a brilliant poet with a new sense of rhythm and *joie de vivre*. "He has everything at his fingertips: the organ grinder's music, the doll on the whore's sofa, the children that are locked in while their mother goes off to work, men from the Hausvogteiplatz for whom the world no longer holds any secrets. . . ." Mehring wrote a tramps' prayer, a thieves' ballad, a chanson for ragpickers and a roundelay for the unemployed. But no sooner had the economy regained its prewar momentum than most people were already overworked, and Berlin acquired the breathlessness described in his *Heimat Berlin* (My Old Berlin Home—or words to that effect):

> *Die Linden lang! Galopp! Galopp!*
> *Zu Fuss, zu Pferd, zu zweit!*
> *Mit der Uhr in der Hand, mit'm Hut auf'm Kopp*
> *Keine Zeit! Keine Zeit! Keine Zeit!*
> *Man knutscht, man küsst, man boxt, man ringt,*
> *Een Pneu zerplatzt, die Taxe springt! . . .*

Along Unter den Linden in a fast gallop
On foot, on horseback or by twos.
Watch in hand, hat on head, with never a stop;
Not a moment to lose, not a moment to lose!
They squeeze, they kiss, they wrestle, they box,
A tire bursts, the taxi rocks!

Tucholsky willingly conceded that Mehring, who was six years his junior, was king of all the cabaret poets, himself included. "Mehring has found verses, rhythms and images that exceed by far anything that would have occurred to me." Everyone had tried to copy him but he was inimitable, with a wealth of words "the like of which is rarely seen in Germany; words that just come flying to him." Still, there was room on the cabaret stages for Tucholsky's harsher, more realistic kind of ballad about putsching generals and munitions-makers, Berlin working girls, love at first sight and Tante Julla's notions of Berlin as the New Babylon. His (or rather Theobald Tiger's) songs were most often to be heard at Rosa Valetti's cabaret *Die Rampe* and Rudolf Nelson's Revue on the Kurfürstendamm (where Josephine Baker created a dancing sensation, dressed only in a bunch of bananas). It was at Nelson's that Tucholsky received his initiation into the realities of the Berlin theater world. Upstairs, in the balcony, there was a box next to the proscenium arch from which one could not see the stage:

If you leaned out so far that you almost fell over the railing you could just see a pair of long, slim legs. And the footlights. Nothing else. I spent many, many evenings in this box—and learned more about the nature of the theater than at many important premieres that I was afterward to review. I didn't see the stage, of course. But I saw something else: the audience.

It was typical of Tucholsky that he should prefer the audience to the performance: "The first thing you see is a whole lot of nostrils. Hundreds of small black nostrils. (Sometimes they are occupied by a finger, but rarely.)" He was fascinated by their reactions— "Mama and Uncle Erich and little Fritz and Dr. Kalkbrenner," lovers holding hands, tired businessmen asleep, but the great majority eagerly devouring the stage with their eyes. . . . Audience and actors, he wrote, complemented one another. "Theater is a duality. One part performs. The other sits there, listens, absorbs, stretches out its antennae, dilates its nostrils and feels that it is a mass; groans with the hero, dances with the girls and always constitutes the true content of every piece of theater."

With its insatiable appetite for novelty, this audience created the preconditions for the great flowering of Berlin theater in the twenties—"Berlin, the greatest theater-city in the world," with its extraordinary constellation of professionals: Brecht, Hasenclever, Georg Kaiser, Ferdinand Bruckner, Leopold Jessner, Berthold Viertel, Piscator, Kurt Weill. . . . Some of the most significant works of those halcyon days were also the funniest: Brecht and Weill's *Threepenny Opera,* of course, but also their other quasi-opera, *Mahagonny,* whose closing scene presents a hilariously menacing prognosis of what would happen to a city taken over by a gang of nihilist strong-arm men:

> *Can't help ourselves, or you or anyone!*
> *Can't help ourselves, or you or anyone!*

Tucholsky happened to be less impressed than most left-wing critics by Brecht's genius for social and political satire (perhaps he was not entirely immune to professional jealousy). "Brecht is a great lyric talent," he wrote of *Threepenny Opera.* "But besides that he is a slapdash workman." And again, "as regards the land of *Mahagonny,* it is a nicely bourgeois country in which grow the walnut and the solid oak from which bookcases are made." Even so, Tucholsky promptly rose to Brecht's defense when Nazis and nationalists began disrupting performances of the *Threepenny Opera* in provincial cities like Kassel and Leipzig, where they could get away with it. "These theater-scandals are a dull-witted expression of resentment," he wrote, for which the opera itself was only a pretext. The "right" side of town wanted to express its hatred of everything new and suspect: "socialism, Jews, Russia, pacifism . . . whatever disturbs their peace of mind and interferes with business, the *Volk,* the commonplace—Pfui! Scandalous! Stop the performance!"

These were the most productive years of the Weimar Renaissance; according to Thomas Mann they witnessed "nothing less than a shift of the cultural center from France to Germany." Yet at the same time a sinister counter-renaissance was already at work, preparing to destroy and dismantle everything that had been accomplished. Tucholsky perceived the struggle for intellectual freedom as "the great conflict of our time," with men like Brecht and Mehring on the one side and the Nazis' ominously named *Kampfbund für deutsche Kultur* (Fighting League for German Culture) on the other. Skirmishes between them took place almost continually in theaters, schools, museums and the law courts. Nearly always, as in the case of the *Reichswehr* v. *George Grosz,* it was the reformers who lost. After the Dada trial, Tucholsky declared that he no longer reposed any faith in the political justice of Weimar Germany. "In all these cases it is not the crime that is being punished . . . but a way of thinking."

He had expected something like even-handed justice from the government of the republic; instead, the old Wilhelmine judges remained in office and the law continued to tilt perceptibly toward the right. The situation is summed up in one of the most concise and ironic of his aphorisms: "Due to unfavorable weather, the German Revolution has taken place in music instead." For a Doctor of Laws with an obsession about justice there was certainly no lack of grievances to write about. He enjoyed belaboring the minor issues as well as the major ones, especially when they bordered on the absurd. Charlie Chaplin's *Shoulder Arms,* for example, was banned by the censors because the dream sequence in which he captures the kaiser singlehanded was deemed insulting to German honor. Tucholsky went to Copenhagen to see it and announced that this sort of antimilitarist satire was precisely what was needed in Germany: "Come across the Rhine, Chaplin, across the Rhine!"

Most of his protest pieces, however, concern far more serious and significant abuses of the law. In 1922 the aging Maximilian Harden, who had been one of the great dissenting journalists of Wilhelmine Germany, was beaten nearly to death by two hired killers; only the timely intervention of a neighbor and an emergency operation saved his life. When one of the would-be assassins and the man who hired him were brought to trial, the defense argued, in effect, that Harden had provoked the attack by his "disloyalty" toward Germany—as a writer of unpatriotic articles, and as a Jew who had changed his name from Witkowski, he had got no more than he deserved. Tucholsky attended the trial and wrote one of his angriest articles about it: "One had to see it in person; had to experience this outrage for oneself for the full three days: this nation, these murderers, this kind of justice. . . . The stench of a whole world was in one's nostrils."

Harden, who had survived four famous libel trials at the turn of the century, spoke on his own behalf on the third day. Though he was still suffering from the effects of his head injuries, he knew that he would have to seize this opportunity to make a public appeal on behalf of the many victims and potential victims of political murder in postwar Germany. Tucholsky called it the most remarkable speech ever made in the Berlin criminal assizes at Moabit:

> Our last well-known European was speaking. A man was speaking in whom a vanished world was resurrected, the representative of an

almost forgotten epoch, a man who still believed in justice, *fair play*, morality and principle even in ideological controversies. "I always fought against the kaiser, from the first day on—but I was not killed under his government." He rose above his personal complaints. He spoke above the heads of the petty bourgeois who sat around him. He spoke the language of the world, not the idiom of this Germany. . . . He spoke of the crime of being Jewish, for which there was no statute of limitations, and of the stupidity of the government, which was equally inexpungable. . . . He challenged the jury at least to agree openly on acquittal if they were of the opinion that inconvenient intellectuals—especially Jews—could be beaten to death with impunity.

As Harden's listeners were aware, most of the prominent victims of political murder in the Weimar Republic were Jews, ranging from leaders of the Left, such as Rosa Luxemburg, Kurt Eisner and Gustav Landauer, to men of the Center like Walther Rathenau, the foreign minister who had been assassinated six months before. Most of these cases had been deliberately allowed to remain "unsolved."* Harden wondered whether this meant that henceforth they would declare open season on Jews: "Then take care that all men who were born as Jews receive the yellow patch, and that they not be allowed to publish magazines and books. But you will not be able to control this terror! Do you not see how far it would reach?"

The jury was unimpressed: there had been "mitigating" (i.e., patriotic) circumstances, and the accused were sentenced to a purely nominal year in prison. Tucholsky (who signed the article with his own name to indicate the seriousness of the occasion), interpreted the verdict as an open invitation to further violence. "It means 'Carry on!' It will encourage the next assassin. . . . We no longer have any justice!" For his audience in the cabarets Theobald Tiger had already written a jaunty but hardly less indignant ballad entitled *Harden* that begins:

> *Ich kann nicht mehr—Sie werden das begreifen—*
> *bei jedem Attentat ein Trauerliedchen pfeifen—*
> *es sind zu viel.*

---

*Statistics compiled by E. J. Gumpel for his survey *Vier Jahre politischer Mord* (Four Years of Political Murder), Berlin, 1922, show that in Germany between 1919 and 1922, 354 persons were killed by right-wing, and 22 by left-wing extremists. All 22 of the left-wing murders were brought to trial: 10 men were executed for these crimes and 28 others received prison sentences averaging fifteen years. Of the right-wing murders, 326 were left unexpiated. Fifty confessed killers were indicted for the remainder: 24 of them were convicted and sentenced to an average of four months; the rest were acquitted or discharged in spite of the fact that they had pleaded guilty.

Es gibt da ehemalige Offiziere,
die schiessen wöchentlich, wie ich taxiere
auf das Zivil. . . .

I can't go on, despite my fascination,
whistling a dirge for each assassination;
the list's too long.
Certain ex-officers among us millions
seem to think taking potshots at civilians
just isn't wrong.

The subject of German justice, or the lack thereof, never ceased to fascinate Tucholsky. It was, he realized, as much a matter of judicial attitudes as of the way the laws were written. "One has only to hear how the judges address the accused to grasp from what source flows this turbid stream of justice." He described "the overbearing tone of the judges, their contemptuous treatment of the defense attorneys, the prima-donna role of the prosecutor, the rudeness of the clerks." There was the Berlin judge who barked at an eleven-year-old prisoner: "Stand at attention with your hands at your seams the way you've been taught!" Tucholsky also quoted from the writings of Robert Heindl, court councilor and author of an important tome on *Strafrechtsreform* (Criminal Law Reform) in which he advocated more rigorous methods of punishment.

Heindl had visited the French penal colony in New Caledonia, where he had learned what struck him as the proper way of dealing with habitual criminals. During his visit a number of prisoners had mutilated themselves in protest against the harsh conditions at the camp. Some had dislocated their arms or cut off a hand or a foot; five men had put out their eyes with thorns. But, as Heindl reported, the commandant had devised exemplary ways of dealing with these malingerers:

> He had a sort of circus erected for blind prisoners and forced them to trot around it every day for eight hours with a sack of sand on their back; the one-armed were yoked to a cart, and similar punishments were devised for the others. Thanks to this new kind of therapy the epidemic of self-mutilation soon came to an end.

Unfortunately, Heindl's book came out several years too late for Kafka to have benefited from its insights into penology. Tucholsky learned from it, however: he remarked that it told him far more about the mentality of the prison authorities *(Strafvollzugsbeamte)* than about ways of reforming the law. Their totalitarian dreams of power always proceeded from the assumption that convicts had forfeited their rights as human beings. He could foresee the day when people like Heindl would have carte blanche to act out their "legitimized sadism" without moral restraints of any kind. The problem, he thought, lay in "mankind's profound mania for cruelty, its *Grausamkeitsdrang*, which finds expression in the law."

In spite of everything he had written about the inequities of Weimar justice, Tucholsky himself was acquitted when the army prosecuted him for an uncomplimentary essay on the officer corps. Occasionally there were other verdicts, too, that gave him grounds for hope that the tide might be running the other way. A major test case, as well as a literary cause célèbre, was the obscenity trial of Schnitzler's *La Ronde* in 1921, in which the defendants were acquitted after five days of acrimonious courtroom debate. Tucholsky advised his readers to buy the book-length transcription of the trial: "I guarantee you some hilarious hours." Among other things the testimony provides a remarkably vivid record of the atmosphere then prevailing in proto-Nazi circles. The case against *La Ronde* had been organized by the *Deutschvölkische Schutz- und Trutzbund* (German Nationalist Watch and Ward Society), and noisy demonstrations against the play had been staged both in and outside the theater, the Berlin Kleines Schauspielhaus:

ATTORNEY FOR THE DEFENSE:	What did you hear in the lobby?
OTHMAR KEINDL (WITNESS)	(44, Administrative Secretary of the Kleines Schauspielhaus, Catholic): Exclusively antisemitic remarks, such as *diese Saujuden*, this vile bunch, this Jewish director, these Jews should all be smoked out, this theater-rabble, the Jews should go to Palestine. . . .
VICTOR SLADEK (DEFENDANT)	(Theatrical Director, born in Hüttendorf, Upper Silesia, Catholic, no previous convictions): Herr Keindl, how did the Tägliche Rundschau refer to me for days and weeks?
WITNESS:	Galician *Saujude*, I believe, but not the Tägliche Rundschau, I think it was another newspaper. Anyhow you were always called *Jude*, black Jew, fat, black Galician Jew was always the expression used.

This was the so-called "Jewish question" at the grass-roots level, in its most banal and incurable form. Tucholsky's response to it had always been unequivocal, but like Kafka he was not really certain of his ground. Technically he himself was now a Protestant. "In 1911 I 'seceded from Judaism,' " he wrote to Arnold Zweig in later years. "I know one can't do anything of the sort, but that was the legal formula. . . . I did it because from early youth I had an instinctive aversion to unctuous rabbis—I sensed, rather than understood, the pusillanimity of these people." Later he tended to think of himself as someone who stood above the battle. "The Jewish question has never really agitated me," he told a friend in 1929. "From my writings you can see that I very seldom touch upon this area, my knowledge of which isn't very great. . . . People who want to hurt the Jew in me are usually wide of the mark."

As a writer, at any rate, he reserved the right to be impartial in his attitude toward Jews. Whenever he had written a particularly eloquent article against antisemitism he would usually redress the balance by composing one of his scathing satires of the Jewish middle class. It was a difficult neutrality to maintain. The trouble was that no one paid much attention to his articles on behalf of tolerance, while nearly everybody—both Jews and Teutonists, though for very different reasons—enjoyed his parodies of Herr Wendriner, the Berlin Jewish businessman with the impossible manners. His sixteen Wendriner sketches are the monologues of a corpulent, loquacious parvenu whose life is an endless series of business maneuvers. He tries to educate his children—"I ask myself just one thing: this fidgeting, this restlessness, these bad manners—where did the boy get them from?" He takes his wife to Paris—"And so I showed my wife Paris; naah, I was never there before. . . ." When he has an affair with a fashion model from a friend's wholesale showroom, it is not so much the girl he notices as her lounging pajamas—violet, with rose trimming—and the way her bedroom is furnished: "an immense bed, from here to there, an English dresser, a very nice carpet and curtains, real lace, handmade, I looked at them very closely, afterward."

Herr Wendriner was an eminently recognizable figure; physically he bore a marked resemblance to Tucholsky, and there were obvious elements of self-caricature in the portrait. One could argue that these sketches were no more malicious than Finley Peter Dunne's Mr. Dooley monologues. But at that perilous moment in German-Jewish relations they could only play into the hands of the Nazis, and many Jews could not forgive Tucholsky his bad timing. The émigré scholar Gershom Scholem remembered them after the war as "a sinister document" of the epoch. Most German antisemitic writings had rung false because their authors lacked all knowledge of the subject, and had no feeling for atmosphere; it had remained for Tucholsky "to accomplish on a definitive level what the antisemites themselves were unable to bring about." Other critics, however, have insisted that Wendriner was merely intended as a sort of object lesson. According to Tucholsky's American biographer, Harold Poor, he created Wendriner "not because he hated Jews but because he wanted there to be no Wendriners among the Jews—because he wanted the Jews to be an exemplary people within the society."* His friend Kurt Hiller also defended him against the charge of having been a "Jewish antisemite":

> Tucholsky always stressed the very qualities that, as far as the antisemites (and the self-hating Jews) were concerned, branded him as typically "Jewish"—his dauntless, analytic way of thinking, his cheerfully critical attitude toward tradition and society's sacred cows, his vigorous intellectualism, his sense of humor, the pepper and salt of his personality. In this he resembled some other notably relaxed and "natural" writers—Ludwig Börne, Heinrich Heine, Alfred Kerr.

Tucholsky himself had said more or less the last word on this question in the final aphorism that he published in *Die Weltbühne* before the Nazis closed down the magazine: "A Jewish man once said, 'I'm proud to be Jewish. If I weren't proud I'd still be Jewish so I may as well be proud in the first place.' " In the same issue he had drawn up a list of some of the other things on which people were congratulating themselves in that era of resurgent patriotism:

> In Europe one is proud of:
> being a German.
> being a Frenchman.
> being an Englishman.
> not being a German.
> not being a Frenchman.
> not being an Englishman. . . .

Like Toller, Tucholsky had already declared his allegiance to "our real fatherland, Europe," and had become a self-proclaimed citizen of the world. (In right-wing parlance he was by definition a

---

*Tucholsky's attitude was similar to that of Walther Rathenau, the first Jewish foreign minister of Germany (and also the first to be assassinated). As a young man, Rathenau had felt an equally pressing need to lecture his brethren about the need to improve their manners and ideals. "Look at yourselves in the mirror," he wrote in a pseudonymous article in Harden's *Die Zukunft* (March 6, 1897). "That is the first step toward self-criticism. Unfortunately one cannot alter the fact that you all look terribly alike, and that the bad manners of one are held against all the rest. Nor does it help to know that your southeastern appearance is not attractive to these northern tribes. It only means that amid these people, whose breeding and education is strict and military, you will have to work all the harder not to make yourselves ridiculous with your crooked posture and sleepy, unkempt bearing. . . ." Along the Tiergartenstrasse on a Sunday morning, or in the theater lobbies at night, his eye would be drawn to "the curious vision of a completely alien tribe of people, conspicuously overdressed, of mobile and hot-blooded gesture. An Asiatic horde here on the sands of Brandenburg!" Later, Rathenau came to regret this caricature, which was duly omitted from his Collected Writings.

member of the *heimatlose Linke,* the homeless Left, while in Soviet terminology he and his kind were to be known as "rootless cosmopolitans," i.e., the modern equivalent of the Wandering Jew.) In 1924 he had gone to Paris for *Die Weltbühne* and the *Vossische Zeitung* and had liked it so well that he decided to stay on. Readers at home, needless to say, were treated to a barrage of invidious comparisons. The magic of Paris, he informed them, derived not from its architecture or its women—"that which determines the atmosphere of this city is its *Menschlichkeit,* its human quality. Visitors from Germany cannot quite understand it at first. . . . Paris has a heart." In Paris, ticket collectors and meter readers were friendly instead of officious. Bumping against a fellow passenger in the Métro during the rush hour was not regarded as "a stain upon the knightly honor that can only be washed away with blood." The French had not developed their *Offensivgeist* and pugnacity to the same extent as the Germans: "I recall, shortly before my departure from Berlin, a scene in a Charlottenburg bakery where everyone was angry at everybody else; the customers, the bakers, the apprentices, the hot cross buns, and all for no reason." And yet he was not entirely without fond regrets for the city of his birth. In a poem written in a café overlooking the Place des Vosges, he wondered, in the refrain, "what do you suppose they're doing at this moment in Berlin?"

> . . . Ich aber denk als alter Spree-Pariser:
> Wie lieb ich dich! Von weitem. Mein Berlin—!

> But I, who come from Paris-on-the-Spree,
> Recall how much I love you! From a distance. My Berlin—!

He was to provide his editors with the best German coverage of French affairs since the days when Heine had lived in Paris. At the same time he went on writing about Germany, for he managed to keep abreast of developments in both countries—and unlike Heine he never wrote for the French public. Late in 1926 he returned to Berlin to take over *Die Weltbühne* following the sudden death of its founder and editor, Siegfried Jacobsohn. After a year as editor, however, he persuaded Carl von Ossietzky to replace him so that he could travel abroad again as a roving correspondent, returning to Berlin often enough to keep a finger on the German pulse. His analyses of German policies remained uncannily accurate no matter where he happened to be. In 1925, for example, after Gustav Stresemann negotiated the Locarno agreements with France, Tucholsky reasoned that Germany would now resume its traditional *Drang nach Osten.* His scenario for a future German chancellor is precisely that which was followed by Hitler a dozen years later:

> At first everything will come off without a hitch. You will accomplish the *Anschluss* of Austria which is indispensable to you: the permeation of Austria with Prussian energy. . . . Czechoslovakia will not be as easy to catch. But it needn't be, in any case. This nation, with its scattered populations of people who are not Czechs, and torn by ethnic conflicts, though remarkably well governed, confronts you with no real danger, since you think only in military terms: "We'll soon be finished with the Czechs." Finished, yes—it's only a question of who will be finished in the end. That leaves Poland. You calculate as follows: For a start the Poles must be overrun. Accordingly, you must first reach an understanding with Russia. The Russians may be counted on for a great many things, but not to make common cause with you against Poland and Rumania—the great business arrangement in which each thinks to betray the other afterward. This is the old German politics; to treat foreign nations as though they were ciphers in a mathematical formula. But sometimes there are miscalculations.

Erich Kästner, the author of *Emil und die Detektive,* once wrote that Tucholsky had wanted to "halt a catastrophe with a typewriter." As long as he still believed that there was at least a chance of averting the disaster, he continued to write—articles, polemics, analyses, buffooneries, cabaret songs about the beer-swilling Nazis and their plans for the establishment of a new and more glorious Reich to take up where the kaisers had left off:

> *Das dritte Reich?*
> *Bitte sehr! Bitte gleich!*
>
> The Third Reich?
> Certainly, Sir! Right away!

Together with John Heartfield, the ex-Dadaist master of caricature-by-photomontage, Tucholsky published a picture book with the ironic title, *Deutschland, Deutschland über alles.* Predictably, it said a lot of scathing things about militarists, Nazis, one-eyed justice and some of the more brutal aspects of German life, such as student-dueling at the universities, but it ended with an unexpectedly passionate profession of love for "this land where we were born and whose language we speak." Though the Teutonists claimed it exclusively for themselves, "it belongs to us as much as to them. . . . We are part of it. We love it quietly, without barrel organs, sentimentality or a drawn sword."

Tucholsky happened to be in Zurich when Hitler came to power, though he was then legally a resident of Sweden. He had moved to Hindås, near Göteborg, in 1929, following the break-up of his second marriage, and it was Sweden that furnished the backdrop for his best-selling novel, *Schloss Gripsholm*, about an emphatically modern holiday *à trois*.

The Nazis lost no time in banning and burning his books—on account of their "insolence and presumption," as Dr. Goebbels announced over the loudspeakers during the first great literary bonfire in Berlin (May 10, 1933). He was denounced in the Nazi press as "the archetype of the man without a country, the many-headed monster, the Jewish *Literatur-sau* Tucholsky." His name, together with thirty-two others such as Heinrich Mann and Ernst Toller, appeared on the first list of those formally deprived of their citizenship (and their assets) under the new Nazi law against "conduct inimical to the Reich." The Nazi Institute for the Study of the Jewish Question devoted a twenty-three-page study to his work, which concluded: "There is nothing of the prophet about him . . . only a gnawing hatred of the national ideal of the people whose bread he eats."

Tucholsky refused to publish a single word in his own defense. Although a *Neue Weltbühne* was started by exiled writers in Vienna and Prague, he declined to contribute. He told his friends that it was too late to do anything for Germany: much of what was happening under the Nazis corresponded to the deepest instincts of the masses, and since the majority of *die kleinen Leute* (the little people) supported Hitler there was no point in preaching to them. Exiled writers could not hope to accomplish from the outside what they had failed to achieve from the inside. In March 1933 he wrote to Walter Hasenclever, "We must see things as they are. We have lost. The only thing for an honorable man to do is to withdraw." Besides, "one cannot write where one only despises." His final entry in the notebook which he used for rough sketches and first ideas is a drawing of three ascending steps, each bearing a single word: *Sprechen, Schreiben, Schweigen*—speaking, writing, silence.

From the isolation of his clapboard house in Hindås he watched the Nazis systematically uprooting what was left of the Weimar Renaissance. Berlin, as Mehring wrote in 1936, had been a *Weltstadt*, a city open to the world—but only so long as Tucholsky was on hand to write about it. Now suddenly it was like a film running backward; all the extraordinary people who had come to Berlin to make it a center of the arts and sciences simply disappeared from the scene, one after the other. The brothers Mann,

Alfred Doeblin, Bertolt Brecht, Walter Hasenclever, Erich Maria Remarque, Mehring, of course, Toller, Hiller, Ferdinand Bruckner, Alfred Kerr; Max Reinhardt, Fritz Kortner, Elisabeth Bergner, most of the stars of the Berlin film studios; Max Beckmann, Kurt Schwitters, Kokoschka, most of the Bauhaus designers, Walter Gropius, Ludwig Mies van der Rohe, Erich Mendelsohn; Paul Hindemith, Schoenberg, Bruno Walter, Otto Klemperer, Erich Kleiber, Artur Schnabel, Rudolf Serkin . . . poets and painters, novelists, critics, actors, directors, philosophers, scientists, architects, composers, singers, publishers; left-wing and right-wing, Christians and Jews, rich and poor, virtually the entire cast of the most brilliant cultural production Germany had ever seen—gone with the wind! The streets of Berlin were filled with shouting mobs but the creative people had left it, if they could, for Prague, Vienna, Paris, London or New York.

Throughout this exodus Tucholsky maintained his self-imposed silence. He was *ein aufgehörter Schriftsteller,* as he said, "a discontinued writer." He intervened in political affairs only once, in March 1935, when the pacifist writer Berthold Jacob, who had exposed the secret rearming of Germany in *Die Weltbühne,* was abducted from France, via Switzerland, by agents of the Gestapo. Tucholsky wrote a letter to the Swiss cabinet urging them to intervene on Jacob's behalf: "This physically insignificant little man has the courage to write about those things where the others stopped." But he was careful not to make this an open letter, and for the rest it was *"Schweigen, Schweigen, Schweigen."* (Jacob, incidentally, was freed when the Swiss insisted that the Gestapo had violated their territory during the abduction—but he was killed by the Gestapo after they caught up with him again in Lisbon five years later.)

In 1911 Franz Kafka had noted Tucholsky's "fear . . . of changing into a melancholic, as he has seen in older Berlin Jews of his type." This fear was to prove justified after all. During his years of silence he became increasingly depressed, and his health was also declining: during the winter of 1934–35 he was operated on five times for a painful nasal infection. Though he was only forty-five he was very tired. "If I had to die now, I would say: 'Was that all?' And: 'I didn't quite understand it properly.' And: 'It was rather loud.' " He felt there was nothing left for him to do. He swallowed poison on December 19, 1935, and after vain efforts to revive him, died in a Göteborg hospital two days later. "I am *au-dessus de la mêlée,"* he explained in a farewell letter to his former wife, Mary Tucholsky. "It is no longer my concern. I am finished."

VII

ULTIMA MULTIS

*The Jews who are librarians and bear witness
to the Redemption.*
                    —CHARLES BAUDELAIRE, Intimate Journals

I n the spring of 1933 Paris became the provisional capital
of German literature. Many of the best-known poets
and novelists of Munich and Berlin were now to be found in the
cafés of Montparnasse and St. Germain, speaking in heavily ac-
cented French in hopes of not appearing overly conspicuous. For
some it was more like a homecoming than an exile: they had always
been drawn to this city, which was the cynosure of all intellectuals, for there was an old tradition—exemplified by Heine and
Rilke—that good German poets, even before they die, go to Paris.
This time, needless to add, they came under more problematic
circumstances. For luminaries like Heinrich Mann and Lion
Feuchtwanger, Paris remained the moveable feast it had been for
their predecessors, the American expatriates, most of whom had
gone home when the twenties bubble burst. They arrived in
France, as Berthold Viertel observed, "like kings who have lost
their thrones," and some of them went on to live like exiled royalty
on the Riviera. But émigré writers without international reputa-
tions learned "to gnaw the bread of poverty and servitude." They
led uncertain, often quasi-illicit lives—i.e., without the requisite
carte d'identité—domiciled in cheap hotels or run-down apartments, doing whatever writers contrive to do when there ceases to
be a market for their writing. One of Walter Mehring's one
hundred fifty exile poems pays rueful tribute to the shabby hotels
in the "ever narrower alleys" where the émigrés went to live; *Die
kleinen Hotels* with their flimsy partitions and peeling wallpaper:

Du musst des Nebenzimmers Pein erdulden,
Dass sie sich schlaflos auf dein Kissen wälz—
Dass dich des Nachbarn Wollust würgt—und alle Schulden
Die prasseln nachts aufs Dach aus vollen Mulden
Auf die kleinen Hotels
Auf die kleinen Hotels
Auf die kleinen Hotels. . . .

You'll learn to bear the sounds of pain and passion
That penetrate from the adjoining room;
They strike your sleepless ear like tocsin bells
Whilst all your debts rain down like thoughts of doom
—in the most disconcerting fashion—
Upon the small hotels, the small hotels.

The émigré author Hans Sahl gives a detailed description of one of them in his autobiographical novel, *The Few and the Many*: "It was the same room I had had five years ago, with the same poisonous-green plush furniture, the smell of moldy wallpaper and dusty velvet curtains, with the bidet in the corner covered by a towel and the view of the Garde Republicaine barracks and the towers of St. Sulpice. There were the same broken and glued wicker chairs, the same bulb hanging from a wire in the ceiling, surrounded by a green glass shade, the same wardrobe with its mirror on the door and its worm-eaten shelves covered by yellowed newspaper. There was the same unaired smell of mold, old walls, and nights of love on freshly disinfected mattresses. . . ."

It was quite possible to write books and articles in such surroundings: the American expatriates had managed it—but they had publishers in New York or Boston waiting to take their manuscripts. The German émigrés, once their books were banned in the Reich, were dependent on a handful of exile publishers who brought out small editions for marginal markets and paid correspondingly insignificant fees. The most brilliant critic among the exiles, Walter Benjamin, was appalled to learn that Klaus Mann's magazine *Die Sammlung* (The Collection) was prepared to pay him only one hundred fifty francs for a major essay on Brecht, and when he had the temerity to ask for two hundred fifty francs— then about ten dollars—the manuscript was returned to him. The only book that Benjamin published during his eight years of exile, *Deutsche Menschen* (German People), a minor literary classic in which he tried to remind the Germans of the humanist moments in their history, was brought out by a Swiss publisher who, to be on the safe side, produced an edition of only two hundred bound copies. Another exiled writer, Franz Schoenberner (the last pre-

Hitler editor of *Simplicissimus*), characterized this method of staying alive with the word *Kleckerbeträge*—payment by dribs and drabs. The writers' wives were usually called on to supply the deficit by making handbags, knitting sweaters, giving piano lessons and such. Regular jobs were out of the question because refugees rarely received work permits. For a foreigner even to apply for a permit was sometimes regarded as sufficient grounds for having him deported. Hence doctors became ghost surgeons, like the hero of Remarque's *Arch of Triumph,* and professors sold artificial flowers from door to door. "Each of us first had to discover some way of staying minimally alive," recalled the poet and essayist Günther Anders. That involved various kinds of permits, a place to sleep, an illicit way of making money, "but above all a living-permit, known as the *permis de séjour.* The hunt for this license to live, which consisted mainly of waiting in corridors, was basically hopeless, for we had come not from rain to sunshine but merely into another kind of bad weather—from one world of unemployment to another world of unemployment." France was going through a depression of its own, with some four hundred thousand registered unemployed, but as Kurt Hiller pointed out in 1935, there were only about forty thousand German refugees in Western Europe, divided among France, Holland, Belgium, England, Czechoslovakia, Switzerland, Scandinavia, Italy and Spain. The total population of these eleven countries was two hundred million. "That means one refugee for every five thousand natives. Is that supposed to represent a threat to the labor market?"

The French academic establishment greeted this sudden influx of German intellectuals with perceptible coolness. "The typical French intellectual, who wanted security and a predictable future for himself and his family, found his way of life threatened by those damned German intellectuals, who did not spend their time drinking aperitifs with their friends but worked twice as hard as the Frenchman," reported Paul Honigsheim, who headed the short-lived Paris branch of the Institute for Social Research. With few exceptions even the prominent intellectuals who actively supported the émigré cause remained socially aloof. As Arthur Koestler writes in his memoirs,

> . . . it depressed me that neither I nor any of my fellow refugees was ever invited to a French house. I knew of course that this reserve was an inherent part of French tradition, and during my previous stay in Paris as a foreign correspondent I had taken it for granted. But poverty and exile made one oversensitive; what a refugee craves most is relief from his permanent feeling of uprootedness. . . . Thus the great

mass of refugees in France lived cut off from French contacts and led a kind of ghetto existence. They read their émigré papers, frequented their émigré-clubs and cafés, lived immersed in their émigré universe, and its inevitable feuds and intrigues. During my seven years as a refugee in France I lived entirely in the company of fellow refugees and continued to write and think in German; yet from the moment when, in 1940, I settled in England, I began to write in English, moved among English friends and ceased to be a refugee.

A few of the émigrés managed to break through this *cordon sanitaire*. Alfred Doeblin, for example, eventually acquired a French passport and an advisory post at the Ministry of Information. Manès Sperber, the novelist-psychoanalyst from Vienna, was befriended by André Malraux and even invited to his house for dinner—a rare privilege which was all the more appreciated because Sperber, then scraping along as a ghost writer, could afford only one meal a day. Once Malraux invited him to meet Gide—just after lunch, as it happened. Sperber had cause to remember the occasion in his autobiography: it was a cold day, but the room was overheated; he himself had eaten neither breakfast nor lunch and was happy to sip a glass of cognac while Gide and Malraux were finishing their meal. Gide, then the most famous and oft-quoted of living French writers, chose to talk to him about the journals of Delacroix. Sperber was rather disappointed that Gide, contrary to expectation, had nothing world-shaking to say on the subject. "And then it happened. I came to with a start and noticed that Gide, somewhat impatiently, was asking me the same question for the second or third time, and that it had nothing to do with Delacroix. I realized that I must have dozed off—from sitting in the warm room and having drunk cognac on a nearly empty stomach. I replied quickly, embarrassed but also amused: that anyone could fall asleep during his first meeting with André Gide was unheard-of in those days. . . ." Sperber adds that he had trouble wiping the idiotic smile off his face, "for I felt all too plainly that this minor contretemps was wholly appropriate to my condition as an intellectual émigré. Particularly to an impoverished one, who receives the fewer invitations the more urgently he needs them."

Walter Benjamin regarded as his greatest Paris coup the fact that the Bibliothèque Nationale permitted him to use its *Enfer*, the department of forbidden books. "This is one of the few successes I have been able to achieve on this soil. It is terribly difficult to obtain." Working at the Bibliothèque, he was on much closer terms of acquaintance with the French writers of the nineteenth century than with his French contemporaries. He had met—and impressed—Gide in the twenties, but in his present circumstances he was reluctant to presume on their acquaintance. "My experience with the French people I knew before has not encouraged me to try to renew erstwhile relationships," he noted in the spring of 1934. Like Heinrich Mann, he was to write some of his finest work not only in but about France. Yet by his own account he was wholly isolated in this very city whose history he wanted to write. "I have hardly ever been lonelier than here," he conceded. "If I wanted to seek out opportunities to sit with émigrés in a café—that would be easy enough to arrange. But I avoid them. . . . When one is wholly destitute, it seems preferable to lose oneself in the anonymity of a big city."

The refugee writers were to take comfort in the fact that they represented *das beste Deutschland,* as Romain Rolland told them in an open letter to the exiled authors' association: "You are the better Germany, the banished, oppressed but unconquerable Germany that suffers but fights on." Heinrich Mann published a pamphlet on *The Meaning of This Emigration* in which he reminded his colleagues that "the Emigration stands for Germany. . . . Its public statements should stress its superiority rather than the injustices it has been made to suffer." They were to hold their heads high because they alone were in a position to "speak the truth and reveal cause and effect." The exiles had become "the voice of the silenced nation." As Hermann Kesten wrote, "the Germany of the generals and the secret police" had driven out "its most famous and meritorious men."

By 1935 so many well-known writers had left Germany that Leopold Schwarzschild, editor of the most widely read of the exile magazines, *Das Neue Tage-Buch,* was moved to boast that literature was "the only German treasure that has been safely transferred out of the Third Reich. . . . It is the only salvaged fortune to remain intact: the whole of German literature, not just pieces or splinters of it, has found refuge beyond the borders of the Third Reich." He doubted whether there had ever been a precedent for this sort of migration, in which "virtually the whole literature of a nation has escaped from the clutches of a regime that threatened to destroy or deform it."

Schwarzschild's comments provoked a major debate in the Swiss press. Eduard Korrodi, critic-in-chief of the *Neue Zürcher Zeitung,* attacked his thesis as a "shameless indecency" that smacked of "ghetto madness." It was a piece of insolence to equate Jewish authors with German literature—not the real poets but only the hack-writers of the "novel industry" had emigrated, and (with

a bow toward Thomas Mann) the "really able writers" living outside Germany preferred not to be identified with the exiles.

Thomas Mann was then living in Küsnacht, on the outskirts of
Zurich. Though he had originally joined the exodus to France, he
had moved back to a German-speaking area, as his wife wrote,
"for the sake of the youngest children, who were still in school."
Unlike Heinrich Mann, whose books had been banned by the
Nazis from the first, Thomas Mann had maintained a discreet silence on political questions since going into exile, and his books
were still being sold in Germany. "He was eager that his books still
be read there," Katia Mann explained, "because he thought this
fact alone would keep many people from throwing themselves in
the arms of fascism." Korrodi's article, however, made it clear to
him that his silence was being misinterpreted. He answered it in an
open letter declaring his unequivocal support for the émigrés;
when it was published in the *Neue Zürcher Zeitung* the Nazis placed
him on their blacklist along with the rest. The gist of it was that
German literature had indeed gone into exile because the Nazis
were attempting "to shake off the ties of civilization," rather than
because all the writers were Jewish: "My brother Heinrich and I are
not Jews. Nor are Leonhard Frank, René Schickele, the soldier Fritz
von Unruh, that authentic Bavarian Oskar Maria Graf, Annette
Kolb, A. M. Frey, or talented younger writers such as Gustav Reg-
ler, Bernhard von Brentano. . . ." Yet it was in the nature of
things "that the Jewish contingent should be numerically strong in
the exile movement: that fact follows both from the sweeping nature of National Socialist racial philosophy and from the revulsion
which the Jewish spirit feels for certain state institutions of our
times." As for Korrodi's contention that he "could not name a
single emigrant poet," what about people like Bertolt Brecht—or
for that matter, "how can you make such a statement, since I know
that you regard Else Lasker-Schüler as a true poet?"

> You say that those who have emigrated are chiefly in the "novel
> industry. . . ." Well, industry implies industriousness, and certainly
> uprooted people, who are everywhere barely tolerated by an econom-
> ically fearful and distinctly ungenerous world,* must be industrious if
> they are to earn their bread. It would be harsh indeed to find fault
> with them for that.

---

*This phrase concealed a well-aimed slap at Korrodi himself, whose "neutrality" did
not prevent him from agitating against Swiss aid for refugee publishers and writers.
In a letter to Hermann Hesse, Mann described him as *eine ganz tückische kleine
Madame* (a thoroughly tricky little number).

The truth of the matter was that German writers in exile could only hope to support themselves if they produced novels that would find a market in other languages. Thomas Mann himself solved the problem with his Joseph tetralogy; Heinrich Mann with his two Henri IV novels, Feuchtwanger with his Josephus trilogy, Alfred Neumann with *Neue Caesar* and *Kaiserreich*, about Napoleon III; Remarque with *Three Comrades* and Joseph Roth with *The Hundred Days* of Napoleon I. Considered as a trend, there was something faintly comical in this parade of costume epics from distinguished novelists. Kurt Hiller accused them of evading the real issue of the day—"How do we clean out the Augean stables of Germany?"—in order to fantasize about "Katherine the Great, Christina of Sweden, Josephine of France, Ferdinand I, Philip II, Napoleon III, the false Nero and the real Peter. . . ." He proposed a list of still unexploited subjects: "Rameses IV, Pippin the In-Between, Winrich of Kniprode, Sultan Suleiman, Melanie the Unusual of Paphlagonia. . . ." But why were the best-known German writers fiddling with the past while civilization was ready to burn? "Hitler will be emperor of Europe the day after tomorrow."

The trouble was that nothing one could say about Nazism in fiction could approach its enormity as fact; on that account the important German literature of exile is to be found not in novels but in the memoirs, letters, diaries: Doeblin's *Schicksalsreise* (which will concern us in the next chapter), Benjamin's letters, Walter Hasenclever's *Die Rechtlosen*, his autobiographical account of "People Without Rights."

The literary escapism of the exiles was also a response to the prevailing indifference to Nazism among those whose immediate interests were unaffected. The rest of the world seemed utterly determined not to know what was then happening in Germany. Stefan Zweig wrote of the "invisible wall" that grew up between the exiles and the people among whom they found asylum because "the thing that had already happened to us had not yet happened to them." In 1937 it was easier to write about Napoleon III than to explain the significance of Hitler to a Des Moines dentist who had just read, in the February issue of the *National Geographic Magazine*, how beautiful and efficient everything was in "Changing Berlin"—how the city's inhabitants were "happy to see the New Age evolving a style of realistic beauty in keeping with today's practical needs," and what remarkable progress was being made in German literature: "It is not only Berlin's physical aspect which is undergoing change today; the language, particularly the written language, is also in a state of evolution. Many writers are abandoning the traditional long-winded style. The tendency is toward crisp, short sentences, American tempo."* Unter den Linden "in gala dress" was decked with swastika banners; cheering crowds lined the avenues as artillery pieces rumbled by on Hitler's birthday; the new German slaughterhouses were wonderfully humane ("Kosher killing is everywhere prohibited"), and "a sturdy race" was being created "to defend Germany in the future":

> Across the bridge, returning from an outing, marches a group of small boys wearing the uniform of the Hitler Youth—short black trousers, brown shirt, and black neckerchief slipped through a braided leather holder. They are singing in accurately pitched, youthful treble that moving modern national song, the "Horst Wessel Lied."

Whether they wrote in short, crisp sentences or the long-winded Thomas Mann variety, the exiles could not hope to shake this beatific vision of Nazi Germany as a sort of gigantic health farm. It was the sheer impossibility of making themselves heard that drove some writers to suicide and others to take mental refuge in the distant past. Zweig, who was ultimately to do both, wrote that he had foreseen the consequences of Nazism "with tortured heart and tormenting clairvoyance," but that the English, among whom he lived for several years, persisted in deluding themselves that "promises were promises, treaties were treaties, and that Hitler could be negotiated with if one but reasoned with him man to man." It was this frightening indifference that explained "why those of us who were already branded by fate had only each other to look to, when the bitter foretaste of the imminent corroded our lips. . . ."

The situation of the exiles was further complicated by their own disunity. Though it never came to the "676 splinter groups" that Tucholsky had predicted in 1933, the old intra-German rivalries flared up again in Prague, Paris and London. "Businessmen don't want to have anything to do with politicians, nor the Social Democrats with the Communists; those who have connections don't want to know about the helpless aliens, and the rich, least of all, are concerned about the poor people with whom they share their exile," wrote the Berlin journalist Wolf Franck in his *Guide to the German Emigration*. "The pride with which they display that hereditary German illness, particularism, is indescribably laugha-

---

*Curiously enough, the favorite American author among German readers of the thirties was the long-winded Thomas Wolfe.

ble, and these schisms have become all the more ridiculous because people constantly bump into each other, involuntarily, at the police bureaus, the committees and the cafés."

Much as they might have preferred some other company, the language kept bringing them together. It was never the same for them, speaking French or English: it they wanted to hear their mother tongue, to have their own nuances fully understood, they were obliged to go to the émigré cafés. "You need two tongues to speak two languages," complained Ferenc Molnar, who spent his days in Paris alternately writing a novel and playing chess, both in the back room of the Café Régence. Refugee children, if they were young enough, could acquire new languages whenever necessary: many of them shifted into French, then into English, without skipping a beat. But for adult writers this problem of language was almost insurmountable. Some of them, indeed, would have liked to dispense with German entirely now that Hitler had become its most prominent speaker. Tucholsky, shortly before his suicide, wrote that he would have nothing more to do with this country, "whose language I speak as little as possible." There were cases of refugees who refused to speak another word of the language once they had escaped from Germany.

But those who were unwilling to go that far—"What were we to do, those of us who were irrevocably committed in writing to the German language?" asked Alfred Doeblin. "We who neither could nor would let go of our language because we knew that language was not just 'language' but thinking, feeling and much else? Could we separate ourselves from it? But that means more than pulling off one's own skin; it means disemboweling oneself, committing suicide. So we remained what we were. . . ." Günther Anders wrote that the German language was "the only piece of home" that the refugees still possessed, "the only evidence that testified (if only to themselves) where they belonged."

In this respect Walter Benjamin was more fortunate than most exiles. He spoke and wrote French fluently; he had always been a passionate admirer of French literature; he had written the best German translations of Proust, Baudelaire and Saint-John Perse, as well as the most important German criticism of French writing since Heinrich Heine. Sometimes he wrote in French for the sheer pleasure of it. Once—just once—he was even invited to write an article for the prestigious Nouvelle Revue Française, though in the end they decided not to publish it. Things usually worked out like this for Benjamin: books stillborn, articles rejected, his most important book left more unfinished than Schubert's symphony. It might have been different if the editors of his day could have foreseen the great Benjamin wave that was to sweep Germany in the 1960s and 1970s, when he had become a culture hero among the students of the New Left and even his most esoteric books could be bought in paperback at any railway bookstall (the ultimate literary accolade). Only then did it become apparent to everyone that this quintessential hard-luck refugee had been, as Philip Toynbee wrote, "one of the great European writers of this century," and that he had achieved precisely what he had set out to make of his life: "The goal I set for myself . . . is to be regarded as the foremost critic of German literature. The trouble is that for more than fifty years literary criticism in Germany has not been considered a serious genre. To create a place for oneself in criticism means to re-create it as a genre."

His conception of literary criticism did not stop at the printed page. As early as 1927 he had first conceived of his fantastic *Passages* project, which was to cut through the cultural history of Baudelaire's time much as the shopping arcades tunneled through the massive masonry of nineteenth-century Paris. The French equivalents of the Gallerias of Milan or the Burlington Arcade, London, were known as *passages*: with their vaulted glass roofs and marble floors they extended through entire blocks of houses, and on each side, as a guidebook pointed out, "there are arrayed the most elegant shops, so that such an arcade is a city, indeed a world, in miniature."

Worlds in miniature were Benjamin's specialty. He possessed Blake's gift, rare in any epoch,

> To see a World in a Grain of Sand
> And a Heaven in a Wild Flower,
> Hold Infinity in the palm of your hand
> And Eternity in an hour.

In the *passages* Benjamin saw not merely the beginnings of the department store but a key to the essential character of the entire century: the new luxury industries supported by a flourishing bourgeoisie, the "fetish of the salable commodity," the emergence of a middle-class culture that "entered upon the historical scene" under Louis Philippe and created a particular style of decoration— "the interior"—in which to display the objects bought in the *passages*. In the construction of the arcades, steel girders were first employed architecturally; they supplied the prototype for the sumptuous exhibition halls of the great Paris world's fairs; they housed the dioramas that led directly to the invention of photography (which, in turn, revolutionized the very concept of art); gaslight was first employed to illuminate them. For Benjamin a stroll through the arcades was a metaphorical passage through the labyrinths of time, with a fresh historical perception to be encountered at every turn. A Freudian analyst might also discover other symbolic motives for his obsession with the *Passages* project. In any case it was to be a portrait of "Paris—the Capital of the Nineteenth Century" as no one else had ever done it, composed of "the most insignificant phenomena, even the scraps, of existence," and of the hundreds of quotations which he collected for it in the course of his voluminous and interminable reading—in literature and art, politics, poetry, philosophy, sociology, economics, psychiatry, technology. Only death could bring to an end this voracious process of ingestion reminiscent, indeed, of a bookworm's passage through a well-stocked, heterogeneous library. Paris, therefore— the Paris of the Bibliothèque Nationale—was the very place where Benjamin would have chosen to live had there been earlier possibilities for him to do so; the Nazi victory in Germany had merely forced him to fulfill a lifelong ambition. It was only his poverty and isolation that sometimes spoiled his enjoyment of it.

Benjamin understood the physiognomy of scraps and objects because he himself was an ardent collector, deriving palpable pleasure from the profusion of objects with which he liked to surround himself. "For a collector," he wrote, "ownership is the most intimate relationship that one can have to objects. Not that they come alive in him; it is he who lives in them." It was true that he had no great luck with his own superb collection of rare books, particularly early illustrated children's books: only a part of it could be smuggled out of Berlin, and there was so little room in the Paris apartment to which he eventually moved, No. 10 rue Dombasle, that it had to be stored in a wooden crate. Above it, however, he was able to hang his most prized possession, Paul Klee's drawing *Angelus Novus*.

But whether it consisted of tangible objects like books, or of intangibles like quotations, "the most distinguished trait of a collection will always be its transmissibility," he wrote, and it was this sense of the inherited and inheritable that constitutes one of the central themes of his writing. His concern for the transmissibility of knowledge—and the continuity of "the never-ending problem"— also provided the motive for his incessant collecting of quotations. He hoped, one day, to put together a book consisting entirely of quotations, so artfully joined together that they would require no bridge passages from the compiler's hand. It would have been a kind of dialogue unbound by time, among writers and thinkers of all ages. Such a collection of ideas, like collections of every kind, involved what Benjamin called "a process of renewal":

> The most profound enchantment for the collector is the locking of individual items within a magic circle in which they are fixed as the final thrill, the thrill of acquisition, passes over them. Everything remembered and thought, everything conscious, becomes the pedestal, the frame, the base, the lock of his property. The period, the region, the craftsmanship, the former ownership—for a true collector the whole background of an item adds up to a magic encyclopedia whose quintessence is the fate of his object. . . .
>
> I fully realize that my discussion of the mental climate of collecting will confirm many of you in your conviction that this passion is behind the times, in your distrust of the collector type. Nothing is further from my mind than to shake either your conviction or your distrust. But one thing should be noted: the phenomenon of collecting loses its meaning as it loses its personal owner. Even though public collections may be less objectionable socially and more useful academically than private collections, the objects get their due only in the latter. I do know that time is running out for the type I am discussing here and have been representing before you a bit *ex officio*. But, as Hegel put it, only when it is dark does the owl of Minerva begin its flight. Only in extinction is the collector comprehended.

Benjamin traced his preoccupation with objects-as-symbols to his own childhood, which he described with Proustian exactitude in a book that became a casualty of the emigration and was first published ten years after his death: *A Berlin Childhood Around 1900.* His father, appropriately enough, was a well-to-do antique dealer who owned an interest in an auction gallery: had there not been a preponderance of poor Jews in the city, one would be tempted to say that Benjamin came from a "typical" Berlin Jewish background. It was typical, at any rate, of the Jewish middle classes—the professional people and businessmen who lived in the western half of Berlin and sent their children to the secular private schools also attended by children of the Gentile bourgeoisie. In his parents' home and at his grandmother's, "where I felt even more secure than at my parents'," he was surrounded by a world of reassuringly solid objects that came to have a certain ritual meaning: the massive dinner table set for company with cups, glasses, goblets; the immaculate white porcelain decorated with a pattern of cornflowers; the special forks for lobster and knives for oysters. . . . There were cupboards filled with silver champagne buckets, soup tureens, Delft vases, majolica ware, bronze urns and glass bowls; years later he still remembered the cases filled with the househould silver, in which everything was multiplied not ten but twenty or thirty times. "And when I looked at these long, long rows of mocha spoons or knife rests, fruit knives or oyster forks, the enjoyment of this profusion struggled with the fear that those who were being expected might all look alike, just as our cutlery did."*

There were other objects that the boy himself brought into the house. "Every stone that I found, every flower I picked and every captured butterfly was already the beginning of a collection, and indeed everything I possessed constituted, for me, one single collection. 'Straightening out' would have meant destroying an edifice of prickly chestnuts that were my morning stars, tin foil that was a hoard of silver, building blocks that were coffins, cactuses that were trees of the dead and copper pennies that were shields." The three Benjamin children were fussily brought up, surrounded by governesses, aunts, a mother, a grandmother. The Benjamins were "well connected" in German-Jewish society. Walter's paternal grandmother was descended from the van Geldern family, which meant that he was related to Heine and, at least distantly, to the Sternheim-Wolfskehl-Lessing galaxy. His mother was a sister of the well-known mathematician, Arthur Schönfliess, who became rector of the University of Frankfurt. His cousin Gertrud Chodziesener (their mothers were sisters) was to become better known under her nom de plume, Gertrud Kolmar (Kolmar was the German name of the Polish village, Chodziesen, from which her father's family had come to Germany). Another literary relative, Günther Stern, changed his name to Günther Anders ("Different") when he became a writer. Anders's recollections of exile have already been quoted; his first wife, Hannah Arendt, was to write the classic essay on Benjamin.

Born on July 15, 1892, Benjamin was still subjected to "the old-fashioned forms of school discipline," including thrashings and public humiliation, that characterized fin-de-siècle education. "Though I experienced them only during my first years at school, the spell of fear that was cast on me during those years was never

---

*Hannah Arendt, in her introduction to Benjamin's *Illuminations,* goes much too far, I think, in comparing this "atmosphere of insecurity and self-consciousness which truly was anything but suitable for the raising of children" with Kafka's arch-oedipal anxiety, and in attributing both to Jewish mores. The anxiety engendered by Wilhelmine upbringing was nonsectarian and stemmed from the authoritarianism of German education as a whole.

lifted." Even so he acquired a reputation as the most brilliant student at the Kaiser Friedrich Schule in Berlin, emerging as a leader and spokesman of the reformist youth movement founded by Gustav Wynekens. His friend and biograp:her Gershom Scholem remembered seeing him for the first time at a student meeting: "His appearance was unforgettable. Without looking at the audience, he spoke with great intensity in words that could have been published without revision, addressing his remarks to one of the upper corners of the auditorium, at which he stared fixedly the entire time."

Later they became fast friends, and Scholem recalls that Benjamin could never sit still when he talked, but would walk around the room until he had reached a conclusion: "then he would stand still and, in his peculiarly intense way, confront you with his position on the question or, more experimentally, with a formulation of a possible position. If you were alone with him he would gaze at you with wide-open eyes." But in public he persisted in addressing the furthest corner of the ceiling: "It gave him an altogether magical appearance."

Although Benjamin was not handsome, Scholem adds, his high forehead, framed by a mass of dark-brown hair, made him an impressive figure. "He had a beautiful speaking voice, which was melodic and memorable. . . . He was of middle height, very slender (as he remained for many years), dressed inconspicuously, and usually walked with a slight stoop. I don't think I ever saw him walk with his head erect. His gait had something unmistakable about it, something pensive and tentative, which was probably due to his shortsightedness." Other friends also commented on the peculiarity of Benjamin's way of walking. "It was both an advancing and a tarrying, or rather a thoroughly personal combination of the two," Max Rychner remembered. "His conversation, however, did not have this rapid to and fro; he was a man of deep reflection who knew how to listen in an exceptionally encouraging way."

There was something about him, Scholem writes, "of the purity and directness, the dedication to the spiritual, of a Scripture scholar who has been transported into the next world and is engaged in the quest for his mystic text." He had deep blue eyes, usually hidden behind thick glasses, a straight nose, a "full, sensuous mouth" surmounted by a bushy mustache, and "beautiful hands, small and expressive." Scholem says that he "looked Jewish" in a quiet, rather retiring way. Courteous and often diffident, he was not at all given to the proverbial Berlin "coldness-of-the-snout" with which the city was afflicted, though he liked to lapse into *Berlinerisch* dialect for comic effect. "In those years,"

Scholem recalls, "his highest word of praise was when he called something 'extraordinary.' . . ."

Benjamin was one of the few young men of his generation whose education was not seriously interrupted by World War I. He managed to persuade an army medical commission that his sciatica and assorted nervous complaints made him unfit for military service, and he obtained an exit visa allowing him to continue his studies in neutral Switzerland. In 1919, after two years at the University of Bern, he became a Doctor of Philosophy with a brilliantly wordy, cerebral dissertation on *The Concept of Art Criticism in German Romanticism*: with 317 citations in 106 pages of text it was already something of a quote-collector's masterpiece. By then he had been married for two years and was the father of a one-year-old son. His wife, Dora Kellner, was the daughter of a prominent Viennese Zionist and Shakespeare authority, Professor Leon Kellner. They had fallen in love while she was still married to her first husband, a Munich businessman, and Scholem describes it as a stormy marriage: "Dora was full-breasted, with a tendency to the Junoesque, very passionate and quick to flare up," with the result that there were constant fireworks. After their divorce, she confided to Scholem that Benjamin was a neurotic whose "intellect stood in the way of his sexuality"—a not uncommon complaint among intellectuals. Yet it was Benjamin's thesis, staunchly defended over the years, that there was no such thing as an unhappy love, and the experience with Dora failed to dampen his enthusiasm for other interesting women. "I have come to know three different women in my life and three different men in myself," he once wrote in his diary. "To write my life story would mean to depict the development and disintegration of these three men, and the compromises that were reached among them." In any event, women never ceased to find him fascinating. "His laughter was magical," reported his friend Olga Parem. "When he laughed a whole world seemed to open up."

Until he was thirty, Benjamin was financially dependent on his parents, whose insistence that he begin to earn his own living he regarded as "petty and tyrannical." As Hannah Arendt has explained, this was an ingrained prewar attitude: since unbaptized Jews were still barred from civil service careers (and hence university professorships), intellectual sons of well-to-do German-Jewish fathers were furnished with private incomes so that they could afford to accept courtesy professorships and become independent scholars. Though the religious requirement was dropped under the Weimar Republic, it was still difficult for someone like Benjamin to obtain a university post. He expected his father to set him up as a private scholar once he had acquired "my proof of public recognition"—his *Habilitation,* so called, which was a sort of second doctoral thesis that served as the ticket of admission to the lower, unsalaried ranks of a university faculty. The elder Benjamin, however, wanted his son to go into something practical, preferably banking. To make matters worse, Benjamin's immensely complex *Ursprung des deutschen Trauerspiels* (Origins of German Tragedy) failed to bring him the expected *Habilitation* at Frankfurt University; the two professors to whom it was submitted claimed not to have understood a word of it. It had been designed to show "the organic power of allegory as the very foundation of the Baroque," but he was not surprised that some of his readers (there were very few) were put off by this plethora of quotations—"the craziest mosaic technique imaginable," as he wrote to Scholem. It was typical of Benjamin that he was proudest of the six quotations that serve as chapter headings: "almost all of them from Baroque writings that can no longer be found—no one could have gathered rarer or more precious ones."

Rychner, who received a copy of the book when it was finally published in 1928, remembered Benjamin asking him, when they next met, whether he had "read the book starting at the beginning, namely with the introduction." When Rychner replied that yes, that was the way he usually read books, Benjamin said that he had gone about it "in just the wrong way, since one could understand the introduction only if one were versed in the kabala. . . . I told him, perhaps somewhat naïvely, that he might have done better, in that case, to have placed the introduction in the back of the book, as an epilogue, if he expected the reader to begin with the main text." Afterward, in a letter to Rychner, Benjamin explained: "I have never been able to think or inquire other than, if I may so put it, in a theological sense—namely in keeping with the talmudic teaching concerning the forty-nine levels of meaning in every passage of the Torah." Under the circumstances it was not surprising that neither the literary nor the academic world knew what to make of this young man who had seemingly read his way through the whole of German Baroque literature—*terra incognita* for everyone else—and who had drawn his *Trauerspiel* illustrations from a collection of six hundred quotations especially assembled for the purpose. The upshot was that not a single critic reviewed the book and Benjamin's plans for an academic career came to nothing. Instead he became a free-lance critic, contributing articles to some of the more intelligent magazines, such as *Der Querschnitt* and *Die*

Literarische Welt. This sort of work struck him as "ignominious writing-for-profit," but he insisted on keeping even the book reviews "on a certain intellectual level, so as not to arouse my own nausea." Among the more than two hundred articles and reviews reprinted in the Collected Works I have been unable to find a single piece of merely routine writing.

As a free-lance writer he was fortunate in combining the tastes of a literary *grand seigneur* with an astonishing serendipity—the knack of finding magnificent surrealist quotations in places where no one else would dream of looking for them. Among the trophies he brought back from his travels, for example, were the dying thoughts of a severed head, communicated at a guillotining to a Belgian mind-reader and recorded by the nineteenth-century Belgian painter Antoine Wiertz: "The severed head saw, thought and suffered. And I saw what he saw, understood what he thought, and felt what he suffered. How long did that last? Three minutes, I was told. The executed man must have thought it was three hundred years. . . ." For Benjamin the severed head fell precisely into that frontier territory between thought and language which was his favorite area of operations: "The man whose head is cut off continues to hope. . . ."

Benjamin had returned to Berlin where, as Scholem notes, his writing had earned him "a great reputation among a small number of people." Hugo von Hofmannsthal had described his essay on Goethe's *Elective Affinities* as "absolutely incomparable." Other literati who knew his work admired him as "an extraordinarily profound and serious, melancholy spirit, a man of great promise whose personality and way of thinking were particularly difficult and idiosyncratic."

He lived apart from the literary Berlin of Dada, Tucholsky and the Kurfürstendamm. "I lead a very lonely life, so that my work, too, suffers from it," he wrote in 1923. He rarely went out except to browse in a bookshop or visit a library: "I lack all means of communication." His one great regret in later years was that he had thus missed the opportunity of getting to know Kafka while he was in Berlin, but it was not until after Kafka's death that Benjamin came to recognize his own elective affinities with Kafka's work. One wonders what sort of friendship might have sprung up between them. Much of what Benjamin wrote about Kafka's writing—"his parables are never exhausted by what is explainable. . . . One has to find one's way in them circumspectly, cautiously, warily"—is equally applicable to his own. And Benjamin perceived Kafka's roots more clearly than any other critic:

In his depth Kafka touches the ground which neither "mythical divination" nor "existential theology" supplied him with. It is the core of folk tradition, the German as well as the Jewish. Even if Kafka did not pray—and this we do not know—he still possessed in the highest degree what Malebranche called "the natural prayer of the soul": attentiveness. And in this attentiveness he included all living creatures, as saints include them in their prayers.

This same unflagging attentiveness to significant detail was also the hallmark of Benjamin's work. For his first nonscholarly book, *Einbahnstrasse* (One-way Street), he availed himself of surrealist license to put together a kaleidoscopic collection of perceptions and intuitions about the world's minutiae. A sign in the park or an advertising billboard is sufficient to launch him into forty-nine artful somersaults of allegory and exegesis.

Ernst Bloch called the result "Philosophy in revue form." The *Pensées* of Pascal might have looked like this had he been a twentieth-century Berliner. *Einbahnstrasse*—writing, of course, is a one-way street—contains Benjamin's Thirteen Theses Against Snobs and his Seven Principles for Writing Thick, Stuffy Books, as well as his considered opinions on the class struggle, amusement parks, happiness, money, publishers, Karl Kraus ("Karl Kraus dances the warrior-dance before the tomb of the German language"), postage stamps ("stamps are the visiting cards that national governments leave in the children's playroom"), art museums ("the facial expressions of people walking through picture galleries reveal an ill-concealed disappointment that nothing hangs there but pictures"), climate ("in summer one notices the fat people, in winter the thin ones") and the art of quotation ("quotations in my works are like robbers by the wayside who make an armed attack and relieve an idler of his convictions"). His attentiveness runs the gamut from life to death. His eye is caught by "the incomparable language of the skull: a complete emptiness of expression—the blackness of the empty eye sockets—combined with the fiercest possible expression, the grinning rows of teeth." His dreams of death are set down with the disarming honesty of a child: "In a dream I took my own life with a rifle. When the gun went off I did not awaken, but saw myself lying there for a time, as a corpse. Only then did I wake up." A chauvinist advertising slogan of the twenties, "Germans, Drink German Beer!" brings him face to face with the phenomenon which was to cost him his life: "The mob is possessed by a frenetic hatred of the intellectual life and regards its own numbers as license to destroy it. Wherever they can, people fall in to form rank and file. . . . No one sees further than the back of the man in front of him, and everyone is proud to serve in a similarly exemplary capacity for the man behind him."

Benjamin's tower of books was not so remote from the world of political events that he could avoid seeing that Germany had taken a dangerous turn toward the militant Teutonism he had always despised. His letters express concern that "the narrow-mindedness with which this nation is trying to prolong its prison-like solitary confinement" was cutting Germany off not only from its European neighbors but from its own humanist traditions. He himself never lost sight "of the profound way in which I am tied" to German tradition: "Nothing leads deeper or binds one more intimately than the study and 'revival' of early German litera-ture. . . ." There was no inconsistency in his being simultaneously attracted to the Jewish tradition. Thanks to Scholem, the foremost modern scholar of the kabala, he knew much more about medieval Judaism than other German-Jewish writers, and he saw many points of contact between the Baroque and Romantic Germany that he loved and the world of Jewish mysticism that he found no less fascinating. "German and Jew," he once wrote, "confront each other as related extremes."

Scholem has pointed out that Benjamin differed markedly from such writers as Schnitzler, Zweig, Werfel and Wassermann, "who took it for granted that they belonged to the German nation." Benja-min never believed in "this terrible and tragic illusion." In Scholem's view, only Freud, Kafka and Benjamin had any real conception of "the distance between themselves as Jews and their German readers." Although they rarely wrote about Judaism as such, "they knew they were German writers but not Germans. However firmly they felt committed to the German language and its world of ideas, they never considered themselves at home there. . . ." Still, Benjamin confessed to feeling happiest when "the Jewish world in my thought" was hedged about with French and German ideas. At one point he firmly resolved to study He-brew because it would open up "a whole new level" of literary possibilities (i.e., untapped sources of quotations). Yet apart from a few trial lessons he could never bring himself to sit down and actually study the language. In much the same way he kept post-poning the voyage to Palestine that Scholem had persuaded him to make. Year after year he would announce his imminent departure and then cancel his plans. "In this matter," he conceded, "I have come up against a pathological indecisiveness that I have also en-countered in some of my other activities."

Competing interests were pulling him in too many different directions. After the failure of his marriage he had fallen in love with Asja Lacis, a Latvian stage director who was an ardent apostle of the Russian Revolution. Under her tutelage he became a Marxist—not, as he told Rychner, because he was an admirer of materialist philosophy, "but because I am trying to direct my thinking toward those areas in which the truth is most heavily concentrated." Marxism seemed closer to the truth than the "eternal verities" of German academic philosophy: at least its attitudes seemed "more humane and fruitful" on most of the important issues of the day. In her memoirs, Asja Lacis was to claim credit for having discouraged his incipient Zionism by persuading him that the road for true progressives led to Moscow, not Jerusalem.* "I can safely say," she writes, "that it was I who prevented Walter Benjamin from going to Palestine." As a counterweight to Scholem she introduced him to Bertolt Brecht, whom he admired more than any other living writer. They confronted each other as mutual admirers and related extremes—the protest-poet and the kabalist-critic, both structuralists at heart. Though Benjamin much preferred the subtler forms of dialectic, he was to write an essay in favor of Brecht's simplistic Marxism—Brecht himself called it *plumpes Denken* (crude thinking)—because political circumstances seemed to require it: "You can't make an omelette without breaking eggs."

Aware that he was "never consistent in the most important matters," Benjamin toyed for a time with the idea of becoming a communist like Brecht; even of joining the party—more or less "experimentally," as he said, in order to find out what it might feel like to be committed to a specific course of political action. In the end his doubts held him back: he wondered whether the Jews would find communism "effective" for solving their particular problems. Rather than relinquish his political independence he decided to retain something of his erstwhile "anarchism." Marxism, he wrote, at least offered a mechanism for understanding what was happening to the masses, but "while anarchist methods are useless, communist 'aims' are nonsense, and nonexistent."

A two-month visit to Moscow in 1926 left him with decidedly mixed feelings about developments in the Soviet Union. In the editorial offices of the *Great Soviet Encyclopedia*, with its five-tier *Apparat* of editors, "I myself was able to observe with how much

---

*We have already seen how dangerous it was for people like Herwarth Walden and Zensl Mühsam to make this assumption. Asja Lacis herself was to spend many years in the Gulag, but lived to tell the tale.

ignorance and opportunism they vacillate between the Marxist program of knowledge and the attempt to secure European prestige." (The article on Goethe which he was commissioned to write for the encyclopedia was chopped to pieces by the editors.) As for the Soviet experiment as a whole, Benjamin wondered "what is to become of Russia now; perhaps a genuinely socialist society; perhaps something quite different. The struggle that will decide this question goes on without interruption."

A visit to Paris, just after Moscow, provided more cogent reasons for remaining in Europe. He was so happy to be in Paris that he even gave up reading for a time, or so he said. He tasted something of literary life in the salon of the Count de Pourtalès, went book-shopping along the Seine and scoured the humbler districts for collectable objects: gingerbread men, old toys, and "the wonderful glass spheres in which thick snow falls" that were for sale at the *foire aux jambons et aux ferrailles,* the ham and old iron market. The idea for the *Passages* project was born on these wanderings through streets that seemed unchanged since Baron Haussmann's day. He had translated Baudelaire and Balzac; now he wanted to translate the whole of nineteenth-century Paris into his precise, unpredictable German prose. The book was to be "a dialectical *féerie*" (a fairy play) and he thought it might prove a precarious enterprise "for never have I written anything at such risk of failure."

Subsequent visits to Paris only increased his anxiety on this point. "The *Passages* project takes on a steadily more mysterious and insistent expression," he reported in 1929. "It howls like a little beast at night if I have not watered it at the most esoteric springs during the day." Determined to explore not only the façade of Baudelaire's Paris but also the interior of his *paradis artificiel,* he arranged to make a series of carefully annotated, medically supervised trips into "the domain of hashish." In this, too, Benjamin was ahead of his time, at least as far as the German writers were concerned, but one wonders what Baudelaire (or William Burroughs, for that matter) would have made of these very fastidious attempts at letting go.

He would have liked to stay on in Paris, but it seemed to offer no possibilities for making a living. After his divorce and the death of his parents, he had to live on whatever he could earn as a writer: "There are some places where I can earn a minimal income, and others where I can live on a minimal income, but not a single one in which these two conditions coincide." Thus he was still in Berlin, writing radio scripts and magazine articles, when the Nazis took over. His intuition had always carried him beyond immediate events: years before he had already foreseen the consequences of the totalitarian attitudes that flourished at the universities, the surreptitious sadism of some of the bureaucrats with whom he had come into contact. The mock curriculum which he drew up in 1924 as a satire on the German university esprit de *Korps* contains, among its more macabre and prophetic entries, an "Introduction to the Theory of Deportation" for students of jurisprudence, a course in "Theory and Practice of Defamation" and a laboratory seminar for medical students: "Practical Studies in Extermination." Yet during the first few weeks of the Hitler era he was undecided whether to stay on; he wanted to resist "the impulse to panic" in that highly charged atmosphere, when thousands of swastika pins suddenly blossomed forth on the lapels of people who had not previously declared their allegiance to Hitler—"this German atmosphere in which one looks first at people's lapels and then preferably not into their faces at all." By mid-March, however, he was persuaded that it was time to leave. (His brother Georg, who failed to follow his example, was shunted in and out of prisons and camps until he was finally killed by the Gestapo.)*

After a stop in Paris he went to Ibiza, the Spanish Mediterranean island where he had spent the spring of 1932. Ibiza and the other Balearics have since become the Miami Beach of Europe, but in the early thirties it was the sleepy backwater described in Eliot Paull's *The Life and Death of a Spanish Town*. Benjamin rented a furnished house and was able to live for about fifty cents a day. In his descriptions of Ibiza he focuses, as usual, on the allegorical relationship between objects and human beings:

> They still plow their fields and raise their animals in an archaic way, and there are no more than four cows on the entire island because the peasants cling to their traditional goat economy; one never sees farm machinery, and the fields are irrigated by ancient well-wheels turned by mules, just as they were centuries ago. The interiors are just as archaic: three chairs on the wall of the room opposite the entrance greet the visitor's eye with the same gravity and assurance as if they were Cranachs or Gauguins on the wall; a straw hat hung on the back of a chair takes on more importance than a drapery of costly Gobelins.

---

*When Georg married "a likable young girl" named Hilde Lange in 1926, Walter Benjamin commented that "his Gentile parents-in-law have had to bite into a doubly bitter apple"—for Georg was both Jewish and an active Communist. Hilde Benjamin became an underground Communist party worker during the war and helped preserve some of Gertrud Kolmar's manuscripts; she served as minister of justice of the German Democratic Republic from 1953 to 1967.

The six months he spent on Ibiza represented the outer circle of his emigration: until his return to Paris in October it was still possible to pretend that he was merely taking a holiday. Yet during his walks through the olive groves he was hard at work on a train of philosophical speculation concerning the fundamental nature of literature, especially the relationship of storytelling to life that forced itself on his consciousness in this austere environment. The narrator's art, he decided, was also "an artisan form of communication," because one man's experience, passed from mouth to mouth (often in a workshop full of journeymen) "is the source from which all storytellers have drawn." And it occurred to him that in the last analysis, "Death is the sanction of everything that the storyteller can tell. He has borrowed his authority from death." Indeed, storytelling as a genre had declined in the nineteenth century to the same extent as the "omnipresence and vividness" of death had been removed from ordinary human experience by the emergence of hospitals and old-people's homes:

> Dying was once a public process in the life of the individual and a most exemplary one; think of the medieval pictures in which the deathbed has turned into a throne toward which the people press through the wide-open doors of the death house. In the course of modern times dying has been pushed further and further out of the perceptual world of the living. There used to be no house, hardly a room, in which someone had not once died. (The Middle Ages also felt spatially what makes that inscription on the sundial of Ibiza, *Ultima multis,** significant as the temper of the times.) Today people live in rooms that have never been touched by death, dry dwellers of eternity, and when their end approaches they are stowed away in sanatoria or hospitals by their heirs. It is, however, characteristic that not only a man's knowledge or wisdom, but above all his real life— and this is the stuff that stories are made of—first assumes transmissible form at the moment of his death. Just as a sequence of images is set in motion inside a man as his life comes to an end—unfolding the views of himself under which he has encountered himself without being aware of it—suddenly in his expressions and looks the unforgettable emerges and imparts to everything that concerned him that authority which even the poorest wretch in dying possesses for the living around him. This authority is at the very source of the story.

This typically Benjaminesque line of reasoning is from the essay on Nicolai Leskov (author of *The Lady Macbeth of Mzensk*), in which

---

*It was not a sundial but the face of the tower clock. Still, the sense is the same: each passing hour is, for many, the last.

he developed the several strands of his thesis that it is death which defines the boundaries of literature. In this essay he also analyzes the relationship between the novel and its reader, who "seizes upon his material" and proceeds to devour it—"Indeed, he swallows up the material as the fire devours logs in the fireplace. The suspense which permeates the novel is very much like the draft which stimulates the flame in the fireplace and enlivens its play." Readers of novels, Benjamin says, are prepared to follow the characters to their death, or at any rate to the end of the book, a figurative death, and it is only then that the "meaning" of a character's life is fully revealed. Once again, therefore, the story derives its ultimate sanction from the manner of its ending:

> "A man who dies at the age of thirty-five," said Moritz Heimann once, "is at every point in his life a man who died at the age of thirty-five." Nothing is more dubious than this sentence—but for the sole reason that the tense is wrong. A man—so says the truth that was meant here—who died at thirty-five will appear to *remembrance* at every point in his life as a man who dies at the age of thirty-five. In other words, the statement that makes no sense for real life becomes indisputable for remembered life. The nature of the character in a novel cannot be presented any better than is done in this statement.

When he wrote these words, Benjamin had already weathered a great emotional crisis that had brought him to the brink of suicide. He had turned forty in 1932, and he was now more prone than ever to the doubts and self-lacerations which the French sum up in a phrase that sounds reassuringly Mediterranean, *la crise du midi* (noonday crisis). He had, by now, lost his youthful élan and become rather stout; people began treating him as a faintly comic figure. The French writer Guy Selz, with whom he spent a lot of time on Ibiza, remembered him as brilliant and unsociable: "Benjamin was corpulent, and his very German ponderousness was in strong contrast to the agility of his mind, which revealed itself in the vivid gleam of his eyes behind their thick lenses." Their long walks through the hilly landscape "took even longer because our conversations constantly caused Benjamin to stand still." Whenever something interested him he would say, *"Tiens, tiens!"* "Then I knew that he would now reflect and also stand still. Sometimes he would also say, as if to himself, 'so, so!' " He would constantly interject *tiens, tiens!* even when speaking to fellow Germans, and this quirk had earned him the nickname Tiens-tiens among the younger Germans. Benjamin developed an understandable aversion to most of these tourists and expatriates: Selz recalled that in the presence of someone he disliked he would barricade himself in his easy chair "like a hedgehog," and at such moments, "nothing could have induced him to break his silence." But his most striking characteristic was his fanatical interest in everything that had to do with his work: "And what was there that didn't concern his work? He seemed unable to interest himself in anything that did not contribute to his writing. In this respect one can describe Walter Benjamin as the fully developed archetype of the wholly intellectual man."

He contracted malaria on Ibiza, and when he arrived in Paris that autumn he lacked the strength "to climb the stairs of the cheap hotels where I am obliged to stay." For a few months he had been kept supplied with ghostwriting assignments for German newspapers, but as the Nazis tightened their grip on the press he was "cut off from everything, even the most modest German sources of income." Eventually he recovered his health and found other ways of supporting himself. The exiled Institute for Social Research, formerly of Frankfurt University but now comfortably established in New York, agreed to pay him a small monthly stipend enabling him to go on with the *Passages* project. He was also expected to contribute articles to the Institute's *Zeitschrift für Sozialforschung*, a journal of Hegelian-Marxist sociology that continued to be published in German—though edited in New York and printed in Paris—until the beginning of the war. Martin Jay has suggested that Max Horkheimer, the institute's director, wanted to keep it that way as a symbolic "link with Germany's humanist past." Admittedly it was also much more convenient for the intellectuals of the institute (among them Herbert Marcuse, Erich Fromm and Benjamin's friend at court, Theodor Adorno) to go on writing in the language they knew best. Since the group's endowment fund had been transferred from Europe to America, they were not really compelled to adapt to their new linguistic environment. They did, however, make one significant concession to the American way: henceforth, in their journal, words like "Marxism" and "communism" were replaced by "dialectical materialism" or "the materialist theory of society."

In spite of his Marxist sympathies, Benjamin himself had never had much use for the special philosophical jargon of the institute's "Critical Theory," so called. The difference between his approach and theirs, as Adorno explained in the 1960s, was that Benjamin's philosophy did not take place "in the realm of concepts" but, rather, in "nonconceptual details, in concrete moments." Though hopelessly at odds with "the classifying, abstract, grandiosely universalist" tendencies of what was then regarded as philosophy,

Benjamin had the happy knack of "unlocking the unopenable as though with a magic key." Yet thirty years earlier it had been none other than Adorno who had rejected the first portion of *Passages* that Benjamin submitted to the institute for publication. Himself a polymath of breathtaking scope, and one of the most prolix masters of "Critical Theory," Adorno possessed the peculiar and unerring talent (so widely distributed in the editorial profession) for finding fault with precisely the best parts of a writer's work. His main objection to the *Passages* was that they were "undialectical," i.e., Benjamin's interpretation of historical cause and effect failed to agree with Adorno's. In a moment of self-awareness he apologized for the "bitchy form" of his criticism, but he went on sniping at the *Passages* anyway: how could the unmethodical Benjamin fail to understand that "the materialistic determination of cultural characteristics is effected only in a collective *Gesamtprozess*?"

Benjamin went back to his table at the Bibliothèque Nationale a wiser but sadder man: "in view of your criticism of my failings, the ground threatens to disappear from under my feet." He had spent years on this project and was determined to see it through; that was why he could not really leave Paris for more than a few weeks at a time, and why he failed to heed the advice of friends who urged him to move on, to either New York or Jerusalem. "The actual writing of this work can probably take place only in Paris," he insisted in 1935. And in 1939, even after war had been declared, he was still insisting that "nothing in the world, for me, could replace the Bibliothèque Nationale." Certainly he spent his happiest hours there, burrowing deeper and deeper into the stacks, and there were days when he experienced a sort of intellectual rapture of the deeps, the feeling of having "won the freedom to pursue my simple pleasures as a reader, free of all literary considerations."

Sometimes, behind his bastion of books, he gave thought to the "new and catastrophic dangers" that threatened the Jews of Europe if they were not rescued and brought to Palestine. Yet he seems to have felt somehow exempt from these dangers. When Scholem visited him in Paris during the summer of 1938, Benjamin realized that the impression he made on his old friend was that "of a man who has, with great difficulty, pried open the jaws of a crocodile and set up housekeeping there." Perhaps his summer visits to Bertolt Brecht, then living in Denmark, gave him a false sense of mobility—the idea that he could get on a train and leave if ever the crocodile's mouth threatened to snap shut. Yet after Hitler's annexation of Austria he took Kafkaesque notes on what was happening to the Jews trapped in Vienna and wondered "how much longer one will be able to breathe the air of Europe." Reading the diatribes of antisemitic French authors like Léon Daudet, he was moved to ask: "When will the alliance between ignorance and infamy, which was formed in Germany . . . also go into action here?"

The war provided an almost immediate answer to that question. Shortly after it began, all males aged sixteen to sixty-seven among the German émigrés in France—legally they were now "stateless" by Nazi decree—were rounded up and sent to French internment camps.* The government was unprepared for this operation, and there were no facilities for housing such a large number of prisoners. In Paris, some six thousand men spent ten days locked up in an open football stadium before being shipped off to makeshift camps further to the south. Benjamin, who was among them, ended up in a so-called "camp of volunteer workers" in Nevers. He would not have minded serving the cause in some way, Benjamin wrote to a French friend, but he had collapsed during the forced march to the camp and "physically I am worth nothing. The camp doctors have placed me *au repos.*" He had already become accustomed to being imprisoned as a "potential enemy of France," but he chafed at the camp routine and the overcrowding: life at Nevers was one long trial of nerves. Hans Sahl, who was interned with him, recalls that it was the prisoners themselves who organized the camp and brought "German" ideas of hygiene and discipline to the deserted castle in which they were housed: "The Boy Scout enthusiasm behind the barbed wire fences swept out the rooms with straw brooms, hung laundry on the line and organized lectures on the difference between Freud and Jung, Lenin and Trotsky." Benjamin entered into the spirit of the thing by offering a course in philosophy "for advanced students": the fee, in the prevailing black-market currency, was three Gauloise cigarettes or a pants button. He also tried to organize a camp journal for intellectuals: the first issue was to be devoted to "The Creation of a Society Out of a Nothing," as he described the sociology of camp life.

But the French P.E.N. Club had interceded on his behalf and he was released before the magazine could be produced. He had told Sahl that "sitting on the terrace of a café and twiddling my thumbs

---

*There were also some bona fide Reich Germans among the internees. As it turned out, these were better looked after than the non-Nazis because they were represented by the International Red Cross and protected by fear of retaliation. The non-Nazis, who lacked legal status, were treated as expendable. Koestler's book about them is entitled *Scum of the Earth.*

is all I still hope for," but when they met again in Paris he was hard at work, writing what were to be the last of his commentaries on the curious ways of mankind, his *Theses on the Philosophy of History*. Among them is his unforgettable description of the Angel of History:

> His face is turned toward the past. Where we perceive a chain of events, he sees one single catastrophe which keeps piling wreckage upon wreckage and hurls it in front of his feet. The angel would like to stay, awaken the dead, and make whole what has been smashed. But a storm is blowing from Paradise; it has got caught in his wings with such violence that the angel can no longer close them. This storm irresistibly propels him into the future to which his back is turned, while the pile of debris before him grows skyward. This storm is what we call progress.

Now that he was at last willing to leave France the exits were closed. His former wife had gone to England but was unable to obtain a British visa for him. He also applied for an American visa, but the mills of the State Department ground slowly.* To complicate matters he was suffering from a minor heart condition evidently brought on by his collapse at Nevers. Now when he walked in the street he was obliged to stop every three or four minutes. A doctor diagnosed myocarditis (a milder form of the disease that had killed Mahler). At the same time he began having Wiertz-like dreams: in one surrealist episode he dreamed of making himself comfortable in a sarcophagus "as though it were a bed," and of turning a poem into a scarf resembling a noose.

When France surrendered to the Germans in June 1940, Benjamin was among the thousands of refugees who poured into the still unoccupied south. He spent several weeks in Lourdes expecting to be arrested at any moment. Under the terms of the armistice, the French government was obliged to "surrender upon demand" any German refugees in France: hence Benjamin's remark, in a letter to Adorno dated August 2, 1940: "I am condemned to read every paper (now they consist of just a single sheet) as though it

---

*Robert Murphy, the American consul in Paris, had received instructions "not to grant too many visas." Recent studies have shown that the State Department official in charge of visa operations, Breckinridge Long, was at that time doing everything in his power to obstruct the entry of Jewish refugees into the United States. Of the 1,137 names of applicants submitted to the State Department between August 5 and December 18, 1940, only 238 received visas. Until he was replaced in 1944, Long worked assiduously, sometimes by deliberately suppressing information and falsifying cables, to prevent the admission of refugees. In this he had the support of powerful politicians like Representative Steven Pace of Georgia, who proposed a bill in Congress whereby "every Alien in the United States shall forthwith be deported." See Henry L. Feingold's *The Politics of Rescue* (New Brunswick, N.J., 1970).

were a ukase addressed to me personally, and to hear in every radio announcement the voice of misfortune. My efforts to reach Marseilles and to plead my case before the consul there were fruitless. For some time now, aliens have been forbidden to change their place of residence." He had, up to now, "remained calm even in difficult moments," but there was no denying "the precarious nature of my present situation," and it seemed to him, quite rightly, that only a handful of refugees would be able to escape from the trap in which they found themselves. His last letters suggest, however, that he was at least equally disturbed at finding himself "totally deprived of books" for the first time in his life.

In September his friends in New York at last succeeded in arranging a visa for him. At that time refugees with American visas and valid tickets from Lisbon to New York had relatively little trouble obtaining the Spanish and Portuguese transit visas required for the rail journey to Lisbon. But a French exit permit was required at the border, and the Vichy authorities, anxious to cooperate with the Gestapo, usually refused to issue these to German émigrés. Benjamin decided that his only chance was to cross into Spain illegally. Arthur Koestler, who had camouflaged his identity by joining the Foreign Legion, ran into him in Marseilles just when both of them were making preparations for escape: "Unable to obtain a French exit permit, he intended to walk into Spain across the Pyrenees, as hundreds of other refugees did. He had thirty tablets of a morphia compound, which he intended to swallow if caught; he said they were enough to kill a horse, and gave me half of the tablets, just in case."

Together with two companions, Benjamin actually reached Port Bou, the first town on the Spanish side, after a strenuous climb. One of the people with him, a Frau Gurland, afterward described their experiences in a letter to Adorno:

> No one knew the path; we had to climb part of the way on all fours. In the evening we arrived at Port Bou and went to the police station to ask them to stamp our papers. Four women and the three of us sat there for an hour, weeping and pleading with the officials; we were desperate. We showed them our perfectly valid documents. But we were all stateless, and they told us that a recently issued directive prohibited stateless persons from traveling in Spain. We were to be allowed to spend a night in a hotel under guard, and we were introduced to three policemen who were to escort us to the French border the following morning . . . for Benjamin that would mean imprisonment in a camp. We all went despondently to our rooms. At seven o'clock in the morning Frau Lipmann called me down to Benjamin's bedside. He told me that he had taken a large quantity of morphine at

ten o'clock the night before, but that I should try to pretend that he was ill. . . . Then he lost consciousness. I called a doctor, who diagnosed cerebral apoplexy and turned down my urgent request that Benjamin be sent to a hospital, in Figueras, on the grounds that he was already dying. . . . I had to call the local priest, and together we prayed on our knees for an hour.

Benjamin died that morning—September 27, 1940—and was buried in a local cemetery not unlike the ones he had known in Ibiza. In retrospect he now seems at every point in his life a man who died at the age of forty-eight. His death, as he had foreseen, was clothed in "that authority which even the poorest wretch in dying possesses for the living around him"; at least it made an impression on the Spanish police, for they allowed the rest of his party to continue their journey after all. The news of his suicide did not reach the outside world until ten days later, and as yet he was so little known that even the New York refugee newspaper *Aufbau* (Reconstruction) described him as "a well-known psychologist." What he would call the "meaning" of his life was not revealed until much later, but it was clear to those who knew him that, in accordance with his own theories, his life had derived its ultimate sanction from the manner of its ending. In the *Passages* he had paraphrased Baudelaire on this point, to the effect that suicide is "an act which seals a heroic will . . . not a resignation but a heroic passion. It is *the* achievement of modernism in the realm of the passions."

Hannah Arendt, in her magnificent essay on Benjamin, calls his suicide "an uncommon stroke of bad luck." Since the Spanish embargo on stateless refugees was lifted again shortly afterward, "only on that particular day was the catastrophe possible." That would imply that Benjamin's death was an isolated phenomenon, and somehow dependent on the vagaries of Spanish refugee policy. Actually it was quite the reverse: only the fortunate few managed to escape; death was the rule rather than the exception; Benjamin had been lucky to get as far as he did. In the last analysis, the "uncommon stroke of bad luck" that cost him his life was the fact that Hitler had become *Führer* of Germany and wielded the power to sweep away all the previously accepted moral standards of European civilization. Benjamin's "catastrophe" had thus been a long time in the making—after the war the Germans were to refer to their whole Hitler epoch as *Die Katastrophe*—and might have happened, in one way or another, on innumerable other days as well. It was not as though his were an isolated case. There were many like him; they differed only in that some of them chose to draw the line somewhat earlier in the process that turned human beings into the quarry of a great international *battu* hunt. Ernst Weiss, the novelist who was a friend of Kafka and a student of Freud, slashed his wrists in his Paris hotel the day the Germans marched into the city. The poet and playwright Walter Hasenclever took Veronal in the internment camp at Les Milles, near Aix-en-Provence, three weeks before his fiftieth birthday. Carl Einstein, the leading German critic of modern and primitive art, ex-officer of the Spanish Republican army and author of an important critique of society, *Die Fabrikation der Fiktion,* drowned himself in the turbulent waters of the Gave de Pau, near Bayonne, to avoid falling into the hands of the Gestapo. For people in this situation, suicide was not an aberration but a rational alternative to being tortured, deported and murdered.

The great majority of émigrés who remained in France were to become victims of the Vichy government, that "alliance between ignorance and infamy" whose emergence Benjamin had foreseen. Some 120,000 Jews were ultimately deported from France to the German extermination camps. Among them, incidentally, were thousands of young German Jews who had, like the novelist Hans Habe, volunteered for service in the French army. Most of them were assigned to three so-called *Régiments de marche de volontaires étrangers* or to regiments of the Foreign Legion. They fought at Narvik, Soissons and elsewhere, but after the fall of France they were demobilized without the rights of native-born soldiers. Most of them were sent to labor camps or concentration camps, whence they were later deported to Auschwitz.* One émigré soldier, still in uniform, demanded of his commanding officer why he and his comrades were being marched off under escort to a French concentration camp. *"C'est parce que vous avez trop aimé la France,"* was the answer.

From the first, refugee inmates of French camps were treated as prisoners rather than internees. There were dozens of camps: official documents referred to them not as *camps de concentration* but as *centres d'hébergement,* "supervised lodging centers" or "reception centers." Some of them were to achieve a certain fame by virtue of the novels or the poetry that were written about them. Walter Mehring, wishing he were back in the small hotels, composed a

---

*Six thousand of the luckier émigré soldiers were sent to three camps in North Africa to work on a Trans-Saharan Railway under what the U. S. Consul in Algiers described as "chain-gang conditions." Nationals of non-Axis countries were released soon after the Allied invasion of North Africa in November 1942, but German and Austrian Jews continued to be held in desert slave-labor camps until July 1943, under the 1938 French law authorizing the internment of "undesirable aliens." See Zosa Szajkowski, *Jews in the Foreign Legion* (New York, 1975).

scintillating vaudeville ballad about the forced-labor camp in which he found himself, Saint-Cyprien in the Pyrenees, better known as "the pest-hole of France." Despite its saintly name, "there is no saint to hear our plea." He writes of its barbed wire and police dogs, of prisoners being beaten, of hunger, fever and scurvy: "France has declared war on the victims." But Mehring's sense of humor, his proverbial *Berliner Schnauze*, has not yet deserted him:

> *Welch ein Triumph! 4000 Juden*
> *Verludern in den Bretterbuden.*

> What triumph this! 4000 Jews
> Condemned to rot in these tar-paper stews!

Most of what was written in and about the "supervised lodging centers" belongs, in the fullest sense, to the literature of the absurd. After his escape from France, Lion Feuchtwanger wrote about his experiences as a prisoner at Les Milles in *The Devil in France*—a book that gave British and American readers their first inkling of life in the French camps. Les Milles was an abandoned brick factory without furniture or washing facilities; the prisoners slept on the floor, and there were seven toilets for three thousand people. "Everywhere you stumbled over bricks, straw pallets, human beings. We squatted and lay one upon another. The crumbling bricks were greatly coveted, and it was only with difficulty that four or five needed to construct something approaching a seat could be got together." Though everyone was covered in brick dust, the prisoners persisted in addressing one another by their German titles: "How do you feel today, Herr Professor?" "How are you this morning, Herr Geheimrat?" Several of the prisoners had been decorated with the *Légion d'honneur*. One man had four sons serving in the French army. Max Ernst was among the painters in the camp; Walter Hasenclever and Franz Schoenberner among the writers. Of the interned veterans of the Foreign Legion, "many had lost an arm or a leg in the cause of France, almost all of them had been decorated. Now they trudged grimly around, their chests covered with ribbons and medals, sleeves dangling over stumps of arms, artificial legs clattering over the dirty floor of the brickworks and of the courtyards."

It was a scene worthy of a Max Ernst collage, but Les Milles was a relatively benign institution, later classified as a "departure" camp for those awaiting legal emigration. (Of 1,659 internees registered for emigration in the first six months of 1942, 129 actually succeeded in getting out.) Conditions were worse at Le Vernet, in the department of Ariège, where Arthur Koestler learned what it was like to do forced labor under the watchful eyes of the fascist *Garde mobile.* The camp had been built as a disciplinary barracks for Spanish Republican refugees and was administered with a "mixture of ignominy, corruption and *laisser-faire.*" Still he was grateful not to be in a German concentration camp: "In Liberal-Centigrade, Vernet was the zero-point of infamy; measured in Dachau-Fahrenheit it was still 32 degrees above zero. In Vernet beating-up was a daily occurrence; in Dachau it was prolonged until death ensued. In Vernet people were killed for lack of medical attention; in Dachau they were killed on purpose. In Vernet half of the prisoners had to sleep without blankets in 20 degrees of frost; in Dachau they were put in irons and exposed to the frost."

One of the worst, and largest, of the French camps was the vast compound at Gurs, *le camp de la mort,* built on swampy ground in the Pyrenees. When it rained the camp was transformed into a sea of mud. Hundreds of its prisoners died of malnutrition, typhus and tuberculosis before they could be turned over to the Gestapo. In November 1940 Gurs held over 15,000 prisoners: 7,200 of them had just been brought from Germany, where the entire Jewish population of Baden (6,900) and the Palatinate (11,500) had been rounded up and transported to Vichy France in an operation described as "a present from Gauleiter Wagner to the *Führer.*" It was only during this nightmarish razzia that many of the more naïve and trusting members of the Rhenish-Jewish community became aware that the Nazis were in earnest: that German antisemitism was no longer a matter of smashed windowpanes but of life and death. The sixty-eight-year-old poet Alfred Mombert and his seventy-two-year-old sister were among the deportees. At first he could hardly believe what had happened to them—turned out of their home without prior warning, transported to the railway station in trucks, then consigned to the unheated barracks of Gurs. The author of *Flowers of Chaos* had been a distinguished member of the Prussian Academy of Arts; a mystic poet whose work was often compared to Yeats's. "Do you suppose anything like this has ever happened to a German poet?" he asked, uncomprehendingly, in a letter from Gurs to a friend in Switzerland. And to think that "everything I wrote so lyrically in my poems (for the 'aesthetic' enjoyment of the Germans) I must now experience in the cruelest reality. . . ."

Mombert was too prominent a figure to be allowed to die anonymously at Gurs like the twelve hundred people, "mainly Jews from Baden," buried in the camp cemetery. In Switzerland the poet Hans Reinhart organized a "save Mombert" campaign to which Hermann Hesse and other prominent writers lent their support. The head of the Swiss police, Heinrich Rothmund, turned down their appeal in March 1941, but finally gave his consent late in autumn: Mombert and his sister were permitted to travel to Switzerland, where he was able to celebrate his seventieth birthday among friends shortly before dying of cancer contracted at Gurs. These final years represented a rude awakening from a life spent in splendid isolation as a "cosmic" poet who had seen himself as a minstrel "playing upon the world-harp." He had written of "the warm generous German earth" and of the linden trees which were, like himself, deeply rooted in it: *Einem schönen Lande zugehörig ganz/ bin ich tief verwurzelt meiner guten Erde. . . .* But now, in his time of exile, "the thoughts that once I thought"—*Gedanken die ich einst gedacht*—were "buried in a deep shaft":

> *Deine Hand greift nach dem Glas—*
> *doch du kannst nicht trinken!*
> *Du siehst die ganze Welt*
> *erschüttert in den Abgrund sinken.*

Your hand reaches for the cup—
But you cannot drink of this;
Before you the entire world
sinks shattered into the abyss.

But it was not only the German Jews who were shattered by the experiences of these years. They had, after all, grown up among fellow human beings, and some of these neighbors were horrified by what they saw of "the Gauleiter's gift to the *Führer*." In Mannheim a young German woman, Irmgard Herrmann, accompanied her "non-Aryan" friend Maria Krehbiel-Darmstädter, to the assembly area where the city's remaining 1,993 Jews were being rounded up for deportation. "The small column of people, escorted by police, was a shattering sight," she remembered later. "Among them were octogenarians and invalids who could no longer walk, dragging themselves along." Surrounded by police, the deportees waited hours for transport to arrive. "At one point the roll was called: were any of those present partners of mixed marriages? Frau Krehbiel spoke up, adding that she was now divorced. A last hope might have flickered up at that moment, but she was told: 'That doesn't count.' " Irmgard Herrmann decided to distribute bread among the deportees: a nearby baker gave it to her without asking for ration coupons. "When I returned with the bread, two of the policemen on guard stopped me and said it was inappropriate for a German girl with such thick blonde braids to help the Jews. They told me that evidently I didn't 'think German,' and that if the roles were reversed these Jews would not lift a finger. I answered that I knew the contrary to be true about the lady whom I had accompanied here, and that German was precisely what I considered my conduct to be. The policemen asked me to point out the 'lady' in question, and then hindered me no more."

Maria Krehbiel-Darmstädter was not a professional writer, but her collected *Letters from Gurs and Limonest,* published in 1970, are among the most important eyewitness accounts of the protracted French phase of the Final Solution. Her letters describe the psychological borderline where the old bourgeois reality ended and the new "final" reality began: a very different state of consciousness from that depicted in Koestler's *Scum of the Earth* or Hasenclever's *People Without Rights.* After forty-eight years of a busy, normal life—a Christian convert, she had been active as a Protestant welfare worker—she suddenly became aware of having lost all freedom of action, as well as her claim to be regarded as a human being. She had relatives in the outside, rational world: a sister in the United States, a brother in Switzerland; neither succeeded in obtaining a visa for her. German friends also tried to help; among them a first lieutenant in the Wehrmacht who prevailed on the Gestapo to grant him an interview with his old friend. Their meeting took place on January 6, 1943, at one of the Gestapo's Paris offices, a confiscated mansion on the Avenue Foch. She had been brought there from Drancy, a camp on the outskirts of Paris from which, as nearly everyone knew by then, the trains ran direct to the death camps in Poland. "We were ushered into a salonlike room furnished with antiques," the lieutenant wrote in the notes he made immediately after their interview:

> "I'm sorry the room is unheated," the [SS] officer said, turning toward Maria. "You'll have to make do. . . ." Her face seemed little changed, but paler, rather sallow, revealing her age. Her eyelids were reddened, as though inflamed; her expression serious, hardened by an effort of will. But she wore the glasses I knew so well, and her eyes shone. . . . The officer retired with a bow, remarking: "I shall leave the *Herrschaften* [lady and gentleman] alone for now," and he asked me to let him know when the conversation was terminated. Maria seemed to lose her self-control for a moment; I asked her to sit down. She buried her face in her hands, sighed *"Ach Gott,"* and cried a little. I stepped up to her and said: "I've brought you a package from your [ex-] husband, who sends you his very best regards. And also some

photos of your godchildren and friends." She looked at the pictures absentmindedly, as though anesthetized, and when she came to the last one she said, "That's one I haven't seen yet. . . ."

They talked for fifteen or twenty minutes. "You could have left Germany in good time," the lieutenant said, as though to reassure her, "but you didn't want to leave your friends or your home." "Yes," she said, "I would not have thought that it is so difficult to give it all up. But I carry it all in my heart. Tell them for me: *Ich vertrete Deutschland gut* [I am a worthy representative of Germany]. Give them all my greetings, all of them; my husband, his wife, his child. Give them this—[a small copy of the Gospel According to St. Matthew]—it is all I have." The lieutenant thought he could detect a discreet noise on the other side of the door. They stood up to tell each other *Auf Wiedersehen*—and "in turning away she said quietly, '*Adieu.*'"

There is something Expressionist in the formality of this interview which Carl Sternheim would certainly have understood: the symbolic farewell of the German and the German Jew, no longer confronting each other as Benjamin's "related extremes" or Wedekind's "two souls in the breast of mankind." The lieutenant writes: *Aus Gründen, die in den besonderen Umständen gelegen waren, schien es mir zweckmässig, Maria mit "Sie" anzureden, obwohl wir stets "Du" zueinander gesagt hatten.* This sentence is purest Sternheim: "For reasons arising from the particular circumstances, it seemed appropriate for me to address Maria with the formal *Sie*, although we had always said *Du* to each other." The I-Thou of the dialogue between friends had, under the pressure of events, been turned into something of an arm's-length transaction: the lieutenant's *Sie* already belongs to the language of her (unwritten) death sentence. The Gestapo officer's bow from the waist is another Sternheim touch: he is a young man of impeccable courtesy, not inappropriately assigned to duty here in the Avenue Foch, in the most elegant district of Paris. Thanks to an understanding reached between him and the lieutenant, Maria was not shipped from Drancy to Auschwitz until February 11, 1943.

The line of exile literature leading from Les Milles to Le Vernet, Saint-Cyprien and Gurs came to an end at Drancy with a book written by a French bystander: Dr. Charles Odic's *Stepchildren of France* (published afterward in an English translation by Henry Noble Hall). At Drancy the prisoners no longer had opportunities to write books of their own. They were searched, deprived of their last possessions, isolated, deported in freight cars. The Gestapo was nothing if not methodical. Fifty persons were herded into each car and each train consisted of twenty cars: if anyone committed suicide during the loading operation, his place was immediately filled with another, living body. "The train," Odic noted, "does not leave till it has its full toll of one thousand." Everything of value, even blankets and overcoats, was taken from the prisoners. Women were stripped and brutally searched by special police units: "It is rare that the search is fruitless; a lock of hair in a medallion, sometimes a little cross of gold, for many Jews are Catholics, a wedding ring. . . ."

> Finally there is a limit to horror, a moment when the features of the tortured express joy no matter what pains the executioners have inflicted. . . . Those who see the deportees go by, say: "The morale of those who left was good." This amazing, this miraculous phrase, I find it in letters and hear it from the lips of witnesses who often add: "Better than ours." Yet the worst is to come. . . . Those cars will stand forgotten for hours or days on sidings; they will roll on through unfathomable nights, in stinking air that no opening can change, shaking up a mass of humanity, torn by suffering, penetrated by death, that voids itself everywhere, a sightless jelly of the living and the dead.
>
> The cars will roll on, carrying their cargo of invading corpses, their darkness where voices become scarcer, leaving in their wake a sickening stench across the German countryside. Later it appears that the enemy did even worse, that he killed whole trainloads by hunger, by gas, that he completed his work with bludgeons and revolvers. Is it not superfluous? . . . They finished off shapeless forms, they could no longer hurt them, they no longer feared anything, they had passed the last limits of suffering, they had written ineffaceable things across the face of German history.

The trains were rolling throughout France. It was hard to avoid seeing them. The police and the Vichy authorities described them as labor transports destined for "the Jewish reservation in Poland." The Geneva representative of the American YMCA, Donald A. Lowrie, made private inquiries into the fate of these missing thousands and drew his own conclusions. As he reported to the secretary of the World's Committee of the YMCA in August 1942, the Germans' ostensible need for labor "does not totally explain this action" since the deportees included children, old people and the sick: "We know of some cases of epileptics, palsied, insane and even bedridden put into the corral for deportation." Lowrie had discovered for himself what the International Red Cross and the U.S. Department of State did not yet care to know, that Hitler's grand design for the new Europe "includes 'purification' of undesirable elements." While other aspects of his program were already behind schedule, particularly the invasion of Russia, "this portion, in the hands of fanatics, is being relentlessly pushed as originally planned. The suffering and panic among Jews in France may be better imagined than described. A considerable portion of these are refugees from Germany. . . ." It was difficult for anyone to mistake the purpose of these deportations if he had seen even one of the trains rolling through the French countryside. "I saw a train pass," wrote a member of the French Resistance for the underground *Lettres françaises*: "In front, a car containing French police and German soldiers. Then came cattle cars, sealed. The thin arms of children clasped the grating. A hand waved outside like a leaf in a storm. When the train slowed down, voices cried 'Mama!' And nothing answered except the squeaking of the springs."

Among those who were ultimately caught in this deadly web of railway trains—not in France, but in Germany itself—was Walter Benjamin's cousin Gertrud Kolmar, who had remained in Berlin to look after her elderly father. She was two years younger than Benjamin; a slender, dark-eyed, dark-haired woman who considered herself plain-looking, though others found her beautiful even when she was in her forties and working as a forced laborer, packing cartons in a factory. Benjamin had always admired his cousin, and he conceded being "extremely impressed" by her poetry. In a short introduction which he wrote for two of her poems in *Die Literarische Welt* in 1928, he went as far as a conscientious critic could go in recommending the work of a gifted relative, saying that he wanted "to win the reader's ear for tones that have not been heard in the work of a German poetess since Annette von Droste" (the foremost lyric poetess of the early nineteenth century). He also did his best to persuade editors like Max Rychner to publish her poetry. But she was not to write her best work until he had already gone into exile, and the bulk of her poetry was not published until 1955, twelve years after her death.

One had every right to expect that this talented young woman "of good family," surrounded by literary influences and fluent in several languages, would produce something worthwhile: a slim volume or two, perhaps of more than passing interest to the historians of German literature, particularly in view of the painful circumstances in which her last poetry was written. And one would expect her verse to say the things that doomed women have a right to say about love, beauty and their autumnal longing for a world to which they know they must bid farewell.* All the more astonished, then, were the postwar critics who first rediscovered her work among the ruins of German literature. Gertrud Kolmar's poetry seemed more like a slap in the face than an album of pressed flowers. *Nicht biegen kann ich. Nur zerspringen*—"I cannot bend, only explode"—she writes in one of her Robespierre poems. The critics who assessed her work agreed that Gertrud Kolmar had been one of the great German poets. Oda Schaefer described her as "an important poetess whose language is powerful in its beauty and its wealth of images like hardly another's." Friedhelm Kemp compared her not only to Annette von Droste but to Christina Rossetti and Emily Dickinson. Rolf Schroers declared that she had written "some of the most vivid and some of the purest and most profound works in the German language." She was called "the third great figure among the German-Jewish poetesses"—together with Lasker-Schüler and Nelly Sachs. Jacob Picard went one step further and wrote that she was unequivocally "the greatest Jewish poetess who ever lived"—in any country. Fortunately there was no need for a *Sängerkrieg* between the admirers of Kolmar and the supporters of Lasker-Schüler: they had belonged to different generations—Kolmar was twenty-five years younger than Lasker-Schüler—and regarded the world from two very different points of view. It is doubtful if Kolmar ever set foot in a literary café; apart from her cousin she knew virtually no other writers (though once, by a macabre coincidence, she met the writer who had won first prize in the "Berlin Gasworks" Poetry Competition). She spent the greater part of her youth living with her parents in one of the garden suburbs of Berlin: her father, Ludwig Chod-ziesner, was one of the most famous defense attorneys in Germany. After earning a teacher's diploma in both French and English, she served as an interpreter in a World War I prisoner-of-war camp. During the postwar years she taught privately and also worked with deaf-and-dumb children. One of the decisive events

---

*Charlotte Salomon, the young art student from Berlin who became an accomplished Expressionist painter during the two years she lived in southern France, deals with all of these themes in her extraordinary cycle of autobiographical paintings, the graphic equivalent of *The Diary of Anne Frank.* One of her last paintings shows Charlotte and her bearded grandfather, each with a small suitcase, arriving at a mountain village in their flight from the French police. "My God how beautiful it is here!" she exclaims. But her grandfather replies irritably: "Will you hurry up! We have to find some place to stay for the night." (Charlotte Salomon; *Ein Tagebuch in Bildern,* Hamburg, 1963, Plate 79.) In September 1943 the painter and her husband, Alexander Nagler, whom she had married in May of that year, were arrested by the Gestapo in Villefranche and deported to Auschwitz.

of these years was the unhappy love affair to which she often alludes in her poetry:

> *Einst*
> *Um die Hälfte der Nacht, der Winternacht,*
> *Erwachte ich und schaute durch Schatten:*
> *Der mich liebte, ruhte auf meinem Lager und schlief.*
> *Sein Atem war Muschelrauschen in Stille.*
> *Ich lauschte. . . .*
>
> Once
> Near the half of the night, the winter night,
> I awoke and gazed through shadows;
> He who loved me lay on my bed and slept.
> His breath was the roar of sea shells in silence.
> I listened. . . .

She wrote a cycle of sonnets about the roses in her garden, *Bild der Rose,* but for Gertrud Kolmar a rose was emphatically *not* a rose, and the sonnets draw careful floricultural distinctions among seventeen specific varieties of rose, from the Captain Harvey-Cant to the Mrs. Henry Morse. Her father raised flowers and dogs while Gertrud, as her sister recalled, "watered the roses and talked to toads." She loved unprepossessing animals, and the totemic beasts that inhabit her imaginary landscape tend to be bats, auks, toads, salamanders, hyenas, weasels, vultures. . . . After her mother's death in 1930 she kept house for her father, but they were forced to sell their suburban villa and move to an apartment in the city when the Nazis came to power. At first her father was determined to "defy all the forces of nature" and to remain in Germany: already in his midseventies, he was convinced that before long "the crooked shall be made straight." Later, when he changed his mind and offered to emigrate on her account, it was already too late. "Believe me," she wrote to one of her relatives abroad, "whatever may happen, I shall not be unhappy or give up hope. I know that I have taken the way that was decided from within me. . . . This emigration would only have been forced on us by outward circumstances. I do not want to flee from that to which I am inwardly committed. I never knew until today how strong I am, and this knowledge makes me happy."*

---

*After the beginning of the war, only Jews with extraordinary connections in neutral countries could still hope to escape from Germany. Nelly Sachs, who was three years older than Gertrud Kolmar, and considerably better known as a poet, received help from one of the most influential women in Sweden, the novelist Selma Lagerlöf, with whom she had corresponded for many years. She was permitted to fly to Stockholm with her mother in June 1940—"one minute past midnight," by her own reckoning. The crushing responsibility of writing an epitaph "for my dead brothers and sisters"

She continued to look after her father until his deportation to Theresienstadt in September 1942. He was then eighty-one, and it is thought that he died there a few months later; she never heard what had become of him. Earlier, like all other German Jews of working age, she had been conscripted for forced labor in an arms factory. Their apartment had been declared a "Jewish billet" and was crowded with other Berlin Jews who had become refugees in their own city: there were times when "the noise in the factory affects me less than the chatter of the people in my own apartment." But there was a gypsy woman at the factory from whom she learned the stern posture of resistance that was to be her last-ditch defense: "an impenetrable isolation, a silence, a distance, into which no word, no glance from the outer world, would still be able to intrude."

She was determined to see it through to the end, though she was in no doubt what that end would be. In her book of interpretive poems on Prussian coats-of-arms, *Preussische Wappen*, published in a tiny edition in 1934, she had analyzed the violent forces at work in their medieval symbolism of towers, swords, eagles. These heraldic images were being revived and distributed throughout Germany as cigarette premiums: for her they were a dream-book from which to prophesy the future. In the coat of arms of Loitz an der Peene, for example, she could perceive the significance of the two massive clubs glittering in gold against a red field:

> Die goldenen Keulen werken Tag und Nacht.
> Sie geben nicht Ruhe: alles wird totgeschlagen.
> Der hört den Bumm, der einsam im Düstern sitzt,
> Und hört das Rollen der ewigen Leichenwagen
> Und sieht das Schreien, das an sein Fenster spritzt. . . .

> The golden clubs work day and night.
> They do not rest: everything is beaten to death.
> He who sits alone in the darkness hears the thud,
> Hears the rolling wheels of the endless wagons of corpses
> And sees the cries that spurt against his window.

Like Kafka, she knew that she was living on murderer's row: *Die Mörder gehen in der Welt herum./ Die ganze Nacht, O Gott, die ganze Nacht!* — "The murderers are abroad in the world; / The whole

---

thus devolved upon her. It was a task to which she devoted nine volumes of poetry that also constitute a sort of epilogue to the German-Jewish literary tradition. In 1966, four years before her death, she shared the Nobel Prize for literature with Josef Agnon.

night, oh God, the whole night!" Still, nothing frightened her. "Even as a child I always wanted to be a Spartan woman," she recalled, and she had once held her hand into the fire, like the Roman hero Mucius Scaevola, to see how brave she could be. Now, as she wrote in December 1942, "I will also step up to accept my fate, be it high as a tower, black as a cloud." She wrote her last letters and poems at midnight or at five in the morning, in the few hours that were left after an exhausting day at the factory. In the letters she wrote to her sister in Switzerland she had to be circumspect: they were subject to censorship and she chose her words with care, disguising the important events in an elaborate private code. But in her poetry she felt no such compunction: she had a defiant vision of herself as Judith bearing aloft the head of Holofernes, the enemy of her people. By the same token she wanted to stay alive and to go on writing until the last possible moment because it fell to her, the trial lawyer's daughter, to write the case for the prosecution—the great *J'accuse* against human cruelty *(Menschheitsgrausamkeit)* whose end she foresees in an apocalyptic poem of the last judgment, *Der Tag der grossen Klage.* Her tone is that of impeachment rather than lament: not mercy but justice is what she demands. "Oh that I could raise my voice like a flaming torch in the dark desert of the world: *Gerechtigkeit! Gerechtigkeit! Gerechtigkeit!"* (Justice! Justice! Justice!). The note of triumph was unmistakable: "I want to be the arch of triumph through which our torments pass."

Gertrud Kolmar kept her poetry a secret from all except one or two trusted "Aryan" friends who undertook to hide her manuscripts from the Gestapo. At the factory she liked to work for hours without speaking to anyone: that was when the poems must have formed themselves in her mind. The other workers had no idea who she was. "One of my two co-workers is an opera singer, the other used to be a well-known actress," she wrote in her last letter to her sister. "We talked about it once. 'We have nothing but famous people, creative talents,' said the cousin of Frau Justizrat Wr[onker], who sat next to me. 'You and I are the only ones who are nothing and don't know anything.' I listened to her without moving a muscle. But another time she remarked that I looked as though I wrote poetry. Again I didn't reply."

At a time when the German poets of the so-called "inner emigration" were taking refuge in veiled allusions or Kierkegaard's "silent despair," Gertrud Kolmar was the last to use the German language, in all its Baroque splendor, to call things by their real names. *Und wenn ein Knebel dir im Mund den blutenden Schrei verhält*—"and though a gag stifles the bleeding cry in your mouth"—she would raise her demonic cry for justice, "the shout that falls into the shaft of eternity":

> *Und Deutschland trägt und Frankreich trägt ein Buch und*
> *   ein blitzendes Schwert,*
> *Und England wandelt auf Meeresschiffen bläulich*
> *   silbernen Pfad,*
> *Und Russland ward riesiger Schatten mit der Flamme auf*
> *   seinem Herd,*
> *Und wir, wir sind geworden durch den Galgen und durch*
> *   das Rad. . . .*
>
> *Knöchel. Ihr schleppt doch Ketten, und gefangen*
> *   klirrt mein Gehn.*
> *Lippen. Ihr seid versiegelt, in glühendes Wachs gesperrt.*
> *Seele. In Käfiggittern einer Schwalbe flatterndes Flehn.*
> *Und ich fühle die Faust, die das weinende Haupt auf den*
> *   Aschenhügel mir zerrt.*
>
> *Nur Nacht hört zu. Ich liebe dich, mein Volk im Plunderkleid.*
> *Wie der heidnischen Erde, Gäas Sohn entkräftet zur*
> *   Mutter glitt,*
> *So wirf dich du dem Niederen hin, sei schwach,*
> *   umarme das Leid,*
> *Bis einst dein müder Wanderschuh auf den Nacken*
> *   der Starken tritt!*

And Germany carries and France carries a book and
    a gleaming sword,
And England's ships ply the ocean's blue and
    silver path,
And Russia casts a giant shadow with the flame of
    her hearth,
And we, we have become what we are through
    the gallows and the rack. . . .

Ankles. But you bear chains and my step clanks
    with prison sounds.
Lips. You are sealed, forced into glowing wax.
Soul. The caged swallow's fluttering entreaty.
And I feel the fist pulling my weeping head
    to the hill of ashes.

Only the night listens. I love you, my people clothed in rags.
Just as the son of pagan Gaea would, when exhausted, glide
    back to his mother the Earth,

Now cast yourself down to the lowly, be weak,
  embrace suffering,
Until that day when your tired wanderer's shoe will tread
  upon the neck of the strong!

On February 27, 1943, the last Jews of Berlin were arrested at the factories in which they were working and deported to Auschwitz. A telegram from the Auschwitz SS concerning this particular group of prisoners has been preserved. It informs the forced-labor section of the *Wirtschaftsverwaltungshauptamt* at Oranienburg that 1,893 Jewish prisoners from Berlin had been received in two train-loads on March 5 and March 7: of these 304 men and 164 women were kept alive for a further period of forced labor; 181 men and 909 women and children were accorded *Sonderbehandlung* ("special treatment" in the gas chambers), and the remaining 335 were, by implication, dead on arrival. Nothing more is known of Gertrud Kolmar's last days.

VIII

A SENSE OF
ASH WEDNESDAY

The Torah and the prayers instruct them in
remembrance. . . .
— WALTER BENJAMIN,
Theses on the Philosophy of History

In 1929 Thomas Mann said of Dr. Alfred Doeblin that he was "in the process of assuming the foremost position in the intellectual movement of Germany." Doeblin was fifty-one years old at the time, and considered to be the only possible German candidate for the Nobel Prize for literature; he had just published his most successful novel, *Berlin Alexanderplatz*, regarded to this day as the *Ulysses* of the city of Berlin. Most contemporary critics agreed that he had written "the most important epic German novel." Forty years later they were to place him among "the great writers of the century"—a "prophet" and "visionary" who had succeeded in "breaking through to a new language." Bertolt Brecht, for one, admitted having "profited enormously from his example"; Arthur Koestler wrote that he had learned more from him than from Tolstoy or Flaubert; Günter Grass, speaking about his literary antecedents, asked that Mann, Brecht and Kafka be placed "respectfully aside" so as to make room for Doeblin, to whom he owed his principal debt. "More than that, I could not imagine my prose without the futurist elements of his work," Grass declared. "I am descended from that Doeblin who . . . saw history as an absurd process."

It is one of the absurdities of literary history, at any rate, that Doeblin's name remains almost unknown to non-German readers.

264

The only one of his major works to appear in English—its title became *Alexanderplatz, Berlin*—was scuttled by an inadequate translation in 1931 and promptly forgotten. Yet he was not, as this might suggest, a one-book author. Indeed, Doeblin was by far the most versatile of all the twentieth-century German writers, producing among other things some of the most readable Expressionist stories and novellas, half a dozen important novels, a volume of theater reviews and another of literary criticism, several collections of political essays and satires, an account of his travels in prewar Poland and another of his flight through France in 1940, a novel in free verse, plays, radio and film scripts. . . . Louis Huguet's *Doeblin Bibliographie* of 1972 runs to 274 pages of fine print and lists nearly three thousand items by and about him. Dr. Doeblin moreover—in contrast to Dr. Kafka, Dr. Tucholsky, Dr. Benjamin and the rest of the betitled literati—was a "genuine" doctor, i.e., of medicine, and wrote his books in his spare time while practicing his profession in one of the shabbier districts of Berlin. He wrote them "on the elevated train, while on night duty in the hospital emergency department, between two consultations, on the stairs before visiting a patient . . ." or again, at a table in the Café Gumpert, where "the confused background noise was pleasant to write by." Doeblin also differed from the others in that he came from a working-class family:

> Did I myself not walk through these dark, narrow streets for many years, across the outer courtyards of the houses and the yards lying behind them, to climb up the stairs of the innermost tenement? The terrible thing I saw was known officially as "substandard housing." Nothing can surpass these bureaucratic clichés; they eclipse the poets. Until my fourteenth year I myself, in the east of the city, slept in a windowless chamber in a bed together with my younger brother (who was afterward gassed, together with his wife, by the proponents of a new kind of progress).

He had been born in the port of Stettin, on the Baltic, on August 10, 1878. His father was a custom tailor who had migrated to Germany from Poland, and it was Doeblin's impression that "ethnologically he was a victim of the transition; all his values were distorted and debased." When Alfred was ten his father ran off to America with a girl named Henriette who worked in the tailor shop. This episode haunted Doeblin for the rest of his life, partly because he sympathized with the runaway: "The man lived very restlessly. He had discovered the breadth of nature and the diversity of the women of Stettin. . . . There are a million women in the world; why should a man be in love with his own wife, of all women?" Frau Doeblin, a strong woman wielding an implacable umbrella, was incapable of "understanding" the situation. "She bore herself with legitimacy and pathos; she made demands. Here were the preconditions for a tragedy."

When her husband decamped, "he was crude enough to leave his family as a burden on his wife's relatives," Doeblin recalled. "Overnight he had plunged us all into need and turned us into paupers. Withal, he was a *Lump*." Yet he could not resist admiring this errant father who, like himself, "possessed a whole arsenal of talents"—besides tailoring he knew how to draw, play the violin and piano, compose music and write poetry. Doeblin's mother, who had to pay the family debts, had a head only for practical concerns and took an understandably dubious view of the arts. "I did not dare, would not have dared, to show her my first writings." Even after the appearance of his first books she asked him: "Why do you do it? After all, you have your business"—she meant his medical practice.

The boy had to drop out of school for a time. Later he won a scholarship to the humanistic Gymnasium. At that point the story takes on familiar features: he hated this school where he was "tortured immeasurably" and the teachers assumed the air of government ministers. "I was treated as a rebel and troublemaker. As an eighteen-year-old I was still beaten. At twenty I was forced to sit on a punishment bench. . . . Once, when Kant and Schopenhauer were found among my books the professor told me to stop wasting my time on such things." Though they treated him as a rebel, he insisted that he was not naturally mutinous; it was just that he always lived in a world of his own. "Kleist and Hölderlin were my spiritual godparents." Despite his nearsightedness he was constantly reading. "I read books . . . the way a flame 'reads' wood." Later he made the acquaintance of Nietzsche's *Genealogy of Morals* and the novels of Dostoyevsky—"only a mighty phenomenon like this Russian could lift us out of the flat, paltry literature of our early days." But he remembered having learned little or nothing about Judaism:

> Within the family our Jewishness was not very noticeable. On the outside I encountered antisemitism and took it for granted. . . . At school we did not participate in the Protestant religious instruction, and Jewish classes were irregular and more voluntary. . . . I learned a little Hebrew, but never got past the initial stages. What, indeed, would have compelled me to learn Hebrew in addition to Latin, Greek and French when the empty formulas of foreign languages had always repelled me anyhow? Having studied the *Iliad* and *Odyssey*,

the Edda, Nibelung and Gudrun sagas, I had little interest in the early history of the tribe of Israel, which was afterward dissolved and dispersed. . . . My mother could read Hebrew, and on the high holidays it was touching to see this hard-working woman—who did so much for us that she hardly had time to read a newspaper—sitting quietly by herself in some corner of the room, holding a book in her hand, reading Hebrew in a low voice. Sometimes it was only a murmur. When I think of Jewish things, it is this picture of my mother that I have before my eyes. She went on running and exhausting herself for us children. . . . then came Parkinson's disease, and she died in the home of our eldest brother, who acted as our guardian. On her tombstone we had them engrave the words: "Love never ceases." Thus was my heart bound to this woman who sat so quietly in a room, book in hand, and prayed.

Doeblin began writing seriously during his last year at the Gymnasium. Unlike Kafka, he felt not the slightest compunction about being entitled to the language he was using, and from the first he used it like a virtuoso. "It stirs and breathes within me quietly. It is as if music had begun to play deep within me, a low humming in the tree. An expanding power wants to find its speech. . . ." He read Schopenhauer and Spinoza, but as a medical student at the University of Berlin, "I found no one who could have played midwife at my spiritual birth." That role was reserved for Herwarth Walden and his friends at the Café des Westens, including Else Lasker-Schüler, who praised his "very, very fine sensibility." At the Café Megalomania "we made fun of the then-idols of the bourgeoisie, Gerhart Hauptmann with his bogus fairytales and the classicist contortions of Stefan George." Walden began publishing Doeblin's essays and short stories in 1910, when he launched his Expressionist magazine *Der Sturm.*

By then Doeblin had completed his medical studies—his doctoral thesis was a sixty-page dissertation on *Loss of Memory in Patients with Korsakoff's Psychosis*—and had joined the staff of the Berlin-Buch psychiatric hospital. Within a few years he had published a series of scientific papers on hysteria, melancholia and the chemistry of the blood. At the same time he wrote a play in which, after a conventional beginning, the actors mutiny against the author, drive the director from the stage and carry the piece to a provocative and bloodthirsty conclusion.

Filippo Tommaso Marinetti came to Berlin in 1912 to introduce Italian Futurist painting to Germany. Doeblin liked the pictures; when they met at the Café Dalbelli he told Marinetti that Futurism represented a marvelous leap into freedom—intense, daring, unconstrained. "If only we had something like this in literature!" Marinetti obliged by issuing his *Technical Manifesto of Futurist Literature*, containing the usual lucubrations about trenches bristling with bayonets, machine guns attractive as femmes fatales and the abolition of things like syntax and adverbs. Doeblin rose to the bait and published an open letter accusing Marinetti of trying to throw out the baby with the bath. "You can't mean," he wrote in *Der Sturm*, "that there is only a single reality, and that the world of your automobiles, airplanes and machine guns is identical with the real world?" His polemic brought him a postcard in fractured German from Guillaume Apollinaire in Paris: "Was very good your article, I congratulate you—long live Doeblinism!"

Modern literature, Doeblin thought, should be austere but not foolish: his "Berlin Program" for writers, published a few weeks later, called for a break with the aesthetics of "beautiful" writing and the egocentrism of the psychological novel. The new novel must be "cinematic" in its precision and objectivity: "its façade cannot be other than of stone or steel." The novelist was to stop writing about himself and to use his "kinetic fantasy" to bring back the art of epic storytelling.

Doeblin himself was already at work on such a novel, having first honed his pen on two volumes of Expressionist short stories. In *The Three Leaps of Wang Lun*, the son of Chinese fishermen begins by founding a nonviolent sect, the "Truly Weak," and ends by leading an abortive peasant revolt. Everything about this book is a tour de force of kinetic fantasy. Doeblin had never been further from home than Freiburg in Breisgau, but his Chinese landscape is drawn in such minute detail that even the Sinologists were impressed. He had culled his information from museums and libraries; had immured himself among the books, in fact, because things had suddenly become very confused in his private life: there was a young nurse who bore him a child, and a rather more formidable medical student, Erna Reiss, to whom he became engaged after tortured scenes, second thoughts and feelings akin to nausea. When he was asked to sing something at the engagement party— he had an excellent voice and could play the piano—he proposed *O Death Thou Art Sweet*. "It was in this crisis, this feeling that I was lost, that I returned to writing . . . a fat Chinese novel."

In preparation for *Wang Lun* he made careful notes on Chinese animals, plants, precious stones; the landscape, cities, folklore, rituals, priestly costumes, dances, games, musical instruments; the titles, administrative structure and examination requirements of the Mandarin system; the eunuch protocol at the imperial palace;

the proverbs and poems of the Ming and Ching dynasties, and much more. These elements are so adroitly fused with the narrative that the prose texture is as hard as Szechwan steel. At the same time the immense psychological distance between author and subject lends a hierarchic gravity to the proceedings, as though a Peking opera were being performed. The critic Walter Muschg called the result "a sorcerer's art; shamanastic poetry," yet it was also the first great crowd novel in German literature. Doeblin himself did not discover its subterranean meaning until he was already well into the book; then it occurred to him, as he noted on the back of one of his sketches, that this story of wandering Chinese outcasts conceals "the Jewish theme. Exiles. The mass of people as a Person."

One of Wang Lun's three "leaps," incidentally, is his decision not to allow himself and the society of the "Truly Weak" to be annihilated without a struggle. "The emperor has issued an edict that we are to be exterminated," he tells one of his followers:

> But who is the emperor? Yes, what is that, an "emperor"? I know bolts of lightning that kill men in rivers, on the water, under beech trees; one can be crushed by landslides; there are floods, fire and wild beasts, snakes. And demons. They all can kill us. There is hardly a way of protecting oneself against them. But who is this "emperor"? This unheard-of, shameless presumption of the emperor, to have us killed, how is it justified? . . . I deny that this is the destiny of the "Truly Weak." I shall not poison myself voluntarily. I shall refuse them. Our community lives on the earth, which belongs to us.

Wang Lun is a political parable—and an eminently musical book. Like Gustav Mahler, Doeblin created a private oriental world where women's voices sang pentatonic melodies to an accompaniment of plucked lutes and bowed zithers—"enveloped by tones, the deep strings murmuring like the tide, the high strings whispering; as the notes grew more vivid one thought to hear a shower of pearls falling on a slab of marble." Clearly this is the literary counterpart of Mahler's *Lied von der Erde** (which had preceded it by only five years); the book no less than the symphony was intended to be "cosmic and inexhaustible like the world and life itself." Perhaps it was merely a coincidence that Doeblin was a small man of Mahler-

---

Wang Lun taught Bertolt Brecht the advantages of China, with its built-in *Verfremdungseffekt*, as a setting for parables like *The Good Woman of Szechwan*. "All things are set into motion," he noted in his diary after reading Doeblin's book. "The relationship of people to one another is projected in unheard-of clarity; like a virtuoso he draws all the gestures and expressions into the psychology and removes everything that is merely scholarly. Technically I was immensely impressed by his use of verbs. Verbs were always my weakest point."

like intensity, perpetually working, moving, gesturing. But he also possessed something of Mahler's passion for vast spaces filled with "the sound of nature"—*In Tönen denkt die Welt* he had written in one of his first essays: "The world thinks in tones." By the same token, both of them were fascinated by the possibilities of mystical religion. The poet Ernst Blass, who wrote the first major essay on Doeblin, in 1922, said that even in the Chinese novel one could detect a mystical longing "for the religious sphere of the Absolute"; that beneath the oriental bacchanalia there was "a secret sense of Ash Wednesday."

Doeblin's attitude toward music reflected his impatience with the whole of the German classical pantheon, from Goethe to Richard Wagner. Though he liked to play the *Liebestod* on the piano and acknowledged its composer as "a great musical and intellectual force," he felt that Wagner's so-called music of the future was only "art for the obedient bourgeois . . . dreadful pomp and circumstance combined with transports of martial delight." He much preferred the dissonances of Béla Bartók "as he roars vehemently through forest and meadow; it is an indescribable pleasure how his music gallops over this terrain; it neighs the way real horses neigh!" When a well-known musician disparaged one of Mahler's symphonies by calling it *Unterhaltungsmusik* (entertainment music), Doeblin took up the issue in the pages of the influential *Neue Rundschau:* "Is that supposed to be a reproach? For such people 'entertainment' is a reproach; 'art' is their shibboleth. . . . For them, making people happy, liberating them, easing their lives, is nothing. They are pseudo-artists, fallen from the tree of life."

He had little use for "art" and what was then called *Kultur.* "I despised literature," and still more anything ornamental, aesthetic, "the school of atelier writing"—"we want no beautification, no decorations, no style, nothing on the surface, only hardness, coldness and fire, gentleness, the transcendental and the earthshaking, without wrapping paper. Packaging belongs to the classics." One of his characters expressed it even more succinctly: "I am not a Greek but a Berliner." And, as a Berliner, Doeblin's loyalties were to the people among whom he had grown up. "It stayed with me that we, that I, belonged to the poor. It determined my character. I belonged to this people, to this nation: to the poor."

During World War I Doeblin served as an army doctor in Lorraine and Alsace. The experience confirmed his aversion to militarism, the officer corps and the Prussian Establishment: "The regular army physician who was told that his patients were suffering from hunger and wanted to prosecute the soldiers who had called his attention to it. Staff doctors who walked through the wards carrying a riding crop; chaplains who rode on horseback and would have liked nothing better than to carry arms; kaiser's birthday celebrations, 'our *heissgeliebter* [hotly beloved] kaiser,' this flummery, this ossification, this aloofness from life, negation of humanity, of people; this loss of direction, this brutality. And this ineptitude!"

For weeks he was stationed within earshot of the artillery at Verdun. While the guns thundered on, Doeblin was at work on a new novel—not about the war on the horizon but about the Thirty Years War and its great "scene-shifter of history," Wallenstein. He had taken the trouble to look into the general's financial background and the result is, among other things, the story of "the army as an investment," as Günter Grass calls it. "Doeblin's rearward-looking vision startles us: long before Krupp pulled off his big business deal at Verdun, Wallenstein invested his fortune in the arms trade. Krupp and Wallenstein each bought themselves an emperor." Doeblin's *Wallenstein*, however, is not a historical novel in the usual sense: he said afterward that the Thirty Years War had remained a closed book to him, just as he had never really "studied" China. "A sympathetic interest in the period? Not that I know of . . . since the Thirty Years War meant nothing to me, and I was prevented from feeling any personal concern in any of these doubtless interesting events, how could I have arrived at a sympathetic interest? . . . I only looked for points of attraction and irritation that would help me." The figure at the center of his *Wallenstein* is not the warlord but the emperor Ferdinand, "a man who no longer knows what is good and bad, who no longer has a sense of 'sin.' " Doeblin explained in an epilogue that what had really concerned him was the struggle for Ferdinand's soul. At the end of the book he disposes of him quite unhistorically by having him killed by a hobgoblin, a medieval forest creature who has somehow survived into the seventeenth century in order to stab the emperor in the back during a moment of blissful suffering.

The real war, meanwhile, had ended with a mutiny in the ranks. Doeblin, like other officers, stripped his uniform of its rank insignia—and became a fascinated observer of the ensuing collapse:

> In front of the yellow kasernes, close by the gate, there is a crowd of nearly a hundred people, shouting, pushing, moving back and forth. As I approach, I see that several windows on the second floor are open. Bareheaded soldiers suddenly appear there, laughing and shouting down to the street. Several of the soldiers lean back and toss

> out masses of boots and equipment; they keep bending backward,
> picking up boots and flinging them in all directions. Everyone rush-
> es toward them, boys run off with single boots, soon everyone is
> jammed together, fighting, screaming, arguing; the carts and wagons
> drive up. There are masses of soldiers at the gates. . . . they no longer
> shoulder their rifles but carry them butt upward in the Russian style;
> their caps, too, have caved in and tend to assume the Russian shape.

He was back in Berlin in time to attend a republican mass demonstration in memory of the war dead. The streets were crowded
with people carrying red flags; "decently dressed" Social Democrats singing choruses to the tune of the *Marseillaise*. "In the endless procession, wreaths with red ribbons, red flags, proletarian
slogans, otherwise nothing that could remind me of a revolution; a
well-ordered petit-bourgeois event magnified to enormous size."
Later he gave vent to his disappointment in an ironic essay for *Die
Neue Rundschau:* "When we came down in the morning the revolution had already happened. Yet we had especially asked them to
wake us when the revolution was on!"

Eventually he settled down as a neurologist-psychiatrist for
working-class patients in one of the grimy districts near the
Alexanderplatz. In his memoirs, Ludwig Marcuse recalls how "the
most amusing of skeptics" appeared during these postwar years,
"a soft hat pressed down over his forehead, a cheerful, impetuous
jack-in-the-box of forty, a quarreler who was always contradicting
everything and who thought heads were meant for running into
walls with." But Marcuse also remembers "how easy it was to get
into a good mood with him; how easily he could put one into a
really fantastic good humor."

He and Erna had begun to raise a family. With three, later four
young boys, "the water was soon at my neck again. It is not easy to
establish a new practice when you don't have the money to sit and
wait." To make ends meet he wrote political pieces for German
magazines and Berlin theater reviews for a Prague German-
language newspaper, the *Prager Tagblatt*. The essays were signed
"Linke Poot" (Left Paw) and delighted independent socialists like
Kurt Tucholsky. "Linke Poot tickles with the epée where Heinrich
Mann wielded a club," Tucholsky wrote in *Die Weltbühne*. "He
concerns himself amiably, wittily, suggestively, 'shamelessly' and
profoundly with the new Germany. He has a completely new
sense of humor, of a sort I have never read before in German." It
was a dry, malicious kind of humor with a penchant for under-
statement: "The republic was brought to the German empire by a

wise man from abroad. What one was supposed to do with it he didn't say; it was a republic without operating instructions."

Linke Poot advocated a socialism which he defined as "freedom, spontaneous association of human beings, refusal of all compulsion, revolt against injustice and compulsion; it is humanity, tolerance and peaceful intentions." In contrast, German communism struck him as hopelessly militarist and simplistic, hence incapable of leading humanity toward "the new natural man." There was no point, moreover, in a socialism that merely "increases production"—to the author of *Wang Lun* it seemed that socialism should resemble "a pagoda full of ringing bells" thronged with worshipers. One had only to read the Communist party's literature to realize they were living in an artificial world: "They hate reality. These clean-thinking historical materialists dare not approach reality. They think it sufficient to wave their little red children's flag over reality." In retaliation, German Communist leaders intervened in Moscow to prevent a planned Russian edition of his work. As an anonymous critic explained in the party magazine *Die Linkskurve,* "A writer who has insulted German proletarian literature in such shameless fashion has no right to be read by the workers of the Soviet Union."

Writers and intellectuals, Doeblin decided, should refrain from joining political parties in order to preserve their independence of judgment. In the language of the professional radicals, this attitude came to be known as *Humanitätsduselei*—i.e., do-good humanism. To Walter Benjamin it seemed amateurish and evasive. Doeblin had said that writers would find their place *at the side* of the workers, "but what sort of a place is that? The place of a well-wisher, an ideological patron. An impossible place."

A more tenable place was his position as a theater critic, which gave him a privileged seat from which to observe some of the most exciting years of Berlin theater. The twenties renaissance had just got under way in an atmosphere of growing tension between Left and Right: many first nights turned into noisy political demonstrations. At the premiere of Toller's *The Machine-Wreckers* there were shouts of "Rathenau!" when the hero was murdered, and the speeches onstage were constantly interrupted by cheering and applause from the audience. "At the start of the intermission," Doeblin reported, "people cheered Toller and shouted, 'Down with the Bavarian government!' (stormy applause). There were heated outbursts for and against the workers; much argument and counter-argument in the crowd."

Perhaps as an antidote to everyone else's social realism, Doeblin's next novel was an immense science-fiction fantasy, the 589-page *Berge, Meere und Giganten* (Mountains, Seas and Giants) published in 1924. His first notes for an outline reveal both its main themes and the gist of his thinking about the modern industrial world:

> The great city. Development of its industry and technology. It is mighty. Mightier than Nature. First came the kings. Song of the knights. The story of this earth. The wars. The sciences. Then came the workers. The great city. Berlin. What lived in them. The conflict between Nature and Technology. The erotic types. How a volcano breaks open in the end. Or how houses are left empty. They will not let themselves be dominated by the houses. The alienation of man from Nature.

His book envisages the apotheosis of the machine a thousand years hence: in a world of technological *Wunderapparate* the volcanoes of Iceland are used to melt the Greenland icecap. But the Prometheans and giants who inhabit this age of supermen have failings that are all too human; man is not only alienated from nature but becomes involved in a disastrous "Ural War."

Doeblin sounded a surprisingly erotic note in this "hymn to the greatness of Nature" (as he described it to a friend). Apparently his newfound sexuality was not unconnected with the fact that he had encountered a "sister soul" *(Schwesterseele)* at last and now found himself poised on the horns of a familiar dilemma—why indeed should a man be in love with his own wife, of all people? He had met the young photographer Yolla Niclas at a Berlin costume ball in 1921, and she was soon to figure as the "ideal inspirer" of his books. According to his friend Robert Minder (afterward professor of German literature at the Sorbonne), between 1922 and 1940 "not a single one of his works was written without her participation." It was to this "mystic bride" that he played the *Liebestod* and sang Puccini arias—but after the experience of his own fatherless childhood nothing could induce him to leave his four sons. "If one asks me to which nation I belong," he once wrote, "I shall say: neither to the Germans nor to the Jews, but to children and the insane."

Gradually he arrived at a compromise whereby he led his "material life" with Erna Doeblin and his "spiritual life" with Yolla Niclas. Friends described the former as a kind of Strindberg marriage. In *Mountains, Seas and Giants*—which is full of such cryptic allusions—he speaks of "human beings who are chained together as enemies in love, interjoined so as to tear each other apart, to bite, to torment. . . ." In one of his later novels a writer is made to say about his wife: "It is her fault that hate and rage and conflict came into our love. Yes I seized her and gripped her with my teeth . . . and then, it was just what she liked. She did not feel really satisfied until I had become enraged."

Yolla Niclas was treated very differently: she appears in his fiction as "the slender, light, floating" woman who is "the human being that I lack, the piece of me that I do not have, the young, gentle woman; the sense of nature that means so much more to me than human society."

Until he was in his midforties, Doeblin had rarely been reminded of his Jewishness. "Why should I have worried about Jews and Jewish problems? I felt they were real, but I was accustomed to going my own way; I was what I was; there seemed no point in thinking about it." In 1923, however, a series of antisemitic incidents occurred in eastern Berlin, not far from Doeblin's office—the same beatings and window-smashings that had shattered Kafka's peace of mind during his stay in Berlin. Doeblin afterward described them as "the Nazis sounding their first cry." It seemed to him suddenly that he should be better informed about Jews. "I didn't know any real Jews. I knew people who called themselves Jews, but I wouldn't have called them that." They were neither Jewish in their beliefs nor could they speak Hebrew. "Perhaps they were the remnants of a vanished people who had long ago been absorbed into their surroundings."

Like Theodor Lessing he decided to make a personal voyage of discovery to Poland, where one could observe "real Jews" in their native habitat. The journal of his explorations appeared, in installments, in the same *Vossische Zeitung* that sent Tucholsky to Paris. Doeblin already knew something of Polish history and about conditions under the monarchy, when Poland was said to have been "a heaven for the nobles, paradise for Jews, hell for the peasants." But nothing had quite prepared him for the realities of this country between East and West: the sight, for example, of a crowd of Orthodox Jews in medieval costume weeping at the graves of their forebears on the eve of the Day of Atonement—"a sea of murmuring, lamentation, women's cries." At the gates of the cemetery an army of beggars lay in wait for the mourners. It was the day of the dead and of the poor: "women in ghastly rags carrying children in swaddling clothes; old yellow Jewesses standing there in their stiff wigs. . . . everywhere wallets and purses are opened, paper and coins fall, some beggars have whole stacks of paper." Doeblin admitted to being profoundly shocked by it all. "It is something dreadful. It is unnatural, atavistic. What does it have to do with Judaism? These are vestiges of primitive superstition, remnants of the fear of the dead, fear of souls that walk abroad. . . . It is a survival of some other religion, animism, the cult of the dead."

Like Kafka he was fascinated by tales of miracle-working Hasidic rabbis—including those of the Gerer Rebbe (who had prevented Kafka's marriage). "I cannot help thinking . . . what an imposing people these Jews! I had not known them before." Yet unlike Kafka he was not tempted to join an Orthodox community. "The Jews carry something medieval with them. They have their Torah, a unique book, but magic and superstition run along with it, anonymously. That resembles Buddhism, which has its own teaching yet allows a world of pagan gods to exist beside it at the same time."

He met Zionists, who were preparing their children for settlement in Palestine by teaching them Hebrew, which sounded to him "like Germans speaking French." He also met passionate Yiddishists of the socialist persuasion who rejected the idea of a Jewish state because it would not solve the economic problems of the majority of Jews. The Zionists might actually succeed in establishing a Jewish state, a young Yiddish writer told him, "But for how many? And what will they have accomplished? They will have soldiers, statesmen, industrial workers, as though the world did not already have enough of those. But they will not produce a Bergson or a Spinoza." Doeblin "felt in his bones" that the man was right, and another solution must be found: *Die Welt muss aufgemenscht werden.* . . . "The world must be made more human. Things are bad not only for the Jews. The Germans, Poles, French, Americans and English are also having a hard time. . . . Everything must be made more human!"

Doeblin's own contribution toward this process, *Berlin Alexanderplatz,* was written during the years that followed. Its theme, as he said, is the sacrificial victim—a *cantus firmus* set against allusions to Abraham and Isaac, to Job, to the slaughterhouses of Berlin and the wanton murder of Mieze, the girl friend of Franz Biberkopf, the antihero. Franz himself is a victim of his own chronic inability to understand reality; a sort of guileless Parsifal of the Berlin underworld. It is a breathtaking book, written "in the Berlin tone of voice" and in a surrealist rush of big-city images: newspaper headlines, advertising slogans, stockmarket reports, weather forecasts, the lyrics of popular songs—the diversity and absurdity of the dingiest, most dangerous streets around the Alexanderplatz, the Piccadilly Circus of old Berlin. Through it all runs the refrain of a sinister folksong: *Es ist ein Schnitter der heisst Tod.* . . . "There is a reaper, his name is Death. Now he whets his knife, it cuts to the life. Watch out, my little blue flower!"

"Everything flows in the stream of living language by which the author is carried along"—as he once described, not his own novel, but the means whereby Homer, Dante and Cervantes had arrived at "the simple great elemental situations of life and the figures of human existence." *Berlin Alexanderplatz* achieves results on a comparable scale of literary magnitude. For once Doeblin himself was wholly immersed in the novel and had "written himself toward the theme" like a hunter stalking his quarry. From Dante he had learned how to "go through his own poem knocking against his characters" by way of participating in the storytelling process, and he wanted the same sense of immediacy for this epic tale of life among the lumpen proletarians. "The reader looks over the author's shoulder as he creates."

It meant taking extraordinary risks, but his twenty years of ministering to the working class had provided him with an immense store of experience for this adventure. "I observed these people in the most varied situations and in the only genuine way of observing them, namely when one lives, works and suffers together with them." Walter Benjamin, who had put street signs and advertising copy to far more arcane use in *One-Way Street*, called it a "monument of the Berlinese precisely because the narrator was not interested in speaking 'for Berlin' in hopes of winning friends for it. He speaks with the city's voice. Berlin is his megaphone. Its dialect is one of the forces with which he assaults the closed structure of the old novel."

Berlin Alexanderplatz became a best-seller and also enjoyed a great deal of success with the critics, who realized at once that it was not only the great urban novel of the century but also the *ultima Thule* of German Expressionism. Some critics took it for granted that his cinematic "montage style" had been borrowed from Joyce, but Doeblin had demonstrably begun writing Joycean German long before the publication of *Ulysses*, and as he said, "Why should I have gone to Joyce, the Irishman, when I learned the method he uses (which is wonderful: I admire it) from the same sources as he did, the Expressionists, Dadaists and so on?" There was now no question that he ranked as the foremost modernist of his generation, and he was unanimously elected to the newly founded Literary Section of the Prussian Academy of Arts. After years of semi-obscurity he had suddenly emerged as the leader of the avant-garde. As Walter Muschg pointed out, "No writer before him had such an eye for the oceanlike flow of reality, for the surging and streaming of existence which surrounds the storyteller and his story." At the same time he was the first "to love the hard, the hardest style, the style without lyricism and ornamentation." Again it was not a documentary novel, of course: Muschg interpreted it as an allegory on Germany's way since its defeat in 1918—and a vision of Sodom on the eve of its destruction. Doeblin ends his parable with an explicit warning from Franz Biberkopf to other little people like himself to whom everything always seems to be happening. Having survived the vicissitudes of petty thieving and the criminal courts, Franz has come safely to rest as an assistant watchman of a small factory. It is the time of the great shoulder-to-shoulder marching mystique cultivated by political parties of both Right and Left:

> Often they march past his window with flags and music and songs; Biberkopf looks coolly out the door and stays well and truly home. . . . They want me to march with them, but later I'll have to pay with my head for what they've decided to do with me. If there's war and they conscript me, and I don't know why and the war just happens to me, then it's my fault and it serves me right. If you're awake, awake, you're not alone. Hail and rain can come out of the air; no one can do anything about it, but against many other things you can defend yourself. So now I won't cry as I used to: it's fate, it's fate! You can't respect that sort of thing as fate; you have to recognize it, seize it and destroy it.

In spite of this excellent advice the Storm Troopers went on marching in ever increasing numbers, but it was not until the day of the Reichstag fire that Doeblin realized the danger he was running by staying on in a land ruled by the Nazis. As he left his apartment that morning he became aware of being shadowed by a man wearing a civilian coat over a Nazi uniform. Doeblin kept cool, got on the subway and managed to lose his pursuer by changing trains in a crowded station. Then, doubling back, he made his way to a railway station where he boarded an express to Stuttgart without being recognized. A friend helped him cross the Swiss border in a private car. From Zurich he submitted his resignation to the Prussian Academy of Arts: "As a person of Jewish descent I would, under the present circumstances, represent too great a liability to the Academy."

At meetings of the Academy he had often had differences of opinion with Ricarda Huch, a well-known poetess and historian of the Romantic age. Once, in a particularly playful mood, he had blinked his doctor's flashlight into her eyes, only to discover that she was not amused. Yet when she heard that he and Heinrich

Mann had been forced to resign she submitted her own resignation
in protest. Max von Schillings urged her to stay on: a writer of her
"profoundly conservative convictions" would be a great asset to
the Academy in "developing a German nationalist literature." She
refused to reconsider the matter. "It is true that I do not agree with
Herr Heinrich Mann and not always with Dr. Doeblin, yet in some
things I did. In any case I wish that all non-Jewish Germans tried as
hard as he does to search for the truth and recognize the right thing
to do, and to be as open, honest and decent as I have always found
him to be." It was not until after the war, as a very old lady, that
she would again agree to participate in any public function.

In Switzerland Doeblin worked furiously on a new fantasy,
clairvoyantly begun in Berlin, about the modern wanderings of an
exiled Babylonian god. "The whole thing," he decided, "wants to
be a series of burlesques, funny, earnest, ironic things; a journey
around a certain world." Published in Amsterdam a year later,
Babylonische Wandrung turned out to be a picaresque mixture of *The
Time Machine* and Heine's *Gods in Exile.* When the ex-god, Konrad,
arrives at a cheap hotel in Paris and hears the sound of rushing
water all about him he believes himself magically transported to
the abode of mermaids and water sprites. But it is only the sound
of the plumbing coming through the flimsy partition: "People
washed themselves, they bathed, they pulled the bell-rope of the
privy place, they rinsed themselves and sprayed water; Paris was
full of dust, the night belonged to the water." Sometimes the satire
comes to a stop and Doeblin launches into a rhapsodic interlude
reminiscent of Mahler's *O glaube, mein Herz, O glaube!* (Believe, my
heart, oh, believe!) from the Second Symphony: "Not yet, no not
yet are you lost, not lost, brother heart! . . . For this is not a world
of robbers and murderers!" But other interludes suggest the very
opposite. He has a vision of human beings massacred by the
thousands as part of a carefully prepared government program. It
is a Babylonian operation, and to heighten the irony Doeblin calls
the victims "Romans"—first 150,000 Romans are scheduled to be
killed, to be followed by "one million Armenians":

> Down on the market place, in the streets, there was indescribable
> hubbub. A vast, gruesome cry arose, a screaming, as when animals
> are being slaughtered. People came pouring out of the houses. . . .
> They did not escape. All were without weapons. Massacre, massacre.
> The bodies screamed, turned, sank to the ground. "There is no point
> in turning away, Konrad. Just this is what you must watch quietly.
> Quietly. You think that people are being slaughtered here. That is
> incidental. What is happening here is very clear, premeditated and

according to plan. Actions are being taken, order is being created. These are Romans, the women, children, all of them Romans, rich merchants, bankers, whatever you like, officials, businessmen. . . . They are being exterminated. The Romans are being annihilated. You believe that defenseless people, especially women and children, are being ruthlessly slaughtered. Nothing of the sort! We're not talking about people. These are Romans, political enemies . . . being destroyed in the course of official operations."

Doeblin had gone to Paris to write the concluding chapters of *Babylonische Wandrung*. In many ways the transition was easier for him than for most refugees, for his reputation had preceded him, and influential friends arranged for him to receive French citizenship in 1936—a rare honor, extended only to a happy few. Still there was the "sour apple" of the language problem and the feeling that he would never fit into this new environment: "I was never a 'German' and will also fail to become a Frenchman." His four boys had not yet completed their schooling, and "Paris is nice for living but nothing for earning money." Though he was not allowed to practice medicine, he found ways of earning a modest living as a writer for exile publishers, and to complete his good fortune Yolla Niclas followed him to Paris, where she opened a photographic studio near the Arc de Triomphe, across town from where Doeblin and his wife had settled in Montparnasse. French civilization was "better, clearer and more closely related to reality than the German," he decided, and it occurred to him that he might even enjoy the Parisians—if only they could speak a little *Berlinerisch*.

Hermann Kesten remembered their years of Paris exile, when he would sit with Doeblin in the cafés of Montparnasse. "He drank coffee and made jokes, and told funny stories from *more* than five continents, and grumbled about God and the world, and looked like a restless foreigner or like a Berlin poet, but not like a prophet. Yet that was what he was." Kesten thought it was Doeblin's second sight that entitled him to a place among the prophets; indeed, he possessed many more of their classic attributes: "He is dark and speaks in the wind and defies the gods; is shortsighted but farseeing; in the midst of confusion he speaks soberly and sees clearly, yet among a preponderance of rationalists his is an ecstatic, intoxicated voice."

Doeblin also availed himself of the prophet's sovereign right to change his mind. Friends who had not seen him for a fortnight would come to him prepared for any eventuality. "Was he Marxist or anti-Marxist, Freudian or anti-Freudian?" Manès Sperber and Arthur Koestler, two very much younger men with whom he used to have long political discussions, bestowed on him the title of *Konfusionsrat*—i.e., Hon. Confusion-Counsel. In his memoirs, Sperber recalls the enthusiasm with which he discussed politics and literature, but if one of his guests expressed his admiration of some other writer, "our host's long, not very lovingly formed face would suddenly become contorted with bitterness and scorn. . . . Doeblin felt himself unappreciated, pushed into the shadow of writers to whom he felt in no way inferior." To salve his pride he resorted to Mahler's cure for snubs and rebuffs, my-time-will-yet-come. "I have a great deal of time," he wrote to the critic Ferdinand Lion in 1938. "I can wait a long time; you know that. People learn from me and they will learn still more."

For several years he contributed articles to a "territorialist" magazine, *Freiland,* published by a group of Yiddishists who were hoping to find some "free land" other than Palestine in which Jewish settlers might establish a homeland. His argument was straightforward enough. "I. Reason for Jewish suffering: lack of land. II. End to Jewish suffering: Jewish land." But although Doeblin knew his Kafka, it never struck him as peculiar that the two places most often mentioned in connection with this enterprise, New Caledonia and Guiana, had previously been known primarily for their penal colonies (Captain Dreyfus having spent five years as the most prominent Jewish settler of Devil's Island, French Guiana). To the "territorialists," Palestine seemed too small to accommodate the rising flood of refugees—Doeblin estimated that only six hundred thousand to a million Jews would be able to settle there. Yet somehow the Jews would have to become strong, for "weakness only serves to attract the thunderbolt." He called for the establishment of a world organization to protect endangered Jews—a "counterforce" to Nazism—so that "those who believe that Jews are fair game will lose their appetite for the hunt."

When he realized his efforts were in vain he went back to writing novels of the imagination. At the Bibliothèque Nationale, where he would go to read Kierkegaard, he discovered the Amazon River. "I plunged into it, this wonderful phenomenon, a stream that is an ocean, a primeval thing. Its banks, the animals and people, belong to it." Without having set foot on South America he wrote a trilogy about the river and the jungle, and Jesuit attempts to establish a Christian republic on the Paraná—*Das Land ohne Tod* (The Land Without Death), *Der blaue Tiger* (The Blue Tiger) and *Der neue Urwald* (The New Jungle).

He had begun working on another series of novels—this one about the failure of the German revolution in 1918—when World

War II broke out. The playwright Jean Giraudoux, head of the newly created Ministry of Information, asked Doeblin to serve as consultant on propaganda addressed to German troops. His two older sons, Claude (Klaus) and Vincent (Wolfgang), were already serving in the French army. (The third, Peter, had gone to New York to work as a typographical designer: Doeblin had visited him there early in 1939, while attending an International P.E.N. Club congress that had included lunch with Mrs. Roosevelt at the White House.) During the "phony war"—or what the French called the *drôle de guerre*—he was busy writing texts for recorded loudspeaker broadcasts designed to persuade German front-line troops that "Your attack will break on the Maginot line, just as Adolf Hitler's garrison state will break into pieces." But the Wehrmacht failed to make the expected frontal attack; instead, their panzer columns rolled through Belgium in May 1940, and within six weeks Paris had fallen.

Doeblin's experiences during the fall of France are set down in a little-known volume of memoirs, *Schicksalsreise* (Fateful Journey), perhaps the most remarkable document of its kind by a major writer since Stendhal's letters from Russia during Napoleon's retreat from Moscow. It is not a conventional account of a military debacle. Doeblin saw only what was happening on the fringes of the war; the tired refugees and the defeated soldiers, the reinforcements being rushed up to a front that no longer existed. What makes this an extraordinary book is the utter honesty and clinical precision with which he described his thoughts and feelings in the midst of the general descent into chaos. Once again, as at the Alexanderplatz, it was a matter of trained and sympathetic observation: the psychiatrist working with a subject he had known intimately for years. Yet the subject's reactions were often unpredictable, even quixotic—and to his surprise Doeblin discovered a self he had never known before. "This whole epoch of my life was unreal. I was never less 'I' than at that time. I was neither 'I' in my actions (most of the time one did not 'act' of one's own volition in any case; either one was driven or one simply went on doing nothing), nor was my way of thinking and feeling the same as before." His reactions were typical of the lethargy and despair that affected thousands of refugees who became victims of the war—the difference was that he lived to write about it. When he did so he "wanted the truth at any price" (something he had admired in Kierkegaard), and as a consequence the *Journey* became his most searching adventure in self-analysis. "During these weeks I had the certainty that I was experiencing very important events," he explains. "That is why I am writing this; to capture and preserve them. For it must not be that such extraordinary events merely pass over me like the beam of a searchlight."

Two weeks before the start of his own journey, Doeblin's wife and their thirteen-year-old son, Etienne, had been evacuated from Paris and sent to live in Le Puy, in central France. Then, as the Germans approached, it was the Information Ministry's turn to leave the city. The propaganda section to which Doeblin was assigned was sent to Tours by rail; already the highways leading south were clogged with refugees. As he stood in the freight yard at Porte d'Ivry waiting for the train it seemed to him that this retreat was somehow *infra dig:* "How improper, how shabby it is to run away and seek one's personal safety. Damn, that one has got in the position of having to flee, to go on fleeing and still fleeing. What a shameful, unworthy destiny. Who has brought me to this?"

After three days in Tours they were evacuated again, this time on trucks, amid scenes of mounting confusion. "I had the impression that our files were becoming less valuable with every move. Now they were being tossed aboard the trucks. I could foresee the day when they would be abandoned on some highway . . . when they would be thrown out and everyone would try to save only his own skin." He was carrying papers of his own—a parcel containing the manuscript of his latest novel and a pair of shoes—as well as a suitcase full of clothes that served as his security ballast, his anchor to windward. After he and his companions had squeezed onto the heavily loaded truck he noticed a subtle shift in their attitudes. "Oh, now we were no longer observers and travelers. We were 'the masses.' It was the first step in our transformation."

Eventually, Doeblin's section was shipped farther south by rail. He and forty others spent three days and nights in a cattle car. "My traveling companions were constantly changing their position, sometimes sitting, sometimes squatting, or again half lying down—until everyone realized (which took time) that actually there was no comfortable way to sit. . . ." He had given up making plans: "Man weaves himself into a situation and attempts to make his life easier. He thinks on a short-term basis and occupies himself with the moment. . . . In the most terrible situations he has a tendency to make jokes." They met trains loaded with artillery heading in the opposite direction, but by now everyone had ceased believing that the Germans could be stopped. Doeblin realized he was suffering from something more than the anxiety that had troubled him since the start of the German offensive: "It was a dark vibration inside me that was partly railway fever, partly fear and sometimes simply sadness. . . . I became aware that this is how defeated people look when they flee, even when they laugh."

During a halt at a small station they learned that the government had sued for an armistice. Everyone had his own thoughts when they heard the news. "One clings to the group for security and at the same time the whole social fabric disintegrates. One has reached a primitive stage of life. For me the feeling is not new. I had experienced it seven years before, when I left Germany. . . . Like the others I feel only a dull, heavy blow. . . . It shakes me to the very roots." The journey came to an end at Cahors, far to the south of the invading army. Here the propaganda section was officially disbanded; as he had foreseen, its files had been destroyed along the way. They learned that the government had prohibited further evacuations and all unauthorized civilian travel. Yet everyone was seized by a sudden desire to act: "I too behaved like a member of the herd and believed that I should now 'do' something."

He obtained a military safe-conduct stating that he was entitled to join his wife and son at Le Puy. Since the trains were no longer running on schedule he had to work his way back toward central France by slow stages, on local trains and buses. "It was not a journey from one French town to another but a journey between heaven and earth." In one small town he was marooned without a place to stay and spent the night sleeping on the steps of the deserted station. He was stopped and questioned by the police: "I, the lone man; during the whole journey I always manage to be the lone man; that in itself is already a blemish, a cause for suspicion." He bought a book of railway timetables in a vain effort to plan his route. "In it I looked day after day where I was and where I wanted to go. Wherever I was, I was not. I always wanted to go somewhere else. My whole being had changed."

He was swept along in the flood of refugees that continued to crowd the roads and railways. "A lasso has been thrown over me; I fight against the coils of the rope that constricts itself around me." At last, after days of wandering, he arrived in Le Puy, unshaven, in mud-spattered clothes. His wife and son had left three days earlier, he was told; they had gone to find him in Bordeaux, where the government had temporarily established its headquarters. He hoped that she might be able to get a ship to England from there. Almost as though this were a comedy by Marcel Pagnol, while he was debating what to do next, he received a telegram addressed to her—the one that he himself had sent two days before. It was so easy to miss connections in this war: "The mails don't work, the trains don't run, and if they do, without timetables. And everyone now lives somewhere else." He felt like Robinson Crusoe stranded on a remote island in the center of France. The effort had exhausted him; he was sixty-one and beginning to feel old. In the town of Mende, not far from Le Puy, he found shelter in a camp for displaced persons. They gave him a bunk in a barracks. For weeks he felt too tired to move on: it was a time for stock-taking. "Whence this emptiness and apathy? I don't really have to search very far. The emptiness already existed. Now it was merely revealed. . . . I realize the valuelessness of everything that had preoccupied me."

He wandered around Mende, watching the first days of a defeated France that, like himself, was in a state of traumatic shock. Groups of disarmed soldiers were waiting to be demobilized. In the garden of the Mende Grand Hotel he saw two of them engaged in some mysterious activity: one was on his knees, the other held two thin branches. "What are they doing? Now they've done it! They've—caught a butterfly!" People were already beginning to praise the Germans as "the new Islam." In the first war they had been known as Huns, Boches, barbarians; now "one speaks of them with respect and, yes, envy." Even their raincoats were said to be actually waterproof.

The camp was on short rations and Doeblin lost a lot of weight. He diagnosed himself as being in a psychologically and physiologically abnormal condition. "This man, a physician, ought to know that. I was genuinely undernourished. I lived in unhealthy surroundings. From time to time I suffered from a certain hallucinatory agitation; one afternoon, as I sat on the edge of my bunk without thinking about anything, I distinctly heard my wife speaking. . . ." He was absorbed in sorting out his life and his relationship to the world:

Do I fear for myself? Do I fear the Nazis? I rarely think about them. I dislike thinking about them, dislike seeing pictures of them. After leaving Germany I could touch a Nazi newspaper only with a feeling of nausea. I remember the physical revulsion I felt when I saw a Nazi gathering with its flag in front of the Charlottenburg Exhibition grounds in Berlin. This Hydra from the German swamps now stretches its multiple arms even as far as this. What deep dishonor and shame for Germany to have produced this monster. I am not a Hercules who could slay a Hydra in the swamps. . . . But what have I myself done against it, what could I still do today, to destroy it? I had recognized this Hydra over the years . . . but what honest weapons did I have? . . . I always asked; I saw no weapons.

When a day of national mourning was declared, Doeblin attended the ceremonies in the local cathedral. For a long time he remained seated before an image of the crucified Christ. An old woman led a weeping boy to the front of the church, and they kneeled to pray. "I question myself and the crucifix but receive no answer. I can go no further. But the weeping woman helps me." Later he was to return to the cathedral many times: "The figure of the crucified Christ will not let me go." It became the symbol for what he now regarded as "our destiny"—"I see Jesus at the cross with his crown of thorns as the incarnation of human suffering, our weakness and helplessness."*

Doeblin eventually mustered up the strength to leave the camp, where the police had already singled him out as a suspicious character. He had received a message from the outside world. "The word *heureuse* jumps out at me. I read the signature. The telegram comes from my wife. She and the boy are living in Toulouse." After weeks of inactivity he resumed his journey: "The last few weeks had passed like an illness, and they left me different from what I had been before." His wife and son were waiting for him at the station in Toulouse, but it was clear that their problems were far from solved. As German emigrants, though with French passports, they were almost certain to be on the Nazi list of aliens who were, according to the terms of the armistice, to be "surrendered upon demand." He cabled his son in New York asking for "three visas and tickets"—as though that were an easy matter to arrange in even the best of times. But if they were to leave France they would need exit visas as well. The local military authorities explained that according to the new regulations, this would be impossible: German refugees were to be held at the disposition of the Germans. Doeblin accepted their decision at its face value; under the circumstances there seemed to be nothing else he could do:

> Had I been alone I would have acquiesced, would have sympathized with the officer who expressed his regret at being unable to help. . . . But my wife stood beside me. She was, for a start, thoroughly disappointed by what had been said. She was indignant, genuinely indig-

---

*About a year later, when it was announced that every Jew in Hitler's domain would have to wear a yellow star of David on his coat, the German Catholic philosopher Theodor Haecker noted in his secret diary that the Son of Man, after all, had sprung from the house of David, and that the swastika would henceforth be known as the symbol of the Antichrist: "Today they are crucifying *Christ as a people* for the second time." Freud, though for quite different reasons, insisted in *Moses and Monotheism* that "the hatred for Judaism is at bottom hatred for Christianity. . . ." Nazi laws required people to prove, not that they were Christians, but that they were *not Jews*.

nant, even beside herself, that we were to be held here for the Nazis—why not arrest us right away and deliver us to the Germans? She could not believe it. The officer's sense of duty was no concern of hers. . . . She was indignant and did not try to hide her indignation. Instead of taking stoic cognizance of the facts, instead of congratulating the officer on his sense of duty, she explained our situation to these officers: two of our sons in the army, one decorated; I a consultant to a ministry. She refused to hold anything back, and she said everything she felt about this "regulation." Standing at the officers' table she called it unheard-of and unbelievable. It was a shameful action to take, and she could not believe that one seriously wanted to detain us, we who had sought refuge in this country and had supported it. She wept. She protested and appealed to the officers, who said nothing. . . . The officers whispered, until one rose and declared he would submit the matter to the general. He took our papers and disappeared. When he returned a few minutes later he said, "You will receive your visa."

Their *visa de sortie* was good for only seven days, and during that time they had to obtain the all-important American visa. A crowd of people was lined up outside the U. S. vice-consul's office in Marseilles. Most of them had some inkling of the odds against them but were making a last desperate effort to save their lives by any means that seemed to offer some hope. For most of them it was an exercise in futility. In Alfred Polgar's rueful phrase, "Hitler was quicker than the consuls on whose moods depended the visas that could save us." Among the waiting refugees were several acquaintances whom Doeblin had known in Berlin and Paris. "Strange how, in their fear and anxiety, each assumed that the Nazis were after him personally. Each tried to remember what he had said or written that was dangerous or subversive. Each recited his catalogue of misdeeds to himself (and to others) and gave himself up for lost."

But once again Doeblin proved to be a special case. His wife had the presence of mind to show the vice-consul her husband's engraved invitation to the White House, carefully preserved from his visit to America the year before. "The official was visibly impressed. He rose and invited us to enter another room, his real office. . . ." Their friends in America had not been idle. Emergency visas had been obtained for them through the Emergency Rescue Committee in New York: one of their steamship tickets from Lisbon to New York had been purchased by a prominent patroness of the arts, Mrs. Dudley Wadsworth; another with funds raised by Erika Mann; a third with the proceeds of a benefit concert given by Lotte Lehmann and Bruno Walter. Yet when all their papers, including the Spanish and Portuguese transit visas, were finally in order, Doeblin learned that he would not be able to draw on his bank account in Paris, which meant they had no way of paying the fare to Lisbon. At the last minute an elderly French school director, to whom they had been referred by a friend of a friend, lent them the four thousand francs they required. "He reached into his breast pocket, took out his wallet and handed us the money. He declined a receipt. We promised to repay him as soon as possible. He refused our thanks; we were in a difficult spot, he regretted not being able to do more, encouraged us, pressed our hand. . . ." They caught the last train that would take them across the border before their visa expired. "What had happened to us reminded me of the sailors in the ancient Greek myth. They had to row through a strait between two movable cliffs that snapped together like jaws. Most of them were caught and crushed to death; hardly one escaped."

It was to save people like Doeblin that the Emergency Rescue Committee had been hastily organized in New York by a group of sponsors that included Frank Kingdon of the University of Newark, William Allan Neilson of Smith College, Alvin Johnson of the New School, Charles Seymour of Yale and George Shuster of Hunter College, as well as Dorothy Thompson, Ingrid Warburg and the radio commentator Raymond Gram Swing. Their purpose, Kingdon declared, was to rescue "outstanding artists and intellectuals endangered by Hitler . . . all those who were trustees of European culture." One of their most important contributions was to loosen, however slightly, the stranglehold on visas exercised by Breckinridge Long at the State Department. During their first year of operation, the committee played a part in saving more than six hundred lives—including those of Heinrich and Golo Mann, Lion Feuchtwanger, Leonhard Frank, Hans Habe, Friedrich Torberg, Alfred Neumann, Fritz von Unruh, Franz Werfel and his wife Alma Mahler, Hans Sahl, Kurt Wolff, Marc Chagall, Jacques Lipchitz, Max Ernst and André Breton.

Varian Fry, the journalist chosen to be the committee's special emissary in unoccupied France, arrived in Marseilles just as Doeblin was leaving it. He came for a month and stayed for a year, operating the so-called Centre Américain de Secours, ostensibly a simple relief organization but actually dedicated to smuggling Fry's "clients" out of a France that was legally obligated to turn them over to the Germans. During that year he stage-managed an endless series of Scarlet Pimpernel escapes under the very noses of the Gestapo and the Vichy police, preparing forged passports and browbeating consuls into visas; arranging illegal passage on ships leaving France, staking out secret routes across the Pyrenees and Spain, obtaining travel funds for refugees through the black market. Altogether the center handled eighteen hundred cases involving four thousand human beings, about one thousand of whom actually succeeded in escaping from France. It was, of course, only a tiny fraction of the tens of thousands who were caught in the trap. "We couldn't help everybody in France who needed help," Fry wrote afterward. "We couldn't even help every intellectual and political refugee who really needed help, or said he did." But he demonstrated how much could be done by even a handful of Americans not content to abide by their government's official indifference. At first, the center was quietly encouraged by an American vice-consul sympathetic to their cause. Later his place as head of the visa section of the U. S. consulate in Marseilles was taken by a man who, as Fry noted, "seemed to delight in making autocratic decisions and refusing as many visas as he possibly could. He was also very weak on modern European history but very strong on defending America against refugees he regarded as radicals." Ultimately the American consul and the Vichy Ministry of the Interior joined forces to have Fry deported from France as an undesirable alien—"*Parce que*," as the chief of the Marseilles police, Rodelle du Prozic, informed him, "*vous avez trop protégé des juifs et des anti-Nazis.*" He was considered important enough to be personally escorted across the Spanish border by an agent of the Sûreté.

Doeblin, with his wife and son, had made the same journey a year earlier and reached Lisbon without further delays. After the blacked-out cities of France, it was a pleasant shock to drive into the city at two o'clock in the morning: "We drove through brilliantly lit streets filled with happy people. Yes, Lisbon welcomed us with light, music and laughter." They had to wait four weeks for a ship to take them to New York. It was, of course, crowded with refugees from Germany, Austria and Czechoslovakia. "All had lost their means of earning a livelihood. . . . What were they to do now? Continue pushing the old cart? They knew only that they were going to America. . . . They were disturbed. All they wanted was to get to America."

A job was already awaiting him in California. Some of the ex-Berlin film people who had preceded him to Hollywood* had established a European Film Fund that worked closely with the

---

*Prominent contributors to the fund included Marlene Dietrich, Peter Lorre, Max Ophuls, Joe Pasternak, Otto Preminger, Erich Maria Remarque, William Wyler, Ernst Lubitsch, Salka Viertel, Paul Kohner, Fritzi Massary, Elisabeth Frank and Gottfried Reinhardt.

Emergency Rescue Committee; they had prevailed on Warner Brothers and Metro-Goldwyn-Mayer studios to help thirteen refugee authors obtain emergency visas by giving them one-year contracts as "screenwriters" at a salary of one hundred dollars a week. At MGM the list included Doeblin, Walter Mehring, Alfred Neumann, Heinrich Mann, Leonhard Frank and Alfred Polgar.

Doeblin had misgivings about the arrangement. "New York was the second emigration, but Los Angeles the third," he wrote wearily to a friend in New York. MGM had no real use for its refugee authors; the contracts had merely been a form of corporate charity. Even so, like the aging Heinrich Mann, he was expected to be physically present in his office every day from ten to five—"but I go home at four," he confided to Hermann Kesten. "Actually one does nothing here. Absolutely nothing. Supposedly we will be asked to work on something, but it is only a rumor. We do our correspondence, call people on the telephone, read newspapers, write our own things. . . . Why that? It's the custom." He wrote most of *Fateful Journey* while on the MGM payroll, and eventually he was asked to do some script writing—on *Mrs. Miniver*, to which, according to the writer who won an Academy Award for the script, George Froeschel, Doeblin contributed forty "masterful" pages of material. Though much of it ended on the cutting-room floor, "the Dunkirk episode is based in large part on his ideas." Later he was brought in as a consultant on *Random Harvest*, the story of an amnesiac who twice loses his memory and falls in love with the same woman each time. "It is a best-seller, a deeply untrue book," was Doeblin's verdict. He, who had written his doctor's thesis on lapses of memory in certain kinds of psychosis, was supposed to watch over the "authenticity" of the script—"Oh woe is me!"

The film contract was not renewed, and Doeblin became one of the gainfully unemployed. "I sit here in the Hollywood branch of the Los Angeles Public Library and browse through books and newspapers. That is what one does in the afternoon instead of going to a café. Every day I stroll over here from three to five with almost astronomic exactitude, and that more or less completes my day. For what is there to do in this steppe with drugstores and shacks that call themselves houses?" Like Schoenberg he failed to qualify for a Guggenheim Fellowship, though Thomas Mann supported his application. For five years virtually every publishing possibility was closed to him as well, and he had to depend on his son Peter, the European Film Fund and some of his émigré friends for the $120 a month on which he managed to live. "It is simply *fatal* for an author to have no money and to live on subsidies as I (and others) are doing. . . ." It seemed to him that he was continuing to write merely to "pass the time." He liked America—"the psychological environment is very different here. They are a friendly people, and they grow up healthier than the Europeans; they put individual freedom in first place, cultivate *freien speech* [*sic*], a robust business sense and the curiously easy and superficial religiosity that belongs to this society." The trouble was that there seemed to be no place for an Expressionist German novelist in all this: "How should we Europeans get in touch with Americans and how can we mean anything to them?"

On his sixty-fifth birthday, in 1943, the Los Angeles émigré colony set out to show Doeblin that he was not forgotten. About two hundred of his admirers met in a Santa Monica auditorium to celebrate the occasion. Heinrich Mann gave a speech, Berthold Viertel read the congratulatory messages, including those from Thomas Mann, Franz Werfel and Lion Feuchtwanger, who were in the audience; Peter Lorre, Alexander Granach and Fritz Kortner read excerpts from Doeblin's books, Hanns Eisler and Ernst Toch played the piano and Blandine Ebinger sang Berlin cabaret songs. But at the end there was a painful scene when Doeblin got up to say a few words. "He spoke so darkly, so mysteriously, that no one understood what he wanted to say," George Froeschel recalled. "Only at the very end did we understand that this was a profession of faith and that Doeblin was telling us that he had experienced a spiritual conversion on his flight through France." No one knew what to make of his speech, and "people left the hall in a subdued, uncertain frame of mind." Ludwig Marcuse remembered that "of all the curious birthday celebrations of the émigré epoch, this was the most grotesque."

Doeblin had, in fact, formally converted to Catholicism in November 1941, but had kept it a "private matter" so as "not to attack my own people in the rear" at a time of crisis. Later he wrote openly about his new faith in *Der unsterbliche Mensch* (Man Is Immortal), which sets forth his ideas about "the metaphysical character of faith" in a series of Socratic dialogues. "I speak of Christianity," he told his friends, "and this is a natural outgrowth of Judaism. One single line runs from one to the other. . . ." The book recapitulates an old Doeblin theme. "After the war," he was certain, "the message that we are all brothers will once again be honored. . . ."

But the reality of postwar Europe failed to fulfill his expectations. Doeblin was one of the very first of the exiled writers to return to Germany: as a French citizen and a former propagandist he was asked to play a role in the reeducation of Germany, at least in the French Zone of Occupation. It was yet another dramatic transformation for the many-faceted Dr. Doeblin. In September 1945 he was still a penniless refugee living in a nondescript apartment on North Citrus Avenue in Hollywood; in November he had arrived in Baden-Baden in a French colonel's uniform to begin carrying out his duties as *chargé de mission* in education and literary adviser to the local occupation authorities.

On the journey from California to New York he had stopped off to see the phenomenon that interested him most on the entire continent—Niagara Falls. "That, ladies and gentlemen, is the American continent, powerful and idiosyncratic as Asia with its Himalayas and Tibet and the Chinese and Indian landscape. . . . It does not stand still. It is not *there*. It comes from three sides at the same time. It ignores all aesthetic demands . . . it knows only how to produce itself, day after day, night after night, to roar and rage, fall and foam, for centuries, millennia." In New York City there was another long-awaited encounter: a meeting with Yolla Niclas, who had escaped from Europe independently of Doeblin and now lived in New York, married to a fellow refugee. "Naturally, Erna was not to know anything about it," Yolla Niclas afterward remembered. "All hell would have broken loose. We had this one opportunity. It was the last time; our last meeting. It was as beautiful and unforgettable as the first." For many reasons, therefore, his ship's departure from New York harbor filled Doeblin with regret:

> *Much has happened to us in this land.*
> *Farewell America.*
> *You did not want me.*
> *Still I love you.*

He had agreed to go back to Germany because "I can do something useful here," but it was not easy for him in Baden-Baden, where he lived and worked in cramped quarters not at all commensurate with his "colonelcy," and rode to work in a crowded streetcar every morning. Erna Doeblin remained in Paris to be with Etienne, who was still at school. Claude had survived the war by joining the Underground* and was living in Nice, but Doeblin had learned at last that his second son, of whom he had heard nothing since June 1940, had taken his own life rather than allow himself to be captured when the Germans overran the French positions in the

---

*Although the word "Underground" has a reassuring ring, it was by no means the safest place to be during the Occupation. Fully 30,000 of the 120,000 Jews deported from France were arrested in connection with their Underground activities.

Vosges. Wolfgang, alias Vincent, had won the *croix de guerre* for gallantry; though only a student he had already made a name for himself as a mathematician with "Doeblin's Central Limit Theorem."

Early in 1946 Doeblin replied to a German acquaintance who wrote to him about her abiding hatred of the Nazis: "I have almost overcome my hatred." He had arrived with no preconceptions other than a great, undiminished passion for his mother tongue. As he wrote to Yvan Goll, "One has to mix with people and hear the language again here on the spot, and speak it again." Still it was not a homecoming such as he might have wished. "When I returned—I did not return. You are no longer the one who went away, and you can no longer find the house in which you used to live." After twelve years of Nazism he found Germany "spiritually starved and hardly aware of it." At first he thought it might be possible to fill the intellectual vacuum that had been created by the exodus of 1933. He founded a literary magazine, *Das Goldene Tor* (The Golden Gate) and a literary academy for anti-Nazi authors. "It was our intention to push back the old 'soldierly' spirit and replace it with something better, one that brought back to Germany the old European, Christian, humanist ethic that had once existed in Germany as well." A few people received him with open arms; the rest were indifferent or hostile to "enlightenment" and good intentions. The problem, as he saw it, was that they had been so inundated with propaganda that they were still unaware of what had happened to them:

> It's as though they had become rusty. They have a very small repertoire of ideas that have been drilled into them, they work with these; it is hard to pull them out of it. It is the legacy of the Nazi regime. And for that reason they disregard all appeals, and the brochures for their enlightenment have no effect and are read indignantly, as though the dictator still ruled the land. And for that reason one cannot discuss the question of guilt with them. Hence too, they resist political discussions with anyone who has other ideas and conceptions.

He was invited to speak in ruined Berlin, where he was remembered as the chronicler of what were now referred to as the city's golden years. Along the Kurfürstendamm one could recognize only the outlines of the once splendid boulevard. "All its wealth had been blown away. In the ruins of the houses, a few shops: they sell household articles, flowers." At the Alexanderplatz the great Tietz department-store "palace" had been bombed to pieces and now looked "like a man whose neck has been broken and whose skull has been pushed down into his chest." Time and the murderers had transformed his city into something with which he could no longer identify: "I ask myself, what am I actually doing here? Should I not run away and see nothing of this? They have allowed themselves to be disgraced." Yet his feelings were those of a mourner. "I mourn the brilliant, tumultuous, promising city which was so full of life. I mourn its unsuspecting, hard-working people!"

After a few years of trying to reeducate Germany, Doeblin came to the conclusion that its "decapitated literature" would take a long time to recover. The continuity of civilization had been violently interrupted: "one will have to chew on this for a long time." In 1953 he wrote to his fellow author Theodor Heuss, who had become the first president of the Federal Republic, that what he had previously described as his "return" to Germany had only been a "somewhat prolonged" and "instructive" visit. He moved to Paris again, embittered by the "boycott of silence" that prevented his books from being reissued, and by the fact that in German public life, "the most important positions, as well as the less important, are filled with Nazis." Though he was now in his mid-seventies and nearly crippled with polyneuritis, "I don't stop writing and writing . . . i.e., thinking and fantasizing." Ludwig Marcuse proposed him for the Nobel Prize in 1953, but nothing came of the idea. The most significant book of his later years, *Hamlet oder Die lange Nacht nimmt ein Ende* (Hamlet, or The Long Night Draws to a Close)—a Dostoyevskian novel of suffering and atonement—was published in East Berlin after being turned down by every West German publisher to whom it was submitted.

When he returned to Germany for the last time it was to become a patient in a sanatorium in the Black Forest. Marcuse went to visit him there shortly before his death. "The doctors had (mistakenly) given him only three days to live. He had to be fed by a nurse—and he conversed brilliantly with me, energetically attacking the Germany of the fifties. He was bitter, too, but above all indestructible; nothing could keep him down." Doeblin died on June 28, 1957, at a hospital in Emmendingen, near Freiburg, and was buried in the Vosges, beside the son he had lost in the war. His death signaled the beginning of a Doeblin revival that was to yield its first concrete results in 1960, when a Swiss publisher brought out the initial volumes of a collected edition of his work which, at this writing, has reached a total of seventeen volumes.

"This lonely, disappointed man, now come to the end of his eventful life"—that was how Doeblin had begun his analysis of the character of Confucius. "He was not permitted to build the house for which he laid the corner stone . . . all things need time in which to ripen." A decade after his death Doeblin had emerged as the great literary model of a new generation of German writers. "He did not lie quietly," explained Günter Grass (who had never known him) in his essay *My Teacher Doeblin.* "Yet he did not 'arrive.' He had been too Catholic for the radical Left, too much of an anarchist for the Catholics, insufficiently prescriptive for the moralists, too inelegant for the radio poetry hour and too rude for the school curriculum." But at the same time, "he will make you uneasy, will trouble your dreams; you will have difficulty in swallowing, he will not taste good; he is indigestible and will not agree with you. He changes whoever reads him."

Doeblin's postwar experiences were typical of what the so-called "remigrants" encountered when they returned to Germany after Hitler's defeat. It was not an easy step for any of the exiles, however much they may have been homesick for the sound of their mother tongue. Those who went back did so with understandable misgivings. Indeed the vast majority of German-Jewish émigrés refused even to entertain the idea of "migrating back to the land of the mass-murderers of our kinsmen," as Einstein wrote to Max Born, one of the few refugee physicists to return home. Still, Born went back to Germany because, as professor of physics, he felt that "here was the chance of making one's influence felt. I regarded this work as my duty, but it also gave me pleasure." By 1965, however, it seemed "more than doubtful to me whether it has had any success. The unteachable are in the ascendency again."

In many ways it was easier for writers of the radical Left, who were warmly welcomed and given generous stipends in the Russian Zone, afterward the German Democratic Republic. Heinrich Mann was about to accept an invitation to East Berlin when he died in California in 1950; Bertolt Brecht received an East Berlin theater of his own, and a generously subsidized company, the Berliner Ensemble, with which to realize the productions he had been dreaming about all his life; Arnold Zweig, Anna Seghers, Alfred Kantorowicz and Ernst Bloch became prominent figures in the East German literary establishment—though Kantorowicz fled to West Germany in 1957 and Bloch followed suit in 1961, after being dismissed from his Leipzig professorship for attempting to teach humanist ideas at a Communist university.

For most non-Communist writers, however, the thought of returning to Germany was almost as traumatic as leaving it had been.

As usual Alfred Polgar found a neatly aphoristic way of summing up the problem: "Those who had accidentally escaped being killed had to make their peace with those who had accidentally failed to kill them." Late in 1945 the exiled novelist Hermann Broch wrote from Princeton to a Swiss friend that he now felt "tolerant toward the Germans and their lack of backbone, but only from a distance. I don't want to see these people any more; the nausea that shook me during my last months in Austria was my worst Hitler experience." Earlier in the year Thomas Mann had received a rather histrionic letter from Walter von Molo asking him to return to Germany as soon as possible; his reply was a long and bitter polemic explaining his reasons for not rushing back to Germany, at least for the time being:

> In the course of all these years Germany has truly become alien to me. You must grant that it is a frightening country. I admit that I fear the sight of German ruins both stone and human. And I fear that communication between one who watched the witches' sabbath from the outside and you who joined in the dance and paid your respects to Old Nick would be difficult in any case. How can I be unresponsive to the effusive letters full of long-repressed loyalty now coming to me from Germany? They are truly emotional events for me—deeply touching. But my pleasure in them is somewhat checked not only by the thought that none of them would ever have been written if Hitler had won, but also by a certain ingenuousness and lack of sensitivity in them, by their naïve assumption that ties can be resumed as if these twelve years had never been.

Most of the émigrés expected some sort of inward transformation from a defeated Germany; a sign that the people as a whole had recognized their share in the deeds that had been committed in the name of *Volk* and *Führer*. Few such indications of what Broch called "a new formation of the German *Geist*" were forthcoming. It was not unreasonable, perhaps, but certainly unrealistic to expect a twelfth-hour conversion from people who had heard only Nazi propaganda for a decade, and who had accepted nationalism as a kind of secular religion. As Doeblin discovered in the course of his work, the impact of Dr. Goebbels had been far greater than anyone imagined:

> . . . this effect would not have been as profound had it not been so well prepared or applied to so receptive an object. There were two nations in one; the one that we knew and cultivated and educated culturally and thus preserved, and the other, which dominated the first and was only tyrannical, violent, power-hungry; this second

Germany had long ago begun using the first to deceive itself with mystic, impertinent dreams. When I returned in 1945, no one with whom I spoke or whose work I read wanted to know anything about what had transpired. . . .

Thomas Mann, on the other hand, delivered a lecture at the Library of Congress in 1945 in which he contended just the opposite, "that there are *not* two Germanys, a good one and a bad one, but only one, whose best turned into evil through devilish cunning. Wicked Germany is merely good Germany gone astray, good Germany in misfortune, in guilt and ruin." It was, at any rate, a purely academic question. Most of the well-intentioned attempts to reeducate Germany were quietly abandoned during the Cold War, when it became apparent that the New Germany would require the expertise of the Old Germany in order to fulfill its ordained role as the West's first line of defense in central Europe. And as the Germans themselves were the first to realize, those who had actually performed the work of the Reich were, as the expression went, *unbussfähig*—i.e., incapable of admitting their guilt or doing penance. The "exigencies of war" could always be invoked to cover all but the most spectacular atrocities. Besides, there was a useful psychological mechanism of repression that had already been described, with great charm and simplicity, in Broch's trilogy *Die Schlafwandler* (The Sleepwalkers), as part of his hilarious character study of a "realist" who has come unscathed through World War I:

> Huguenau had committed a murder. He forgot it afterward; it never came into his mind again, while every single business *coup* that he had successfully brought off . . . remained accurately imprinted in his memory. And that was only natural; for none of our actions remains alive except those that consort with our reigning system of values, and Huguenau had reverted once more to the commercial system.

The Huguenaus of World War II exonerated themselves in much the same fashion, and the twelve-year Reich was permitted to remain an *unbewältigte Vergangenheit*, an undigested, unexpiated past. Even if the occupying powers had taken a greater interest in the problem, the exiles and remigrants could have done very little about it—in the eyes of those who had stayed at home, they were merely carpetbaggers or Germanophobes. The so-called *Emigrantenhetze* of the 1950s and 1960s was directed not only against people like Thomas Mann and Doeblin but against Willy Brandt and Fritz Bauer, the refugee lawyer who had returned to Germany to become chief public prosecutor for the State of Hesse. Enlightenment, such as it was, eventually came from within Germany: from a new generation that began asking impolite questions of its elders, and from writers like Grass who provided some of the liberating answers in the form of parables such as *The Tin Drum*. The dividing line between those raised on Goebbels and the postwar generation is clear-cut. The American correspondent George Bailey, who interviewed scores of Germans at the time of the Eichmann trial in 1961, recalls that from the people who were then over forty, "as often as not we heard the frankly stated opinion that the Jews had brought the Final Solution on themselves. How so? 'Because they crucified our Lord Jesus Christ!' "

When Thomas Mann eventually returned to Europe, he chose to live in Switzerland rather than Germany. Since the Swiss government had reversed its wartime policy toward ex-German writers, several other prominent exiles adopted the same expedient of a quasi-return, among them Alfred Neumann, Walter Mehring, Erich Maria Remarque and Carl Zuckmayer. But nearly all the intellectuals who had gone to England or America chose to stay where they were. By then it had become apparent to most of them that the emigration had a raison d'être and direction of its own. Although, as a group, the refugees had failed to influence the course of events in postwar Germany, their other achievements were not inconsiderable, and perhaps of more lasting significance.

They had, for one thing, taken their Expressionist compassion beyond the borders of Germany and joined it to the Blakean humanist tradition of the English-speaking world. In exile they had created a body of work that brought the "Periclean age" of German culture to a dazzling conclusion. Schoenberg's *A Survivor from Warsaw*, Thomas Mann's *Doctor Faustus*, Benjamin's *Passages* project, Doeblin's *Schicksalsreise*, Broch's *The Death of Virgil* and Lasker-Schüler's *Mein blaues Klavier* establish beyond all doubt that a renaissance can gather strength even against a background of human tragedy. They had, moreover, fulfilled Karl Mannheim's injunction that a refugee must serve as "a living interpreter between different cultures" and create "living communication between different worlds which so far have been kept apart."

Mannheim's own influential career as a sociologist at the London School of Economics and the University of London typifies the kind of bridge-building he had in mind. It was a process for which people with a dual heritage were particularly well equipped, and it took place on many levels, in schools, theaters, laboratories, publishing houses. The musicologist Alfred Einstein's Princeton lectures on the Italian madrigal could be cited as a more esoteric example, or the *Theory of Games and Economic Behavior* by John von Neumann and Oskar Morgenstern, Herbert Marcuse's *Eros and Civilization*, Erich Kahler's *Man the Measure* and the psychoanalytic teaching of Franz Alexander, Karen Horney and Erich Fromm, as well as Kurt Weill's *September Song* (or for that matter, all of his music for *Knickerbocker Holiday*, *Lady in the Dark* and *Lost in the Stars*) and Billy Wilder's *Some Like It Hot*, which turned an old Bavarian farce into a Hollywood classic. Laura Fermi, wife of the Nobel Prize physicist Enrico Fermi, has written a comprehensive account of what was achieved in the arts and sciences by the hundreds of *Illustrious Immigrants*, like herself, who settled in America—"a new phenomenon in the history of immigration."

Ironically enough, at a time when the Weimar Renaissance was being brutally annihilated at home, it was the refugees who carried its ideas abroad, disseminating German culture more widely than ever before. Schoenberg at UCLA, Ernst Cassirer at Yale, Bruno Bettelheim at the University of Chicago were far more influential in their new surroundings than if they had remained in Berlin, Hamburg or Vienna. This was something like the German Diaspora that Goethe had once proposed, facetiously, as a way to "'develop the good" in his countrymen: "Like the Jews, the Germans must be transplanted and scattered all over the world!" It was an exercise in cultural diffusion carried out principally by German-Jewish refugees, but with the aid of a moral quorum of friends and sympathizers like Thomas Mann, Paul Klee and Kurt Schwitters—Christians who had, in the Nazis' ugly vocabulary, become *weisse Juden*. In this Diaspora, incidentally, German Christians and Jews could at last deal with one another as Wedekind's "two souls in the breast of mankind." Their age-old love affair—"the deep affinity that prevails between these two ethical nations," as Heine said—found its logical consummation in places like the New School or the University of Chicago, or in the living room of Thomas Mann's home in Pacific Palisades, where a typical evening might find him in conversation with Theodor Adorno, Bruno Walter, Alfred Neumann and Arnold Schoenberg.

By the same token, it was the refugees who built "the ark for German decency when the Nazi flood began to rise," as Gershom Scholem said of Walter Benjamin's book *Deutsche Menschen* (German People)—which is, at long last, being widely read in the Germany of the 1970s. Not the least bizarre aspect of their history is that, while half the German Jews were being murdered in the name of a greater Germany, many of the rest continued to think of themselves as ambassadors of the German *Geist*. "Leaving with us," Theodor Lessing was certain, "are Goethe, Schubert, Dürer, Hölderlin. . . ."

There was another, more important task, which the refugees accomplished with brilliance and distinction: as Manès Sperber had written during the war, "We shall become the walking cemeteries of our murdered friends." In the age of the Final Solution it remained for the survivors to speak for the victims and to erect a suitable memorial to the dead. This responsibility for remembrance was part of their tradition as people of the book; converts like Doeblin or *Grenzjuden* like Sperber were as assiduous as any talmudist in fulfilling their obligation. They wrote the epic of their own lives and those of their dead friends with great art and honesty. Sometimes—one thinks of Benjamin, Lessing, Hasenclever—they were prepared to serve as insightful observers even at their own execution, like something from a surrealist painting by Antoine Wiertz. They saw "writing as a vehicle of remembrance, as a means of clarification, as a purely private act that no longer had anything to do with the creation of 'a work of art' "—as Hermann Broch characterized his work on *The Death of Virgil*, part of which was written in a Nazi prison after the annexation of Austria. Beyond this, too, there was Kafka's "writing as a form of prayer." In *Schicksalsreise*, Doeblin says of his stories and novels, "In a certain sense all of them were prayers."

They had, demonstrably, arrived at a point not very far from where they started. They may have been "pioneers of Jewish modernity," yet even their avant-garde conveyed a secret sense of Ash Wednesday. Walter Benjamin always stressed the element of "transmissibility" in his quotations and ideas: "Actually, inheritance is the soundest way of acquiring a collection." But inheritance is also a form of that *noblesse qui oblige*. Karl Wolfskehl declared that in his art he felt "under obligation to the past and responsible toward the future"—*der Vergangenheit verpflichtet und der Zukunft verantwortlich*. For that matter, their very modern insistence on social justice—Toller's, Tucholsky's, Benjamin's, Doeblin's—ultimately derives from Isaiah's "I will make judgement the measuring line and righteousness the plummet." Consciously or not, their gift of prophecy derived from the same transmissible sources. Kafka, as Benjamin pointed out, drew on the kabalists for his key to the present and the future: "This most recent world of experience was conveyed to him precisely by this mystical tradition. . . . Kafka's world, frequently of such playfulness and interlaced with angels, is the exact complement of his era which is preparing to do away with the inhabitants of this planet on a considerable scale."

Writing as a vehicle of remembrance or as a form of prayer both constitute a kind of preparation for death. The very theme of Broch's great novel—"my private discussion with death"—had suggested itself to him because "the threat of death through Nazism assumed increasingly concrete forms" during the years just preceding the war. The political atmosphere of Austria during the late thirties concentrated his mind wonderfully—not on contemporary events but on the life of Virgil, and the legend that the poet had wanted to burn the *Aeneid* before he died. Broch was in his early fifties at the time, but the most important part of his writing career still lay ahead of him. He had been trained as a textile engineer—his father was a self-made textile magnate who owned the largest spinning mill in Austria—and it was only by an effort of will that he had been able to leave the family business so that, in 1927, he could at last devote himself to the things that really interested him—writing, mathematics, philosophy and psychology. The three novels comprising *The Sleepwalkers,* completed in 1932, gave him something of a literary reputation: they were published in a one-volume English translation a year later.

After his brief imprisonment by the Gestapo in 1938 Broch's English friends helped him escape to London (though there was no way for him to get his mother out, and she ultimately perished in a concentration camp). Thomas Mann was instrumental in bringing him to America, and a German friend helped smuggle his manuscripts out of the Reich. For several years he was passed from hand to hand on the American "arts and letters" circuit: Guggenheim and Rockefeller fellowships, a summer at Yaddo, a month with Einstein in Princeton, lectures at Yale. He received a grant for writing a study of mass psychology and "meta-politics," but his life as a writer had begun to revolve around *The Death of Virgil,* which he had brought to America in an eighty-page version and which he now expanded into an immense polyphonic composition on themes of life and death. "The German text," he explained to Thornton Wilder, "is an attempt to broaden the German expression by a rather individual use of the German language. . . ." Like *Ulysses* it depicts twenty-four hours in a man's life, but while Joyce had dealt with the psychopathology of everyday life, Broch focused on what Hannah Arendt calls "the least commonplace of days," the day of death.

At the core of this book was his own experience with imminent death. "I wrote this book exclusively for myself . . . and in a sense a private preparation for death and with no thought of a public. It was an attempt to drive myself, by means of the imagination, to experience death as nearly as possible. . . ." His Virgil resembled a figure from the ancient Mediterranean myth of Proteus the sea magician; a figure rather like Broch himself. The novel's mythological framework allowed him to write for five hundred pages about "the subject with which *all* art has always concerned itself . . . the great pacemaker of all metaphysical knowledge . . . for myth remains mankind's closest approximation to the knowledge of death." The figure of Virgil, he told Aldous Huxley, struck him as "a kind of pre-Christian saint, and indeed worthy of grace. . . . He was not yet the prophet who announces the new truth, but he belongs to those who are necessary in order that the prophet shall appear. . . . He was a pre-prophet, and probably felt himself as such. And therefore one can presume that he was very lonely."

The history of German-Jewish literature comes to an end with this immensely complex synthesis of pagan, Jewish and Christian images and symbols. After *The Death of Virgil*—and indeed, after Broch's own death in 1951, six years after its publication—there were to be no more major landmarks in this astonishing tradition that had begun with a love song in 1821, with Heine's *Buch der Lieder*. Broch, writing "in such apocalyptical times," was fully aware that this was to be a kind of farewell; that there could be nothing like it again. That is another reason, perhaps, why he gave no thought to the public as he was working; why he conceived of it not as a "novel" but "just as *something* that arose from the constellation of its own problems by necessity." The effect of letting the reader "reexperience how a person draws near to the knowledge of death (draws near but never reaches it while still alive)" could not be achieved by ordinary rational statement; instead, it came to him "in the form of litany-like sentences"—like the long, unbroken cantilenas that Mahler had used in the Second Symphony: *O glaube, mein Herz, O glaube*—"Believe, my heart, oh believe; nothing will be lost to you!" Indeed some of Broch's sentences, as his translator Jean Starr Untermeyer points out, "are probably among the longest in the world's literature." His cadences rise and fall like the chanting of a prayer, rising slowly, slowly rising, into a great Kaddish for all the living and the dead:

> . . . that which sounded was more than song, more than the striking of the lyre, more than any tone, more than any voice, since it was all of these together and at once, bursting out of the nothing as well as out of the universe, breaking forth as a communication beyond every understanding, breaking forth as a significance above every com-

prehension, breaking forth as the pure word which it was, exalted above all understanding and significance whatsoever, consummating and initiating, mighty and commanding, fear-inspiring and protecting, gracious and thundering, the word of discrimination, the word of the pledge, the pure word; so it roared thither, roaring over and past him, swelling on and becoming stronger and stronger, becoming so overpowering that nothing could withstand it, the universe disappearing before the word, dissolved and acquitted in the word while still being contained and preserved in it, destroyed and recreated forever, because nothing had been lost, nothing could be lost, because end was joined to beginning, being born and giving birth again and again; the word hovered over the universe, over the nothing, floating beyond the expressible as well as the inexpressible, and he, caught under and amidst the roaring, he floated on with the word, although the more he was enveloped by it, the more he penetrated into the flooding sound and was penetrated by it, the more unattainable, the greater, the graver and more elusive became the word, a floating sea, a floating fire, sea-heavy, sea-light, notwithstanding it was still the word: he could not hold fast to it and he might not hold fast to it; incomprehensible and unutterable for him: it was the word beyond speech.

NOTES

I. A FAMILY RESEMBLANCE

Page	Line	Source
1	1	HEI-2, vol. 3, pp. 658–59.
	21	EIN-1, p. 180.
	22	Ibid., p. 181.
2	13	LEO-2, vol. 6, p. 130.
	23	HEI-1, p. 196.
	29	KRO, p. 143n.
3	4	GRO, vol. 8, p. 116.
	11	MAL, p. 2.
	23	KAU, p. 447.
	30	DIS, vol. 3, pp. 85–86.
5	1	CLA, p. 20.
	2	EIN-1, p. 183.
	3	Ibid.
	20	FOR, pp. 635–36.
	32	Ibid., p. 659.
	39	HEI-3, p. 486.
6	4	FOR, p. 658.
	13	BERL-2, p. 295.
	26	HEI-3, p. 134.
	28	HEI-2, vol. 2, p. 332.
	35	HEI-3, pp. 113–14.
7	3	HEI-2, vol. 1, p. 322.
	11	BUT, p. 228.
	20	HEI-2, vol. 2, p. 550.
	33	FREU-3, p. 367; and LEO-2, vol. 2, p. 227.
	42	LEO-2, vol. 12, p. 76.
8	3	Ibid., p. 83.
	10	WAS, p. 126.
	16	STER, p. 74.
	33	WEIN, p. 413.

Page	Line	Source
9	2	Ibid., p. 431.
	9	ALT, p. 21.
	23	ADO, p. 42.
	27	BEN-3, vol. 1, p. 162.
	37	GOE-1, p. 149.
	40	FIT, p. 69.
10	4	MOS-1, p. 20.
	11	FREU-3, pp. 68–69.
	16	Ibid., p. 86.
	26	DEV, p. 65.
	34	Ibid., pp. 64–66.
11	10	BAU, p. 66.
	16	WALT-B, p. 7.
	31	BAU, p. 172.
	42	Ibid., p. 57.
12	10	Ibid., p. 58.
	19	STER, p. 25.
	28	MAL, p. 31.
	41	Ibid., p. 61.
13	4	DEV, p. 69.
	10	CAR, p. 97.
	14	Ibid., p. 157.
	20	Ibid., p. 179.
	33	Ibid., p. 245.
	42	BAR, p. 200.
14	3	CAR, p. 245.
	17	MARX, p. 366.
	25	MOS-1, p. iv.
	27	WAL, p. 111.
	32	REIC, p. 15.
15	7	FREU-3, p. 39.
	11	JON-2, p. 365.
	16	FREU-3, p. 277.
	20	JON-2, p. 366.
	21	Ibid.

Page	Line	Source
16	11	KAH-2, p. 100.
	14	Ibid., p. 120.
	16	SOM, p. 134.
	24	STE, p. 93.
	27	BENN-2, p. 534.
	34	LAS-6, p. 72.
17	5	SPA, p. 48.
	11	JAY, p. 33.
	17	CAS, p. 28.
	25	Ibid., p. 176.
	28	SAL, no. 10–11, p. 70.
	36	RAT, p. 108.
18	6	TOL-1, p. 3.
	26	STO, p. 63.
	34	KAF-7, p. 117.
	37	KAF-9, p. 376.
19	1	DURZ, p. 11.
	17	KOR, p. 19.
	32	FREU-3, p. 93.
20	34	SLO, p. 121.
	37	BERL-1, p. 316.
21	7	CAN-1, p. 178.
	15	BENN-1, p. 42.
	18	Ibid., p. 43.
	26	Ibid., p. 47.
	30	LEO-2, vol. 2, p. 237.
	38	Ibid.
22	3	Ibid., p. 238.
	10	Ibid., pp. 238–39.
	31	MUS-1, p. 68.
	36	KAF-1, p. 27.
23	5	WIL, p. 75.
	11	CAT-4, p. 28.
	28	BUL, no. 50, p. 77.
24	1	CAT-4, p. 27.
	14	Ibid., pp. 27–28.
	24	BUL, no. 50, p. 76.
	29	Ibid., p. 79.
	35	Ibid., p. 78.
	36	Ibid.
25	5	KAF-9, p. 406.
	8	LAS-4, vol. 1, p. 58.
	9	MEY, p. 13.
	15	SEY, p. 245.
	28	CAT-4, p. 61.
	30	MEY, p. 64.
	40	CAT-4, p. 34.
26	3	SCHA, p. 159.

Page	Line	Source
	11	ZWEI, p. 214.
	19	MUS-1, p. 15.
27	7	HEIN, p. 352.
	43	OGD, p. 195.
28	8	MANN-T-4, p. 55.
	10	Ibid., pp. 55–56.
	24	LEO-1, p. 20.
30	2	FISH, p. 54.
31	6	BOE, p. 225.
	36	KAF-7, p. 37.
32	22	LEO-2, vol. 18, p. 133.
	25	ENG, p. 122.
	29	Ibid., p. 248.
33	8	HELM, p. 120.
	12	ROH, p. 111.
	20	MANN-E, title page.
	23	MUS-1, p. 8.
	27	Ibid., p. 10.
	39	Ibid., p. 11.
34	34	CEL, p. 39.
35	5	HIL-2, p. 61.

II. FROM THE VERY HEART OF NATURE

Page	Line	Source
36	8	FREU-7, p. 342.
	19	JON-2, p. 279.
37	7	REIK, p. 343.
	15	Ibid., p. 344.
	26	MAH-1, p. 157.
	28	Ibid., p. 158.
	41	BAU, p. 8.
38	1	MAH-1, p. 159.
	9	Ibid.
	18	REIK, p. 347.
	29	BAU, p. 172.
	30	NEL, p. 56.
39	6	FREU-2, vol. 4, p. 197.
	34	JON-1, vol. 2, p. 89.
40	13	BAU, p. 151.
	19	Ibid., p. 147.
	33	FREU-2, vol. 4, p. 184.
	39	BAU, p. 119.
41	1	Ibid., p. 141.
	6	Ibid., p. 144.
	35	FREU-1, p. 105.

Page	Line	Source
	42	Ibid., p. 75.
42	5	LAG, p. xxiii.
	19	FREU-3, p. 406.
	23	JON-2, p. 381.
	31	FRE, p. 11.
	37	JON-2, p. 14.
43	7	LAG, p. 17.
	22	BAU, p. 53.
	26	Ibid., p. 166.
	32	WALT-B, p. 115.
	36	SPE, p. 169.
44	14	Ibid., p. 164.
	19	LAG, p. 18.
	29	FREU-5, p. 41.
	36	FREU-3, p. 368.
45	3	FREU-5, p. 42.
	9	MAH-2, p. 20.
	11	Ibid., p. 21.
	21	MAH-3, p. 8.
	35	WALT-B, pp. 94–95.
	38	BAU, p. 129.
46	19	WALT-B, p. 28.
	22	SPE, p. 40.
	27	MAH-2, p. 97.
	32	Ibid., p. 138.
	42	BAU, p. 54.
47	14	Ibid., p. 60.
	21	Ibid., p. 31.
	24	MAH-2, p. 144.
	37	LAG, p. 898.
48	3	MAH-1, p. 90.
	19	WALT-B, p. 38.
	22	MAH-1, p. 103.
	36	Ibid., p. 102.
	39	Ibid., p. 103.
49	4	MAH-2, p. 365.
	11	Ibid., p. 393.
	24	Ibid., p. 418.
	26	Ibid., p. 446.
	29	Ibid., p. 432.
50	4	MANN-KA, p. 64.
	11	Ibid., p. 62.
	15	Ibid., p. 63.
	19	Ibid., p. 64.
	33	MAH-1, p. 274.
	35	MANN-KA, p. 65.
	38	JON-2, p. 217.
	43	BAU, p. 90.
51	10	FREU-3, p. 250.

Page	Line	Source
	14	Ibid., p. 241.
	16	JON-2, p. 171.
	19	NEL, p. 90.
	26	JON-2, p. 299.
	29	FREU-3, p. 307.
	38	NEL, p. 56.
52	9	FREU-6, p. 165.
	29	JON-2, p. 353.
	30	FREU-3, p. 215.
	40	FRE, pp. 70–71.
53	8	FREU-6, p. 347.
	14	BAK, p. 47.
	25	FRE, p. 65.
	33	FRAE, p. 203.
	37	KUB, p. 187.
54	5	FRI, p. 258.
	16	FRAE, p. 434.
	22	WIE, no. 34–35, p. 25.
	28	ZWEI, pp. 27–28.
	38	Ibid., p. 28.
55	23	SCHI, p. 68.
	27	Ibid., p. 69.
	31	WEI, p. 328.
	31	LEO-2, vol. 16, p. 170.
56	1	HAA-1, p. 22.
	7	FREU-2, vol. 4, p. 197.
	12	FREU-3, p. 259.
	16	DIEF, no. 376–77, pp. 20–22.
	26	HAA-1, p. 24.
	36	FREU-3, pp. 344–45.
57	12	SCHE, p. 66.
	31	SCHN, p. 274.
58	5	SCHE, p. 78.
	19	ZEN, vol. 6, p. 10 (1933).
	28	HAN, p. 226.
	35	ZEN, vol. 7, pp. 8–10 (1934).
	40	JON-2, p. 367.
59	36	Ibid., p. 10.
	38	Ibid., p. 11.
	40	Ibid.
60	4	HAN, p. 225.
	19	Ibid., p. 219.
	25	Ibid., p. 224.

Page	Line	Source
60	34	MAX, p. 120.
61	3	FREU-7, p. 258.
	15	JON-2, p. 480.
	29	ZWEI, p. 317.
	35	FREU-2, vol. 3, p. 179.
62	11	GID, vol. 2, p. 299.
	24	FREU-2, vol. 5, p. 173.
	35	NEL, p. 51.
63	10	MANN-T-6, vol. 2, p. 218.
	13	CAT-8, p. 32.
	16	JON-2, p. 496.
	26	FREU-1, p. 61.
	34	JON-2, p. 492.
64	2	Ibid., p. 513.
	13	LOE, p. 146.
	24	FRAE, p. 210.
	29	FREU-3, pp. 441–42.
	33	Ibid., p. 443.
	38	JON-2, p. 527.
	42	Ibid., p. 529.
65	3	ZWEI, pp. 317–18.
	36	Ibid., p. 318.
66	3	AUD, pp. 215–18.

III. TURN TOWARD THE LIGHT FOR A MOMENT

Page	Line	Source
67	1	CAT-6, p. 150, and plate 1.
	16	Ibid., pp. 144–45.
68	7	WOLF-2, p. 5.
	16	SWI, p. 272.
	20	KAH-1, p. 168.
	26	CAT-6, p. 180.
	28	Ibid.
69	7	WOLF-1, p. 158.
	14	Ibid., p. 185.
	25	LEO-2, vol. 8, p. 177.
	27	Ibid.
	32	CAT-6, p. 11.
70	6	Ibid., p. 19.
	21	KAH-1, p. 166.
	30	CAT-6, p. 19.
71	11	SCHON, p. 89.
	30	KAL, pp. 333 *ff.*
	35	REI, p. 102.
	40	Ibid., p. 103.

Page	Line	Source
72	5	KALT, p. 337.
	29	SCHON, p. 87.
	30	Ibid.
	38	Ibid., p. 88.
73	15	LEO-2, vol. 8, p. 181.
	21	WOLF-1, p. 186.
	23	WOLF-3, vol. 1, p. 60.
	32	CAT-6, p. 13.
74	13	WOLF-3, vol. 2, p. 62.
75	5	Ibid., p. 64.
	10	CAT-6, p. 21.
	16	Ibid., p. 42.
	23	WOLF-3, vol. 2, p. 396.
	38	CAT-6, p. 253.
76	8	WOLF-3, vol. 2, p. 518.
	13	Ibid., p. 521.
	19	Ibid., pp. 334–37.
	26	WOLF-1, p. 12.
77	3	HER, p. 169.
	23	WOLF-4, p. 323.
	35	Ibid.
	37	Ibid., p. 325.
	42	Ibid., p. 323.
78	4	Ibid., p. 325.
	8	Ibid., p. 279.
	13	Ibid., p. 323.
	16	Ibid.
	28	WOLF-1, p. 79.
	40	Ibid., p. 80.
79	6	LES-3, p. 249.
	12	Ibid., p. 77.
	22	Ibid.
	29	Ibid., p. 66.
	40	Ibid., p. 83.
80	1	Ibid., p. 85.
	7	Ibid., p. 94.
	14	Ibid., pp. 95–96.
	24	Ibid., pp. 86–87.
81	10	Ibid., p. 118.
	20	Ibid., p. 156.
	24	Ibid., p. 143.
	27	Ibid., p. 135.
	39	Ibid., p. 137.
82	10	Ibid., p. 341.
	19	Ibid., p. 147.
	22	Ibid.
	28	Ibid., p. 257.

Page	*Line*	*Source*
	30	LES-3, p. 257.
	36	Ibid., p. 259.
83	4	Ibid., p. 306.
	6	Ibid., p. 161.
	16	LES-1, p. 17.
	22	LES-3, p. 275.
	40	SEG, p. 55.
84	10	Ibid., p. 17.
	22	LES-1, p. 15.
	26	Ibid., p. 17.
	31	Ibid., p. 16.
	38	Ibid., p. 11.
85	8	Ibid., p. 26.
	16	Ibid., p. 38.
	26	LES-3, p. 321.
	41	Ibid., p. 326.
86	15	HIE, p. 29.
	25	LES-4, p. 19.
	28	Ibid., p. 22.
	29	Ibid., p. 23.
	40	HIE, pp. 31–32.
87	2	LES-3, p. 251.
	9	LES-2, p. 31.
	17	MUEN, October 31, 1958.
	30	MANC, September 1, 1933.
	39	DEU, November, 1956.
	40	MANC, September 15, 1933.
88	10	LES-3, p. 30.
	29	KAR, pp. 57–58.
89	12	STERN-2, vol. 6, p. 16.
	23	Ibid., p. 495.
	29	Ibid.
	35	Ibid., p. 478.
	42	Ibid.
90	4	Ibid., p. 479.
	12	Ibid., p. 482.
	22	Ibid., p. 423.
	35	Ibid., pp. 499–500.
91	12	Ibid., p. 500.
	26	Ibid., p. 554.
	37	KAR, p. 29.
92	2	STERN-2, vol. 6, p. 567.
	10	Ibid., p. 570.

Page	*Line*	*Source*
	14	KAR, p. 16.
	24	STERN-1, p. 124.
	27	Ibid., p. 20.
	43	STERN-2, vol. 6, p. 580.
93	8	Ibid., p. 559.
	16	Ibid., p. 556.
	22	HAA-3, p. 148.
	27	MANN-KL-2, p. 88.
	40	ZUC, p. 332.
94	1	BLE, p. 168.
	4	STERN-2, vol. 6, p. 523.
	20	Ibid., p. 64.
	28	CAT-4, p. 194.
	33	KAF-6, p. 661.
95	7	STERN-3, p. 24.
	14	MANN-KL-2, p. 90.
	26	KAR, pp. 9–10.
	39	MANN-KL-2, p. 90.

IV. AN ANGEL AT THE GATE

Page	*Line*	*Source*
96	1	LAS-1, p. 604.
	2	Ibid., p. 605.
	4	SCHUE, p. 77.
	9	DIEF, no. 454–56, p. 37.
	12	BENN-2, vol. 1, p. 534.
	14	COH, p. 35.
97	3	MUE-2, p. 26.
	3	Ibid., p. 58.
	5	TOL-2, p. 187.
	12	WALL, p. 62.
	16	KAF-2, p. 296.
	19	Ibid.
	21	Ibid.
	36	LAS-6, p. 13.
	38	LAS-5, p. 15.
	40	Ibid., p. 52.
	41	Ibid., p. 171.
98	4	Ibid., p. 51.
	11	LAS-1, p. 295.
	19	WEIC.
	24	BENN-2, vol. 1., p. 538.
	31	Ibid.
	37	KES, p. 114.

Page	Line	Source
98	40	KES, p. 114.
	43	BENN-2, vol. 1, p. 534.
99	3	LAS-1, p. 564.
	7	Ibid., p. 264.
	14	Ibid., p. 318.
	19	HAS, p. 41.
	23	LAS-1, p. 31.
	26	Ibid.
	31	Ibid., p. 302.
	34	LAS-6, p. 173.
	38	LAS-1, p. 151.
100	10	Ibid., p. 574.
	26	LAS-6, p. 119.
	31	LAS-3, p. 12.
	38	LAS-1, p. 237.
	41	Ibid., p. 251.
101	5	Ibid., p. 234.
	11	LAS-5, p. 74.
	22	LAS-1, p. 575.
	26	Ibid., p. 232.
	43	Ibid., p. 250.
102	10	Ibid., p. 254.
	24	Ibid.
	29	Ibid.
	31	Ibid., p. 255.
	38	MUS-2, p. 145.
	42	LAS-1, p. 67.
103	5	LAS-4, vol. 2, p. 758.
	6	Ibid., vol. 1, p. 333.
	11	COH, p. 22.
	12	Ibid.
	19	LAS-4, vol. 3, p. 10.
	24	LAS-3, p. 104.
	25	LAS-1, p. 283.
	29	BIT, p. 356.
	37	LAS-1, p. 330.
	39	FREU-2, vol. 1, p. 83.
104	1	LAS-1, p. 66.
	7	Ibid., p. 64.
	9	Ibid.
	17	LAS-4, vol. 3, p. 75.
	30	MUE-2, p. 38.
	30	Ibid., p. 31.
105	1	Ibid., p. 55.
	6	Ibid., p. 54.
	17	DIEF, no. 313–14, p. 31.
	21	Ibid.

Page	Line	Source
	24	LAS-4, vol. 1, p. 164.
	35	DIEF, no. 313–14, p. 36.
106	19	WEIC.
	25	LAS-5, pp. 67–68.
	31	LAS-6, p. 81.
	38	LAS-1, p. 515.
107	14	DOE-2, p. 465.
	21	DUR, pp. 107–8.
	34	LAS-1, p. 515.
	38	LAS-5, pp. 22–23.
	42	Ibid., p. 44.
108	9	LAS-4, vol. 2, p. 402.
	13	LAS-6, p. 71.
	30	LAS-4, vol. 1, p. 189.
109	16	Ibid., p. 270.
	25	LAS-1, p. 213.
	38	Ibid., p. 78.
110	5	LAS-5, p. 113.
	11	Ibid.
	24	Ibid., p. 117.
	30	LAS-6, p. 281.
	39	LAS-5, p. 172.
	43	Ibid., p. 149.
111	3	Ibid., p. 182.
	18	Ibid., p. 180.
	32	LAS-1, p. 224.
112	13	LAS-6, p. 89.
	18	LAS-5, p. 115.
	24	Ibid., p. 188.
	31	LAS-1, p. 140.
113	5	LAS-5, p. 221.
	7	Ibid.
	10	FIS, p. 136.
	16	LAS-5, p. 216.
	39	LAS-2, p. 92.
114	1	Ibid., p. 71.
	8	Ibid., p. 86.
	25	LAS-6, p. 130.
115	2	LAS-5, p. 275.
	6	Ibid., p. 253.
	13	Ibid., p. 230.
	14	Ibid., p. 256.
	23	Ibid.
	35	Ibid., p. 37.
	38	LAS-6, p. 46.
116	5	MUE-3, p. 76.
	35	LAS-4, vol. 3, p. 83.
	41	MUE-5, p. 44.

Page	*Line*	*Source*	*Page*	*Line*	*Source*
117	8	BLA, p. 291.		27	MUE-5, p. 14.
	10	Ibid., p. 630.		37	ROC, p. 7.
	13	Ibid., p. 211.	127	3	Ibid., p. 8.
	15	MUS-2, p. 119.		9	Ibid.
	17	BLA, p. 712.		22	MUE-5, p. 42.
	20	FIS, p. 174.		26	Ibid., p. 9.
	22	MUE-1, p. 474.		31	Ibid., p. 13.
	31	Ibid., p. 472.		34	Ibid., p. 41.
	35	BLA, p. 149.	128	10	Ibid., p. 56.
	41	MUE-2, p. 148.		24	Ibid., p. 57.
118	11	Ibid., p. 472.		33	BUB, p. 143.
	17	DIEF, no. 202, p. 9.	129	13	TOL-2, p. 232.
	25	Ibid.		17	MUE-1, p. 476.
	28	Ibid.		25	EHR, p. 195.
	37	Ibid., no. 206, p. 15.		27	Ibid., p. 196.
	40	Ibid.		35	Ibid.
119	3	MUE-5, p. 52.		40	LAS-4, vol. 3, p. 84.
	7	Ibid., p. 69.	130	7	TOL-1, p. 5.
	13	MUE-4, p. 74.		13	Ibid., p. 1.
	30	MUE-5, p. 68.		29	Ibid., p. 3.
	39	Ibid.		35	Ibid., p. 13.
120	13	Ibid., p. 71.		37	Ibid.
	25	MUE-4, p. 88.		39	Ibid., p. 14.
121	7	MUE-2, p. 136.	131	1	Ibid., pp. 281–82.
	12	Ibid., p. 137.		30	Ibid., p. 26.
	17	MUE-5, p. 71.		40	Ibid., p. 38.
	23	SIM, vol. 10, no. 45.	132	11	Ibid., pp. 77–78.
122	2	MUE-2, p. 12.		27	Ibid., p. 78.
	9	MUE-5, p. 71.		31	Ibid., pp. 78–79.
	10	Ibid., p. 34.	133	9	Ibid., p. 82.
	21	NIE, p. 38.		15	LEO-2, vol. 15, p. 218.
	23	MUE-1, pp. 446–47.			
	29	Ibid., p. 449.		23	Ibid., p. 216.
123	11	EIS, p. 201.		42	TOL-1, pp. 168–69.
	20	KAF-1, p. 274.	134	11	Ibid., p. 179.
	24	Ibid., p. 275.		32	TOL-2, p. 52.
	33	HAF, p. 170.	135	3	TOL-1, p. 212.
	39	NET, vol. 2, p. 730.		22	Ibid., p. 284.
	41	Ibid.		23	TOL-2, p. 278.
124	14	TOL-1, p. 264.		27	TOL-1, p. 287.
	28	MUE-5, p. 6.		30	Ibid., p. 288.
125	8	MUE-1, p. 6.		36	EHR, p. 198.
	15	MUE-5, p. 53.	136	10	TOL-3, p. 193.
	22	Ibid., p. 26.		17	LAS-4, vol. 3, p. 82.
	28	Ibid., p. 23.		21	Ibid.
	33	MUE-3, p. 76.		22	Ibid.
	38	SEY, p. 36.		25	Ibid., p. 84.
126	1	MUE-3, p. 189.		29	TOL-3, p. 5.
	12	MANN-E, pp. 18–19.		40	Ibid., pp. 271–72.

Page	Line	Source
137	10	KEST-3, p. 158.
	14	MANN-KL-1, p. 278.
	22	KES, p. 277.
	30	TOL-3, p. x.
	35	Ibid.
138	6	WIE, vol. 18, April 1964, p. 25.
	14	EHR, p. 199.
	29	LOE, p. 216.
	33	SPEN, p. 258.
	36	Ibid.
139	3	MANN-KL-1, p. 352.
	6	KEST-1, p. 96.
	12	MAR, p. 253.
	26	WIE, vol. 18, April 1964, p. 25.
	30	LAS-4, vol. 3, p. 84.
	32	Ibid.
140	5	HAES, p. 227.
	13	LUD, p. 82.
	22	LAS-6, p. 187.
	27	LAS-1, p. 510.
	30	BUL, no. 7, p. 164 (1959).
	41	Ibid., pp. 164–65.
141	9	LAS-6, p. 187.
	18	LAS-4, vol. 3, pp. 45–46.
	39	HAES, p. 282.
	43	BAU, p. 141.
142	1	LAS-5, p. 14.
	18	HAES, p. 225.
	21	LAS-1, p. 216.
	26	LAS-5, p. 281.
	33	Ibid., p. 279.
	35	HAES, p. 338 and passim.
	40	ELL, p. 750.
143	5	LAS-3, p. 75.
	23	LEO-3.
	30	LAS-5, p. 317.
	34	Ibid., p. 276.
	37	LAS-1, p. 184.
	43	LAS-4, vol. 3, p. 104.
144	3	Ibid.
	6	LAS-6, p. 191.
	10	LAS-4, vol. 3, pp. 163–64.
	22	LAS-6, p. 212.

Page	Line	Source
	23	Ibid., p. 162.
	24	Ibid., p. 212.
	25	LAS-4, vol. 3, p. 154.
	27	Ibid., p. 162.
	35	LAS-6, p. 199.
	37	LAS-1, p. 153.
	43	Ibid., p. 162.
145	4	LAS-6, p. 170.
	22	LAS-4, vol. 3, p. 165.
	25	LAS-1, p. 181.
	29	Ibid., p. 180.
	33	Ibid., p. 103.
	36	LAS-3, p. 13.

V.   LES INDÉSIRABLES

Page	Line	Source
146	20	FRAN, p. 177.
147	6	SCHO-1, p. 122.
	13	MUSIK, p. 311.
	15	WUL, p. 469.
	17	Ibid., pp. 43–44.
	40	CLA, p. 557.
148	10	EIN-2, p. 101.
	13	Ibid., p. 102.
	30	FRAN, p. 290.
	40	EIN-3, p. 114.
149	1	CLA, p. 569.
	7	CEC, p. 226.
	14	CLA, pp. 605–6.
	30	FRAN, p. 199.
	32	EIN-2, p. 133.
150	4	MUSIK, p. 327.
	10	Ibid., p. 320.
	19	GEO, p. 154.
	24	MUSIK, p. 321.
	32	SLO, p. 162.
	33	Ibid., p. 148.
	34	Ibid., p. 158.
	36	MUSIK, p. 324.
	40	SPE, pp. 29–30.
151	3	MUSIK, p. 324.
	7	SLO, p. 163.
	11	CLA, p. 326.
	17	KES, p. 157.
	25	STU, p. 140.
152	5	THU, p. 138.
	12	MANNH, p. 278.
	27	THU, p. 161.
	36	WAS, p. 118.

Page	Line	Source
153	4	FREU-2, vol. 5, p. 173.
	11	KARD, p. 121.
	17	Ibid.
	26	MOS-1, p. 223.
	33	FRAN, p. 27.
154	9	LEO-2, vol. 10, p. 274.
	23	HOF, p. 59.
	33	MOS-1, p. viii.
	38	WIC, p. 31.
155	3	Ibid., p. 17.
	5	Ibid., pp. 31–32.
	7	Ibid., p. 32.
	12	Ibid., p. 14.
	21	RUF, p. 133.
	28	MUSIK, p. 319.
	43	SCHOLS, p. 453.
156	26	SCHO-1, p. 20.
	28	RUF, p. 185.
	41	ZIL, p. 80.
157	1	STU, p. 71.
	12	SCHO-1, p. 31.
	18	WEB-1, p. 47.
	23	STU, p. 45.
	28	Ibid., p. 82.
	35	MUSI, vol. 38, no. 4, p. 527.
	38	SCHO-3, p. 447.
158	2	PEY, p. 7.
	16	THE, p. 5.
	22	(left) RUF, passim.
	22	(left) WIC, passim.
	22	(right) EIN-1, passim.
	35	FRAN, p. 210.
	39	WIC, p. 25.
	41	MOS-2, p. 179.
159	15	SCHO-1, p. 154.
	26	STU, p. 140.
	31	BER, p. 16.
	34	WEB-2, p. 24.
	40	CAG, p. 93.
160	7	MOS-1, p. 68.
	20	WIC, pp. 60–61.
	31	BROD-2, p. 314.
	38	WIC, p. 65.
161	3	FRAN, p. 141.
	14	KES, p. 233.

Page	Line	Source
	29	FRAN, p. 154.
	31	EIN-1, p. 171.
162	5	ROL, p. 36.
	18	EIN-3, p. 35.
	23	FRAN, p. 196.
	31	TUC-2, vol. 10, p. 63.
	36	WIC, pp. 85–86.
175	4	SCHO-1, p. 91.
	12	Ibid., p. 90.
	26	SCHO-2, pp. 89–93.
176	27	Ibid., p. 112.
	30	SCHO-1, p. 136.
177	3	SCHO-5, no. 6.
	12	Ibid., no. 2.
	28	SCHO-1, p. 154.
	34	SCHO-4, act 2, scene 4.
	39	Ibid.
	42	SCHO-1, p. 70.
178	10	CAT-2, p. 335.
	14	SCHO-2, p. 196.
	18	SCHO-1, p. 214.
	23	CAT-2, p. 60.
	26	SCH, p. 131.
	36	MIL, p. 245.
179	1	ARM, p. 98.
	7	KLE, p. 47.
	26	SCHO-1, p. 219.
	37	Ibid., pp. 219–20.
180	6	VIE, p. 207.
	20	Ibid., p. 208.
	27	Ibid.
	36	MOD, p. 250.
181	13	MANNH, p. cxxv.
	21	MANN-E, p. 250.
	35	EIN-3, p. 128.
	43	Ibid., p. 182.
182	9	CLA, p. 38.
	26	Ibid., p. 672.
	42	HOF, p. 210.
183	6	EIN-3, p. 144.
	11	Ibid., p. 158.
	15	Ibid., p. 149.
	25	EIN-1, p. 150.
	32	Ibid., p. 188.
	39	Ibid., p. 177.
184	1	Ibid., p. 199.
	7	CLA, p. 750.
	13	EIN-1, p. 171.

Page	Line	Source
184	25	RUF, p. 73.
	35	SCHO-1, p. 194.
	39	STU, p. 131.
185	3	CAT-2, p. 357.
	5	ZIL, p. 106.
	10	Ibid.

VI.   TRIALS AND TRIBULATIONS

Page	Line	Source
186	12	BROD-2, p. 109.
	16	KAF-9, p. 58.
	20	Ibid.
187	8	Ibid.
	16	TUC-2, vol. 4, pp. 52–53.
	23	KAF-9, p. 15.
	34	KAF-11, p. 54.
188	2	TUC-2, vol. 7, p. 199.
	4	Ibid., p. 200.
	18	KAF-11, p. 168.
	25	TUC-2, vol. 7, p. 275.
	31	Ibid.
189	1	BROD-1, p. 75.
	4	CAN-2, p. 83.
	8	KAF-11, p. 251.
	10	BEN-4, p. 129.
	14	KAF-9, p. 428.
	15	KAF-6, p. 257.
	17	KAF-9, p. 14.
	19	KAF-6, p. 294.
	22	Ibid.
	26	BEN-4, p. 129.
	28	Ibid., pp. 129–30.
190	4	KAF-3, p. 191.
	13	WEINS, p. 12.
	14	SCHUM, vol. 1, p. 188.
	15	KAF-9, p. 18.
	19	Ibid.
	22	KAF-5, p. 132.
	25	DOE-1, p. 286.
	29	TUC-2, vol. 4, p. 374.
	41	KIE, p. 19.
191	7	KAF-9, p. 230.
	10	KAF-5, p. 348.
	12	KAF-9, p. 406.
	16	KAF-6, p. 517.
	18	KAF-7, p. 50.
	24	Ibid., p. 51.

Page	Line	Source
	34	STO, p. 23.
	41	TRA, p. 139.
192	6	STO, p. 97.
	10	Ibid., p. 81.
	11	KAF-6, p. 517.
	15	KAF-1, p. 337.
	21	Ibid.
	25	Ibid., p. 338.
	31	Ibid.
	36	KAF-10, p. 173.
	40	CAN-2, p. 82.
193	2	KAF-10, p. 175.
	5	Ibid., p. 173.
	14	Ibid., p. 183.
	19	Ibid.
	22	Ibid.
	27	KAF-8, p. 17.
	34	KAF-9, p. 476.
194	2	KAF-3, p. 184.
	9	Ibid.
	10	KAF-1, p. 404.
	12	KAF-9, p. 302.
	15	KAF-6, p. 502.
	16	Ibid.
	23	KAF-9, p. 154.
	24	Ibid.
	36	BROD-1, p. 16.
	38	Ibid., p. 19.
195	3	Ibid.
	4	HAA-1, p. 30.
	7	WAG, p. 13.
	13	KAF-6, p. 55.
	20	Ibid., p. 525.
	26	KAF-9, p. 88.
	37	KAF-3, p. 168.
196	1	KAF-9, p. 64.
	5	Ibid.
	8	Ibid., p. 65.
	8	Ibid., pp. 65–66.
	18	Ibid., p. 129.
	25	Ibid., pp. 103–4.
	41	Ibid., p. 399.
197	4	Ibid., p. 292.
	10	Ibid.
	13	HEL, p. 206.
	18	HAA-1, p. 34.
	22	HAA-2, p. 67.
	25	KAF-9, p. 481.
	27	Ibid., p. 393.

Page	Line	Source
	28	Ibid., p. 392.
	29	Ibid., p. 393.
	30	Ibid.
	34	BEN-5, p. 266.
	40	BLA, p. 617.
198	3	BROD-1, p. 82.
	6	Ibid.
	12	KAF-9, p. 230.
	16	BROD-1, p. 84.
	23	Ibid.
	30	KAF-10, p. 196.
	36	Ibid., p. 197.
	38	Ibid.
199	2	TUC-2, vol. 2, p. 344.
	5	Ibid., p. 344.
	9	Ibid., p. 345.
	11	Ibid., pp. 345−46.
	35	BROD-1, p. 162.
	39	WOL, p. 46.
	41	KAF-3, p. 37.
200	1	Ibid.
	5	KAF-9, p. 404.
	8	KAF-3, p. 183.
	10	KAF-9, p. 393.
	14	Ibid., p. 230.
	16	Ibid., p. 405.
	23	KAF-3, p. 188.
	25	Ibid., p. 11.
	28	KAF-9, p. 394.
	37	EHRE, p. 81.
	42	Ibid.
201	2	Ibid., p. 82.
	5	Ibid., p. 81.
	10	WAG, p. 126.
	12	Ibid.
	18	KAF-9, p. 395.
	20	KAF-6, p. 390.
	21	Ibid., p. 381.
	22	Ibid., p. 389.
	24	KAF-1, p. 14.
	29	Ibid., p. 439.
	30	Ibid., p. 447.
	34	Ibid., p. 451.
	40	Ibid., p. 448.
	42	Ibid., p. 453.
202	6	KAF-4, p. 144.
	8	KAF-1, p. 464.
	11	Ibid., p. 468.
	14	Ibid., p. 455.

Page	Line	Source
	18	BROD-1, p. 208.
	20	Ibid.
	35	Ibid., p. 212.
	39	TUC-2, vol. 4, p. 186.
	40	Ibid., vol. 3, p. 92.
	40	Ibid, vol. 4, p. 374.
203	2	Ibid., p. 186.
	18	Ibid., vol. 5, p. 434.
	19	Ibid.
	24	Ibid.
	25	Ibid.
	30	Ibid.
	34	Ibid., vol. 2, p. 151.
204	8	POO, p. 33.
	11	TUC-2, vol. 2, p. 144.
	20	Ibid., p. 228.
	25	Ibid., p. 112.
	27	TUC-1, p. 395.
	30	TUC-2, vol. 2, p. 374.
	33	Ibid.
205	1	Ibid., p. 375.
	4	Ibid., vol. 3, p. 241.
	7	Ibid.
	13	Ibid., vol. 2, p. 107.
	22	MEH-1, p. 68.
	30	Ibid., p. 51.
	36	BUB, p. 94.
206	4	KES, p. 64.
	7	TUC-2, vol. 2, p. 383.
	12	Ibid., p. 26.
	16	Ibid., p. 432.
	23	CAT-5, p. 9.
	33	TUC-2, vol. 7, pp. 54−55.
207	8	Ibid., vol. 2, p. 447.
	11	Ibid.
	26	Ibid., p. 449.
	28	Ibid.
	38	MEH-2, p. 13.
208	9	TUC-2, vol. 7, p. 101.
	11	Ibid.
	24	Ibid., vol. 8, p. 84.
	31	Ibid., p. 85.
	34	Ibid., p. 86.
	37	Ibid.
209	11	BRE-1, p. 32.
	15	TUC-2, vol. 7, p. 69.
	17	Ibid., vol. 6, p. 60.
	23	Ibid., vol. 8, p. 105.

Page	Line	Source		Page	Line	Source
209	26	TUC-2, vol. 8, p. 105.			31	SCHU, p. 165.
	31	MANN-T-2, p. 389.			34	POO, p. 202.
	36	TUC-2, vol. 8, p. 106.		219	17	TUC-1, p. 339.
210	2	Ibid., vol. 3, p. 28.			23	CAT-7, p. 24.
	8	Ibid., vol. 8, p. 346.			30	KAF-9, p. 58.
	18	Ibid., vol. 5, p. 228.			36	SCHU, p. 169.
	30	Ibid., vol. 3, p. 296.			40	TUC-1, p. 251.
	42	Ibid., p. 302.				
211	20	YOU, p. 254.		**VII.**	**ULTIMA MULTIS**	
	28	TUC-2, vol. 3, p. 304.				
	33	Ibid., p. 224.		220	15	SCHW, p. 274.
212	12	Ibid., vol. 5, p. 206.			18	Ibid.
	14	Ibid., p. 205.		221	1	MEH-3, p. 220.
	18	Ibid., vol. 6, p. 144.			15	SAH, p. 188.
	31	Ibid., p. 182.		222	2	WALT-H, p. 225.
213	3	Ibid., vol. 7, p. 255.			13	SCHW, pp. 173–74.
	15	Ibid., vol. 3, p. 281.			25	WALT-H, p. 364.
	22	HEIN, p. 164–65.			28	JAY, p. 38.
	41	TUC-1, p. 333.			38	KOE-1, pp. 247–48.
214	3	TUC-3, p. 50.		223	25	SPER, pp. 196–97.
	20	TUC-2, vol. 4, p. 91.			33	Ibid., p. 197.
	23	Ibid., p. 431.			39	BEN-3, p. 669.
	27	Ibid., p. 234.		224	2	Ibid., p. 600.
	38	POO, p. 219.			8	Ibid., p. 599.
	41	Ibid.			15	CAT-3, p. 161.
215	2	Ibid.			19	Ibid.
	7	HIL-2, p. 106.			24	Ibid., p. 162.
	16	TUC-2, vol. 10, p. 116.			30	BERM, p. 114.
	21	Ibid., p. 115.			35	Ibid.
	29	Ibid., vol. 6, p. 84.			40	Ibid., p. 115.
	34	RAT, p. 92.			43	Ibid.
	43	Ibid., p. 89.		225	1	Ibid.
216	8	TUC-2, vol. 3, pp. 396–97.			6	MANN-KA, p. 95.
	13	Ibid., p. 397.			10	Ibid.
	16	Ibid.			19	MANN-T-3, p. 248.
	22	Ibid., p. 413.			20	Ibid., pp. 245–46.
	24	Ibid.			25	Ibid., p. 247.
217	4	Ibid., vol. 4, p. 67.			33	Ibid.
	22	POO, p. 23.			41	HES, p. 64.
	28	TUC-2, vol. 8, p. 127.		226	11	CAT-3, p. 166.
	38	Ibid., vol. 7, p. 312.			18	Ibid.
	40	Ibid., p. 314.			31	ZWEI, p. 314.
218	7	RAD, p. 129.			38	NAT, pp. 131–70, passim.
	10	CAT-7, p. 13.		227	8	Ibid., p. 170.
	15	RAD, p. 121.			20	ZWEI, p. 314.
	17	POO, p. 203.			25	Ibid., p. 315.
	29	TUC-1, p. 250.			32	CAT-3, p. 169.
				228	8	MOL, p. 196.

Page	Line	Source
	19	CAT-7, p. 32.
	22	SCHW, p. 303.
	30	Ibid., p. 176.
229	7	BEN-5, back cover.
	9	BEN-3, p. 505.
	23	BEN-1, p. 158.
	28	BLA, p. 431.
	36	BEN-1, p. 167.
230	7	Ibid., p. 155.
	8	BEN-3, p. 685.
	24	BEN-5, p. 67.
	35	Ibid., p. 66.
231	3	Ibid., p. 61.
	4	Ibid., p. 60.
	12	Ibid., pp. 66–67.
	37	BEN-4, vol. 4, p. 257.
232	3	Ibid., p. 287.
	9	Ibid., p. 286.
	32	BEN-2, p. 97.
	38	BEN-5, p. 29.
233	5	SCHOL, p. 10.
	12	Ibid., p. 16.
	21	Ibid.
	28	ADO, p. 28.
	33	SCHOL, p. 70.
	37	Ibid., p. 17.
	43	Ibid., p. 18.
234	18	Ibid., p. 72.
	21	Ibid., p. 122.
	26	Ibid., p. 223.
	31	Ibid., p. 235.
	36	BEN-3, p. 292.
235	2	Ibid., p. 293.
	11	Ibid., p. 366.
	14	Ibid.
	17	Ibid.
	22	ADO, p. 25.
	30	BEN-3, p. 524.
236	1	SCHOL, p. 188.
	14	BEN-4, vol. 4, p. 806.
	20	Ibid., p. 807.
	23	ADO, p. 36.
	25	BEN-5, p. 3.
	26	ADO, p. 36.
	31	BEN-3, p. 319.
	33	Ibid.
	40	Ibid., p. 124.
237	1	Ibid., p. 134.
	15	SCHOL, p. 176.

Page	Line	Source
	21	BEN-4, vol. 4, p. 121.
	23	Ibid., p. 137.
	25	Ibid., pp. 138–39.
	27	Ibid., p. 125.
	28	Ibid., p. 138.
	32	Ibid., p. 112.
	36	Ibid., p. 133.
	41	Ibid., p. 105.
238	7	BEN-3, p. 311.
	11	Ibid., p. 309.
	12	Ibid.
	20	Ibid., p. 151.
	23	ADO, p. 154.
	27	Ibid.
	29	Ibid.
	33	BEN-3, p. 461.
	35	Ibid., p. 173.
	41	SCHOL, p. 194.
239	6	BEN-3, p. 523.
	10	Ibid.
	13	LAC, p. 45.
	23	BEN-6, p. 81.
	24	BEN-3, p. 425.
	26	Ibid.
	30	Ibid., p. 426.
	32	Ibid.
	34	Ibid.
	39	Ibid., p. 444.
240	5	Ibid., p. 439.
	14	Ibid., p. 421.
	21	Ibid., p. 455.
	25	Ibid., p. 472.
	31	Ibid., p. 456.
	39	Ibid., p. 563.
241	6	BEN-4, vol. 4, p. 442.
	11	BEN-3, p. 567.
	14	Ibid.
	28	Ibid., p. 548.
	39	Ibid., p. 409.
242	8	BEN-5, p. 91.
	10	Ibid., p. 84.
	12	Ibid., p. 94.
	15	Ibid., p. 93.
	18	Ibid., pp. 93–94.
243	3	Ibid., p. 100.
	13	Ibid.
	30	ADO, p. 38.
	34	Ibid., p. 39.
244	1	Ibid., p. 42.

Page	Line	Source		Page	Line	Source
244	4	ADO, p. 42.			36	SZA-1, p. 168.
	10	BEN-3, p. 595.		252	4	KOE-2, p. 107.
	13	Ibid., p. 626.			6	Ibid., p. 94.
	25	JAY, p. 114.			15	MEI, p. 110.
	40	ADO, p. 14.			23	HAES, p. 74.
	41	Ibid.			35	SCHW, p. 107.
	42	Ibid.			42	SZA-1, p. 242.
245	9	BEN-3, p. 679.		253	10	HEN, p. 20.
	12	Ibid., p. 683.			10	DER, p. 471.
	14	Ibid., p. 785.			14	SEY, p. 168.
	17	Ibid., p. 792.			16	Ibid.
	22	Ibid., p. 659.			31	KRE, pp. 18–19.
	25	Ibid., p. 839.		254	29	Ibid., p. 332.
	29	Ibid., p. 711.			32	Ibid., pp. 332–33.
	33	Ibid., p. 712.		255	4	Ibid., p. 335.
	37	Ibid., p. 767.			7	Ibid.
246	1	Ibid., p. 777.			14	Ibid.
	4	Ibid., p. 753.			21	Ibid., p. 332.
	19	Ibid., p. 827.		256	4	ODI, p. 100.
	26	UNS, p. 77.			8	Ibid., p. 110.
	34	Ibid., p. 80.			11	Ibid., pp. 111–12.
	38	Ibid., p. 78.			33	SZA-1, p. 121.
247	6	BEN-5, pp. 259–60.			40	Ibid.
	25	BEN-3, p. 829.		257	1	Ibid.
	31	FRY, p. x.			9	PAX, p. 183.
	33	BEN-3, p. 861.			24	BEN-3, p. 504.
	35	SZA-1, p. 92.			28	BEN-4, vol. 4, pp. 803–4.
	44	FEI, p. 149.				
248	5	BEN-3, p. 861.		258	6	KOL-2, p. 217.
	6	Ibid., p. 862.			10	WIEC.
	11	Ibid., p. 860.			14	Ibid.
	22	KOE-1, pp. 420–21.			18	KOL-2, p. 339.
	32	SCHOL, pp. 279–80.			27	KOL-1, p. 207.
249	11	BEN-5, p. 94.		259	3	KOL-2, p. 320.
	17	AUF, October 11, 1940.			20	Ibid., pp. 340–41.
	22	BEN-1, p. 75.			27	KOL-1, p. 217.
	26	BEN-5, p. 18.			28	Ibid.
	28	Ibid.			31	KOL-2, p. 339.
250	29	SZA-1, p. 24.			43	BAC, p. 77.
	34	Ibid., p. 21.			44	SAC, p. 43.
	40	SZA-2, p. 97.		260	8	KOL-1, p. 186.
251	3	SZA-1, p. 248.			12	Ibid., p. 114.
	3	MEH-2, p. 60.			25	KOL-2, p. 285.
	6	Ibid.			35	Ibid., p. 69.
	8	Ibid.		261	2	KOL-1, p. 160.
	20	FEU, p. 32.			21	KOL-2, p. 103.
	26	Ibid., p. 40.			24	Ibid., p. 65.
	32	Ibid., p. 23.			31	KOL-1, p. 207.
					43	KOL-2, p. 64.

Page	Line	Source	Page	Line	Source
262	4	Ibid., pp. 64–65.		24	Ibid., p. 136.
263	13	KOL-1, p. 224.		28	DOE-1, p. 362.
				30	Ibid., p. 18.
				30	Ibid., p. 9.
VIII.		**A SENSE OF ASH WEDNES-**		34	DOE-5, p. 58.
		DAY		36	MIN-1, p. 179.
				41	DOE-16, p. 75.
264	2	MANN-T-6, p. 167.	271	11	DOE-1, p. 387.
	8	MUS-2, p. 203.		13	GRA, p. 17.
	9	HUG, p. 203.		21	DOE-1, p. 338.
	10	Ibid., p. 205.		21	Ibid., p. 340.
	11	Ibid., p. 204.		39	Ibid., p. 66.
	12	BRE-2, p. 66.	272	10	DOE-16, p. 70.
	16	GRA, p. 8.		11	Ibid., pp. 70–71.
	17	Ibid.		16	Ibid., p. 83.
265	17	DOE-10, p. 57.		21	MAR, p. 277.
	21	DOE-15, p. 449.		30	DOE-1, p. 365.
	24	DOE-10, p. 225.		36	TUC-2, vol. 3, p. 127.
	36	DOE-14, p. 355.		42	Ibid., p. 128.
	40	DOE-10, p. 136.	273	3	DOE-7, p. 141.
266	2	Ibid.		8	Ibid., p. 199.
	5	Ibid., p. 138.		9	DOE-16, p. 172.
	9	Ibid., p. 140.		13	Ibid., p. 252.
	13	Ibid., p. 141.		19	MUEL, p. 253.
	20	KREU, p. 19.		28	BEN-6, p. 93.
	28	DOE-15, p. 159.		38	DOE-11, p. 96.
	30	DOE-1, p. 340.	274	7	DOE-1, pp. 349–50.
	32	Ibid., p. 368.		21	DOE-6, p. 123.
	36	DOE-15, pp. 157–58.		24	MIN-1, p. 189.
267	18	DOE-1, p. 357.		28	Ibid., p. 190.
	22	Ibid., p. 385.		30	Ibid., p. 189.
	25	LAS-5, p. 14.		32	Ibid., p. 190.
	26	DOE-1, p. 385.		34	Ibid., p. 189.
268	1	Ibid., p. 9.		37	Ibid.
	7	Ibid., p. 10.		41	DOE-4, p. 90.
	11	CAT-1, p. 109.	275	2	DOE-13, p. 469.
	17	DOE-1, p. 17.		7	DOE-18, p. 43.
	37	MIN-2, p. 111.		12	DOE-6, p. 19.
269	7	MUS-2, p. 213.		19	DOE-15, p. 164.
	12	Ibid., p. 219.		20	Ibid.
	16	DOE-9, p. 427.		32	DOE-14, p. 73.
	18	Ibid., pp. 427–28.		36	Ibid., p. 91.
	30	Ibid., p. 368.		39	Ibid., p. 92.
	36	LAG, p. 646.		43	Ibid., p. 93.
	39	BRE-2, pp. 65–66.	276	7	Ibid., p. 137.
270	3	MIN-2, p. 99.		9	Ibid., p. 110.
	8	KRO, p. 74.		16	Ibid., p. 140.
	14	DOE-7, p. 181.		20	Ibid., p. 331.
	16	Ibid.		25	Ibid.
	18	DOE-16, p. 148.			

Page	Line	Source
276	37	DOE-1, p. 391.
	43	DOE-5, p. 517, and passim.
277	3	DOE-1, p. 132.
	6	Ibid.
	9	Ibid., p. 123.
	11	Ibid., p. 114.
	14	Ibid., p. 123.
	18	PRA, p. 43.
	23	BEN-4, vol. 3, p. 233.
	34	DOE-1, p. 391.
	42	MUS-1, p. 88.
278	2	Ibid., p. 90.
	14	DOE-5, p. 528.
	36	DOE-6, p. 176.
279	3	DIEW, p. 168.
	5	Ibid., pp. 170–71.
	14	DOE-6, p. 192.
	22	DOE-3, p. 551.
	28	Ibid., p. 627.
	35	Ibid., p. 613.
	36	Ibid., pp. 612–13.
280	14	DOE-6, p. 201.
	15	Ibid., p. 193.
	17	Ibid., p. 219.
	24	Ibid., p. 191.
	28	KEST-3, p. 99.
	34	Ibid.
	40	KEST-2, p. 291.
281	5	SPER, pp. 220–21.
	10	DOE-6, p. 222.
	17	DOE-12, p. 5.
	28	DOE-18, p. 402.
	30	Ibid.
	34	DOE-1, p. 393.
282	12	DOE-16, p. 416.
	32	DOE-15, p. 27.
	40	Ibid., p. 163.
	42	Ibid., p. 27.
283	12	Ibid., p. 24.
	18	Ibid., p. 37.
	28	Ibid., p. 38.
	31	Ibid., p. 49.
	36	Ibid., p. 52.
	43	Ibid., p. 57.
284	6	Ibid., p. 61.
	16	Ibid., p. 72.
	22	Ibid., p. 76.
	26	Ibid., p. 78.

Page	Line	Source
	30	DOE-15, p. 81.
	34	Ibid., p. 90.
285	1	Ibid., p. 119.
	8	Ibid., p. 132.
	17	Ibid., p. 170.
	19	Ibid., p. 171.
	25	Ibid., p. 183.
	32	Ibid., pp. 153–54.
286	5	Ibid., p. 131.
	7	Ibid., p. 182.
	9	Ibid., p. 180.
	14	Ibid., p. 193.
	17	Ibid., p. 220.
	25	Ibid., p. 262.
	32	Ibid., p. 275.
	40	HAE, p. 173.
	42	FREU-4, p. 145.
287	24	SCHW, p. 274.
	27	DOE-15, p. 282.
	36	Ibid., p. 283.
288	6	Ibid., p. 295.
	12	Ibid.
	23	SPA, p. 215.
289	7	FRY, p. 31.
	15	Ibid., p. 215.
	21	Ibid., p. 224.
	28	DOE-15, p. 313.
	32	Ibid., p. 348.
290	7	DOE-6, p. 245.
	12	Ibid., p. 248.
	21	Ibid., p. 585.
	22	Ibid., p. 586.
	26	Ibid., p. 253.
	29	Ibid., p. 254.
	31	Ibid., p. 273.
	42	Ibid., p. 280.
291	2	Ibid., p. 290.
	2	Ibid., p. 288.
	9	Ibid.
	21	DIEZ, June 15, 1962.
	26	Ibid.
	27	MAR, p. 278.
	31	DOE-6, p. 259.
	34	DOE-8, p. 243.
	35	DOE-6, p. 406.
	38	DOE-8, p. 280.
292	11	DOE-15, pp. 389–90.
	20	DIEZ, May 26, 1978.
	26	DOE-15, p. 391.

Page	Line	Source
	30	DOE-6, p. 327.
	41	SZA-1, p. 101.
293	6	DOE-6, p. 335.
	9	Ibid., p. 386.
	11	DOE-15, p. 391.
	14	DOE-6, p. 348.
	19	DOE-15, p. 405.
	27	Ibid., pp. 417–18.
	38	Ibid., p. 442.
	42	Ibid., p. 447.
294	3	Ibid.
	6	Ibid.
	10	DOE-6, p. 351.
	12	Ibid., p. 453.
	16	Ibid., p. 458.
	17	Ibid., p. 485.
	19	Ibid., pp. 431–32.
	21	Ibid., p. 454.
	31	MUEL, pp. 393–94.
	42	DOE-17, p. 8.
295	4	GRA, p. 26.
	20	EIN-3, p. 199.
	24	Ibid., p. 203.
	26	Ibid.
296	2	SCHW, p. 277.
	5	BRO-1, pp. 234–35.
	14	MANN-T-3, p. 481.
	31	BRO-1, p. 282
	38	DOE-6, p. 456.

Page	Line	Source
297	7	MANN-T-1, p. 64.
	25	BRO-4, p. 637.
298	7	BAI, p. 158.
	33	MANNH, p. cxxv.
299	11	FER, p. 3.
	21	GOE-2, vol. 22, p. 523.
	36	SCHOL, p. 252.
300	1	LES-4, p. 23.
	6	SPER, p. 44.
	17	BRO-1, p. 244.
	22	KAF-5, p. 348.
	24	DOE-15, p. 168.
	26	LEO-2, vol. 11, p. xx.
	29	BEN-5, p. 66.
	32	CAT-6, p. 42.
	40	BEN-5, p. 146.
301	5	BRO-1, p. 376.
	35	Ibid., p. 181.
	40	BRO-3, p. 9.
	43	BRO-1, p. 214.
302	7	Ibid., p. 185.
	11	Ibid., p. 217.
	22	Ibid., p. 181.
	26	Ibid., p. 215.
	28	Ibid., p. 214.
	31	Ibid.
	35	BRO-2, p. 486.
	39	Ibid., pp. 481–82.

BIBLIOGRAPHY

(Sources Quoted in the Text)

ADO	Adorno, Theodor W., et al. *Über Walter Benjamin*. Frankfurt, 1968.
ALT	Altenberg, Peter. *Semmering 1912*. Berlin, 1913.
ARM	Armitage, Merle, ed. *George Gershwin*. New York, 1938.
AUD	Auden, W. H. *Collected Poems*. London, 1976.
AUF	*Aufbau* ("Reconstruction"). New York, 1936–45.
BAC	Bachmann, Ingeborg, ed. *Nelly Sachs zu Ehren*. Frankfurt, 1961.
BAI	Bailey, George. *Germans*. New York, 1972.
BAK	Bakan, David. *Sigmund Freud and the Jewish Mystical Tradition*. New York, 1965.
BAR	Barzun, Jacques. *Darwin, Marx, Wagner*. Boston, 1941.
BAU	Bauer-Lechner, Natalie. *Erinnerungen an Gustav Mahler*. Leipzig, 1923.
BEN-1	Benjamin, Walter. *Charles Baudelaire: A Lyric Poet in the Era of High Capitalism*. Translated by Harry Zohn and Quintin Hoare. London, n.d. [c. 1977].
BEN-2	Benjamin, Walter. *Berliner Chronik*. Frankfurt, 1970.
BEN-3	Benjamin, Walter. *Briefe*. Edited by Gershom Scholem and Theodor W. Adorno. Frankfurt, 1966.
BEN-4	Benjamin, Walter. *Gesammelte Schriften*. Frankfurt, 1972.
BEN-5	Benjamin, Walter. *Illuminations*. Translated by Harry Zohn. London, 1973.
BEN-6	Benjamin, Walter. *Understanding Brecht*. Translated by Anna Bostock. London, 1973.
BENN-1	Benn, Gottfried. *Doppelleben*. Wiesbaden, 1950.
BENN-2	Benn, Gottfried. *Gesammelte Werke*. Wiesbaden, 1959.
BER	Berg, Alban. *Bildnis im Wort*. Zurich, 1961.

BERL-1   Berlioz, Hector. *Evenings in the Orchestra.* Translated by Charles E. Roche. New York, 1929.

BERL-2   Berlioz, Hector. *Memoirs.* Translated by Rachel and Eleanor Holmes. New York, 1935.

BERM   Bermann-Fischer, Gottfried. *Bedroht, Bewahrt.* Frankfurt, 1971.

BIT   Bithell, Jethro. *Modern German .Literature, 1880–1938.* London, 1939.

BLA   Blake, William. *Complete Writings.* Edited by Geoffrey Keynes. London, 1969.

BLE   Blei, Franz. *Zeitgenössische Bildnisse.* Amsterdam, 1940.

BOE   Boehlich, Walter. *Der Berliner Antisemitismusstreit,* Frankfurt, 1965.

BRE-1   Brecht, Bertolt, and Weill, Kurt. *The Rise and Fall of the City of Mahagonny* (opera libretto). New York, n.d. [c. 1960].

BRE-2   Brecht, Bertolt. *Tagebücher.* Frankfurt, 1975.

BRO-1   Broch, Hermann. *Briefe.* Zurich, 1957.

BRO-2   Broch, Hermann. *The Death of Virgil.* Translated by Jean Starr Untermeyer. London, 1946.

BRO-3   Broch, Hermann. *James Joyce und die Gegenwart.* Frankfurt, 1971.

BRO-4   Broch, Hermann. *The Sleepwalkers.* Translated by Willa and Edwin Muir. London, 1932.

BROD-1   Brod, Max. *Franz Kafka.* New York, 1947.

BROD-2   Brod, Max. *Streitbares Leben.* Munich, 1960.

BUB   Buber-Neumann, Margarete. *Als Gefangene bei Stalin und Hitler.* Stuttgart, 1968.

BUL   *Bulletin des Leo Baeck Instituts,* Nos. 1–51. Jerusalem, 1958–75.

BUT   Butler, E. M. *Heinrich Heine.* London, 1956.

CAG   Cage, John. *Silence.* Middletown, Conn., 1961.

CAN-1   Canetti, Elias. *Crowds and Power.* London, 1962.

CAN-2   Canetti, Elias. *Kafka's Other Trial.* Translated by Christopher Middleton. London, 1974.

CAR   Carmichael, Joel. *Karl Marx.* London, 1967.

CAS   Cassirer, Toni. *Aus meinem Leben mit Ernst Cassirer.* New York, 1949.

CAT-1   Catalogue, *Alfred Doeblin, 1878–1978.* Schiller Nationalmuseum, Marbach, 1978.

CAT-2   Catalogue, *Arnold Schoenberg Gedenkausstellung.* Edited by Ernst Hilmar. Vienna, 1974.

CAT-3   Catalogue, *Exil-Literatur, 1933–1945.* Deutsche Bibliothek, Frankfurt, 1965.

CAT-4   Catalogue, *Expressionismus.* Schiller Nationalmuseum. Marbach, 1960.

CAT-5   Catalogue, *George Grosz: Frühe Druckgraphik.* Berlin, 1971.

CAT-6   Catalogue, *Karl Wolfskehl, 1869–1969: Leben und Werk in*

Dokumenten. Hessische Landes- und Hochschulbibliothek, Darmstadt, 1969.

CAT-7   Catalogue, *Kurt Tucholsky, 1935–1975.* Deutsche Bibliothek, Frankfurt, 1976.

CAT-8   Catalogue, *Verbannt, Verboten –Verdrängt?* Ausstellung der Stadtbibliothek Worms zum 40. Jahrestag der Bücherverbrennung am 10. Mai, 1933. Worms, 1973.

CEC   Cecil, Robert. *The Myth of the Master Race: Alfred Rosenberg and Nazi Ideology.* London, 1972.

CEL   Celan, Paul. *Mohn und Gedächtnis.* Stuttgart, 1952.

CLA   Clark, Ronald W. *Einstein.* New York, 1971.

COH   Cohn, Hans W. *Else Lasker-Schüler.* Cambridge, 1974.

DER   *Der Morgen,* "Monatsschrift der Juden in Deutschland," vol. 12, no. 10, Berlin, January 1937.

DEU   *Deutsche Rundschau,* November 1976.

DEV   Devrient, Eduard. *My Recollections of Felix Mendelssohn-Bartholdy.* Translated by Natalia MacFarren. London, 1869.

DIEF   *Die Fackel,* vols. 1–922, Vienna, 1898–1936.

DIEW   *Die Wandlung,* vol. 4, no. 2, Heidelberg, 1949.

DIEZ   *Die Zeit,* Hamburg, 1960–78.

DIS   Disraeli, Benjamin. *Tancred.* London, 1847.

DOE-1   Doeblin, Alfred. *Aufsätze zur Literatur.* Olten, 1963.

DOE-2   Doeblin, Alfred. *Autobiographische Schriften.* Olten, 1977.

DOE-3   Doeblin, Alfred. *Babylonische Wandrung.* Amsterdam, 1934.

DOE-4   Doeblin, Alfred. *Berge, Meere und Giganten.* Berlin, 1924.

DOE-5   Doeblin, Alfred. *Berlin Alexanderplatz.* Berlin, 1930.

DOE-6   Doeblin, Alfred. *Briefe.* Olten, 1970.

DOE-7   Doeblin, Alfred. *Der deutsche Maskenball.* Olten, 1972.

DOE-8   Doeblin, Alfred. *Der unsterbliche Mensch.* Freiburg im Breisgau, 1946.

DOE-9   Doeblin, Alfred. *Die Drei Sprünge des Wang-Lun.* Berlin, 1920.

DOE-10   Doeblin, Alfred. *Die Zeitlupe.* Olten, 1962.

DOE-11   Doeblin, Alfred. *Ein Kerl muss eine Meinung haben.* Olten, 1976.

DOE-12   Doeblin, Alfred. *Flucht und Sammlung des Judenvolks.* Amsterdam, 1935.

DOE-13   Doeblin, Alfred. *Hamlet oder Die lange Nacht nimmt ein Ende.* Berlin, 1956.

DOE-14   Doeblin, Alfred. *Reise in Polen.* Olten, 1968.

DOE-15   Doeblin, Alfred. *Schicksalsreise.* Frankfurt, 1949.

DOE-16   Doeblin, Alfred. *Schriften zur Politik und Gesellschaft.* Olten, 1972.

DOE-17   Doeblin, Alfred, ed. *The Living Thoughts of Confucius.* London, 1942.

DOE-18   Doeblin, Alfred. *Unser Dasein.* Berlin, 1933.

DUR   Durieux, Tilla. *Eine Tür steht offen.* Berlin, 1969.

DURZ   Durzak, Manfred. *Hermann Broch.* Hamburg, 1966.

EHR   Ehrenburg, Ilya. *Memoirs, 1921–1941.* Translated by Tatania Shebunina in collaboration with Yvonne Kapp. New York, 1963.

EHRE   Ehrenstein, Albert. *Ausgewählte Aufsätze.* Edited by M. Y. Ben-Gavriel. Heidelberg, 1961.

EIN-1   Einstein, Albert. *Ideas and Opinions.* Translated by Sonja Bargmann. New York, 1964.

EIN-2   Einstein, Albert. *Mein Weltbild.* Frankfurt, 1955.

EIN-3   Einstein, Albert, and Born, H. and M. *The Born-Einstein Letters.* Translated by Irene Born. London, 1971.

EIS   Eisner, Kurt. *Welt werde froh!* Berlin, 1929.

ELL   Ellmann, Richard. *James Joyce.* New York, 1959.

ENG   Engelmann, Bernt. *Deutschland ohne Juden.* Munich, 1970.

FEI   Feingold, Henry L. *The Politics of Rescue: The Roosevelt Administration and the Holocaust, 1938–1944.* New Brunswick, N. J., 1970.

FER   Fermi, Laura. *Illustrious Immigrants.* Chicago, 1968.

FEU   Feuchtwanger, Lion. *The Devil in France.* London, n.d.

FISC   Fischer, Grete. *Dienstboten, Brecht und andere.* Olten, 1966.

FISH   Fishberg, Dr. Maurice. *Die Rassenmerkmale der Juden.* Munich, 1913.

FIT   Fitzgerald, F. Scott. *The Crack-Up.* New York, 1956.

FOR   Ford, Ford Madox. *The March of Literature.* London, 1947.

FRAE   Fraenkel, Joseph, ed. *The Jews of Austria: Essays on Their Life, History and Destruction.* London, 1967.

FRAN   Frank, Philipp. *Einstein: His Life and Times.* London, 1948.

FRE   Freud, Martin. *Glory Reflected: Sigmund Freud—Man and Father.* London, 1957.

FREU-1   Freud, Sigmund. *Civilization and Its Discontents.* Translated by Joan Riviere. New York, n.d.

FREU-2   Freud, Sigmund. *Collected Papers,* vols. 1–5. Translated under supervision of Joan Riviere. New York, 1959

FREU-3   Freud, Sigmund. *Letters.* Edited by Ernst L. Freud; Translated by Tania and James Stern. London, 1970.

FREU-4   Freud, Sigmund. *Moses and Monotheism.* New York, 1949.

FREU-5   Freud, Sigmund. *Selbstdarstellung.* Frankfurt, 1971.

FREU-6   Freud, Sigmund. *The Interpretation of Dreams.* Translated by A. A. Brill. New York, 1913.

FREU-7   Freud, Sigmund, and Jung, C. G. *The Correspondence Between Sigmund Freud and C. G. Jung.* Edited by William McGuire. Translated by Ralph Manheim and R. F. C. Hull. London, 1974.

FRI   Friedell, Egon. *Ecce Poeta.* Berlin, 1912.

FRY   Fry, Varian. *Surrender on Demand.* New York, 1945.

GEO   George, Stefan. *Poems.* New York, 1943.

GID   Gide, André. *Journals*, vol. 2. Translated by Justin O'Brien. London, 1948.

GOE-1   Goethe, Johann Wolfgang von. *Maximen und Reflexionen.* Munich, 1963.

GOE-2   Goethe, Johann Wolfgang von. *Werke, Briefe und Gespräche.* Zurich and Stuttgart, 1948.

GRA   Grass, Günter. *Über meinen Lehrer Doeblin und andere Vorträge.* Berlin, 1968.

GRO   Grove, Sir George, ed. *A Dictionary of Music and Musicians.* 5th ed., edited by Eric Blom. London, 1954.

GUM   Gumpel, E. J. *Vier Jahre politischer Mord.* Berlin, 1922.

HAA-1   Haas, Willy. *Die Literarische Welt.* Munich, 1957.

HAA-2   Haas, Willy. *Fragmente eines Lebens.* Frankfurt, 1960.

HAA-3   Haas, Willy. *Gesicht einer Epoche.* Munich, 1962.

HAB   Habe, Hans. *A Thousand Shall Fall.* London, 1942.

HAE   Haecker, Theodor. *Journal in the Night.* Translated by Alexander Dru. London, 1950.

HAES   Häsler, Alfred A. *Das Boot ist voll: Die Schweiz und die Flüchtlinge, 1933–1945.* Zurich, 1967.

HAF   Haffner, Sebastian. *Failure of a Revolution: Germany 1918–19.* London, 1973.

HAN   Hannah, Barbara. *Jung, His Life and Work.* New York, 1976.

HAS   Hasenclever, Walter. *Gedichte, Dramen, Prosa.* Edited by Kurt Pinthus. Hamburg, 1963.

HEI-1   Heine, Heinrich. *A Biographical Anthology.* Edited by Hugo Bieber. Translated by Moses Hadas. Philadelphia, 1956.

HEI-2   Heine, Heinrich. *Sämtliche Werke*, vols. 1–4. Munich, n.d. [c. 1970].

HEI-3   Heine, Heinrich. *The Poetry and Prose of Heinrich Heine.* Edited by Frederic Ewen. New York, 1948.

HEIN   Heine, Wolfgang, ed. *Der Kampf um den Reigen.* Berlin, 1922.

HEL   Heller, Erich. *The Disinherited Mind.* New York, 1959.

HELM   Helm, Everett. *Bartók.* Hamburg, 1965.

HEN   Hennecke, Hans. *Alfred Mombert.* Wiesbaden, 1952.

HER   Herzfelde, Wieland. *John Heartfield.* Berlin, n.d. [c. 1965].

HES   Hesse, Hermann, and Mann, Thomas. *Briefwechsel.* Frankfurt, 1968.

HIE   Hieronymus, Ekkehard. *Theodor Lessing.* Hanover, 1972.

HIL-1   Hiller, Kurt. *Leben gegen die Zeit.* Hamburg, 1969.

HIL-2   Hiller, Kurt. *Profile.* Paris, 1938.

HOF   Hoffmann, Banesh (with the collaboration of Helen Dukas). *Albert Einstein, Creator and Rebel.* New York, 1973.

HUG   Huguet, Louis. *Bibliographie Alfred Doeblin.* Berlin, 1972.

JAY   Jay, Martin. *The Dialectical Imagination.* London, 1973.

328   Bibliography

JON-1   Jones, Ernest. *Sigmund Freud, Life and Work,* vols. 1–3. New York, 1955.
JON-2   Jones, Ernest. *The Life and Work of Sigmund Freud.* Edited by Lionel Trilling and Steven Marcus. London, 1961.
KAF-1   Kafka, Franz. *Briefe, 1902–1924.* Frankfurt, 1975.
KAF-2   Kafka, Franz. *Briefe an Felice.* Frankfurt, 1976.
KAF-3   Kafka, Franz. *Briefe an Milena.* Frankfurt, 1966.
KAF-4   Kafka, Franz. *Briefe an Ottla und die Familie.* Frankfurt, 1974.
KAF-5   Kafka, Franz. *Hochzeitsvorbereitungen auf dem Lande.* Frankfurt, 1953.
KAF-6   Kafka, Franz. *Letters to Felice.* London, 1974.
KAF-7   Kafka, Franz. *Shorter Works,* vol. 1. Translated by Malcolm Pasley. London, 1973.
KAF-8   Kafka, Franz. *The Castle.* Translated by Willa and Edwin Muir. London, 1970.
KAF-9   Kafka, Franz. *The Diaries of Franz Kafka.* Edited by Max Brod. Translated by Joseph Kresh and Martin Greenberg. London, 1972.
KAF-10   Kafka, Franz. *The Penal Colony.* Translated by Willa and Edwin Muir. New York, 1948.
KAF-11   Kafka, Franz. *The Trial.* London, 1976.
KAH-1   Kahler, Erich. *Die Verantwortung des Geistes.* Frankfurt, 1952.
KAH-2   Kahler, Erich. *The Jews Among the Nations.* New York, 1967.
KAL   Kalow, Gert, ed. *Sind wir noch das Volk der Dichter und Denker?* Hamburg, 1964.
KALT   Kaltenbrunner, Gerd-Klaus. *Zwischen Rilke und Hitler— Alfred Schuler* [in: *Zeitschrift für Religion und Geistesgeschichte,* vol. 19, no. 4]. Cologne, 1967.
KAR   Karasek, Hellmuth. *Carl Sternheim.* Hanover, 1965.
KARD   Kardiner, Abram, and Preble, Edward. *They Studied Man.* New York, 1961.
KAU   Kaufmann, Walter, ed. *The Portable Nietzsche.* New York, 1954.
KES   Kessler, Count Harry. *The Diaries of a Cosmopolitan.* Edited and translated by Charles Kessler. London, 1971.
KEST-1   Kesten, Hermann. *Deutsche Literatur im Exil: Briefe Europäischer Autoren, 1933–1949.* Vienna, 1964.
KEST-2   Kesten, Hermann. *Lauter Literaten.* Munich, 1966.
KEST-3   Kesten, Hermann. *Meine Freunde die Poeten.* Vienna, 1953.
KIE   Kierkegaard, Søren. *Either/Or.* Translated by David F. Swenson and Lillian Marvin Swenson. New York, 1959.
KLE   Klemperer, Otto. *Minor Recollections.* London, 1964.
KOE-1   Koestler, Arthur. *The Invisible Writing.* New York, 1954.
KOE-2   Koestler, Arthur. *Scum of the Earth.* New York, 1941.

KOL-1   Kolmar, Gertrud. *Briefe an die Schwester Hilde, 1938 –1943.* Munich, 1970.

KOL-2   Kolmar, Gertrud. *Das lyrische Werk.* Heidelberg, 1955.

KOR   Kortner, Fritz. *Aller Tage Abend.* Munich, 1959.

KRE   Krehbiel-Darmstädter, Maria. *Briefe aus Gurs und Limonest, 1940 –1943.* Heidelberg, 1970.

KREU   Kreutzer, Leo. *Alfred Doeblin: Sein Werk bis 1933.* Stuttgart, 1970.

KRO   Krojanker, Gustav, ed. *Juden in der deutschen Literatur.* Berlin, 1922.

KUB   Kubizek, August. *Young Hitler.* Maidstone, England, 1973.

LAC   Lacis, Asja. *Revolutionär im Beruf.* Munich, 1971.

LAG   LaGrange, Henry-Louis de. *Mahler,* vol 1. London, 1974.

LAS-1   Lasker-Schüler, Else. *Dichtungen und Dokumente.* Munich, n.d. [c. 1951].

LAS-2   Lasker-Schüler, Else. *Die Wupper; Arthur Aronymus und seine Väter.* Munich, 1965.

LAS-3   Lasker-Schüler, Else. *Eine Einführung in ihr Werk und eine Auswahl.* Edited by Werner Kraft. Wiesbaden, 1951.

LAS-4   Lasker-Schüler, Else. *Gesammelte Werke in drei Bänden.* Edited by F. Kemp and Werner Kraft. Munich, 1959−61.

LAS-5   Lasker-Schüler, Else. *Lieber gestreifter Tiger.* (Briefe, vol. 1.) Munich, 1969.

LAS-6   Lasker-Schüler, Else. *Wo ist unser buntes Theben.* (Briefe, vol. 2.) Munich, 1969.

LEO-1   Leo Baeck Institute. *Perspectives of German-Jewish History in the 19th and 20th Century.* Jerusalem, 1971.

LEO-2   Leo Baeck Institute. *Year Book,* vols. 1−21. London, 1956−77.

LEO-3   Leo Baeck Institute Library Clipping File.

LES-1   Lessing, Theodor. *Der jüdische Selbsthass.* Berlin, 1930.

LES-2   Lessing, Theodor. *Deutschland und seine Juden.* Prague, 1933.

LES-3   Lessing, Theodor. *Einmal und nie wieder.* Prague, 1933.

LES-4   Lessing, Theodor. *Hindenburg.* Berlin, 1925.

LOE   Löwenstein, Prince Hubertus zu. *Towards the Further Shore.* London, 1968.

LUD   Ludwig, Carl. *Die Flüchtlingspolitik der Schweiz in den Jahren 1933 bis 1955.* Bern, 1957.

MAH-1   Mahler, Alma. *Gustav Mahler, Memories and Letters.* Translated by Basil Creighton. New York, 1946.

MAH-2   Mahler, Gustav. *Briefe.* Berlin, 1925.

MAH-3   Mahler, Gustav. *Ein Bild seiner Persönlichkeit in Widmungen.* Edited by Paul Stefan. Munich, 1910.

MAL   Malcolm, Norman. *Ludwig Wittgenstein.* London, 1958.

MANC   *Manchester Guardian*, September 1, 1933.
MANN-E   Mann, Erika and Klaus. *Escape to Life*. Boston, 1939.
MANN-KA   Mann, Katia. *Unwritten Memories*. Edited by Elisabeth Plessen and Michael Mann. Translated by Hunter and Hildegarde Hannum. New York, 1975.
MANN-KL-1   Mann, Klaus. *Der Wendepunkt*. Frankfurt, n.d. [c. 1952].
MANN-KL-2   Mann, Klaus. *Die Heimsuchung des europäischen Geistes*. Munich, 1973.
MANN-T-1   Mann, Thomas. *Addresses Delivered at the Library of Congress*. Washington, D.C., 1963.
MANN-T-2   Mann, Thomas. *Doctor Faustus*. New York, 1948.
MANN-T-3   Mann, Thomas. *Letters, 1889–1955*. Translated by Richard and Clara Winston. New York, 1971.
MANN-T-4   Mann, Thomas. *Werke: Autobiographisches*. Frankfurt, 1968.
MANN-T-5   Mann, Thomas. *Werke: Miszellen*. Frankfurt, 1968.
MANN-T-6   Mann, Thomas. *Werke: Schriften und Reden zur Literatur, Kunst und Philosophie*, vol 2. Frankfurt, 1968.
MANNH   Mannheim, Karl. *From Karl Mannheim*. Edited by Kurt H. Wolff. New York, 1971.
MAR   Marcuse, Ludwig. *Mein zwanzigstes Jahrhundert*. Munich, 1960.
MARI   Marinetti, Filippo Tommaso. *Selected Writings*. London, 1972.
MARX   Marx, Karl. *Dokumente seines Lebens*. Leipzig, 1970.
MAX   Max-Müller, Friedrich. *Biographies of Words and the Home of the Aryas*. London, 1888.
MEH-1   Mehring, Walter. *Berlin Dada*. Zurich, 1959.
MEH-2   Mehring, Walter. *Der Zeitpuls fliegt*. Hamburg, 1958.
MEH-3   Mehring, Walter. *Grosses Ketzerbrevier*. Munich, 1975.
MEI   Meier, Maurice. *Briefe an meinen Sohn*. Zurich, 1946.
MEY   Meyer, Alfred Richard. *Die Mär von der Musa Expressionistica*. Düsseldorf, 1948.
MIL   Milhaud, Darius. *Notes Without Music*. London, n.d. [c. 1952].
MIN-1   Minder, Robert. *Dichter in der Gesellschaft*. Frankfurt, 1972.
MIN-2   Minder, Robert. *Wozu Literatur?* Frankfurt, 1971.
MOD   *Modern Music*, vol. 23, no. 3. New York, 1946.
MOL   Molnar, Ferenc. *Companion in Exile*. London, n.d. [c. 1950].
MOS-1   Moszkowski, Alexander. *Conversations with Einstein*. London, 1970.
MOS-2   Moszkowski, Alexander. *Einstein, Einblicke in seine Gedankenwelt*. Hamburg and Berlin, 1921.
MUE-1   Mühsam, Erich. *Auswahl—Gedichte, Drama, Prosa*. Zurich, 1962.
MUE-2   Mühsam, Erich. *Namen und Menschen: Unpolitische Erinnerungen*. Leipzig, 1949.

MUE-3	Mühsam, Erich. *Sammlung, 1898–1928.* Berlin, 1928.
MUE-4	Mühsam, Erich. *War einmal ein Revoluzzer.* Hamburg, 1978.
MUE-5	Mühsam, Erich. *Zum 40 Todestag.* Europäische Ideen, vols. 5 and 6, edited by Andreas W. Mytze. Berlin, 1974.
MUEL	Müller-Salget, Klaus. *Alfred Doeblin.* Bonn, 1972.
MUEN	*Münchener Jüdische Nachrichten,* Munich, October 31, 1958.
MUS-1	Muschg, Walter. *Die Zerstörung der deutschen Literatur.* Munich, n.d. [c. 1960].
MUS-2	Muschg, Walter. *Von Trakl zu Brecht.* Munich, 1961.
MUSI	*Musical Quarterly,* vol. 38, no. 4. New York, 1952.
MUSIK	*Musikblätter des Anbruch,* vol. 6, "Arnold Schoenberg zum fünfzigsten Geburtstage." Vienna, 1924.
NAT	*National Geographic Magazine,* vol. 71, no. 2. Washington, D.C., 1937.
NEL	Nelson, Benjamin, ed. *Freud and the 20th Century.* New York, 1957.
NET	Nettl, J. P. *Rosa Luxemburg,* vols. 1 and 2. London, 1966.
NIE	Nietzsche, Friedrich. *Der Fall Wagner.* Leipzig, 1888.
ODI	Odic, Charles. *Stepchildren of France: A Doctor's Account of Paris in the Dark Years.* Translated by Henry Noble Hall. New York, 1945.
OGD	Ogden, James. *Isaac D'Israeli.* London, 1969.
PAX	Paxton, Robert O. *Vichy France: Old Guard and New Order, 1940–1944.* London, 1972.
PEY	Peyser, Joan. *The New Music: The Sense Behind the Sound.* New York, 1971.
POO	Poor, Harold L. *Kurt Tucholsky and the Ordeal of Germany, 1914–1935.* New York, 1968.
PRA	Prangel, Matthias, ed. *Materialien zu Alfred Doeblin Berlin Alexanderplatz.* Frankfurt, 1975.
RAD	Raddatz, Fritz J. *Kurt Tucholsky.* Munich, 1961.
RAT	Rathenau, Walter. *Schriften.* Berlin, 1965.
REI	Reich, Wilhelm. *The Mass Psychology of Fascism.* London, 1972.
REIC	Reich, Willy. *Alban Berg.* Zurich, 1959.
REIK	Reik, Theodor. *The Haunting Melody.* New York, 1953.
ROC	Rocker, Rudolf. *Der Leidensweg von Zensl Mühsam.* Frankfurt, 1949.
ROH	Roh, Franz. *Entartete Kunst.* Hanover, 1962.
ROL	Rolland, Romain. *Der freie Geist.* Zurich, n.d. [c. 1960].
RUF	Rufer, Josef. *The Works of Arnold Schoenberg.* Translated by Dika Newlin. Glencoe, Ill., 1963.
SAC	Sachs, Nelly. *Das Buch der Nelly Sachs.* Edited by Bengt Holmquist. Frankfurt, 1977.
SAH	Sahl, Hans. *The Few and the Many.* Translated by Richard and Clara Winston. New York, 1962.

SAL   *Salmagundi Quarterly* (Skidmore College, Pennsylvania),
            "The Legacy of the German Refugee Intellectuals," nos.
            10–11, 1969/70.

SALO   Salomon, Charlotte. *Ein Tagebuch in Bildern.* Hamburg,
            1963.

SCH   Schaber, Will, ed. *Aufbau—Reconstruction: Dokumente einer
            Kultur im Exil.* Cologne, 1972.

SCHA   Schardt, Alois J. *Franz Marc.* Berlin, 1936.

SCHE   Scheible, Hartmut. *Arthur Schnitzler.* Hamburg, 1976.

SCHI   Schick, Paul. *Karl Kraus.* Hamburg, 1965.

SCHN   Schnitzler, Arthur. *Der Weg ins Freie.* Berlin, 1932.

SCHO-1   Schoenberg, Arnold. *Briefe.* Mainz, 1958.

SCHO-2   Schoenberg, Arnold. *Letters.* Edited by Erwin Stein. Trans-
            lated by Eithne Wilkins and Ernst Kaiser. New York,
            1965.

SCHO-3   Schoenberg, Arnold. *Harmonielehre.* Leipzig, 1911.

SCHO-4   Schoenberg, Arnold. *Moses und Aron.* Mainz, 1957.

SCHO-5   Schoenberg, Arnold. *Six Pieces for Male Chorus a Capella,
            Opus 35.* Berlin, 1930.

SCHOL   Scholem, Gershom. *Walter Benjamin—die Geschichte einer
            Freundschaft.* Frankfurt, 1975.

SCHOLS   Scholes, Percy A. *The Mirror of Music.* London, 1947.

SCHON   Schonauer, Franz. *Stefan George.* Hamburg, 1960.

SCHU   Schultz, Klaus-Peter. *Kurt Tucholsky.* Hamburg, 1959.

SCHUE   Schümann, Kurt. *Im Bannkreis von Gesicht und Wirken.*
            Munich, 1953.

SCHUM   Schumann, Robert. *Gesammelte Schriften über Musik und
            Musiker.* Leipzig, 1888.

SCHW   Schwarz, Egon, and Wegner, Matthias, eds. *Verbannung:
            Aufzeichnungen deutscher Schriftsteller im Exil.* Hamburg,
            1964.

SEG   Segel, Benjamin. *Die Entdeckungsreise des Herrn Dr. Theodor
            Lessing zu den Ostjuden.* Lemberg, 1910.

SEY   Seydel, Heinz, ed. *Welch Wort in die Kälte gerufen: Die Juden-
            verfolgung des Dritten Reiches im deutschen Gedicht.* Berlin,
            1968.

SIM   *Simplicissimus,* vol. 10, no. 45. Munich, 1906.

SLO   Slonimsky, Nicolas. *Lexicon of Musical Invective.* New York,
            1953.

SOM   Sombart, Werner. *Judentaufen.* Munich, 1912.

SPA   Spalek, John M., and Strelka, Joseph, eds. *Deutsche Exil-
            literatur seit 1933,* vol. 1: Kalifornien. Bern, 1976.

SPE   Specht, Richard. *Gustav Mahler.* Berlin, 1913.

SPEN   Spender, Stephen. *World Within World.* London, 1951.

SPER   Sperber, Manès. *Bis man mir Scherben auf die Augen legt.*
            Vienna, 1977.

STE   Sterling, Eleaonore. *Judenhass.* Frankfurt, 1969.

STER   Stern, Fred B. *Ludwig Jacobowski.* Darmstadt, 1966.

STERN-1 Sternheim, Carl. *Die Hose; Der Snob.* Frankfurt, 1970.

STERN-2 Sternheim, Carl. *Gesammelte Werke,* vols. 1–6. Berlin, 1965.

STERN-3 Sternheim, Carl. *1913.* Stuttgart, 1963.

STO   Stölzl, Christoph. *Kafkas böses Böhmen.* Munich, 1975.

STU   Stuckenschmidt, H. H. *Arnold Schoenberg.* Translated by Edith Temple Roberts and Humphrey Searle. New York, 1959.

SWI   Swinnerton, Frank. *The Georgian Literary Scene.* London, 1935.

SZA-1   Szajkowski, Zosa. *Analytical Franco-Jewish Gazetteer, 1939–1945.* New York, 1966.

SZA-2   Szajkowski, Zosa. *Jews in the Foreign Legion.* New York, 1975.

THE   *The Étude,* Philadelphia, January 1947.

THU   Thüring, Bruno. *Albert Einsteins Umsturzversuch der Physik,* in: *Forschungen zur Judenfrage,* vol. 4. Hamburg, 1940.

TOL-1   Toller, Ernst. *I Was a German.* Translated by Edward Crankshaw. London, 1934.

TOL-2   Toller, Ernst. *Letters from Prison.* Translated by R. Ellis Roberts. London, 1936.

TOL-3   Toller, Ernst. *Seven Plays.* London, 1935.

TRA   Trachtenberg, Joshua. *Jewish Magic and Superstition.* New York, 1974.

TUC-1   Tucholsky, Kurt. *Ausgewählte Briefe, 1913–1935.* Edited by Mary Gerold Tucholsky and Fritz J. Raddatz. Hamburg, 1962.

TUC-2   Tucholsky, Kurt. *Gesammelte Werke,* vols. 1–9. Hamburg, 1975.

TUC-3   Tucholsky, Kurt. *The World is a Comedy.* Edited and translated by Harry Zohn. Cambridge, Mass., 1957.

UNS   Unseld, Siegfried, ed. *Zur Aktualität Walter Benjamins.* Frankfurt, 1972.

VIE   Viertel, Salka. *The Kindness of Strangers.* New York, 1969.

VOL   Volke, Werner. *Hugo von Hofmannsthal.* Hamburg, 1967.

WAG   Wagenbach, Klaus. *Franz Kafka.* Hamburg, 1964.

WAL   Walker Puner, Helen. *Freud.* London, 1949.

WALL   Wallman, Jürgen P. *Else Lasker-Schüler.* Mühlacker, 1966.

WALT-B Walter, Bruno. *Gustav Mahler.* New York, 1958.

WALT-H Walter, Hans-Albert. *Asylpraxis und Lebensbedingungen in Europa: Deutsche Exilliteratur, 1933–1950,* vol. 2. Darmstadt, 1972.

WAS   Wassermann, Jakob. *Mein Weg als Deutcher und Jude.* Berlin, 1921.

WEB-1   Webern, Anton. *Der Weg zur Neuen Musik.* Vienna, 1960.

WEB-2   Webern, Anton. *Weg und Gestalt.* Zurich, 1961.
WEI   Weigel, Hans. *Karl Kraus oder Die Macht der Ohnmacht.* Munich, 1968.
WEIN   Weininger, Otto. *Geschlecht und Charakter.* Vienna, 1922.
WEINS   Weinstock, Herbert. *Chopin.* New York, 1949.
WIC   Wickert, Johannes. *Albert Einstein.* Hamburg, 1972.
WIE   *Wiener Library Bulletin,* vols. 18–28. London, 1964–75.
WIEC   Wiener Library Clipping File.
WIL   Willett, John. *Expressionism.* London, 1970.
WOL   Wolff, Kurt. *Briefwechsel eines Verlegers, 1911–1963.* Frankfurt, 1966.
WOLF-1   Wolfskehl, Karl. *Briefe und Aufsätze, München 1925–1933.* Hamburg, 1966.
WOLF-2   Wolfskehl, Karl. *An die Deutschen.* Zurich, 1947.
WOLF-3   Wolfskehl, Karl. *Gesammelte Werke,* vols. 1–2. Hamburg, 1960.
WOLF-4   Wolfskehl, Karl. *Zehn Jahre Exil: Briefe aus Neuseeland, 1938–1948.* Heidelberg, 1959.
WUL   Wulf, Josef. *Musik im Dritten Reich.* Hamburg, 1966.
YOU   Young, Harry F. *Maximilian Harden, Censor Germaniae.* The Hague, 1959.
ZEN   *Zentralblatt für Psychotherapie,* vols. 6–7. Leipzig, 1933–34.
ZIL   Zillig, Winfried. *Variationen über Neue Musik.* Munich, 1959.
ZUC   Zuckmayer, Carl. *Als wär's ein Stück von mir.* Frankfurt, 1969.
ZWEI   Zweig, Stefan. *The World of Yesterday.* London, 1943.

ACKNOWLEDGMENTS

This book would not have been possible without the assistance of numerous people and institutions to whom I should like to express my heartfelt thanks. I owe a particular debt of gratitude to the Wiener Library, London, and to the three ladies who allowed me to clutter up their reading-room tables for weeks on end: Mses. Christa Wichmann, Gita Johnson and Janet Langmaid, and their assistants. Ms. Bertha Cohen of the Wiener Library and Mr. Arnold Paucker of the Leo Baeck Institute, London, also contributed bibliographic advice. I received invaluable aid from the staff of the London Library, St. James's, notably Messrs. Douglas Matthews, Colin Stevenson and Paul Perman, and Mses. Cynthia Forbes and Ann Holland. Mrs. Gibbings, the then-librarian of the Reform Club, London, also helped me in many ways, and I should like to tender my thanks collectively to the staffs of the British Library, the New York Public Library, the Leo Baeck Institute Library, New York, and the Library of Congress.

For help in obtaining photographs I am particularly indebted to Dr. Joachim W. Storck of the Deutsches Literaturarchiv, Schiller Nationalmuseum, Marbach A. N., and to the museum's photographic department; to Hans Joachim May of the Staatsbibliothek Preussischer Kulturbesitz, Berlin, and to Dr. Roland Klemig of the Bildarchiv Preussischer Kulturbesitz; to Frau Gunnemann of the Stadt und Landesbibliothek, Dortmund; to Dr. Prilop of the Stadtbüchereien, Hanover; Mr. J. Bröning of the Hessische Landes und Hochschulbibliothek, Darmstadt; Ms. Karin Wagner of the Walter Verlag, Olten, and Dr. Gershom Scholem, Jerusalem.

This is primarily a literary history, and many authors are quoted in the foregoing pages. The principal sources are duly indicated on the copyright page, but I should like to thank personally those copyright holders who were particularly generous and forthcoming in the matter of assistance and permissions: Mrs. Mary Tucholsky, the widow of Kurt Tucholsky; Mrs. Ruth Gorny, the daughter of Theodor Lessing; Mrs. Katia Mann and Dr. Golo Mann; Ms. Gerda Niedieck, who manages the copyrights of Alfred Doeblin; Mrs. Alice von Kahler, the widow of Erich Kahler, who permitted me to quote from her husband's work and also allowed me to use her superb portrait of Hermann Broch; Mr. Lawrence Schoenberg; Mr. Andreas Mytze of *Europäische Ideen*, Berlin, who has undertaken to revive Erich Mühsam's work; Dr. Hans Sahl, who provided me with a copy of his novel, *The Few and the Many;* and Mr. Sidney Kaufman, who manages the copyrights of Ernst Toller. I am also under obligation to the Hogarth Press, Basic Books, Inc., Random House, Harcourt Brace Jovanovich, Inc., the Macmillan Publishing Company, the Bodley Head, the Nonesuch Press, Cassell & Co., Hutchinson & Co., the Jewish Publication Society of America, Faber and Faber Ltd., Alfred A. Knopf, Inc., Pantheon Books, Crown Publishers, Routledge & Kegan Paul Ltd., Martin Secker & Warburg, Schocken Books, the Seabury Press, A. D. Peters & Co., Suhrkamp Verlag, Rowohlt Verlag, Bote & Bock, Kösel Verlag, Claassen Verlag, Econ Verlag, Musikverlag B. Schott's Söhne, Williams Verlag, Hermann Luchterhand Verlag, F. A. Herbig's Verlagsbuchhandlung, International Creative Management, Macmillan Administration (Basingstoke) Ltd., Belmont Music Publishers and the Arnold Schoenberg Archives at California State University.

Friends, relatives and acquaintances provided sage counsel and various kinds of logistical support during the preparatory stages of this book. Without Ann O'Sullivan's bibliography it could never have been finished. In New York I had the help of Mrs. Edith Tietz and Mrs. Marga Land, as well as that of Jesse Simons, Anita Hart, Paul Krause and Foster V. Grunfeld; in Munich that of Mrs. Kitty Neumann; in Berlin that of John Evarts, Alfredo del Monaco, Gerald Gert and the late Hans Wollenberg; in London that of Ian and Philippa Fraser, John and Harriet Sackur, Anthony and Kit Van Tulleken, Lawrence and Edith Malkin and Anthony Smith. For advice and encouragement I am also indebted to Professor and Mrs. Henry H. Remak, and to Svea Gold. Nor can I conclude this (only partial) listing without mentioning the help I have received from my long-suffering editors, Tom Wallace, Philippa Harrison and Trent Duffy, as well as Alice van Straalen, who bore with me patiently throughout the inordinately long time it took to complete this book.

INDEX

A Note on the Author

Frederic V. Grunfeld is a critic of the arts and a former roving editor of *Horizon*, New York, and *Queen* magazine, London. His most recent book—*Berlin* in the "Great Cities" series—was described by the *Times* of London as "the best book in English on present-day Berlin," and his social history of Nazism, *The Hitler File*, was widely recognized as the most revealing study of its kind. A graduate of Columbia and the University of Chicago, he was written on many other aspects of art, music and cultural history, including *The Art and Times of the Guitar* and *Games of the World*.

Catalog

If you are interested in a list of fine Paperback
books, covering a wide range of subjects
and interests, send your name and address,
requesting your free catalog, to:

McGraw-Hill Paperbacks
1221 Avenue of Americas
New York, N.Y. 10020